Japan's Book Donation to the University of Louvain

▲ Stone image of a lion-dog, holding a red shield emblazoned with a
chrysanthemum, on one of the stepped side gables of the University of
Louvain library (built 1921-1928). Although it is not a heraldic animal in
the strict sense of the word, the architect Whitney Warren (1864-1943)
borrowed the image of the Japanese mythological animal *koma-inu* (lion-
dog) as supporter to a red shield, emblazoned with the golden chrysanthemum of the Japanese imperial crest. He thus combined diverse elements into an approximation of a Japanese coat of arms, suitable to take
its place in the sequence of national coats of arms which he had placed on
each of the steps of the stepped gables. The coats of arms were intended
to serve as emblems of the victor nations of the First World War. On the
other two steps of the gable we see the Scottish unicorn symbolizing the
United Kingdom and the Gallic rooster as the emblem of the French Republic. Photograph by Christine Vande Walle.

Japanese Cultural Identity and Modernity in the 1920s

Japan's Book Donation

to the University of Louvain

Edited by
Jan Schmidt,
Willy Vande Walle
and Eline Mennens

LEUVEN UNIVERSITY PRESS

Table of Contents

▲ Catholic University of Louvain Rector Paulin Ladeuze (left) addressing
words of welcome to Crown Prince Hirohito (to the right) in the ruins
of the burnt-out university library (20 June 1921). Standing to the left
and slightly behind the crown prince is Cardinal Mercier. Further to the
back are the two escorting Belgian officers, Raoul Pontus (left) and Aloïs
Biebuyck (right), both veterans of the Great War. Photograph courtesy of
Emilie Vilcot, UCLouvain – Libraries Heritage Collections.

KU Leuven and UCLouvain's Co-operation Strengthened by Japan

The University of Leuven/Louvain is almost six centuries old and many of Europe's leading scholars refined their talents back here. Writing the European continent's intellectual history, without paying due attention to great minds like Erasmus, Vesalius, Mercator and many other Lovanienses, is next to impossible. Leuven is where Georges Lemaître formulated his Big Bang theory and Christian de Duve conducted research that won him the 1974 Nobel Prize in Medicine.

In 1968 the bilingual University of Leuven/Louvain was split into the Dutch-speaking KU Leuven and the French-speaking UCLouvain. Hailed as Europe's most innovative university, KU Leuven offers a myriad of disciplines that all proudly belong to the top 100 in their field. Its publication record puts KU Leuven at the forefront of the global conversation. UCLouvain is one of the highest ranked universities in the francophone world. Fifty years after the scission, the two universities have grown very close together, relating to each other like daughters of one and the same mother. Unity in diversity, that is the reality of today. There is intense research collaboration, the two sisters co-invest in multilingual programs and joint research, and they position themselves jointly in the capital city of Brussels and on the international forum. The two together form an academic powerhouse in Europe. Between them, they educate over 90,000 students of more than 160 nationalities. Both universities have successful research cooperations and student exchanges with partners around the world, among which Japanese universities are of eminent importance.

Today, the two universities are once again united in their common objective of further strengthening links with Japan and Japanese universities and maximizing the value of the Japanese book collection donated to the university in the 1920s. The precious collection was donated by Japan to symbolize the friendship between Japan and Belgium, after the university's library had been destroyed during the First World War. Today, the collection also represents the intense collaboration and intertwining of the two parts of the Universitas Lovaniensis. One hundred years after the donation, Japan once more reunites KU Leuven and UCLouvain with the Special Exhibition on "Japan's Book Donation to the University of Louvain: Japanese Cultural Identity and Modernity in the 1920s," hosted in the KU Leuven University Library. In addition to a fundraising campaign to support the digitization of the collection and to create a position for a specialist in the book history or visual history of the Edo period, this book, which accompanies the exhibition, is published to serve as a lasting introduction to the magnificent book donation and its historical background, and as a reference for further research in the future.

Prof. Dr. Luc Sels, Rector KU Leuven
Prof. Dr. Vincent Blondel, Rector UCLouvain

特命全権大使　安達峯一郎

大正10年5月31日　　（大使館しよう格）

31. 5. 1921

▲ Adachi Mine'ichirō, promoted to the rank of ambassador on 31 May
1921. The photograph, showing him in full regalia with various decorations
pinned to his chest, dates from 1928 or later. Courtesy of the Japanese
embassy in Belgium.

Message by the Ambassador
of Japan to Belgium

The horrendous destruction of the University Library of Leuven/ Louvain in the night of August 25, 1914, sent shock waves through the cultural and political world and was a direct attack on the city's long academic tradition. Right after this tragedy, already in 1915, Japan expressed its will to help with the restoration and reconfirmed this intention during the Paris Peace Conference. Japan quickly seized the historic momentum to offer something transcending mere financial aid, something of a magnitude befitting the university's rich cultural history.

Despite the unprecedented devastation brought upon by the Great Kantō Earthquake of 1923, efforts to build up this symbol of friendship continued, and from 1924 to 1926, the precious collection of almost 14,000 rare volumes exemplifying the Japanese heritage finally arrived in Belgium. It was meant to provide Belgian and, to a larger extent, Western scholars with an extensive window into Japanese culture, offering a nearly endless source of materials for studying Japan and its traditions. I feel grateful for the efforts that were made in the past on both sides to bring the collection to the university. I strongly believe the collection's importance as a token of friendship will only increase in the years to come.

One could spend a lifetime perusing the treasures of the collection and still not be able to fathom its true depth and richness. I am very much looking forward to seeing that, through the upcoming exhibition, this remarkable proof of friendship between Japan and Belgium will be known to the wider public in Belgium. As Ambassador of Japan to Belgium, I wish to extend my deepest gratitude toward those who contributed to the realization of this project.

SHIMOKAWA Makita, Ambassador of Japan to Belgium

Jan Schmidt, Willy Vande Walle and Eline Mennens

Introduction

This publication is a companion to the Special Exhibition "Japan's Book Donation to the University of Louvain. Japanese Cultural Identity and Modernity in the 1920s" (October 2022-January 2023), held at the University Library of the University of Leuven (KU Leuven) in close collaboration with l'Université catholique UCLouvain to commemorate the centennial of the book donation made by Japan to the University of Louvain in the 1920s. The publication serves a double purpose: it is a catalogue for the exhibition, which besides a selection of the donated books also includes items from 1920s Japan that represent the contemporary culture, society, and politics of Japan, while at the same time adding further background information and context through five essays. The focus of this publication is to introduce a carefully selected number of the more than 3,000 book titles consisting of almost 14,000 volumes donated by Japan to the University of Louvain – the ancestor of KU Leuven and UCLouvain – in the 1920s, and to explain the history of the donation as part of the international effort to rebuild the university library, which had been destroyed soon after the outbreak of the First World War.

All too often Japanese historical books and artworks are exhibited without contextualizing them or explaining the – very modern – background of their arrival in Europe. One only needs to think of the iconic *ukiyo-e* print of the famous wave by Hokusai or colorful prints of actors and courtesans in exhibitions throughout Europe, where until recently not much attention was being paid to the context of the time these books or prints arrived in Europe nor to the contemporary circumstances in Japan. In the case of the Japanese donation to the University of Louvain this

is even more problematic since the books donated were carefully selected by a Japanese National Committee comprising prominent Japanese academics and businessmen, which had entrusted the task to Wada Mankichi, the renowned Head of the Imperial Libraries Association and Director of the Library of Tokyo Imperial University. The donated books have therefore to be seen also in the political, socio-economic, and cultural context of their own time – the years from the Paris Peace Conference in 1919, when Japan committed to participate in restoring the library of the University of Louvain, to 1928, when the new library was inaugurated. They were an expression of how "Japanese culture" was conceived by the donors in the 1920s, and thus of their – quite elitist – vision of Japanese cultural identity and how it should be displayed to a Western audience.

The core of this publication, conceptualized and written by Willy Vande Walle, engages with the historical background of the donation and offers a careful description of a selection of 65 books and works of art that are representative of the enormous breadth of the donation, ranging from history, religion, art, and literature to what today would be the natural sciences. His essay is so far the most exhaustive account of the history of the donation, including many hitherto unknown facts, for instance about the background of the selection of books by Wada and others, as well as about the miraculous way the book donation survived the second fire that ravaged the university library again in 1940 after the outbreak of the Second World War, a fact the details of which were long shrouded in mystery.

In addition, a different part of the exhibition and, hence of this book, is the section curated by Jan Schmidt, which presents objects related to aspects of the larger context of 1920s Japanese

13

politics, society, and culture, designed to offer a glimpse into the complexity of Japanese cultural identity and modernity during the years when the donation arrived in Leuven. This will also provide hints why the donation was subsequently almost forgotten even in Japan. An obvious reason for that long neglect was that after the fire of 1940 and the devastations of the Second World War in general in Europe and in the Asia-Pacific region that ended with Japan's formal capitulation on September 2, 1945, around the globe more urgent matters were pressing. Thus, the 1920s donation was neither on the priority list in Belgium nor in Japan for decades to come. But as the explanations about 1920s culture and modernity in Japan in this publication will show, the donation, which was essentially a project of the political, economic, and academic elites of late 1910s and early 1920s Japan, was in a way already an event on the margins of the immense cultural and socioeconomic dynamics that swept through Japan and everywhere else at the time when the last books arrived in Leuven in 1926. The political currents of the time, too, which can be associated with mounting socioeconomic inequality, the rise of leftwing radicalism as well as of a growing tendency on the political right towards "ultra-nationalism", but also with the countervailing tendencies of democratization and cosmopolitanism of the 1920s, affected the – never homogeneous nor holistic – attempts to define a "Japanese cultural identity" in such a way that there was for decades no follow-up on the donation. The books remained – well preserved and in pristine condition – largely unused and unnoticed. There were notable, but again elite, exceptions, such as the donation of an academic chair to the University of Louvain in 1927 by Satsuma Jirōhachi, the wealthy son of a textile dynasty residing in Paris and engaging in philanthropy. This "Satsuma Chair," designed to fill the Japanese book donation with life by way of lectures on Japanese culture, religion and history, is still extant. It is hosted by the two sister universities KU Leuven and UCLouvain, regularly inviting guest speakers and guest lecturers. It is an occasion of great joy that now, celebrating the centennial of the 1920s Japanese book donation against all challenges posed by the COVID-19 pandemic, the special exhibition and this publication could be realized.

Aside from the core part carefully laying out the history of the donation in a long essay and introducing a comprehensive range of representative examples of the books and artworks donated in the 1920s in careful descriptions provided by Willy Vande Walle, and the descriptions of objects on the culture, society, and politics of 1920s Japan, four more essays invite the readers to deepen their understanding of the background to the Japanese donation:

The first essay by Jan Schmidt on "The First World War as the Precondition to the Japanese Donation to the University of Louvain" argues that the First World War (1914-1918) not only simply caused the destruction of the library and elicitated in its wake the international contributions to build a new library in which Japan participated, but had other distinctive effects in Japan that are important for understanding the book donation. Firstly, the war catalyzed a shift in the perception of the world among the wider Japanese public towards a more self-confident stance vis-à-vis the European countries including Belgium, which had been an ally of Japan and won widespread solidarity for its fate during the war. This formed an important background for a wave of philanthropic efforts by the Japanese state and private actors in the wake of the war. This shift was also fueled by the fact that the war for Japan had not brought widespread destruction, in contrast to so many regions of Europe and some of the European colonies, especially in Africa. It had instead ushered in a period of unprecedented economic boom, which helped to fund such philanthropic efforts and unprecedented projects of cultural diplomacy. The war was also highly mediatized in Japan, similarly to the rest of the world. This sparked an upsurge of sympathy and moral support for Belgium, which had been hit hard by the devastations of military actions and by the harsh German occupation. This mediatized attention further facilitated mutual relief efforts and symbolic acts that started during the war, for instance when a precious Japanese sword was presented to the Belgian King Albert I in 1915 by a Japanese newspaper, while in 1921 the then-Japanese crown prince and later emperor Hirohito visited many sites associated with the war, among them also the ruins of the old library in Leuven that had been set ablaze by German troops in August 1914. In return, the Japanese support during the First World War and its aftermath, triggered enormous solidarity throughout Belgium when one of the most devastating earthquakes in modern history, the Great Kantō Earthquake, destroyed large parts of Tokyo and

Yokohama on 1 September 1923 and claimed around 100,000 lives. This support from Belgium, including books sent from the University of Louvain, which was still recovering from the destruction of 1914, fueled the decision in Japan not to discontinue the book donation in the face of the enormous loss of books there in fires caused by the earthquake.

In his essay "An Empire of the Mid-Tier: The Japanese Ministry of Foreign Affairs and the New Mass Public-Focused Diplomacy of the Early Twentieth Century" Lieven Sommen argues that the 1920s Japanese book donation must be seen in the perspective of the diplomatic efforts of the Japanese Empire trying to redefine its position among the other existing empires and the so-called Great Powers. Since the 1890s, Japan had put itself on the map as a fledgling empire. This development coincided with the advent of mass media, which in turn caused diplomacy to change, as it was now required to not only appease the officials of the other nations but also the 'international public opinion'. This chapter explores how from the early 1900s on the Ministry of Foreign Affairs tried to adapt to the need to promote Japan abroad via mass media. The essay explains how propaganda press offices established during the First World War made the promotion of the empire through public diplomacy a mainstay of international politics, and how from the early 1900s on the Japanese Ministry of Foreign Affairs realized that its methods for shaping this public diplomacy effectively proved deficient at the Paris Peace Conference in 1919. It further argues that in the 1920s Japan actively played its role in the new internationalism as a permanent member of the League of Nations (the predecessor of today's United Nations), and that the young Crown Prince Hirohito, the later Shōwa Emperor, could function in this form of diplomacy as the new and international face of Japan via modern mass media when he made a trip to Europe in 1921.

In her essay on "Japanese Art in Belgium in the 1920s: Hidden Treasures and Public Celebrations," Freya Terryn argues that the book donation can be seen in the context of the 1920s being an important decade for the celebration and appreciation of Japanese culture and its arts in Belgium. This study explores the fascination with Japanese art in the interwar period in Europe, by focusing on two main examples: the first is a print series by Tsukioka Yoshitoshi preserved in the Royal Museums of Art and History (recently renamed: Art & History Museum), and the second are paintings by Fujita Tsuguharu, known as Léonard Foujita in Europe, today in the collection of the Royal Museums of Fine Arts of Belgium. The study sets out to examine the acquisition of Tsukioka's woodcuts in the larger context of the longstanding appreciation for Japanese prints in Europe since the 1860s. Even in the 1920s, Belgian museums continued to acquire prints, prompting the Japanese donors to include woodblock-printed illustrated books of the Edo period in the collection donated to the University of Louvain. The essay further discusses how during the 1920s there was significant interest in art painted by Japanese artists in Europe, and how this led to several exhibitions of Japanese artists, primarily based out of Paris. Especially the works of Fujita Tsuguharu were received positively by the European audience. He combined Western-style oil painting and *sumi-e* techniques to create cross-cultural art and managed to garner much praise for this synthesis. Fujita was the president of the (short-lived, since it came into existence and folded again within 1929) French Japanese Artists Association, which was in large part funded by Satsuma Jirōhachi. In this way, Fujita's work is indirectly connected to the 1920s book donation because aside from both having Satsuma involved in them, they also show how there was a continuing interest in Japanese culture within Belgium throughout the 1920s.

In his essay "Japan's Sonic Modernity: Popular Music and Culture in the 1920s" Aurel Baele adds important contextualization to the selection of 1920s objects and their significance for understanding the culture, society, and politics of 1920s Japan. He argues that in the 1920s Japan went through a transformation into a society of mass culture and mass consumption. Jazz and other popular tunes that reverberated through Japan's society marked the tempo and energy by which this change was taking place. The essay briefly discusses the places where popular music was consumed, and the role and influence of the culture industry, to illustrate the pervasiveness of this sonic modernity in Japan. It is this vibrant modernity that is often forgotten when Japanese prints, books or artworks are displayed. They were produced in previous centuries but, as in the case of the Japanese book donation to the University of Louvain, found their way to Europe in times of changing and multidimensional cultural identity and modernity.

⬆ 2. Section of the original stacks made to shelve the Japanese book donation, as re-used when the Chinese-Japanese library of KU Leuven was moved into the KU Leuven University Library in 1981. Photograph KU Leuven Digitisation and Document Delivery.

▲ 3. View of the present East-Asian Library in the KU Leuven University Library, with part of the original stacks for the donation still in use. Photograph KU Leuven Digitisation and Document Delivery.

The exhibition and this publication would not have been possible without the support of numerous institutions and individuals. Above all, we thank the rectors of KU Leuven and UCLouvain, Luc Sels and Vincent Blondel, for their continuous support to the exhibition, to this publication, as well as to the Japan fundraising campaign, which was initiated concurrently, with the ultimate goal of facilitating the full digitization of the precious 1920s Japanese book donation and establishing a position for a researcher specializing in the Edo period (1600-1868), in which the majority of the books was originally printed. In addition, the immense support of Emilie Vilcot of the UCLouvain Libraries Central Service, and of Charles-Henri Nyns, UCLouvain Chief Librarian, was crucial. On the KU Leuven side, we are particularly indebted to Hilde Van Kiel, Director of the KU Leuven Libraries, and her team, as well as to Demmy Verbeke, Head of KU Leuven Libraries Artes. An extensive list of the many institutions and persons who supported the exhibition and this publication can be found in the acknowledgements. In case anybody involved has accidentally been omitted, our utmost gratitude will still be with them.

If this publication with its five essays and the two sections containing descriptions of the objects displayed during the exhibition manages not only to catch the interest of its readers but also to serve as a basis for further research into the fascinating history of the donation and of the books and artworks donated, we as editors would see our mission more than fulfilled. Now, at the time of the centenary of the 1920s book donation, we all realize that once again major challenges for humankind lie ahead of us, including the threat of climate change, pollution and extinction, rising social inequality, the chances offered and dangers posed by artificial intelligence, and geopolitical tensions. But the history of the 1920s Japanese Book Donation, realized after the First World War and in the midst of another devastating pandemic, the so-called "Spanish flu", which claimed several times more lives than the war before it, provides also an example of mutual aid across continents in times of global reconstruction. It may be hoped that in the coming years such mutual assistance will be able to play a role in preventing another devastating failure like the one that occurred at the end of the Interwar period.

大正三年八月二十五日
第三種郵便物認可

大正五年二月二十五日印刷納本
（每月二回五日廿五日發行）

歐洲戰爭實記

第五十四號　　二月廿五日

博文館

Jan Schmidt

The First World War as the Precondition to the Japanese Donation to the University of Louvain

Without the First World War there would have been no Japanese donation to the University of Louvain, the ancestor of today's KU Leuven and UCLouvain,[1] in the 1920s. What might initially seem to state the obvious, though, merits further elaboration, since the war in many ways created factors that would lead to the donation.

In the first place, of course, it was the destruction of the university library and large parts of the city – not to mention the indiscriminate killing of more than two hundred citizens of Leuven by German troops in August 1914 – that had led to an international outcry. The Empire of Japan, which had declared war on Germany on 23 August, just two days before Leuven was put to the torch, was no exception: news of the city's destruction reached Japanese newspapers soon after, and even cinemas were quick to put images presenting the destruction onto the screen. The news was met with many expressions of pity and solidarity from the Japanese public for the plight of Belgium, which had just become a wartime ally of Japan, both being part of the Entente war coalition against the Central Powers. Moreover, certainly a favorable feeling toward Belgium had built up already in the decades long before the war, in combination with genuine expressions of anger about violence against civilians and the destruction of the centuries-old university library. Such sentiments were important factors in the favorable reception by the elite Japanese politicians and businessmen of an originally French proposal to rebuild the university library. That initiative soon grew into an international effort, which Willy Vande Walle explains in more detail in his essay in this volume.[2]

Yet aside from these circumstances, the complex impact of the First World War on Japan itself also provided other important structural preconditions for the 1920s donation by Japan to the University of Louvain.[3] The following essay will discuss several of these antecedent conditions in order to further contextualize the Japanese donation. As will become evident below, it was inherently and to a large extent a complex product resulting both from the impact of the First World War and from more long-term developments within the modern history of Japan, which had first arisen in the late nineteenth century.

The First World War and Belgium in the Shifting World Perception among Japanese Mass Media

In Japan, as the historian Yamamuro Shin'ichi has argued convincingly,[4] the First World War accelerated a paradigm shift in the perception of the wider world and Japan's relation to it. This change has to be seen as the result of three currents that had started in the last decades of the nineteenth century: the first trend built on an already high level of literacy compared to the international standard, which had resulted from the ubiquitous temple schools (*terakoya*), merchant schools, and schools for the offspring of the *samurai* in the early modern era (roughly late sixteenth century to mid-nineteenth century).[5] With the introduction of compulsory elementary school education in Japan in 1872, along with the steady growth of institutions of secondary and tertiary education, not only did the number of students and teachers on all levels continuously rise, but, parallel to it, the number of readers for newspapers and magazines rose as well.[6] The ever burgeoning market and readership for these media, as well as for books, introduced the wider world to a public

◤ 1. Cover of the illustrated war magazine *Ōshū sensō jikki* (True account of the European War), No. 54, 25 February 1916. Source: private collection Jan Schmidt.

版八

歐洲戰爭實記

第一號

東京
博文館

growing larger than ever, while building on the vibrant book printing culture of the seventeenth, eighteenth, and early nineteenth centuries (various examples of which can be found in this publication). With the development of a modern book market in the wake of the Meiji Restoration of 1867/68 came numerous translations of an enormous variety of Western fiction and non-fiction books. This larger world came to be keenly interpreted, moreover, by many Japanese authors, possibly best represented by intellectuals – like Fukuzawa Yukichi (1834-1901) – associated with the "Civilization and Enlightenment" (bunmei kaika) movement of the 1870s.[7] Not unlike the mass media in Europe and many other parts of the world, Japanese newspapers and magazines quickly started to diversify. From around the turn of the twentieth century, these media included more sensationalist journalism catering to a broader audience, with elements such as serialized novels, crime stories, and also more pages exclusively targeting a female readership.[8]

A major boost to the circulation of newspapers and magazines were the modern wars in which Japan was directly involved: the First Sino-Japanese War (1894-95) and the Russo-Japanese War (1904-05). The widespread and popular coverage of both wars also accelerated the use of drawings and maps as well as increasingly numerous photographs to convey current events.[9] The Japanese mass media therefore had already developed a certain routine in covering wars when the First World War broke out in 1914. At the time, Japan's direct military participation was limited to occupying the German-leased territory around the port city of Qingdao in China and the German island colonies in Micronesia, in addition to sending Japanese war ships to the Mediterranean. Even so, the Japanese mass media covered the war in all its aspects continuously, including many lengthy, elaborate commentaries by Japanese journalists, politicians, businessmen, and academics.[10]

In 1914, all major national daily newspapers sold in the hundreds of thousands, in both their morning and evening editions. More recent research by the media historian Ariyama Teruo has shown, furthermore, that even in remote rural villages at least around half of the households frequently purchased one, in many cases two newspapers – a national and a regional publication – and occasionally also popular "general magazines" (sōgō zasshi), such as Taiyō (The Sun).[11] In addition, coinciding with the beginning of the First World War, a wave of illustrated photo magazines flooded the market – the predecessors of the big graphic magazines with their rich photo collages of the 1920s.[12] One of these was the Rekishi shashin (History in Photos), which aspired to document 'history' in the making. By conveying photographs from Japan and from the entire world, it provided information about political events; celebrities; catastrophes, such as wars, large accidents, and natural disasters; trends in consumption and technology; and sports. Within the extensive coverage given to the First World War, the fate of Belgium during the war was discussed widely, and the magazine "History in Photos" proved no exception. As can be seen in the pages reproduced here, very often it was the plight of the Belgian civilians that was the focus of attention: Belgian refugees leaving Ostend shortly before the arrival of the German troops, depicted in the February 1915 issue of the magazine, for instance, and Belgian war orphans in Calais about to be sent to Britain for shelter, in the March 1916 issue.

Already in late 1914 and in early 1915, the destruction in Belgium was being shown in "actuality films" in Japanese cinemas as well. According to film historian Peter B. High, these

▲ 2. Cover of the illustrated war magazine Ōshū sensō jikki (True account of the European War), No. 1, 25 August 1914.
Source: private collection Jan Schmidt.

documentary portrayals evoked much solidarity amongst the cinema-goers, leaving many in tears.[13] This observation in itself is interesting, since it alludes to an emotionality in which the pictures of despairing civilians with their houses destroyed were perceived as part of a world that, despite being thousands of kilometers away, felt "utterly real" and contemporaneous, as Yamamuro Shin'ichi wrote.[14]

Throughout the war, the Japanese public was consuming fictional films, too, such as the US silent movie *The Belgian* (1918). Directed by Sidney Olcott, it depicted the tragic situation of Belgium in the war through the perspective of two lovers who for the good of Belgium must work together against wily German spies, while waiting to be liberated by US troops. As can be seen on a film program flyer for the cinema Patē-kan in Tokyo, Europe was perceived to be under attack by German militarism, while the "Belgian Spirit" (as

the Japanese translation of the film title, *Berugī-damashii*, went) was hailed for withstanding such brutal violence.

It was further said that an expression of "worldwide sympathy" had allegedly led to full cinemas in 9,740 venues across the twenty-one allied countries where the film was screened.

Similar to other countries, in Japanese mass media, too, the Belgian King Albert I became a popular figure, often depicted in military uniform as a fighting king. It is therefore not a coincidence that it was not the Japanese state but, rather, the newspaper companies Ōsaka asahi shinbunsha and the Tōkyō asahi shinbunsha that donated a precious Japanese sword to King Albert I in January 1915. This move proved to cause an even larger spike in circulation once the gift was announced in their newspapers. Both newspapers designed a *laterna magica* show that projected images depicting the plight of the Belgian population, which was connected to relief fundraising organized by them.[15] The sword was

▲ 3. *Haori* 羽織 coat with images of the First World War in Europe including the special edition of the newspaper *Ōsaka asahi shinbun* reporting the German declarations of war on France and Russia of 3 August, 1914. Source: Museum Fünf Kontinente, Munich, Kimono no. 2017-64-15.

民難避の後最るけ於にドンテスオ國白

The last refugee to leave Ostend for England was a baby, who is shown being carried backwards down a ladder from the quay to a sailer. This photo was taken right a few minutes before the German arrived, and the photographer himself escaped on a fishing boat.

（號月二年四正大眞寫史歴）　22

迭移利吉英の兒孤義白

No one can look at this picture without any sympathetic emotion toward Belgian orphans who were deprived of their paternal stems on account of the raid of Germans on their native country since the outbreak of the war. Photo taken at Calais station in France shows the orphans to be taken to England.

（號月三年五正大眞寫史歴）　2 の後

▲ 4. Page of the illustrated magazine *Rekishi shashin* (History in Photos), February 1915, p. 22, depicting the "last refugee" from Belgium, a baby, leaving Ostend for Britain. Source: private collection Jan Schmidt.

▲ 5. Page of the illustrated magazine *Rekishi shashin* (History in Photos), March 1916, p. 2 (verso), depicting Belgian orphans waiting in Calais to be shipped to Britain. Source: private collection Jan Schmidt.

handed to the king by the Japanese journalist Sugimura Sojinkan (1872-1945), who had been reporting directly from Belgium and later from France during the first months of the war. Sugimura was one of the many Japanese war correspondents sent by Japanese newspapers at great cost throughout the years 1914 to 1918. Their reporting, together with the propaganda by Japan's allies, often put German war crimes and the very real hardships of the occupation in Belgium at the forefront, thus further fueling several additional donation campaigns in Japan for disabled veterans in Belgium and other Entente allies.[16] For Japan, participating in humanitarian relief in this way was also a means to demonstrate the stature of the Japanese Empire vis-à-vis the Western powers. The symbolic character of such campaigns for Belgium or, for instance, for Polish orphans - not to mention the dispatch of seventy-five Japanese Red Cross nurses to London, St. Petersburg, and Paris, as covered widely in the Japanese mass media - cannot be overestimated.[17]

When tracing these gestures of solidarity, it should not be forgotten that only a few decades earlier, in the 1850s and 1860s, Japan had been forced at gunpoint to open its ports to Western powers and to accept 'unequal treaties' infringing upon its sovereignty. The aforementioned humanitarian acts during the First World War were - in visual terms, too, particularly in an age of ever accelerating mediatization - important also in light of rampant anti-Asian racism. Photos of Japanese nurses tending to the maimed bodies of gravely wounded Western soldiers, or of a Japanese sword handed to a Western king, depicted watershed moments in the emancipation from the Eurocentric world order of the 'long nineteenth century', with all its future consequences. They came about at a historical moment when what historian Sandra Wilson has called "the discourse of national greatness" reached an early peak in the pre-1945 history of Japan.[18] This atmosphere of lending support to its Western allies during the First World War, as well as the mass media coverage of such actions, very plausibly influenced the idea of supporting international efforts to rebuild the library of the University of Louvain in the form of a book donation - an initiative that would be readily adopted by the Japanese elites in the direct aftermath of the war.

The First World War Economic Boom in Japan and Its Consequences

The war led to an unprecedented economic boom in Japan between mid-1915 and early 1920, in particular because of the demand for supplies by its allies. As markets in China and South-East Asia, for instance, were temporarily vacated by the European competition, the state - and the Japanese Empire in toto, as well as the Japanese business world - was able to acquire a budget surplus that could be used for more than just immediate necessities and reinvestment.[19] This development was crucial for gaining the financial means and fostering the willingness of political and business elites to engage in cultural diplomacy and philanthropy inside and outside Japan. The modern Japanese state, for the first time in its existence since 1868, shifted from being a debtor nation to becoming a creditor on the financial markets. Aside from funding major infrastructure projects, the sharply rising tax revenue meant that considerable funding could be provided domestically to cultural endeavors such as the compilation of multi-volume local histories of prefectures and cities. These projects helped support an ongoing process of creating new local historical identities in the wake of long decades of turbulent change, during which the numerous feudal fiefdoms evolved into the modern administrative units created in the 1870s.[20] Similarly, Japanese industrialists engaged in large-scale domestic philanthropy throughout the war, an era that was called the age of the *narikin*, the *nouveaux riches*.[21]

The acceleration of socio-economic change due to the wartime boom also gave a major boost to academic institutions, as the demand for higher education was rising. The last year of the war witnessed the "University ordinance" (*Daigaku-rei*), which elevated many institutions of higher learning, including state- or prefecture-level colleges, to university status. Likewise, the already established, prestigious Imperial Universities also saw major expansion. The Japanese state actively and intentionally reinvested part of the high tax revenue that the wartime economic boom had created into the expansion of higher education, especially in natural sciences, technology, medicine, and social sciences.[22] The war had powerfully demonstrated the value and rising necessity of these fields for the Japanese ministerial bureaucracy and the military, both of which had studied the wartime mobilization of academia closely.[23]

狼藉の破壊せるホテルの惨状

此圖本年二月初旬比國海岸一大砲戰之時某旅館受獨軍砲撃之慘狀也

寫眞は大正二年二月初旬白耳義海岸の一大砲戰に於て獨軍の一行により破壞せられし某ホテルの惨狀を示せるものなり
Wreckage of a hotel damaged by German shells at the time of a decided cannonade on the Belgian coast in the early part of Feb, 1915.
（歴史寫眞大正四年四月號）21

Japanese universities – similar to their counterparts all over the world – eagerly used this recognition to attract state funding for expanding their faculties or creating new ones. In that respect, almost the entire, steadily growing corps of university professors had studied at European universities and thus they were part of transnational networks in their respective fields. It is therefore not surprising that the leading academic institutions – represented by the members of the Imperial Academy as well as the rectors of several Imperial universities and of the most prestigious private universities – became involved after the war in the National Committee to support the international effort to rebuild the library of the University of Louvain, one of the oldest and most prestigious European universities.

Enabled by the wartime gains, several state-run or privately financed research institutes were founded, many of which belong to the leading institutions in their field worldwide to this very day. The arguably most renowned is the Rikagaku kenkyūjo, nowadays known to the world as RIKEN, the Institute of Physical and Chemical Research, founded in 1917. Another example would be the Ōhara shakai mondai kenkyūjo, the Ōhara Institute for Social Research, founded in 1919 by the entrepreneur and philanthropist Ōhara Magosaburō (1880-1943) from Kurashiki, a city close to Okayama in western Japan. Ōhara had made a fortune with the production of silk fabric, as a banker, and as the head of a major electric company, all of which saw major expansion during the First World War. Since its creation, the institute has been distinguished for having been home to or been supported by many of the most renowned sociologists and economists of modern Japan. Its research on labor and society, social movements, and economics, as well as its sophisticated statistics regarding aspects of labor in modern society, are internationally famous. Nowadays, it is part of Hōsei University in Tokyo and an important archive for the documentation of social movements, including rare materials such as political posters, several of which can be found in this catalogue (see pp. 254-271).[24]

As part of Japan's new self-confidence and financial possibilities in the wake of the First World War, many other successful businessmen and their families started to engage in philanthropy outside of Japan as well. In the early 1920s, as Willy Vande Walle mentions in his

▲ 6. Page of the illustrated magazine *Rekishi shashin* (History in Photos), April 1915, p. 21, depicting the war damage in a Belgian hotel. Source: private collection Jan Schmidt.

essay, substantial financial support from the Iwasaki family (behind the Mitsubishi conglomerate), the Mitsui family, the Sumitomo family, the Furukawa family, and others for the Japanese book donation to the University of Louvain needs to be seen in the context of the aforementioned substantial economic gains during the First World War. Of course, they had already engaged in philanthropic acts before, but it was in the direct wake of the First World War that the scale significantly changed. In this regard, other representative examples would be the donation of a "Chaire d'Histoire de la Civilisation Japonaise" by "Baron Mitsui et autres notables Japonais" to the Université de Paris, Sorbonne in 1920; later on, the same decade also saw the donation of a

"Maison du Japon" to the Cité internationale universitaire de Paris (built 1927-1929) as well as the chair for Japanese Studies to the University of Louvain, both donated by Satsuma Jirōhachi, the heir to another industrial fortune residing in Paris.[25]

The actual manner chosen for contributing to the reconstruction of the university library - a donation of almost 14,000 volumes of Japanese books, the majority of which were premodern titles - is discussed in greater detail in Willy Vande Walle's essay. In connection to the First World War, it should be briefly mentioned that the war - at least within the political, economic, and cultural elites - catalyzed a shift in perception of Japan's own historical and cultural identity, one that had

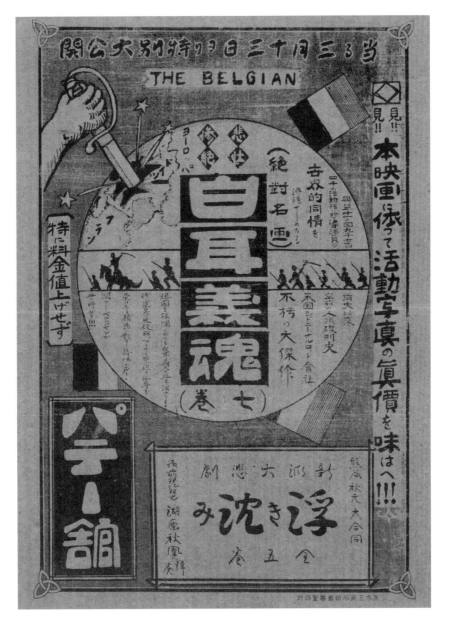

▲ 7. Japanese cinema program leaflet for *The Belgian* (1918), a US film directed by Sidney Olcott about two lovers who must work together against wily German spies for the good of Belgium while waiting to be liberated by the United States. Source: private collection Jan Schmidt.

been in the making for decades. This argument is difficult to prove empirically, to be sure, for there never was and almost certainly never will be a homogenous collective 'cultural identity'. One should be careful even trying to frame such a - constructed - thing, since it usually comes as a set with central elements of national ideology often imposed by a tiny fragment of the population without being at all contested. Nevertheless, it is safe to say that at least Japan's conservative elites in politics, business, and academia - and very likely also a growing middle class - underwent a fundamental change in early twentieth-century Japan in their collective perception and ideological use of national history and cultural heritage.

It is therefore no coincidence that most of the books donated to the University of Louvain stem from the Edo period (1600-1868). At the beginning of the modern nation-state in the late nineteenth century, the Edo period had been denounced as a feudal past that had to be overcome, in order to be on a par with European 'civilization'. However, in the early twentieth century, the Edo period experienced a renaissance and became perceived as part of the essence of Japanese 'culture' (*bunka*) in the years before the First World War. This re-evaluation was to an extent also indebted to the trend of 'Japonisme' in European art in the late nineteenth century, not to mention the successful creation of the image of 'samurai values'. As the alleged core of Japanese premodern culture, these qualities were depicted as exerting their influence into modern times in publications such as Nitobe Inazō's book *Bushido: The Soul of Japan*, first published in English in 1899, which also proved successful in its later Japanese version.[26] Elements of the cultural production of the Edo period such as the *ukiyo-e* and *nishiki-e* prints - discussed here in the essay by Freya Terryn - became a prized item for collectors all over the world, and were more and more seen as the epitome of Japanese culture. That more than ninety percent of the Japanese population in the Edo period had not been part of the warrior class, and that the selection of Edo period cultural production that became so appreciated in modern times was very eclectic, is not surprising. It serves, rather, as a mechanism that can be observed in many modern nation-states, one that historians Eric Hobsbawm and Terence Ranger have pointed out as part of their concept of the "invention of tradition".[27] In her classic text on "The Invention of Edo", the renowned historian

of modern Japan Carol Gluck has argued that one of the most prevalent appearances of the bygone Edo period in modern times can be seen in its consumption in popular culture. That cultural production included, for instance, the hundreds of *chanbara eiga*, sword-fighting films enacting the Edo period which were produced by Japanese film companies in the 1910s and 1920s.[28] For the Japanese National Committee that created the donation to the University of Louvain and whose members were recruited from the political, academic, and economic elite, however, the Edo period books donated had the purpose of "transmitting Japanese culture (*Nihon bunka*) to the West", as their official final report from 1926 stated.[29]

The enormous economic gains of the First World War years had helped to facilitate this paradigm shift by enabling not only private connoisseurs, but also the state and the regional governments of Japan to invest in ambitious publication projects and collections as part of a drive to redefine Japanese 'culture'. In that sense, the First World War was essential as a major facilitator for (re)forming a Japanese cultural identity. At the same time, however, the socio-economic changes accelerated by the war propelled a modern way of life, of urban mass culture, and of mass consumption that was detrimental to highly elitist projects such as the donation to the University of Louvain. The latter development and the following disruptive period of the Asian-Pacific War (1931-1945) are crucial in understanding why the donation was almost forgotten afterwards.

Mutual Belgian-Japanese Relief Efforts as Part of the Legacy of the First World War

In many ways the First World War years had a fundamental influence on the international nature of the Interwar Period. To be sure, diverging interests among the former wartime coalition of the Entente and Associated Powers led to tensions between Japan and Great Britain, for instance, and between Japan and the USA. By and large, however, the so-called Versailles-Washington System - building on the treaties concluded in Paris in 1919 and, for the Asia-Pacific region, in Washington 1921/22 - ushered in an atmosphere of international cooperation with the newly created League of Nations at the center of expectations.

8. Commemorative plate with the flags of the Allied Powers. The Japanese characters on the plate read, from right to left: "The Empire celebrates victory in war". Plates like these had already been manufactured in Japan since the victories in the First Sino-Japanese War (1894-95) and the Russo-Japanese War (1904-05). Source: Collection Research Group Japanese Studies, KU Leuven Faculty of Arts.

As explained in this volume by Lieven Sommen, cultural diplomacy became more important for Japan, too. In many countries that had been its wartime allies, Japan could advance foreign relations with favorable recent memories of the support given by Japan and the Japanese people, and Belgium was no exception. It is noteworthy that in Japan as well as among its wartime allies the perception of this wartime alliance can also be traced to material culture. It may seem ephemeral at first, but on many objects the flags of Japan, Britain, France, Italy, the US, and also of Belgium were displayed together, with Japan as the only non-Western member among the 'Five Great Powers' (whereas Russia's status was unclear after the Bolshevik Revolution, with the emerging Soviet Union thus excluded from being embedded in such commemorative culture). Objects like the commemorative plate on display in the exhibition and shown here were common, while in the Royal Library in Brussels a rare

◥ 9. First World War commemorative pin in the form of an airplane with allied flags including Japan. Source: Royal Library of Belgium (KBR), Inv. II, 2189.

▶ 10. First World War commemorative pin with allied flags including Japan. Source: KBR, Inv. II, 1604.

ベルギー首府ブリュッセル市の北停車場御著。皇帝陛下と御同乗、王宮に向はせらる。（六月十日）

collection of commemorative pins also shows that Japan was seen in Belgium as an integral part of the coalition during the war and in its immediate aftermath.

The fact that the Imperial Seal of Japan can be seen together with the flags of Britain, France, Italy, and the US on the façade of the new library building of the University of Louvain at its inauguration in 1928, resulted not only from the Japanese book donation but also from the integral part Japan played in the commemoration of the First World War alliance in more general terms.

As Willy Vande Walle lays out in his essay, it was deemed to be only logical that Japanese Crown Prince Hirohito (1901-1989), the later Shōwa emperor (r. 1926-1989), when travelling through the countries of the wartime alliance, would visit not only battlefields of the First World War in Ieper/Ypres and in Luik/Liège, but also Leuven/Louvain, which was still in the process of reconstruction. Guiding the young Crown Prince through the ruins of the old university library were Cardinal Désiré-Joseph Mercier (1851-1926) – a popular figure of resistance against the German occupation in the Japanese mass media during the war – and Rector Paulin Ladeuze (1870-1940). Many documents and objects related to his visit remain in Belgian and Japanese archives. The Crown Prince was received by the King of Belgium and Belgian notables in Brussels at a gala dinner, and

the meticulous preparations for his itinerary in Belgium show once more the traces of the First World War. The visit to the destroyed landscapes of Ieper/Ypres and to a panorama painting in Brussels of the drearily muddy IJzer/Yser front seems to have left a genuinely strong impression on Hirohito and his entourage, and soon after his return to Japan the Imperial Household Ministry donated 10,000 yen, a sizeable sum at that time, to the effort of the National Committee. This sum became the core of other financial donations from affluent Japanese families, which then were used to purchase the book donation to the University of Louvain, which arrived between 1924 and 1926. The visit by the Crown Prince was also an immensely popular topic with the Japanese public, covered by the Japanese mass media in great detail.

Even the arguably most critical situation in the process of the preparation of the donation and the way it unfolded can be attributed partially to the First World War. Namely, on September 1, 1923, the Great Kantō Earthquake hit the Tokyo-Yokohama region. Along with the subsequent ubiquitous fires, this massive earthquake destroyed large parts of the Japanese capital region and killed about 100,000 of its inhabitants.[30] Many contemporary Japanese observers immediately commented in the mass media that the flattened, charred landscape of Tokyo resembled the images of the battlefields of Ieper/Ypres, the Somme, or Verdun. These were well known

▲ 11. Crown Prince Hirohito after having arrived at North Station, Brussels, in a carriage together with King Albert I., 10 June 1921. Source: Futara, Yoshinori/ Sawada Setsuzō, *Kōtaishi denka go-gaiyū-ki.* Tōkyō: Tōkyō nichinichi shinbun 1924, private collection Jan Schmidt.

to the Japanese public through the many photos and films that had been in the media during the war, not to mention the images conveyed to the Japanese audience from Crown Prince Hirohito's visit in 1921. Several "actuality films" that were shot by Japanese media companies or by British and French film companies also had shown the Crown Prince walking over the moonscapes of the former battlefields. They proved to be very popular, with movie-goers in the millions and, thus, with several screenings a day lasting into the night even at smaller, local cinemas in Japan. Very likely, then, images of that kind had become such a part of the collective memory that the idea (mentioned above) could be voiced that now Japan had its own Ieper/Ypres. The Japanese capital region, it was said, needed a complete reconstruction modeled after the postwar reconstruction in West Flanders or other sites of wartime destruction.[31] Internationally, the news – and the images – of the destroyed Tokyo-Yokohama landscape and of the hundreds of thousands of domestic refugees displaced from their dwellings evoked immediate willingness for a donation campaign, coordinated in Belgium by the Belgian Red Cross. Part of this campaign was a "Japanse Dag te Antwerpen"/"Journée Japonaise à Anvers", and it is not a coincidence that it took place on November 11, 1923, that is, on Armistice Day. A rare two-minute, forty-nine-second film of the event – in the possession of the Antwerp City Archives and stored in the Royal Film Archive of Belgium – shows citizens of Antwerp dressed as Japanese at the head of a solidarity parade, carrying a banner of the Union amicale d'Anvers launching a "Hulp aan Japan"-"Aide au Japon" campaign.

Another material trace of this can be found in the Royal Library in Brussels, where a voluminous album contains the signatures of about 15,000 pupils from schools in Tokyo and Yokohama expressing their gratitude for the considerable financial donations made by Belgians as part of the international relief effort after the earthquake.

The University of Louvain, where the new university library was not yet even built, also participated by sending books to Tokyo Imperial University, which had lost its library to the fires after the earthquake. It was this atmosphere of mutual Belgian-Japanese relief efforts, interwoven in the commemoration of the alliance of the First World War, that caused the National Committee in Japan to decide to continue the preparations for the book donations to Belgium, regardless of the enormous loss of books in Tokyo in 1923.

Conclusion

The First World War provided, in several ways, structural preconditions for the 1920s Japanese donation to the University of Louvain. It transformed the way the Japanese public viewed the world in an age of ever intensifying mediatization, including the perception of Belgium. The Japanese mass media followed the development of the war closely and actively provided extensive commentary, often highlighting humanitarian and symbolic acts of solidarity such as the dispatch of seventy-five Japanese Red Cross

▲ 12. Still from the film 'Japanse Dag te Antwerpen' of parts of a parade with citizens of Antwerp dressed as Japanese as part of a Red Cross charity event on Armistice Day (11 November) 1923, to collect money for the victims of the Great Kantō Earthquake in Japan of 1 September 1923. Source: Felixarchive, Stadsarchief Antwerpen.

▲ 13. Still from the film 'Japanse Dag te Antwerpen' of citizens of Antwerp dressed as *geisha*. Source: Felixarchive, Stadsarchief Antwerpen.

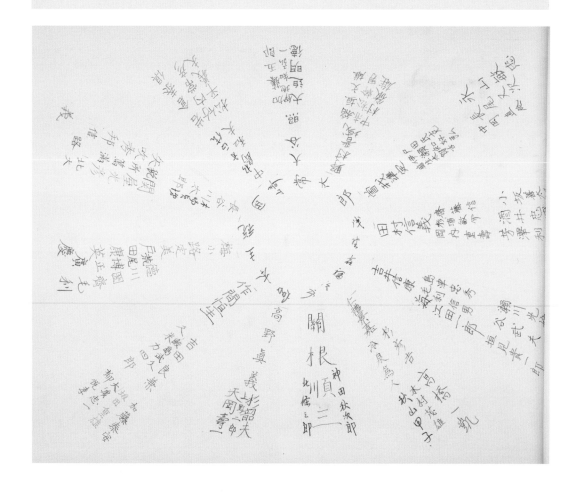

▲ 14. "Letter of Gratitude to the Belgian People" in French in a register with signatures of pupils of schools in Tokyo expressing their gratitude for the Belgian aid in the aftermath of the 1923 Great Kantō Earthquake, 1924, KBR, Manuscripts Department, Ms. II 5974.

▲ 15. Signatures of pupils of schools in Tokyo arranged as a Japanese flag, KBR, Manuscripts Department, Ms. II 5974.

nurses to Britain, France, and Russia, as well as the donation of a Japanese sword to King Albert I of Belgium by Japanese newspaper companies. By at least symbolically reversing the originally Eurocentric world order of the nineteenth century, these acts were part of a process of emancipation, as the Empire of Japan now supported its besieged European allies.

The economic boom of the war years in Japan also served as a precondition for the 1920s donation: firstly in a very direct, material way, by allowing the creation of surplus earnings that could be invested in cultural diplomacy by the state and in philanthropy by private entrepreneurs; secondly, by strengthening Japanese universities and research institutes, which elevated the standing and self-confidence of these institutions, many of which became supporters of the donation by joining into a public-private partnership with the aforementioned philanthropic entrepreneurs. Although empirically somewhat hard to prove, it can also be argued that the economic gains and the accompanying socio-economic changes, in addition to the elevated international standing of the Empire of Japan in the postwar order, also might have catalyzed an already ongoing shift in collective 'cultural identity' – at least within the elites – leading to the impulse to "transmit Japanese culture" actively outside of Japan and to represent it abroad in the form of such donations.

Moreover, several concrete Belgian-Japanese relief efforts can be seen as part of the legacy of the First World War. They were embedded in an atmosphere commemorating the wartime alliance, with symbols such as the national flags visible in the material culture of both countries in the early 1920s. Crown Prince Hirohito's visit to Belgium – and, as part of it, to the sites of wartime destruction in Ieper/Ypres, Luik/Liège, and Leuven/Louvain – also is a direct outcome of the First World War. In the case of his visit to Leuven, this led to the contribution of a considerable sum by the Imperial Household Ministry to the Japanese donation as part of the international effort to rebuild the library of the University of Louvain, thereby encouraging affluent Japanese entrepreneurs to follow suit. The visit also had a deeper impact on the visual collective memory in Japan, given the many photographs and the films of Crown Prince Hirohito's visit to the former battlefields of the First World War. These representations cemented the image of large-scale wartime destruction of cities and entire landscapes

that had already been previously conveyed by the Japanese mass media during the war. This image was subsequently turned to when the Great Kantō Earthquake devastated large parts of the Tokyo-Yokohama area in September 1923. In the aftermath of the earthquake, the Belgian contribution to international relief efforts through financial donations by citizens and of books by the University of Louvain further strengthened the wartime atmosphere of mutual support and led to the decision by the National Committee coordinating the Japanese donation not to abandon the project, despite the fact that the earthquake had destroyed many major libraries in Tokyo, including the one at Tokyo Imperial University. The structural nexus between the First World War and the 1920s Japanese donation to the University of Louvain was made all the more manifest in the fact that major fundraising events in Belgium to participate in the disaster relief after the 1923 earthquake in Japan were staged on November 11, 1923, on Armistice Day. These traces of an ongoing commemoration of wartime alliances, of which the Japanese book donation is a part, faded towards the end of the 1920s when new global challenges appeared. Only too soon afterward would the Japanese donation become a – nearly – forgotten chapter in the legacy of the First World War.

31

▲ 16. Map of the Japanese Empire, ca. 1920, Alexander Gross F.R.G.S., London. Source: private collection.

FÊTES DE LA VICTOIRE
Gal. Japonais et son Etat-Major

Lieven Sommen

An Empire of the Mid-Tier:
The Japanese Ministry of Foreign Affairs and
the New Mass Public-Focused Diplomacy
of the Early Twentieth Century

Introduction

In 1868, Japan's feudal regime under the Tokugawa 徳川 clan was replaced by the Meiji government in what is known as the *Meiji Ishin* 明治維新, the 'Meiji Restoration', signaling the start of Japan's newly increased participation in world affairs and starting a period of rapid change for the country. From the perspective of Japan's foreign relations, there were two main phases between Japan's re-opening and its defeat in the Pacific War in 1945. In the first phase, until the First Sino-Japanese War of 1894-1895, the Meiji regime spent much of its resources trying to prove to the outside world that Japan was a developed nation along the lines envisioned by the Western powers, in an attempt to have the 'Unequal Treaties' (*fubyōdō jōyaku* 不平等条約) reversed. These were treaties that had been imposed on Japan by the U.S., Britain, France, and other Western countries, including Belgium, in the 1850s and 1860s. In the second phase, the island nation surprised many by winning wars against Imperial China in 1894-1895 and Czarist Russia in 1904-1905. From this point on, Japan vied to become an empire amid a changing world order, turning Taiwan and Korea into colonies in 1895 and 1910, respectively. Heading into the Paris Peace Conference of 1919, where the Japanese delegates sat at the victors' table as one of the so-called Five Great Powers, it seemed as though Japan was poised to consolidate its position as a burgeoning new empire within East Asia.

However, at the Paris Peace Conference, the Japanese diplomats met fierce opposition from the Chinese delegation, and heading into the 1920s there was still a long road ahead before Japan could have considered itself the equal of the United States or Great Britain on the world stage. As historian Akira Iriye describes the situation,[1] in the two decades following the First World War, a sentiment of internationalism swept across the globe, while at the same time the resurgence of nationalism and isolationism cannot be ignored, either. The Japanese diplomats struggled to find their place within this changing diplomatic landscape in the 1920s especially, as they were caught between a desire to forge better foreign relations with the U.S. and other powers on the one hand, and a desire to try to gain acceptance of Japan's ambitions to become the dominant power within East Asia on the other. This essay will give a brief overview of the obstacles Japanese diplomats faced before and after the conference at Versailles and of the diplomatic strategies taken in response. In this way, it serves to show the context in which the 1920s book donation to the Leuven library was made after the First World War.

Improvements in Mass Communication Technologies Made Diplomacy More Public

The 1800s saw the rise of mass media, which first emanated out of the Western countries but were soon a global phenomenon. In many countries, with Germany and Britain at the vanguard, improved production technology for newspapers and weekly magazines caused the prices for them to drop. This change coincided with the appearance of a growing level of literacy that allowed the general population to consume these media. In Japan, the creation of new educational institutions also allowed for the growth of mass media there, but equally important is that Japan already had a high level of literacy in comparison to many other countries during the Edo Period, as

1. Postcard showing Japanese mounted officers at the victory parade on the Champs-Élysées in 1919 on the occasion of the Paris Peace Conference. Source: Collection CEEJA/Pauer, Alsace, France.

has been shown by Peter Kornicki.[2] Within this global context, politics became something that the general population participated in ever more, and politicians who wished to retain their positions of influence had to account for the nebulous 'public opinion' that from now on legitimized their political clout.[3]

The same held true in Japan, where the founders of the Meiji regime did their best to withhold authority from the parliament, which came into being along with the Meiji Constitution of 1889. Nonetheless, heading into the 1890s and 1900s, the government gradually had to abide a political system in which political parties gained more and more influence. In 1925, suffrage rights (the ability to vote in elections) were extended to all Japanese males over 25. Much in the same way, foreign relations and the way diplomacy was carried out also changed as a result of this new, more connected world.

New Communication Technologies and the 'Old' Versus the 'New' Diplomacy

In general, the diplomatic sphere incrementally changed in two ways in the period between the 1880s and 1945. On the one hand, the ubiquity of media made it so that information travelled very fast and, in combination with the increased importance of satiating (foreign) public opinion, a new type of international politician had to be put forward who could both defend his nations' interests and appeal to a global audience. Due to ceaseless scrutiny by a host of different media, which were ever evolving technologically, backroom diplomacy became significantly more difficult. A balance now had to be struck between compromises that could be reached between the various countries' leaders and the expectations that the public behind these negotiating parties had.[4]

On the other hand, there was also the shift from what has been called 'old diplomacy' to the 'new diplomacy'. In January 1918, Woodrow Wilson gave a speech to Congress outlining his Fourteen Points, in which he called for such ideas as free trade, democracy, and a willingness by governments around the world to create agreements with each other that were transparent to the public. This set of ideas was then legitimized as it became the main thrust of the Paris Peace Conference that was soon to happen. Wilson actually never proposed the idea of the 'self-determination of nations', despite this phrase having become associated with his peace proposals. Rather

than give individual states high levels of freedom, Wilson's designs instead focused on a collective participation by the world's various powers both large and small, in order to achieve global consensus over various issues.[5]

'Old diplomacy' may be understood, then, to mean a world order in which only the great powers with colonies have a say in how the power balances evolve through bilateral or trilateral agreements, whereas new diplomacy was purported to be more inclusive. In it, the various countries of the world would be granted more freedom by each other to hold sovereignty, while also being part of an international network to support one another.[6] However, it must be noted that these idealistic propositions by Wilson had an element of *Realpolitik* to them, as they were meant to consolidate the United States' growing diplomatic power within the aftermath of the First World War.

The First World War and the Institutionalization of Propaganda

Though both of these transitions occurred over a longer period of time, the advent of the First World War threw them into stark relief. Propaganda came to be an essential weapon in warfare during the First World War and was recognized as such in the eyes of many contemporary writers. Among them was Komatsu Taka'aki (小松孝彰), a bureaucrat who became the head of Japan's Cabinet Information Bureau (*naikaku jōhōbu* 内閣情報部) in 1937. He saw evidence of propaganda's critical role in the fact that countries like Britain (the War Propaganda Bureau at Wellington House) and the U.S. (the George Creel Committee) had instituted propaganda-spinning agencies during the war, and that after the war these institutions had not gone away. Rather, intelligence-gathering and the spinning of information for diplomatic gains was now common practice for governments around the world, Japan included.[7]

At the same time, the utter ruthlessness of the war had shown both the fighting nations and those that witnessed it from the sidelines that the perception of the Western major powers had changed. Whereas power had lain with a small number of empires in the West, in Versailles the liberalism of Wilson now combined with a desire for internationalism that looked like it might give the newly forged Empire of Japan the opportunity to join the other great powers. While Japan already had colonies, including Korea, Taiwan, and

South Sakhalin, the main goal of certain factions within the government and the Japanese Army was to expand Japan's influence in Manchuria and China at large.[8]

For its participation in the First World War on the side of the Allies, Japan got a seat as one of the Five Major Powers at the Paris Peace Conference of 1919, where the postwar order would be decided. With regard to China, the U.S. and Britain sought in Versailles to maintain the Open Door Policy, which had been negotiated by U.S. Secretary of State John Hay in 1899, and stated that the great powers would have equal access to the resources and opportunities they identified for themselves in China. The continuing existence of this status quo was a large obstacle to Japan's ambitions in the region as a new empire, which the other powers tried to keep from getting a large foothold in China.[9] The Japanese Ministry of Foreign Affairs had to learn quickly how to make use of new media in order to strengthen Japan's diplomatic position, therefore, and convince the other powers that the Japanese were justified in building an empire of their own.[10]

The Paris Peace Conference: The Public-Facing Diplomacy of the Chinese Delegation and Japan's Pyrrhic Victory in the Shandong Issue

The Japanese delegation included such figureheads as the diplomats Makino Nobuaki 牧野伸明 (1861-1949) and Ijūin Hikokichi 伊集院彦吉 (1864-1924). These men had already been spending time thinking about the representations of Japan in foreign relations matters since 1900. For this reason, the Japanese Ministry of Foreign Affairs sent along a 'media team' that had to advise the delegates on how certain messages would be received. Among this team were Matsuoka Yōsuke 松岡洋石 (1880-1946), who would later become head of the delegation of Japan to the League of Nations to Geneva and Minister of Foreign Affairs, as well as the Irishman John Russell Kennedy, who had been a key part of the *Kokusai* news agency.[11]

At the Paris Peace Conference, the Japanese delegation had two main objectives. It wanted to have a 'racial equality clause' written into the Covenant of the newly created League of Nations, the prewar predecessor of today's United Nations. Such a clause would symbolically declare the Japanese citizens to be on an equal level with the peoples of the major powers. The delegates

also wanted the concessions held by Germany in China to be transferred to Japan. However, on both fronts they encountered resistance. When it came to the subject of racial equality, the Australian delegation was heavily opposed, and ultimately it was defeated.[12] The previously German-held concessions in Shandong were contested by the Chinese delegation, which used the 'self-determination of nations' espoused by Wilsonianism to argue that these concessions should be returned to China rather than be passed on to the Japanese. The Chinese diplomats were aided in these efforts by a team of American journalists that advised them on the media angle of their interventions. In general, the Chinese diplomats, like Wellington V.K. Koo, spoke English far better than their Japanese counterparts did. Furthermore, outside of the halls of the conference, they also made use of techniques such as interviews, the printing of flyers defending their cause, and the enlisting of support from foreign journalists through bribes.[13]

Before the Paris Peace Conference, the growing Japanese Empire had looked poised to seat itself alongside the other major powers in global politics. However, the conference turned out to be a bitter disappointment. With the rejection of the 'racial equality clause', it became clear that Japan would only partially be allowed to enter into the circle of imperial nations and that its citizens would remain the target of discrimination based on race, even when emigrating to other member states of the League of Nations. With regards to the German-held concessions, the Japanese delegation's tactics to promote itself to a global audience also turned out to be deficient.

The conference made many diplomats realize that Japan would need to do more to promote itself in a more appropriate manner, were it to have any hope of joining the club of the most powerful nations and, in so doing, be allowed to expand its influence in East Asia. It became clear to the younger generation of Japanese diplomats in Paris, that Japan was not yet at this point; as a result, much of the public and cultural diplomacy that would follow in the 1920s and early 1930s was created with this goal in mind. After 1919, the Ministry of Foreign Affairs would seek to rapidly professionalize its understanding of how to promote Japan.[14] The book donation to Leuven must be seen within this context of the Japanese diplomats' attempts to be a part of this internationalist atmosphere.

Participating Actively in the New Internationalism: The League of Nations

There were members of the Japanese government who had considerable misgivings about joining the new League of Nations during the Paris Peace Conference, especially in light of the other powers' unwillingness to declare the equality of citizens of members states of other 'races'. Nevertheless, Prime Minister Hara Takashi 原敬 (1856-1921) still felt that joining the League was essential in mending the relations with Britain and the U.S., which had suffered during the war.[15]

During the 1920s, Japan cooperated energetically with the League of Nations. It became one of the four permanent members of the League Council. A League of Nations association was established very quickly after the war in Japan, and subcommittees of the League of Nations were also headed by noted internationalists like Nitobe Inazō 新渡戸稲造 (1862-1933), who was the delegate of Japan to the League in 1921. These subcommittees showed how having international conferences on a wide variety of subjects, such as the arts, journalism, science, and foreign relations, was becoming the new global norm. Experts were coming together across the boundaries of their own nations, and the League of Nations was the strongest symbol of this desire to share knowledge without borders.[16]

However, the League stood for maintaining the status quo, and Japan tried to balance its contribution to the existing situation with attempts to establish regional dominance for its empire. Eventually, this ambivalent position turned out to be untenable due to growing ultra-nationalism within Japan, which resulted in the country's leaving of the League in 1933. In September 1931, namely, the Japanese Army had staged what became commonly known as the 'Manchurian Incident' as a pretense for intervening in northeastern China. Yet the League of Nations rejected the validity of the ensuing invasion of Manchuria, and Matsuoka Yōsuke was forced to lead the Japanese delegation from the League's council chambers.[17]

▲ 2. Commemorative photograph of Ambassador Plenipotentiary Saionji Kinmochi and his retinue after the Paris Peace Conference, taken at the Hotel Le Bristol in Paris, June 1919. Citing bad health, Saionji remained in the background, however, and the delegation was led de facto by Makino Nobuaki. Saionji is sitting front and centre, holding a light coloured hat. Source: Image from Wikimedia Commons under license Creative Commons CC 1.0.

An Example of Public Diplomacy in the 1920s: Crown Prince Hirohito's 1921 Visit to Europe

Aside from Japan's considerable contributions to the League of Nations in the 1920s, other attempts were also made to foster good relations with the Western powers. In this subsection, an example of public diplomacy that relates to this goal will briefly be explained: Crown Prince Hirohito's 裕仁皇太子 (1901-1989) visit to various European countries in 1921.[18] In the wake of the Paris Peace Conference and throughout the 1920s, the above-mentioned internationalists in the Ministry of Foreign Affairs felt that it was essential to create better relations with the U.S., in particular, and to make Japan better understood by people in Europe and America.

In this context, Crown Prince Hirohito (who became the Shōwa Emperor in 1926) would make an official visit to Britain, France, Belgium, the Netherlands, and Italy between March and September of 1921. The Crown Prince was only 20 years of age at this time, showing how the Japanese government wished to put forward a face of

youth in their international image. Leaving from the port of Yokohama with two ships for himself and his entourage, Hirohito would call at primarily British-controlled colonies' ports along the way, including those of Hong Kong, Singapore, British Ceylon, Egypt, Malta, and Gibraltar.[19]

The trip, which was managed by the Ministry of the Imperial Household (宮内省, hereafter *Kunaishō*) in cooperation with the Ministry of Foreign Affairs and the Home Ministry (内務省), was notable for two reasons. First, it was intended as a form of education for the prince, as his educators felt he made a stiff impression during social contact. Furthermore, the Taishō Emperor (大正天皇) was a sickly man, and Hirohito was expected to take over from him soon. Exploring various countries and seeing the world was therefore also a good way to prepare Hirohito for his duties as sovereign in a world that was becoming increasingly connected through mass media. He would need this experience and knowledge of the modern world, for at that time many traditional monarchies were in existential crisis in Europe: The Russian Revolution (1917-1923) was bringing

Czarist rule to an end, while the Austrian and Ottoman Empires and their monarchs vanished as well.[20] Though there were many in the Japanese government and *Kunaishō* who felt that the crown prince should not be taught the ways of Western countries, in the end the internationalists won out and he was allowed to leave for Europe.[21]

The other important aspect of the 1921 visit to Europe is its place in the history of the Japanese imperial family's relation with mass media. Historian Komura Akira has stated that this media element was not a large part of the original decision to send Hirohito away by Japanese government and *Kunaishō* officials. As Akira also observes, however, this aspect did start to play an increasingly big role in the lead-up to the trip. The Crown Prince was quite interested in new media technologies such as film reels (called 活動写真 – "moving photos" – at this time in Japan), and he made a positive impression in both the Japanese and foreign media. Accordingly, the officials supporting him realized they should put him in front of cameras and have him appear in newspapers more often.[22] The films that came out of the trip represent the first time a core member of the Japanese Imperial family was allowed to be filmed.[23]

By the time the two ships set sail from Yokohama, four Japanese news companies had been given permission to send along correspondents who would cover the trip and report it to the Japanese people. Six Japanese news and film companies were made responsible for feeding news reels back to Japan. News would come in with a delay of a few weeks to a month, but to the contemporary audience it must have felt as though they could watch the prince travel around Europe in real-time.[24]

The worries about foreign media and how they might portray Crown Prince Hirohito turned out to be unfounded, as the young man was a striking figure who left a good impression. Before the departure, it had been decided by the *Kunaishō* that the Japanese newspaper companies could not have their correspondents ride with the royal entourage on the two ships, and instead they had to race ahead to the planned ports of call in order to be there before Hirohito himself arrived. However, as the trip went on, the officials waiting on the prince allowed him to engage with these journalists more and more. Through his figure, a vision was projected of Japan as being a prominent part of the new post-Versailles global order, with an energetic ruler who was interested in media and new technologies, as well as in other countries' cultures and traditions.[25] In this way, the visit may also be seen in both the contexts of the rise of mass media and mass culture, as well as the internationalism of the 1920s, both of which many foreign policy elites within the Japanese Ministry of Foreign Affairs were keen to slot into.

Activities such as Hirohito's trip were made even more critical because of the United States' Immigration Act of 1924, also known as the 'Asian Exclusion Act'. This legislation banned all immigration from Asia and was a blow to Japan. Japanese notables like Nitobe Inazō and the Japanese ambassador to the U.S., Matsudaira Tsuneo 松平恆雄 (1877-1949), thus made attempts to heal relations. The creation of the Institute of Pacific Relations, in which Japan and the U.S. played key

▲ 3. Crown Prince Hirohito being guided through the ruins of the University of Louvain hall and library during his visit to Belgium in 1921. Source: Koninklijk Museum van het Leger en de Krijgsgeschiedenis, B.1.111. 115 | 28515, No.: 201871636.

roles, as well as cultural diplomacy, speeches, and extensive news propaganda were all tactics to give the Japanese empire the positive image that would allow it to achieve its goals.[26]

Conclusion

In the early 1900s, Japan was a new and burgeoning empire trying to find its place in the global order. As a result of key developments in communications technology, approaches to diplomacy had to change for all the world powers, because now the public could track of the movements of the state and express its opinions on it. This was coupled with a groundswell of liberal and pacifist sentiment in the early twentieth century for which the First World War acted as a considerable catalyst. These two evolutions made for the rise of the 'new diplomacy', in which the direction of foreign relations would not be decided by a select group of colonizing 'great powers' alone. As a result, propaganda and the advertising of one's country to audiences in other nations through mass media became a normalized feature in the policies of governments around the world.

Through the creation of news agencies in the 1910s, the Japanese foreign policy elites showed that they understood the need to adapt to the new realities of mass public-based diplomacy. Japan had already been working on improving its own propaganda efforts since the First Sino-Japanese War (1894-1895), and its diplomats arrived at the

▲ 4. 'Elder Statesman' and former Prime Minister Saionji Kinmochi (1849-1940), who led the Japanese delegation to the Paris Peace Conference in 1919 and who vowed to support the international effort to rebuild the library of the University of Louvain. Portrait photo taken around 1928. Source: Creative Commons CC 1.0.

Paris Peace Conference of 1919 thinking that they were poised to break into the ranks of the world's most powerful players.

However, the Paris Peace Conference of 1919 made it clear that Japan was still a second-rank nation when compared to the established major powers. The diplomats themselves did not know how to appeal to the foreign media that were present in Paris in order to strengthen their case. This was in stark contrast to the Chinese delegation, which knew how to steer their image in Western media, and which constituted the opposition in the discussion surrounding the rights to concessions in Shandong. The conference caused young Japanese diplomats to realize that Japan would have to do better at promoting itself to the world, and in the 1920s they did their best to participate in a wave of internationalism spreading across the globe.

The Japanese diplomats acted as an important part of the greatest symbol of this internationalism, the League of Nations, becoming one of its four permanent members in an attempt to foster closer relations with the Western powers. As has been described above, they also undertook 'cultural diplomacy' through such endeavours as Crown Prince Hirohito's visit to Europe. The 1924 Immigration Act was a blow to internationalists in Japan, but in general the Japanese Ministry of Foreign Affairs went to great lengths to engender better relations with various western countries, and the United States in particular, during the 1920s. With this goal in mind, young diplomats with internationalist ideas worked to go along with a wave of internationalism that swept the globe during this decade. Though it may cynically be concluded with the benefit of hindsight that they did so in order to further Japan's capacity for war, many of them simply believed that Japan should be part of a connected world order, and that the nation should find its rightful place within it.

The book donation to the library of the University of Louvain may in this context be seen as a clever way to present Japan's culture to readers in the West, but it also symbolized the Japanese desire to be included among the major nations, with a culture that deserves to be shared. Though isolationist voices within Japan ultimately won out over the internationalist ones and led the nation into war, the donation should be seen as an attempt to connect, as well as to become an open part of a global world order.

Willy Vande Walle

The Japanese Book Donation to the University of Louvain

The Destruction of the Library in 1914

On the fateful night of August 25, 1914, the Louvain[1] University Library was set ablaze and laid to waste in the 'sac de Louvain', the phrase used in reference to the 'Strafgericht' meted out by the German troops occupying the city of Leuven. They ransacked and burned hundreds of buildings in the old city centre, as well as executed civilians in retaliation for the actions of alleged *francs-tireurs* who had shot down German troops. An estimated 250,000 volumes, including 950 manuscripts and 800 incunabula, all went up in flames.[2] Virtually no book was left intact. Both KU Leuven and the Université Catholique de Louvain (UCLouvain) keep in either their archives or rare book collections a few specimens of charred, now illegible volumes – all that remains from the library as it then was.

International Solidarity for the Reconstruction

The burning down of the library was condemned throughout the world as an act of barbarism and a blow to civilization itself. Response was quick, first in Belgium, where the Flemish writer Emmanuel de Bom (1868-1953), already in September 1914, in yet unoccupied Antwerp, collected 800 books for donation to the university's library. In November 1914 Robert Fruin (1857-1935), director-general of the State Archives of the Netherlands (*algemeen rijksarchivaris*) and acclaimed historian, launched the *Leuvensch Boekenfonds*, which may rightly be considered the first national committee of solidarity towards the university.[3] It was soon eclipsed in early 1915 by the initiative of the Institut de France and the French Academy, which launched an international appeal, calling upon the Allies as well as the neutral nations to help in rebuilding the library and restore its holdings. Japan responded very quickly to the French appeal. On July 19, 1915, Baron Kikuchi Dairoku 菊池大麓 (1855-1917), member of the Privy Council and the then president of the Imperial Academy of Japan, wrote to Étienne Lamy (1845-1919), perpetual secretary of the Académie française as well as president of the newly established *Comité* (subsequently called: *commission) d'initiative de l'Oeuvre internationale de Louvain*. Kikuchi confirmed to Lamy that the Imperial Academy was prepared to join the international effort to reconstruct the library of the University of Louvain.[4] As a result, on the sidelines of the Paris Peace Conference in 1919, a *Comité International de l'Oeuvre de Louvain* was constituted, comprising leading personalities from the political and scholarly world. It was to coordinate the various activities for the *Oeuvre internationale de Louvain,* the overarching name given the initiatives taken up by national committees in many countries of the world, those similarly in solidarity for the University of Louvain, as well as in support of the library's reconstruction and the reconstitution or substitution of its holdings. Mgr Simon Deploige (1868-1927), professor in the Faculty of Law and president of the Institute of Philosophy at the University of Louvain, was appointed commissioner-general of *Le Comité International pour la restauration de l'Université de Louvain*. He was aided by a secretariat set up within his institute.[5]

Japan Joins *l'Oeuvre internationale de Louvain*[6]

Japan's Minister Plenipotentiary to Belgium Adachi Mine'ichirō 安達峰一郎 (1870-1934)[7] urged the Japanese Ministry of Foreign Affairs to pledge

41

AMBASSADE IMPÉRIALE
DU
JAPON

BRUXELLES, LE 30 MAI 1925.
1, BOULEVARD MILITAIRE
TÉLÉPHONE : 311.25

Monseigneur,

J'ai l'honneur et le très grand plaisir de vous informer qu'un troisième envoi de 16 caisses, dont l'une contient un vase à fleurs, don de S.A.I. le Prince Hirohito, destinées à la Bibliothèque de votre Université et embarquées à bord de S. S. Suwa-Maru, arrivera vers mi-juin à Anvers.

Comme pour les précédents envois, j'ai prié notre Consul à Anvers de vous envoyer directement les caisses en question dès qu'elles arriveront en Belgique.

Je vous remets sous ce pli la liste des livres constituant l'envoi des 15 caisses annoncées et l'explication du vase à fleurs.

Vivement désireux de savoir si ces caisses vous sont parvenues sans incidents et sans avarie, je vous serais très reconnaissant de vouloir bien me faire envoyer un petit mot à ce sujet dès que vous serez en leur possession.

Très heureux de pouvoir vous annoncer cette bonne nouvelle, je vous prie d'agréer, Monseigneur, l'assurance de ma très haute considération et de mes sentiments très respectueux.

Monseigneur LADEUZE.

▲ 2. Letter from the Japanese Ambassador to Belgium Adachi Mine'ichirō to Mgr. Paulin Ladeuze, rector of the University of Louvain. Source: Universiteitsarchief KU Leuven, Archief rector magnificus Paulin Ladeuze, C163.2

its participation in the projected international *Comité d'initiative*. He proposed a list of fifteen members, including Saionji Kinmoch 西園寺公望 (1849-1940) and Hozumi Nobushige 穂積陳重 (1855-1926) as honorary members of the International committee, in addition to thirteen other prominent academics as regular members. Saionji, scion of a noble family and senior statesman, who had been prime minister in 1906-1908 and 1911-1912, was Japan's chief delegate to the Paris Peace Conference; while Hozumi, a professor of philosophy of law at Tokyo Imperial University, was the incumbent president of the Imperial Academy of Japan. The other academics were mostly presidents of universities and members of the Imperial Academy.[8] From May through July 1919, the committee gathered in Paris. Japan was represented at the meetings by Captain Yamamoto Shinjirō 山本信次郎 (1877-1942),[9] naval attaché to the Japanese delegation to the Paris Peace Conference,[10] a man whom we shall meet again below. While in Paris, Saionji Kinmochi made the promise to Jules Van den Heuvel (1854-1926), plenipotentiary delegate of the Belgian Government at the Conference and professor of law at the University of Louvain, that he would undertake to set up a national committee in Japan. The Japanese members of the international committee held their first meeting in Tokyo in March 1920.

Adachi, promoted to the rank of ambassador to Belgium in 1921,[11] had a clear vision of what the Japanese contribution to *l'Oeuvre internationale de Louvain* would ideally have to be: He wanted a spacious room exclusively reserved for books and documents "concernant la civilisation du Japon et de l'Extrême Orient".[12] He argued that a small amount of money would not do, given the important donations that the other major nations intended to make. In order to avoid unfavourable comparisons with these countries, he not unwisely proposed to make a contribution in kind. Japan was to donate books and models that would explain aspects of Japan's unique culture. The models would be put in a small museum annex to the library. Initially, as Rector Paulin Ladeuze (1870-1940) stated in a letter to Adachi, the university would have preferred a financial contribution.[13]

Visit of Crown Prince Hirohito to Belgium and the Ruins of the Louvain Library

In 1921, Crown Prince and future Emperor of Japan Hirohito made a tour of Europe. In those days, battlefields and spectacular ruins were fixed fare on the menu for important foreign visitors. Consequently, a visit to the library's ruins could not be missing from the itinerary of the Japanese crown prince.[14] Accompanied by his great-uncle Prince Kan'in no Miya Kotohito 閑院宮載仁 (1865-1945) and Yamamoto Shinjirō, who had been designated Hirohito's teacher of French and his personal aide, he visited the ruins on June 20, 1921.[15] Yamamoto's counterpart in Louvain was Louis de Schaetzen van Brienen (1900-1958), the second secretary of the university (from 1931 to 1958), and the secretary of *l'Oeuvre internationale de Louvain* on the Louvain side. Incidentally, Yamamoto was a devout Catholic, who allegedly harboured the conviction that his country should convert to Catholicism wholesale and subsequently lead the Far East along the same path of conversion.[16] After Japan had established diplomatic ties with the Vatican, he did indeed become *chargé de mission* to the Holy See.

On March 17, 1922, a meeting was held in Tokyo by the Japanese members of the international committee to pass the following resolutions:

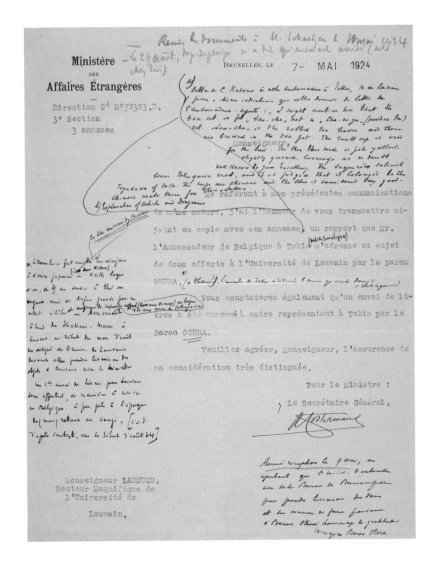

▲ 3. Letter from Foreign Ministry of Belgium to Mgr. Paulin Ladeuze, rector of the University of Louvain. Source: Universiteitsarchief KU Leuven, Archief rector magnificus Paulin Ladeuze, C163.2.

1. It would donate books and periodicals published in Japan, of old printed books, classical documents, and drawings of ancient works of art. The donations were to be placed in a room especially reserved for the Japanese donation.

2. A committee for the restoration of the library was to be set up. It would consist of the Japanese members of the international committee as well as illustrious persons from all walks of life.

3. An appeal was to be launched to schools and academic institutions, libraries, and private persons, calling for the donation of books and money.

4. A vetting committee was to be charged with the selection and the classification of the donated books and objects.

5. An executive committee was to be set up to carry out the project.[17]

The Japanese National Committee

On October 23, 1922 the international committee formally instated what was literally called a domestic committee (*Naikoku iinkai* 内国委員会), but which we will henceforth call the "National Committee", charged with the implementation of Japan's contribution to the *Oeuvre internationale de Louvain*. On its first meeting the Committee appointed the business tycoon Shibusawa Eiichi 渋沢栄一 (1840-1931) as its chairman; Furuichi Kimitake 古市公武 (1854-1934) as vice-chairman; Saionji as honorary chairman; and Hozumi and Adachi as honorary vice-chairmen. Shibusawa's function was de facto equally honorary. It was actually Furuichi who was the driving force in this National Committee. He was a civil engineer and entrepreneur and Japan's first doctor of engineering. Both he and Shibusawa had connections with France, and this at least partly explains their interest and involvement in this enterprise, which had been initiated by the French Academy.

By end 1922, the National Committee apparently had already collected the estimated equivalent of 700,000 Belgian francs. It wanted to use this money for the purchase of "classical books" and "old drawings", but it also wanted to spend part of the amount for interior decoration and for furnishing the special room that was to be reserved for the Japanese donation.[18] On July 27, 1923, the National Committee held its first working session in the Ministry of Education.[19]

The Great Kantō Earthquake

However, another disaster was lurking. A good month later, on September 1, 1923, the Great Kantō Earthquake hit. In the Kantō area many libraries and bookshops went up in flames; several millions of books and manuscripts were lost. The Tokyo Imperial University Library was completely lost and was now itself in need of donations, but since so many offers of support had come in from the West, the Japanese National Committee decided that it had to carry on with its work. On January 8, 1924, a secretariat was set up in the library of the Tokyo Academy of Arts in Ueno Park,[20] which sent out an appeal for donations of money, books, and works of art.[21] Wada Mankichi 和田万吉 (1865-1934) - formerly head of the Tokyo Imperial University Library - and

▲ 4. A colorized postcard showing the Japanese Crown Prince Hirohito and King Albert I leaving 'a Brussels museum'. Source: National Museum of Japanese History, Sakura, H-546-1-3-331.

TRENTE-SEPTIEME ANNÉE — N° 26   PROVISOIREMENT : 40 CENTIMES LE NUMÉRO | 26 JUIN 1921.

LE PATRIOTE ILLUSTRÉ
REVUE HEBDOMADAIRE

ABONNEMENTS 1921

POUR LA PUBLICITÉ
s'adresser au bureau du Journal
18, MONTAGNE-AUX-HERBES-POTAGÈRES, 18.
BRUXELLES
Téléphone : Br. 2380

ICI FINIT LA CULTURE ALLEMANDE

Trois civilisations sont représentées dans ce tableau, auquel les murs calcinés de la Bibliothèque de l'Université de Louvain servent de cadre historique. Le prince Hiro-Hito et sa suite représentent l'Orient, le Cardinal Mercier et les hautes personnalités qui l'entourent, notre civilisation Occidentale. Quant à la Culture allemande, on n'y voit que trop les traces de son infamie. Le futur Mikado, (à droite du cardinal), dans son pèlerinage aux ruines de la Bibliothèque est accompagné par le cardinal et Mgr Ladeuze, recteur de l'Université.

Le Prince Impérial du Japon visite les ruines de la Bibliothèque de l'Université de Louvain

Urushiyama Matashirō 漆山又四郎 (1873-1948) - specialist in Japanese literature and translator of classical Chinese poetry - were put in charge of the actual selection and acquisition of the books.

The secretariat started its activities in January 1924, thanks to substantial financial contributions from the Ministry of the Imperial Household (*Kunaishō* 宮内省) and the entrepreneur Sumitomo Kichizaemon 住友吉左衛門 (fifteenth head of the Sumitomo family, 1865-1926), who presided over the Sumitomo conglomerate. Other support came from the Iwasaki 岩崎, Mitsui 三井, Furukawa 古川, and Suenobu 陶延 families, all of whom led industrial conglomerates or other major businesses and contributed 10,000 yen each. The Shibusawa 渋沢 family contributed 1,000 yen and the Bank of Japan 2,000 yen, while a number of universities, individual academics, and other institutions or citizens contributed smaller sums. The total monetary donation amounted to about 63,000 yen, a considerable sum in the 1920s.

In the first phase, the Committee drew up a "standard list of books"[22] that it wanted to purchase and donate to Leuven. Yet in the aftermath of the 1923 Great Kantō Earthquake in the Tokyo-Yokohama area, books, either new or antiquarian, were hard to come by. To fill in the big gaps, the secretariat of the Committee ventured into the areas of Kyoto, Osaka, and Nara.[23] By May 1924 it had managed to collect a few thousand volumes.

▲ 5. Front page of *Le Patriote Illustré*, showing a picture of the visit of Crown Prince Hirohito to the ruins of the University of Louvain library. Source: *Le Patriote Illustré* 26 June 1921, KU Leuven Libraries, Special Collections, J684.

It decided to hold an exhibition of the acquisitions and to invite the Belgian ambassador Albert de Bassompierre (1873-1956), the members of the Committee, and all others who were involved in or connected with the enterprise, as well as the metropolitan press (May 21, 1924).[24] This kind of exhibition was subsequently repeated every time a major batch of books was being readied for shipment. Before being shipped, the books were given a (new) fitting wrapper (or: protective book covering, *chitsu* 帙) in order to keep the many fascicles that constitute one book together. On the back of the wrappers was pasted a rectangular slip bearing the title of the book. Tailoring the wrappers and restoring the binding of old books took a considerable chunk of the budget.[25] A clerk wrote out index cards in twofold, one to be sent to Leuven with a view to classifying and cataloguing the books once they had reached Leuven, one to be kept in Tokyo as reference. For the scrolls, the Committee had wooden boxes made.[26]

Vetting and Classifying the Donations

The selection of the books reflected the vision of Wada Mankichi and Urushiyama Matashirō on what was deemed essential in Japanese culture. They determined what had to be purchased, vetted books that were donated, and compiled a catalogue to go with the donation. In that catalogue,

they organized the collection into twenty-six divisions, allocating each physical title to one of the divisions, and within each division they listed the entries in alphabetical order. The catalogue was printed in a limited edition, and copies of it were presented to the donors involved. In 2000, Yamazaki Makoto 山崎誠 from the National Institute of Japanese Literature compiled a new catalogue, adopting the same organising categories, evidently using a copy of the original catalogue he had been able to secure. We will return to this catalogue later on.

What kind of classification system did Wada adopt? None of the other authors who have studied the collection give the problem more than a passing thought, but as a regular user of the collection, I remained puzzled by the arrangement Wada and Urushiyama employed. In the early days after the Meiji Restoration (1868), there was no standard classification method in Japan. Libraries created their own taxonomy in accordance with the size and type of their holdings. In 1887 (Meiji 20) the Tokyo Library (later the Imperial Library, *Teikoku toshokan* 帝国図書館) adopted the so-called "Eight gates" (*Hachimon* 八門) classification system. However, this was a bibliographical classification used only for compiling a classified catalogue, and it lacked a classification code. In the Imperial Library, regardless of the subject of the materials, books were arranged in the order of size and intake ("fixed shelving method", *kotei haika-hō* 固定排架法, in a "closed stacks system" *heika-shiki* 閉架式, similar to the one also used at the Louvain/Leuven University Central Library until the 1970s). There was no particular need to reflect the location of the materials in the subject code.

To be sure, many large libraries with closed stacks at that time also adopted this system. However, as the number of books on the shelves increased, the fixed shelving method increasingly hampered circulation and reference requirements, and the need for a systematic arrangement of the materials on the shelves according to the subject was increasingly felt. It was then that the Dewey Decimal Classification (DDC) came into the picture. In 1929, then, the librarian Mori Kiyoshi 森清[27] (1906-1990) published his "Japanese Decimal Classification: Common Classification Tables and Indexes for Japanese, Chinese, and Western Books", the *Nihon jisshin bunrui hō: wa-kan-yō-sho kyōyō bunrui-hyō oyobi sakuin* 日本十進分類法：和漢洋書共用分類表及

▲ 6. Portrait photograph of the Belgian ambassador to Japan Albert de Bassompierre. Source: Collection Verbeke-Kuliś.

索引.[28] The English name is "Nippon Decimal Classification" (NDC). It was both based on DDC, and on US librarian Charles Ammi Cutter's (1837-1903) Expansive Classification System, which uses alphabetic tables to abbreviate authors' names and generate unique call numbers, called 'Cutter numbers'. The date of publication was August 25, 1929, the birthday of Mori. The publication of this NDC definitely had a huge impact on the library community and was hailed by many – though not by Wada Mankichi, then an advisor to the Japan Library Association 日本図書館協会. He argued, "It is quite good to be able to make a good classification table", but "I do not desire nor is it desirable to create a method that is valid for 500 or 1,000 years and shared by a myriad libraries."[29] Wada's criticism can be seen as representative of those who were skeptical of a standardized taxonomy. Notwithstanding this opposition from a luminary in the librarian community, the NDC gradually gained acceptance and was ultimately adopted by libraries nationwide. However, in the 1920s, NDC was still just one of several library taxonomies. It was not until after the Second World War that it was generally accepted as the standard taxonomy.

My hypothesis is that the system Wada opted for when classifying the Louvain donation was a mixture of Cutter's Expansive System and the system used by the Imperial Library in Tokyo. Since the Imperial Library was the first "modern" library in Japan, which served as a point of reference for other prefectural and local libraries, its classification system quite naturally was widely adopted as it was (or with some minor adaptations).

In the 1920s Cutter's system was still considered the most scholarly in Japan.[30] That Wada was an advocate of Cutter's system transpires from the way he describes it in one of his works. He is full of praise for the system because it is very flexible and allows for gradual and limitless expansion. He describes it as "common sense and modern, clear and easy to adapt".[31] Especially the fact that it is so easy to adapt to the size of any library was a very attractive feature in his eyes. That is no doubt the reason why he chose it for Louvain. Since he did not know which way the Japanese collection might develop in the future, and since the collection would at any rate be in the hands of a Louvain librarian, he had to ensure that the system chosen at the outset did not require specialized know-how.

It is therefore no coincidence that there are twenty-six divisions (as a matter of fact Wada calls them "gates")[32] in the catalogue of the Louvain collection. He has arranged the divisions contained within the "gates" of the Imperial Library in such a way that he ended up having twenty-six of them (i.e. one for each letter of the alphabet). He no doubt believed that by arranging the catalogue that way, there would be the least trouble in the future in the event of further additions and expansion at Louvain. Traces of the effort to forcibly reach a total of twenty-six divisions may be seen in the fact that he has included a division 'Education' which actually contains only one category of books, namely "educational books for the populace dating from before the Meiji period". Other features that speak to this effort is the fact that the fifteenth division is 'Statistics', normally not expected on the primary division level. Moreover, it only includes five items, all published in the Taishō period (1912-1925). Perhaps even more surprising is the sixteenth division, labelled 'Colonies' and listing a meagre three items, one dating from the late Meiji period and two from the Taishō period (See list on p. 291). In the printed catalogue, the lowest level of classification is the alphabetical order of the first letter of the romanised title of the books.

Wada and Urushiyama wanted a selection that would adequately reflect "Japanese classical civilization" in the eyes of the Western public, and they even cherished the secret hope that the old Japanese books would somehow replace the incunabula lost in the fire of 1914.[33] They selected books in the widest possible range of the human sciences, including philosophy, Shintō, religion, literature, fine arts, history, geography, economy, law, physics, arts and crafts, industry, sports (entertainment, games), and so forth. In addition to the printed catalogue mentioned above, which allocated all physical titles to one of the twenty-six divisions, they made out in twofold what they called an index card catalogue, with each card corresponding to a single virtual title (one physical title often contains numerous virtual ones). Each card was allocated to one of the many rubrics each major division was further divided into. Although in card format, this instrument amounted to a real detailed catalogue, comprising a total of between 13,000 and 14,000 cards.[34] One of the two index card catalogues, contained in a wooden filing cabinet (on display in this exhibition), along with a now lost copy of the printed catalogue were sent to Louvain. The filing cabinet with the index cards is still extant, but the level of subdivisions has basically been done away with by Joseph Mullie (see below). Fortunately, the original printed catalogue included a chart that shows the entire classification structure.

In the late 1990s, however, the aforementioned bibliographer Yamazaki Makoto stumbled on a rare copy of the original printed catalogue in an antiquarian bookshop in Tokyo. Curiosity set him on a voyage of discovery to Louvain-la-Neuve, where, during a month's stay, he took a photograph of the title page, the frontispiece, the colophon, or some other prominent page of each physical title in the collection.[35] With these data in his camera, he returned to his institute and checked each title with the corresponding item in the huge database of the National Institute of Japanese Literature. Thus, he was able to supplement the bibliographical information given in the original printed catalogue with additional bibliographical data for each item culled from the database, such as alternative title(s), classification rubric of the National Institute of Japanese Literature, and so on, and published the result in a hefty volume.[36] In it he has replicated the twenty-six major divisions of the original printed catalogue. Within each division he has not tried to reconstruct the subdivisions of the card index (which would have been impossible anyway), but

simply listed the items alphabetically, as in the original printed catalogue. In addition, he has added the shelf mark (call number) that the items presently bear in UCLouvain, noting the fictitious shelf mark 00000 if the item is now missing. As we shall explain further on, the present shelf marks, printed on oval labels, were devised and attached to the books by missionary and specialist in Chinese linguistics Joseph Mullie CICM (1886-1976). We shall therefore henceforth refer to them as the 'Mullie numbers'. Yamazaki's catalogue is faithful both to Wada and to Mullie. He is faithful to Wada in the sense that he replicates Wada's original classification structure and faithful to Mullie in that he has also included the Mullie numbers in the data for each item, as well as adding a new division entitled 'Supplement' to include books, unrelated to the Japanese donation, that were later added and also given a shelf number by Mullie.

Precious Items

In a letter (dated May 22, Taishō 13 [1924]), Wada sent to his son-in-law, the political scientist, journalist and postwar politician Sassa Hiroo 佐々弘雄 (1897-1948), we read the following passage:

> I am presently overseeing the work of the Japanese book donation which is part of an international enterprise for the reconstruction of the Louvain Library, and which includes among others Great Britain, France, the United States, and Italy. Thanks to the collaboration of the Imperial Household Ministry and others, we have already collected more than 5,000 titles, including a *Hyakumantō darani* 百万塔陀羅尼, printed in 770 A.D., and a manuscript Buddhist scripture from 740 A.D., commissioned by Empress Kōmyō, the Kōmyō Kōgō go-gankyō 光明皇后御願経.[37]

According to the final report of the National Committee,[38] the selection included indeed several rare and precious manuscripts as well as printed editions, listed by the Committee under the twenty-fifth division 'Rare books'. By far the oldest were two specimens of the *Muku Jōkō-kyō Darani* 無垢浄光経陀羅尼, dating from the first year of Hōki 宝亀 (770 AD), two copies which belonged to the so-called *Hyakumantō Darani*. There was also the manuscript Buddhist scripture mentioned by Wada in his letter dating from the twelfth year of Tenpyō 天平 (740 AD), commissioned by Empress Kōmyō 光明 (701-760). Additionally, there were three *Gozan* 五山

▲ 7. Portrait photograph of Father Joseph Mullie CICM. Source: Archief van het F. Verbiest Instituut KU Leuven vzw.

(Five Mountains)[39] impressions dating from the fourteenth century, including *Eigen Jakushitsu Oshō Goroku* 永源寂室和尚語録, compiled about the sixth year of Jōji 貞治 (1367) and printed in the third year Eiwa 永和 (1377), acquired by the Committee for the price of 400 yen, a handsome amount in those days. It also included several copies of *kokatsujiban* 古活字版, books printed in movable type during the first half of the seventeenth century. These books were printed in limited editions, so that nowadays examples are very rare.

In the printed catalogue of the National Committee, we find indeed the two copies of *Muku Jōkō-kyō*, one entitled *Muku Jōkō-kyō Jishin Darani* 無垢浄光経自心陀羅尼 and the other *Muku Jōkō-kyō Sōrin Darani* 無垢浄光経相輪陀羅尼, both dated first year of Hōki, but unfortunately neither of them seems to be extant.

These *darani* (Japanese from Sanskrit *dhāraṇī*) - Buddhist incantations written in Sanskrit or Pali - rank among the oldest extant printed texts in the world. There is indeed only one text that has an earlier date: a *dhāraṇī*, bricked into one of the stone pagodas of Pulguk-sa (Bulguksa) in Korea in 751, discovered in 1966. The two *darani* donated by the Committee originally were part of a set of *darani* known as *hyakumantō darani* 百万塔陀羅尼 (i.e. a million *dhāraṇī* encased in a million pagodas). In the course of the year 764, the ruling Empress Shōtoku 称徳 (713-770) decided to have one million miniature pagodas made that were to serve as reliquaries for one million *dhāraṇī*. The execution of the commission would take approximately six years. In making this huge gesture of devotion Shōtoku took her inspiration from a Buddhist scripture (*sutra*), generally known in Japan by its abbreviated title: *Muku Jōkō-kyō* 無垢浄光経. This sutra taught the magic means to prolong life, to strengthen political rule, to prevent betrayal, and to eliminate enemies.

To achieve these worldly goals, the *Muku Jōkō-kyō* recommended writing out *dhāraṇī* and storing them in pagodas. Each *dhāraṇī* was placed in the upper, hollowed-out part of a miniature wooden pagoda that opened and closed at the spire. The pagodas were not all of the same type; most had three levels (height around 15 cm), but some (one in 10,000) counted seven and others (one in 100,000), thirteen. When this monumental work was completed, the *dhāraṇī* stored in their pagodas were divided into groups of one hundred thousand and distributed among ten great monasteries of that time. Among these monasteries, only the Hōryūji 法隆寺 temple currently has around one hundred examples preserved. Others are scattered throughout the world in public and private collections. We can admire one copy in the Royal Library Albert I in Brussels, which has a three-level pagoda in its possession. Thus spreading across the globe, these documents and their reliquaries are an important testimony to the beginnings of printing and a typical manifestation of the international character that the printing press always had: these *dhāraṇī* are written in an Indian language, transliterated in Chinese characters, and committed to paper in Japan.[40]

Similarly, the seventh scroll of a collection entitled *Sonbasumitsu Bosatsu Sho-shū* 尊場婆須蜜菩薩所集 (dubbed *Tenpyō-kyō* 天平経, "a sutra from the Tenpyō era" in the catalogue), with a dedication by Empress Kōmyō and dated twelfth year of Tenpyō (740) is listed in the Committee's catalogue, but cannot be traced in the present collection. The three *Gozan* editions, however, are still extant. The report does not mention any particular title in the category *kokatsujiban*, but the catalogue includes quite a few, most of them still extant. Some of them are included in this exhibition. Worth mentioning are editions of the Zen classic *Hekiganroku* 碧巌録; the historical chronicle *Eiga Monogatari* 栄華物語; the Buddhist dictionary *Honyaku Myōgi Shū* 翻訳名義集 by the Chinese monk Hōun (Fayun 法雲; 1088-1158), said by the Committee to date from the Keichō-Genna 慶長・元和時代 era (1596-1624); the *Ressenden* (*Liexianzhuan*) 列仙伝, comprising biographies of immortals attributed to the Chinese historian and bibliographer Ryū Kō' (Liu Xiang) 劉向 (77-6 BC); *Ryūkō Bukkyō Hennen Tsūron* 隆興仏教編年通論, a history of Buddhism in China by the monk Soshū 祖琇; *Shūmon Shōtōroku* 宗門正燈録, a collection of traditional biographies of Zen teachers compiled by Tōyō Eichō 東陽英朝 (1428-1504) and edited by his distant successor Gudō Tōshoku 愚堂東寔 (1579-1661); and *Teikan Zusetsu* 帝鑑図説, an illustrated mirror of good and bad conduct for rulers.

The donation also included a number of old printed editions that are not mentioned either in *Kokusho Sōmokuroku* 国書総目録[41] or in *Kokubungaku Kenkyū Shiryō-kan Tenkyo Fairu* 国文学研究資料館典拠ファイル, the database of the National Institute for Japanese Literature used by Yamazaki Makoto[42] - that is, the two union catalogues *par excellence* for books produced in Japan before the Meiji Restoration (1868). They include such titles as *Ogura Sansō Shikishi Waka* 小倉山荘色紙和歌, a collection of poetry written in Japanese, dated fourth year of Genna 元和 (1618); *Sagoromo* 狭衣 (date unknown), a story of the love affairs of a man named Sagoromo; and *Shida* しだ (date unknown), a libretto to a recitative dance.

The donation further contained a fine assortment of *Meisho Zue* 名所図会 – illustrated topographical descriptions of scenic beauty and famous places in Japan – including *Kyō Warabe* 京わらべ by the Nakagawa Kiun 中川喜雲 (1636-1705), published in the fourth year of Meireki (1658); *Edo Meisho-banashi* 江戸名所はなし, published in the seventh year of Genroku (1694); and *Miyako Meisho-zue* 都名所図会, compiled by the Akisato Ritō 秋里離島 (?-?) and illustrated by the Takehara Shunchōsai 竹原春朝斎 (?-1801), published in the ninth year of An'ei (1780) (see descriptions in the following chapter 'Selected Books from the 1920s Japanese Donation').

In addition, Wada made a consistent effort to include representative samples of the various genres representative of the ebullient popular literature produced during the Edo period.[43]

In the category of manuscripts the final report mentions Buddhist texts from the archives of the temples Nakatomidera 中臣寺, Chūsonji 中尊寺, Jingoji 神護寺, and Tamukeyama Hachimangū 手向山八幡宮. The original catalogue lists indeed two manuscripts from the Jingoji temple, *Bussetsu Ben'i Chōjashi-kyō* 仏説弁意長者子経 and scroll 35 of *Daichidoron* 大智度論, apparently both lost now. It also lists one from the Chūsonji 中尊寺, entitled *Dai'i Riki Usushima Myōō-kyō Shinmitsuji-hō* 大威力烏蒭瑟摩明王経心秘密法, adding that it is commonly known as the Hidehira scripture (dubbed *Hidehira-kyō* 秀衡経 in the original catalogue), equally missing at present. The manuscript in the original catalogue listed as bearing the seal of the Nakatomidera is scroll 16 of a Buddhist scripture entitled *Mishasokubu Goburitsu* 弥沙塞部五分律第, also missing at present. The same holds for the two scrolls of the *Daihannya Haramita-kyō* 大般若波羅蜜多経, which according to the catalogue bear the seal of the Yakushiji 薬師寺 temple. The manuscript that the final report mentions as being from the Tamukeyama Hachimangū 手向山八幡宮 is scroll 476 of the Buddhist scripture *Daihannya Haramita-kyō* 大般若波羅蜜多経. It is said to bear a seal "Tōdaiji Hachimangū" 東大寺八幡宮, i.e.

the Hachimangū shrine in the Tōdaiji temple. This linking of a Shintō shrine and a Buddhist temple must be explained in light of the fact that the Shintō deity of Tamukeyama Hachimangū was the tutelary deity of Tōdaiji temple in the city of Nara, until the separation of Buddhist temples and Shintō shrines in the early Meiji period. This manuscript too I have not been able to retrieve so far. Also from the Tōdaiji temple is a manuscript containing scroll 342 of the same *Daihannya Haramita-kyō*, but not of the same set as the aforementioned one. The colophon at the end of the scroll mentions that it underwent a second revision in the first year of Gennin 元仁 (1224). This manuscript, still extant today, has been restored and remounted on a scroll by the National Committee.

As also mentioned by the final report, a few handsome *Nara Ehon* 奈良絵本 were indeed included in the donation. The ones listed in the catalogue and still extant today are *Hachikazuki* はちかつき, *Ohara Gokō* 小原御幸, and *Urashima* うらしま. *Nara Ehon* are horizontal woodblock print books, measuring approximately 16 cm x 22 cm, with hand-printed or printed illustrations of stories. The covers of the books or scrolls are decorated with mist and cloud forms on dark blue paper, often with flowers and grasses painted in gold. The catalogue also mentions a manuscript of the *Ise Monogatari* 伊勢物語, though apparently now missing. *Ohara Gokō*, datable around 1661-1672, is possibly a unique copy. Although not mentioned in the final report, the manuscript entitled *Shōjūsan-shō* 正宗賛鈔 and datable about the year 1500 is equally rare and precious. It is a Japanese commentary on a text by the Chinese Buddhist monk Shaoyun 紹雲, who lived during the Song period (960-1279). Equally worth mentioning is the manuscript of a Japanese commentary on a Chinese anthology, dated from the first year of Meiō 明応 (1492) and entitled *Shoju Senkai Kobun Shinpō Kōshū* 諸儒箋古文真玉後集.

It is striking that quite a few manuscripts, marked by Wada and Urushiyama as "rare", are missing in the collection as it has come down to us today. I will be suggesting a possible explanation below.

Moreover, the donation also included large series, comprising primary resources for historical research, such as *Koji Ruien* 古事類苑 in 355 volumes, *Gunjo Ruijū* 群書類従 in 660 volumes, and *Honzō Zufu* 本草図譜 in 95 volumes.

Imperial Donations

The Committee had also received gifts from the Imperial Household, several government agencies, and a number of private individuals. The Prince Regent Hirohito[44] contributed nineteen titles in 301 volumes as well as "an album" from the Library of the Imperial Household, in addition to a porcelain flower vase by Seifū Yohei III 清風与平三代 (1851-1914), a potter from Kyoto,[45] and a gift of 10,000 yen from the emperor.[46] In the Department for Archives and Mausolea (*shoryōbu* 書陵部) of the present Imperial Household Agency (*Kunaichō* 宮内庁), there are two files related to the donation of Japanese books to the Louvain Library.[47] From these sources, we learn that the books donated included fine editions of the Six National Histories, including *Nihonshoki* 日本書紀, *Shoku Nihongi* 続日本紀, *Nihon Kōki* 日本後紀, and other important historical and literary works, both printed editions and manuscripts, as well as a few Meiji era publications.

Objets d'Art

Baron Ōkura Kihachirō 大倉喜八郎 (1837-1928) donated a writing-case with ink slab and a tea set, both dating from the beginning of the eighteenth century. The tea set was stored in a lacquer cabinet that featured the crest of the Mito branch of the Tokugawa clan. It included two canisters engraved by Kanō Natsuo 加納夏雄 (1828-1898), a great master in the field, as well as a set of five cups in blue and white stamped with a Chinese imperial mark. They were destined not for the tea ceremony *cha no yu* 茶の湯 but for *sencha* 煎茶, the Chinese style of tea drinking, used when drinking *gyokuro* 玉露, for instance.[48] The writing case was made of gold lacquer and decorated with a barge and fishes "in the style of Utamaro" according to a contemporary newspaper article.[49] In the repository of the university we have been able to identify the case: In point of fact, it is an ink slab (*suzuri-ishi* 硯) whose top section features two embossed carps. The slab is contained in a lacquer box whose lid is decorated with a funerary barge. A contemporary notice in French reads: "Ecritoire à encre de Chine orné de poisons à la Outa Maro (sic). Sur le couvercle barque funéraire d'un samurai. XVIII e. Don du Baron Okura, de Tokio."

The Vision of the Donors

To what extent did the selection reflect the vision of the Japanese donors? The proper answer would be: to a considerable degree, but certainly not one hundred percent. They simply could not bring together their dream list, even if they had one, because books were in great dearth in the wake of the Great Kantō Earthquake. Additionally, the money was not forthcoming as they had expected. Wada himself admitted that the Committee in the end barely managed to raise one fourth of the original amount they had budgeted.[50]

They had thus to settle for less than their dream list presumably, and the selection somehow came together. Quite a few individuals and institutions donated books. In the Japanese context, it would certainly have been difficult to spurn such an act of goodwill in times of great distress, to refuse the donation out of hand, or to discard it from inclusion. I assume that they rejected some books if they were in poor material condition, or too vulgar, or of mundane content. In order to avoid unpleasant surprises or donation of doubles, the Committee had stipulated in its call that before donating books, the prospective donor had to send in a list of the titles concerned. It expected in the first place books written and published in Japanese, but books in Chinese, English, French, German, Dutch, and other languages were also acceptable provided they were published in Japan.[51] It would be interesting to see if, despite all these preconditions, donations were rejected; and if so, which; and how they were disposed of.

Meiji and Taishō Reprints

The Taishō period (1912-1926) is known for its social mood of relative freedom and emancipation. At the same time, it is a period when the reappraisal of Japan's cultural tradition reached an unprecedented height. That is reflected in the great editorial enterprises of the day: the Buddhist Tripitaka *Taishō Shinshū Daizōkyō*, the reprints of *Gunsho Ruijū* and its sequels, to name but a few. Furthermore, it included recently edited series and reprints such as those published by Seigeisha 精芸社, Hakubunkan 博文館, and by the Kokusho kankōkai 国書刊行会. There were more than ten of such series, practically all reprints of classical texts. Also reflecting this tendency is the inclusion of reproductions of sixty-five classical paintings on seventy-six scrolls, especially paintings that are connected with the Zen tradition, published by Dōkōkai 同好会.

We also must note the sizeable inclusion of original publications from the Meiji and Taishō periods, that is, from the decades immediately preceding the time of the donation or contemporary to it. They were mainly on scholarly subjects, including legal and institutional subjects, but upon closer inspection it turns out that the Committee has included original publications from the Meiji and Taishō period in each of the twenty-six divisions. This act suggests a deliberate effort not only to donate an antiquarian heritage but also to promote the fruits of contemporary Japanese scholarship,[52] which in those days was largely ignored by the Western academic community. The donation thus stands as a monument to both Japan's cultural heritage and its contemporary scholarship. Admittedly, the latter is strictly limited to the humanities. We do not see any representative titles of science and technology or cosmopolitan medicine. There is, for instance, no trace of Takamine Jōkichi 高峰譲吉 (1854-1922), who was the first to isolate and purify the hormone adrenaline from animal glands, becoming the first to accomplish this for a glandular hormone. Likewise absent is Kitasato Shibasaburō 北里柴三郎 (1853-1931), co-discoverer of the infectious agent of bubonic plague in Hong Kong in 1894, and co-discoverer of the diphtheria antitoxin serum.[53]

The duality between pre-Meiji and Meiji is also observable in the material make-up of the books. 1868, the year of the Meiji Restauration, marks a watershed in the history of Japan, as it does in that of Japanese printing and publishing. Books before 1868 were bound in one of the traditional Japanese styles of binding. From 1868 onwards, these types of binding became gradually marginalized and were in the end nearly completely supplanted by Western style binding. In the late nineteenth and early twentieth centuries traditional binding was increasingly limited to special editions, when the publisher wished to give his publication a retro, arty, archaic, bibliophile, or antiquarian aspect. The aforementioned mood of reappraisal of traditional pre-modern culture during the Meiji and Taishō eras also manifested itself among other things in publishing books on heritage topics, and among them we find many publications in traditional Japanese binding. Traditional technology and topics connected with *Yūsoku kojitsu* 有職故実 - a body of exquisitely bland pseudo-science about codified techniques, precedents, and rules that typified the pre-modern lifestyle of the aristocracy and the samurai class - were popular subjects in this niche of publications. Good examples are *Shōka Kojitsu Roku* 匠家故実録 and *Kōshō Gijutsu no Futokoro* 工匠技術之懐, treatises

on traditional carpentry and wooden building technology, which are Meiji reprints of earlier books.[54] Another example worth mentioning is *Tōki Zukan* 陶器図鑑, which highlights traditional decorative designs on ceramics.

That duality in terms of material make-up and format was present in the mind of the donors. In their eyes, books from before 1868 were heritage, whereas books from after that date, certainly in the case of books in Western binding, were data carriers and information resources. I believe that they wanted to impart both those senses in their donation. Due to the earthquake and the resulting scarcity on the book market, we will never know how deliberate their selection was and how much was due to coincidence and expediency. Therefore it is not possible to determine apodictically what vision is embodied in the selection as it came to Leuven.

As a rule Yamazaki's catalogue, mentioned above, includes photographs of the title page or frontispiece or first page, and/or an illustration of a book if it is Japanese bound (*wasōbon* 和装本) and predates 1868. For books published after 1868 he does not include a photograph if they are a Western bound book (*yōsōbon* 洋装本), but he does include photographs of Meiji and Taishō era (1868-1912) books if they are Japanese bound. This practice enables the user of the catalogue to evaluate the quality of the collection, including the portion belonging to the Meiji and Taishō periods. One somehow gets the impression that the National Committee intended to conflate the pre-modern and modern periods, to suggest some measure of continuity between the two. This is borne out, for instance, by the fact that in the second of the twenty-six divisions, entitled 'Philosophy', we come across items on *Eki* 易 (i.e. the *Book of Changes)*, on divination, and on *bokuzei* 卜筮, fortune-telling, along with "serious" Western-style treatises. The sixth of the twenty-six divisions, 'Literature', also includes translations of Shakespeare by eminent writer and literature critic Tsubouchi Shōyō 坪内逍遥 (1859-1935).[55] There is no doubt that these are masterly translations or rather renditions, literature in their own right indeed. Was this the reason for their inclusion in the donation, though, or was this simply a case of expediency, a donation hard to refuse? Likewise, the treatises on Roman law by Viscount Suematsu Kenchō 末松謙澄 (1855-1920) were included more likely owing to the prestige and background of the family who donated them (the books bear the stamp "donation from the family of viscount Suematsu") rather than on account of their connection with classical Japanese culture.

The Packing and Shipping of the Donations and Their Reception in Leuven

From the National Committee's final report we also learn that the donation was sent in six shipments. The shipping company Nihon (Nippon) Yūsen 日本郵船 took on the shipping at half the regular rate. The first shipment of 324 titles in 1,977 fascicles/tomes was shipped on August 7, 1924; the second of 587 titles in 3,354 fascicles/tomes on December 8, 1924; the third of 560 titles in 3,175 fascicles/tomes, including the vase donated by the crown prince, on April 14, 1925; the fourth of 810 titles in 2,818 fascicles/tomes on October 15, 1925; the fifth of 791 titles in 2,194 fascicles/tomes on April 5, 1926; the sixth of 130 titles in 164 fascicles/tomes on August 30, 1926. Even after the final shipment, a number of books still had to be sent on by mail, because they had been ordered but not yet published at the time of shipment.[56] It totalled 3,202 titles, in 13,682 volumes. In that enumeration, each fascicle belonging to a title in traditional binding was counted as one, whereas an entire collection or series of books in Western binding was counted as only one. Conversely, in the index cards, there was only one card for one title in traditional binding; notwithstanding how many fascicles they may have comprised, they constituted just one title. A collection, series or even single tome in Western binding comprise multiple individual titles, and so here each title was given an index card. Hence, the number of physical tomes or fascicles in total exceeded 20,000.[57] Scrolls, maps and rubbings were counted as one title and one volume each. In addition, the donation also included ten printing blocks (hangi 版木) of classical works.[58] Each index card mentioned at the top of the first line the title of the book in romanized transcription to make searching easy for a Western reader. In Japan it is customary to search for Japanese and Chinese books by title, and one generally does not search by the author's name. Wada assumed it was best to follow the Japanese practice for Japanese books. Only in the twenty-sixth division, 'Works in Western languages', did he follow the Western practice of arranging in alphabetical order by the initial of the author's family name. This cabinet was shipped to Leuven to serve as the catalogue

for the collection there. Since no cataloguer in Louvain could be expected to read Japanese, the cabinet was essential because it contained on index cards the virtual catalogue in romanised transcription of the collection. Even so, the Committee planned to send an expert to Leuven to classify and arrange the books *in situ* once the new library building would be completed. The plan, however, never materialized.

Apart from the financial contributions already mentioned, books were donated by prominent individuals, various universities, associations, government departments, and regional administrations. In March 1926 the Committee sent out a communiqué to the European legations and embassies, as well as to Ambassador de Bassompierre. The total sum of donations to the Committee was 63,189 yen and 90 sen. It spent 36,005 yen and 67 sen on the purchase of books; 3,728 yen and 99 sen on restoration and binding; 899 yen and 75 sen on tools and index cards; 1,507 yen and 15 sen on shipping to Leuven; 18,314 yen and 28 sen on personnel costs; and 408 yen and 62 sen on sundry costs. 2,325 yen and 44 sen were donated to Louvain University with an eye to fitting out and decorating the 'Japanese room'.[59]

The fate of the donation after its arrival in Leuven

In his article Koyama Noboru 小山騰 (1948-) has rightly stated that this sizeable donation of Japanese books to Leuven, which included a considerable portion of manuscripts and rare printed books, was probably the largest such donation to an overseas library before the Second World War.[60] Moreover, it is also remarkable for its high profile, involving as it did prominent personalities, and its high degree of organization. Although not directly financed by the government, it may arguably have been the first case of organized support by Japan for Japanese Studies abroad.

After having arrived in Leuven the books first remained in the cases until the library was ready. They were probably unpacked according to packing lists that went with the cases. That might explain the orderly arrangement of the books on the only photograph we have of the collection *in situ* before the Second World War. This photograph, a picture postcard of the "Collection japonaise Japaneesche verzameling" by Ernest Thill (Brussels), was taken some time between

1928 and 1933 (see below), and features wooden 'orientalist' stacks, in addition to some of the reproductions of classical paintings hanging on the wall. On the far end of the room, we also see the vase of Seifū Yohei III and an illustrated narrative hand scroll hung up against the wall. On the side of the nearest right-hand stack hangs what looks like a sword, whose provenance and whereabouts since are unaccounted for. On the photograph it is even possible to discern some book titles. From a sample of readable titles, it is clear that the books were not arranged according to Wada's catalogue, because we can discern books from widely differing divisions arranged close to another. Quite readable is, say, the title *Sakai Manroku* 茶会漫録 from the 'Entertainment/sports/games' division next to *Man'yōshū Daishōki* 万葉集代匠記, a book in the 'Literature' division.' What they have both in common, however, is that they are Meiji period publications. Other books close by – such as *Yōkyoku Tsūkai* 謡曲通解 and, on the shelf below, *Tokugawa Jūgodai-shi* 徳川十五代史 – are likewise Meiji publications. They were all shipped in the third shipment, as can be confirmed from the alphabetical packing list preserved in the archives. They are not put in alphabetical order, however, which suggests that they were simply taken out of their boxes and arranged on the shelves in the order of unpacking.

The Satsuma Chair

During the period leading up to the First World War, more and more languages and cultures had been added to the curriculum of both the Faculty of Theology and the Faculty of Letters at the University of Louvain, where numerous eminent Oriental Studies scholars were trained and subsequently taught. The number of Orientalists in Belgium had grown sufficiently large for the rector Monsignor Paulin Ladeuze (1870-1940) to found the "Belgian Society of Oriental Studies" in 1921. The eminent Buddhologist Louis de la Vallée Poussin (1869-1938) became its first president and the Egyptologist Jean Capart (1877-1947) its first vice-president. On the ever-growing list of courses offered, though, neither Japan's language nor its culture was included until the year 1928. Previously, in 1927 – the year the university celebrated its 500th anniversary (after a two-year delay, see illustration) – the university had awarded an honorary doctorate to Mr Adachi Mine'ichirō, who in that year changed

his post as the ambassador to Belgium to France. The honour was given him as a token of gratitude for Japan's generous help in the reconstruction of the university library after its destruction during the war, as well as in recognition of his personal contribution.

A few days after receiving his honorary doctorate, Ambassador Adachi informed the chancellor of the university that one of his fellow countrymen intended to endow a chair for the study of the history of Japan's civilization. Already the *Commission d'initiative* had proposed that the various national committees were welcome to endow chairs to teach their national language(s), history, and literature.[61] The donor in question was Satsuma Jirōhachi 薩摩次郎八 (1901-1976),[62] commonly known in the West as "Baron Satsuma", the son of a well-known Tokyo industrialist, who resided in Paris and had previously made his intention known to Baron Édouard Descamps (1847-1933), professor at the University of Louvain and vice-chairman of the Belgian Senate. (Satsuma had in fact also been present at the celebration of the 500th anniversary of the university in July 1927.[63]) Baron Descamps, Ambassador Adachi, and Rector Ladeuze were the threesome who defined the format the chair would and could take. Satsuma's endowment was 100,000 BF – according to Descamps' note not enough to sponsor a regular course of study, but only adequate to pay a series of six lectures, though this was apparently deemed sufficient. The Belgian side did not ask for much and was not overly ambitious. In his letter of November 21, 1927, Adachi writes that he has recently met "Satsuma fils" (Satsuma Jirōhachi), who has declared himself prepared to increase the endowment.

It would seem, however, that the request for an increase was actually never made. Nevertheless, the academic authorities immediately approved the proposal and decided to inaugurate the proposed chair in the academic year 1927-1928. Due to circumstances, the chair could not be inaugurated until the beginning of the academic year 1928-1929. The first incumbent appointed was R.P. Pierre Charles (1883-1954), a professor of missiology at the Gregorian University of Rome who had a strong interest in the history of religions and ethnology. During the subsequent quarter century he was to fill the chair until his death, apart from the war period (1940-1945), during which time the courses of the Satsuma Chair were suspended.[64]

The forgotten Chinese Donation

It is less well known that the Chinese Republic likewise participated in the *Oeuvre internationale de Louvain*. Quite early, as of October 1920, the Chinese Legation in Brussels notified the university that it was donating a collection of books, including the Chinese classics, the history of the Qing dynasty, catalogues, dictionaries, and books by individual authors. The National University of Peking would also make a donation, and the famous scholar, philosopher, and politician Hu Shi 胡適 (1891-1962) would donate a set of his own works. The Chinese donation also included a Chinese typewriter together with instructions for use.

In 1927, Lou Tseng Tsiang (Lu Zhengxiang) 陸徵祥 (1871-1949),[65] former Minister of Foreign Affairs and Prime Minister of the Republic of China, entered the Benedictine convent of Saint-André near Bruges. His monastic name was Dom Pierre-Célestin Lou O.S.B. He befriended King Albert I (1875-1934), Cardinal Désiré-Joseph Mercier (1851-1926), members of the clerical elite, the diplomatic elite, and others. He cherished the hope to get Chinese Studies started in Belgium, more specifically "dans le monde laic", for he evidently was well aware of the Chinese proficiency of the Belgian missionaries, but their expertise was of little use to Belgian society. Before leaving the diplomatic service, he visited Rector Ladeuze to donate his personal Chinese library to the university as "un premier modeste fond d'une section de sinology en Belgique".[66] We learn this from a letter he addressed to Raoul Pontus, chairman of the *Institut Belge des Hautes Etudes Chinoises*.

A Japanese Room

The new library, rebuilt with American funding, was inaugurated on the symbolic date of July 4, 1928, an event that was even covered in a Chinese newspaper founded by the Belgian missionary Vincent Lebbe in 1915.[67] However, from that moment on, little is heard of the Japanese collection. In the annual report made for 1927-28, the librarian Van Cauwenbergh cursorily mentions the arrival of the Japanese books, but in the subsequent yearly reports about the activities of the library, nothing is reported on them, not even on the Japanese room. Strangely enough, between 1929 and the outbreak of the Second World War, not once did he refer to the Japanese library in the wing along the Blijde Inkomststraat. Here the administration was located on the ground floor, while the

upper floors housed the Japanese room, the precious works room, and a few seminar rooms.[68] Admittedly, if the room was more or less a closed one, and the collection was equally closed, there was little to report. Nevertheless, some sporadic additions were made, like the books by the bibliographer and cultural historian Kawase Kazuma 川瀬一馬 (1906-1999), sent by the Yasuda Library (*Yasuda Bunko* 安田文庫); moreover, there was the major batch of books that made up the *Da Qing shilu* (*Daishin Jitsuroku*) 大清実録 (chronicling the Manchu dynasty), a superb piece of movable type printing from Japan's Ministry of Finance. While both additions were sent and received in 1937,[69] no mention of them is made in the yearly reports.

All this seems to suggest that the Japanese room was something of a sealed salon. Since there was no foot traffic going in or out, it was always a neatly arranged interior and therefore ideal for showcasing. Although not a soul could read the books, they were nevertheless an object of pride. A special issue of the periodical *Le blé qui lève*,[70] whose manifest aim was to highlight the vibrant life and scholarship of the Catholic University of Louvain among its readership, bears out this function as a salon, utilising the very same Ernest Thill photograph of the "Collection japonaise Japaneesche verzameling" without even mentioning that it was the Japanese collection. Since there was no Japanese Studies programme, the special issue cannot have aimed to promote this particular discipline, but this manifestly impressive arrangement of stacks was presumably the university library's 'best room'. At any rate, this special issue of the above mentioned periodical proves that the Japanese Room was put in place between 1928 and 1933.

The Orientalist Institute

With the Satsuma Chair established, the university now offered a course of study that could claim to cover the further end of the Asian continent. However, all courses related to Asia in the broadest sense of the term remained scattered over two faculties and did not lead to a regular degree in Oriental Studies as such. Some felt that the time had come to bring lecturers and courses together under one and the same roof. Thus, the *Orientalist Institute* was established in 1936, integrating all branches of Oriental Studies conducted in the faculties of Theology and Arts into a programme of philological instruction for

all ancient languages and the critical instruction of the history of the ancient peoples of East Asia.

The new set-up hardly affected the status of Japanese Studies, however. It remained restricted to the one Satsuma Chair. Nevertheless, Far Eastern Studies, including the study of China, in the broad sense did make a step forward thanks to the monumental contribution of Professor Étienne Lamotte (1903-1983).

The Second Burning of the Library

At the beginning of the Second World War, the library again fell victim to enemy bombs. Starting with May 14, 1940, the Germans had been bombing the town of Leuven. On May 17, the day the German army entered the town, at half past one in the morning, fire broke out in the library. The building sustained massive damage. The tower had been hit some twelve times during the bombardment. Little more remained of the magnificent building than calcined walls, twisted beams, and heaps of scrap. Of the 900,000 volumes in its holdings, of its rich collections, of its 3,000 series of journals, very little could be kept from the flames: Only 15,000 volumes were saved from the blaze in the tower, and in some rooms on the first and the second floor, in the wings that run along the Arendstraat and along the Blijde Inkomststraat respectively.[71] The reader will notice that the number of 15,000 volumes comes close to the number of items in the Japanese donation. Yet the Japanese collection was not the only one to be saved. The 'Toponymie' collection was likewise rescued, but I have not been able to verify how many volumes this category included.

The Japanese Donation Saved

When the dust had settled, the occupying forces turned over the books and objects that had been recovered from the ruined library to the town burgomaster and the librarian. The inventory of the transfer, written in German,[72] includes a page entitled "Japanische Bibliothek", which lists five items:

1. 5346 Bände und Broschüren
2. 108 Faksimile-Schriftrollen
3. 10 Druckplatten
4. Eine Schreibmaschine
5. Eine Kartothek.

The figures given in the inventory of transfer by the German command do not seem to tally with the figures we have mentioned above, but this is not surprising. The Germans no doubt counted wrappers, physical tomes and fascicles, whereas the printed catalogue lists physical titles and the index card catalogue inventories all virtual titles (in many cases one tome includes multiple titles). I assume *Bände* denotes both wrappers (*chitsu* 帙) as well as tomes in Western-style binding. *Faksimile-Schriftrollen* refers no doubt to the reproductions of Japanese classical paintings, while *Druckplatten* obviously to the 10 printing blocks, *Schreibmaschine* to the Chinese typewriter, and *Kartothek* to the filing cabinet. *Broschüren* is less straightforward, but it probably refers to the Japanese-style fascicles. The fact that the Chinese typewriter is mentioned here suggests that it was placed in the Japanese room, presumably together with all the Chinese books that had been donated by the Chinese Legation in Brussels in the early 1920s and by Dom Lou. Though not mentioned in the German list, the vase (now at KU Leuven) had also escaped unharmed. The fact that it was not mentioned was probably because it had been transferred to the section of mainly Chinese ceramics, which was housed elsewhere. It seems that the vase had even been mistakenly considered a piece of Chinese porcelain.

Although it is hard to verify whether the Japanese collection was saved in its entirety, that it was rescued at all remains something short of a miracle - as well as not without a measure of irony, given the fact that Japan was a member of the Axis Powers. If the arrangement of the Japanese library in wooden stacks on a parquet floor was permanent, as depicted in the Ernest Thill's photograph, how could it have survived the flames? In addition, if it did, how did it withstand possible degradation from dampness or rain, even given the fact that the spring and summer of 1940 were exceptionally fair? Indeed, according to the annual report of 1941-42 by Van Cauwenbergh, it took two months before the Germans released the ruined library. Does that mean that the two only surviving collections, 'Toponymie' and the Japanese donation, remained in the ruins, exposed to the elements for two months? Perhaps not. In the same report the Japanese library is said to have been salvaged and transferred to the University Hall.[73] That only *seems* to contradict the claim of the German document that the Japanese library had been transferred to the city authorities, since the University Hall was and still is property of the municipality of Leuven.[74] It was however not safe there, either.

On May 11, 1944, the University Hall sustained heavy damage, this time from Allied bombing. On the next leg of its journey, the Japanese library was located in the subterranean floor (*sous-sol*) of the *Institut de Spoelbergh*. The Spoelbergh Institute is the building at Krakenstraat 3, where the general administration (*Algemeen Beheer*) for KU Leuven is now located.

The question whether the Japanese donation escaped unscathed is relevant in regard to the present collection. Namely, twenty-six items listed under the twenty-fifth division 'Rare books' in the original catalogue (and the Yamazaki catalogue) are missing. They include the two *Muku Jōkōkyō Darani*, the *sūtra* dedicated by Empress Kōmyō, two Buddhist manuscripts from the Jingo-ji temple, two from the Yakushiji temple, one from the Nakatomidera, one from the Hachimangū, and one from the Chūsonji temple. As already mentioned, these are some of the precious items explicitly mentioned in the final report of the National Committee. Perhaps the absence of at least some of these items ties in with the report about damages and losses that the university authorities filed with the *Commissariat provincial du Brabant*, at the request of the *Commissariat general à la Restauration du pays*, on December 24, 1942.[75] In this report there is an item labelled "Fonds Lefort et Japonais" in the category "Manuscrits". Obviously, we can only surmise what this may have meant. Fact is that numerous items classified under the twenty-fifth division 'Rare books' in the catalogue happened to be manuscripts. Being manuscripts, they may have been separated from the main collection and, together with the Fonds Lefort, stored with the manuscripts on the underground level of the library. On that level during the fire, molten glass flowing down from the stack rooms reduced everything to ashes. The estimate of the loss in the amount of 169,750.00 Belgian francs is, in comparison with other categories, not particularly high; therefore, the envisaged number of manuscripts subsumed under this line item cannot have been very high, again confirming my assumption. Though the lost Japanese manuscripts represent a sizeable proportion of the "rare" category within the Japanese donation, in absolute terms it was a modest number, much lower than for the collections of Western manuscripts.

In total about fifty items appear to be missing from the collection as it now stands. About what was lost in 1940, the only information I have

▲ 9. View of the room housing the Japanese book donation in the Central Library of the University of Louvain (before 1933). Source: Studio Ernest Thill, Bruxelles, collection KU Leuven Universiteitsarchief, Topografisch-Historische Atlas. Verzameling Prentbriefkaarten. Reproduced by KU Leuven Digitisation and Document Delivery.

▲ 10. Tentative reconstruction of arrangement on a shelf as seen on the nearest right-hand stack in the Ernest Thill picture postcard (Ill. 9). Source: Photograph by Willy Vande Walle

▲ 11. Tentative reconstruction of arrangement on a shelf as seen on the nearest right-hand stack in the Ernest Thill picture postcard (Ill. 9). Source: Photograph by Willy Vande Walle.

found is the following letter from the librarian Van Cauwenbergh to the rector:

Monseigneur,

[...]

Dans l'incendie de la bibliothèque, le 17 mai 1940, ont péri 6 rouleaux manuscrits japonais sur fond noir et d'autres, à images de Nara, fortement coloriés, de l'époque de Yedo et 3 fragments de manuscrits du canon bouddhique du 9ᵉ et du 10ᵉ siècle, provenant des temples de Nakatomidera, de Chusonji et de Jingoji. Tous les livres ont été sauvés, mais des officiers allemands en ont emporté quelques-uns à titre de souvenir...

Le service à thé et le service à encre de Chine (écritoire) offerts à l'Université par le baron Okura en mai 1923, par l'intermédiaire du Baron de Bassompierre, ont été sauvés.

Il en est de même du vase en porcelaine Satsuma[sic], offert par l'Empereur du Japon et ramené comme les deux autres objets, par Mr de Bassompierre.

[...]

Van Cauwenbergh

While this letter sounds surprisingly knowledgeable for someone with no background at all in this regard, it is addressed to a 'Monseigneur,' who can be none other than Rector Monseigneur Van Waeyenbergh. It was in fact the reply to an enquiry by the latter, who had been asked for information about the whereabouts of the donation by Ambassador de Bassompierre.[76] However, the number of the items listed by Van Cauwenbergh does not nearly add up to fifty, and the majority remains unaccounted for. Yet another question concerns what happened to the Taishō-period reproductions of the classical paintings, many of which are now missing as well. Were some of them kept outside the Japanese room, thus falling victim to the flames?

The Restoration of the Library

Very soon after its destruction, new plans for the restoration of the burnt-out building were drawn up, with construction authorized by the Germans already in 1941. Thanks to the work of the Comité tot Herstel der Bibliotheek van de Universiteit te Leuven, led by Professor Jan Vanderheyden, the library could boast a book fund of inventoried and catalogued items between 250,000 and 300,000 by the end of 1944.[77]

When the restoration was completed in 1950, the Japanese collection was returned to the library and returned to its pre-war location.

Floor plans of the building, which were drawn up in connection with a fire insurance policy taken out in 1959, confirm that the Japanese library was located on the third floor of the wing along the Blijde Inkomststraat.[78] Its pre-war location on the second floor cannot be ruled out, but Vanderheyden says it was the top floor (i.e. the third). The Seifū Yohei vase was exhibited in the *Petit Musée*, an exhibition room within the library, above the general reading room, as is evidenced in a contemporary photograph.

Before the war, the Japanese books had been arranged on wooden 'orientalist' stacks, but during the turbulent phase between 1940 and the return to the restored library in 1950, the stacks were apparently separated from the books and stored somewhere else. When around 1950 the restoration was complete, and all the books were moved back into the Warren Whitney building on the Ladeuzeplein, the 'orientalist' stacks were apparently not recovered and, from the look of it, metal stacks were chosen instead, as can be seen from another unique photo, "Vue intérieure de la Section japonaise", reproduced in Rodica Doina Pop's book.[79] It is to my knowledge the only photograph of the Japanese library between 1950 and its transfer to Louvain-la-Neuve in the 1970s. One notices the slanted ceiling of the room on the third floor along the Blijde Inkomststraat,[80] which now houses the "Illuminare Centre for the Study of Medieval Art". The bookshelves are not the original historical 'orientalist' bookshelves, but more modern, ostensibly metal ones, standing back to back in double rows. On the side of the nearest stack, one notices a Japanese hanging scroll (*kakemono*), a reproduction of a classical painting. On a low table a hand scroll is half-unrolled. This is manifestly a staged photograph.

Mullie's Classification System

If we compare the Ernest Thill photograph (before 1933) with the Rodica Pop photograph (1958), we notice that in contrast to the former, the books on the latter photograph bear what looks like oval labels. These are the shelf marks that were applied to the books by Joseph/Jozef Mullie (1886-1976), as already pointed out at the beginning of this essay. He was a Scheut missionary active in Northern China from 1909 to 1931. He was trained as a philologist in Leuven by Colinet, and before he left for China, he had already studied Chinese, Manchu, Mongol, and Tibetan. He discovered the imperial tombs of the Liao dynasty (eleventh century), collaborated with Sven Hedin and Teilhard de Chardin, and published numerous contributions in European and Chinese journals. After his return to Europe, he was appointed extraordinary professor of Chinese language and literature at the University of Utrecht (1939-1956) and inducted as member of the Royal Flemish Academy (1955).

Mullie had no status at the university, but had permission to work in the library. Ostensibly having no knowledge of the Wada catalogue, he set out to rearrange the books according to his own system, integrating them into a more comprehensive library of Far Eastern Studies. He conceived the classification system that is embodied in the oval labels, but it remains puzzling. To some extent it puts books of the same or related subject together, but some books end up in a totally 'alien' environment. Although he was a consummate sinologist, he did not know Japanese and may have read wildly different meanings into some of the Japanese characters. When his reading was correct, he usually put the books with germane

titles in the same order on the shelves. On the other hand, the arrangement also suggests that he was following the system of fixed shelving in a closed stacks system, thus putting books of the same size together. The order of chronological intake obviously did not apply to the Japanese donation, since it was terminated. However, by merging it with new arrivals and the donation of his own sizeable collection of Chinese books, he gradually developed it into a comprehensive library for Far Eastern Studies. Since by now there were two professors dealing with the Far East, the aforementioned Mgr Étienne Lamotte and Robert Shih, it gradually took on the function of the putative research library, or seminar library, of the 'Section de l'Extrême Orient'.

As already pointed out, the Chinese donation and the Dom Lou donation must have been put in the same room as the Japanese donation at an early stage. The fact that for instance the Chinese typewriter is mentioned together with the Japanese books in the inventory of the German command suggests that they were in the same

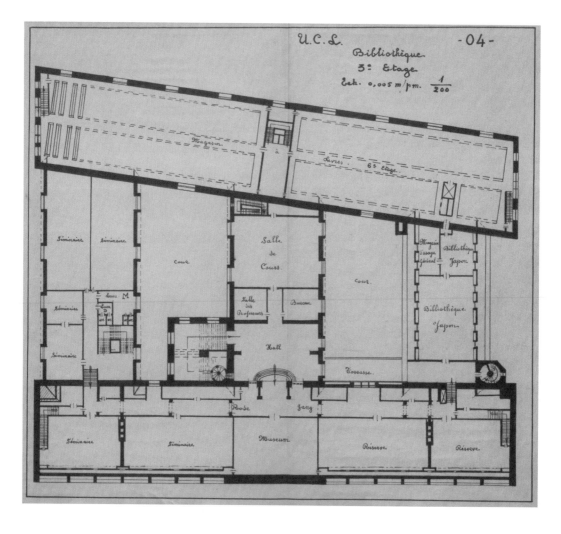

▲ 12. Floor plan showing location of the Japanese library in 1959.
Source: UCLouvain Archives de la Bibliothèque centrale, Fonds FI 067\ 13

room. If the Chinese typewriter was in the same room, then the Chinese books must have been in the same room as well. The annual report of Van Cauwenbergh also bears that out.

That Mullie is the author of the classification with the oval labels is confirmed both by his own statement to that effect,[81] and by a letter from Jacques Ryckmans (1924-2005), president of the *Institut Orientaliste*, to the Head Librarian of the University (i.e. Professor Joseph Ruwet).[82] This letter is also instructive regarding the make-up of the library. Writing at the time of the split of the university, Ryckmans significantly calls it the 'séminaire japonais', a point which confirms my interpretation about the transformation of the nature of the library into the research library of the 'Section de l'Extrême-Orient'. The letter gives a list of six specific divisions constituting the library in the 'séminaire japonais':

1. A sizeable collection of Chinese works published in Japan [*sic*] and given by the Japanese government after the First World War (these books have escaped the fire of 1940). They are arranged on stacks that bear numbers ranging

▲ **13. Interior view of the Japanese section in the 1950s.**
Source: Rodica Doina Pop, *Bibliothèque de l'Université catholique de Louvain: trentième anniversaire de la première restauration (4 juillet 1958) et Lettre de son excellence Mgr Honoré Van Waeyenbergh, évêque titulaire de Gilba, évêque auxiliaire de Malines, recteur magnifique*, Louvain: UCLouvain. Centre international de dialectologie générale, 1958.

from 1 to 68. The volumes bear an oval label with the number of the stack, of the shelf, and of the volume (summary catalogue drawn up by Father Mullie). Some of these numbered stacks (notably no. 9) contain works belonging to the collection described below under no. 6.

2. Gift by Dom Lou before his death in 1949. The gift includes two series of original boxes (with accompanying inscribed wooden panels), arranged to the left and right of the door, containing the texts of the "collection des quatre dépôts". Other boxes (against the wall on the left) contain works of calligraphy and of Chinese seals.

3. Gift of Mgr Lamotte. Collection of 47 volumes of a historical series in blue and brown binding, offered to Mgr Lamotte by Mr Tsiang Fu-Tsung, director of the Central Library of Taipei. These books are placed at the far end of the seminar, opposite the entrance. These volumes do not bear any shelf mark, but some of them bear the label "Non Evertetur" of the library, with the indication D.D. E. Lamotte. This gift is claimed on behalf of the UCLouvain in the accompanying letter.

4. The collection *Hien Tai Kouo Min Ki Pen Tche Che Ts'ong Chou* (book of the fundamental knowledge of present-day citizens), a donation

61

from the government of the Republic of China (Taiwan) [...].

5. A collection of Buddhist texts ordered by the library at the request of Mgr Lamotte and R. Shih.

6. Brochures and varied works sent since 1955 by the Chinese government to the *Institut Orientaliste* at the request of R. Shih. These works are dispersed across certain shelves of the numbered stacks of the Japanese donation.[83]

From this list, one important component is missing: the Chinese, Mongolian, and Tibetan books owned by Mullie and added in the course of time to the library in the 'séminaire japonais'. Indeed, at the time of the split – on October 19, 1969, to be precise – Mullie had had his books removed from the library of the 'séminaire japonais'. Numbered 60A1 through 68G63 and numbered 57B1 through 57G40, they were donated to the Katholieke Universiteit Leuven,[84] along with his Mongolian and Tibetan books.[85] They could therefore not figure on the list of Jacques Ryckmans, writing in February 1971. This brings us

▲ 14. View of part of the donation of Dom Lou, now in the Réserve Précieuse, UCLouvain. Photograph by Willy Vande Walle.

directly to the split of the unitary university of Leuven/Louvain.

'La Splitsing': The Division of the University and Its Library

Writing in 1960, Gonzague Ryckmans (1887-1969) had concluded his article "Bis Diruta, Bis Restituta" on the two fires that destroyed the library in the course of the first half of the twentieth century, with a pious wish. He noted that the second half of the century had started under much luckier stars, and he prayed that his successors in the year 2000 might bless God for having allowed them to pursue their work in serenity and peace in the shadow of the library tower.[86] In the year 2000, to be sure, the library did indeed offer a spectacle of busy professors, students, and library personnel in unprecedented numbers and ditto scale, if not of serenity or peace. Before the decade of the sixties was over, however, the library had to face yet another ordeal, which has often ironically been dubbed "the third fire".

During the 1960s the university went through a period of fast growth. The student population increased spectacularly and its structure encompassed a French-speaking and a Dutch-speaking section, which gradually expanded into two separate entities. The division of the university was not unlike a divorce, painful and acrimonious, a story that has been told elsewhere.[87] In 1968, as the result of a political decision, the two entities became two legal persons. The decision also entailed the eventual relocation of the French-speaking entity. The Dutch-speaking university would remain in Leuven, the French-speaking university would, after a period of transition, move out to the French-speaking part of Belgium, to a site renamed Louvain-la-Neuve. The unitary Orientalist Institute was divided along the same linguistic lines. Awaiting its transfer to Louvain-la-Neuve, it relocated to Redingenstraat 16.

The split of the former unitary library proved to be a Gordian knot. The central holdings were divided in half, but separate collections were adjudicated to one or the other university.

Where does that leave the Japanese donation? As I have pointed out, the library in the 'séminaire japonais' had gradually evolved into a research library serving the professors of the 'Section de l'Extrême Orient'. On the Dutch-speaking side there was no one teaching or doing research in that field. As Jacques Ryckmans stated in the letter quoted above:

The teaching of Buddhist languages (Chinese and Tibetan) has been assured since 1934 only by Mgr Lamotte; the courses of Classical Chinese and Introduction to Chinese Philosophy have been given by Mr Shih, the courses of Japanese have been given by Mr Durt, and subsequently, since 1964, by Mr Van Campenhoudt. KUL[euven] has not been able to appoint a teacher for any of these courses since the split. The gift of the Japanese government has been made at a period when there was no Dutch-speaking section. Moreover, the three doctorates that have been submitted to the Far Eastern division of the Orientalist Institute (Masson, Hofinger, Durt) have been defended in the French-speaking section. It seems to me that these considerations must be taken into account in the event of deciding to divide the content of the Japanese seminar.[88]

The few professors involved in the study of the Far East were indeed French-speaking and had always been, and the donation had indeed been done at the time of the monolingual French-speaking university. These arguments seem to have weighed heavily with Head Librarian Prof. J. Ruwet. It was his judgment that the Japanese donation and the donation of Dom Lou were destined for UCLouvain.[89] In April 1971 part of the library of the 'séminaire japonais' was transferred to 16 Redingenstraat.[90] The Far Eastern section, together with the Japanese donation, eventually moved to the new site of Louvain-la-Neuve, where Lamotte, Shih, and Van Campenhout continued to teach Buddhist languages, Classical Chinese, and Japanese.

Two Sister Universities

The Japanese books were thus transferred to UCLouvain, but the Japanese *objets d'art* remained at the Katholieke Universiteit Leuven, and so did the 'orientalist' bookshelves, which had presumably been stored in the attic since the 1950s. As one of the few remaining items of historical furnishings from the University Library during the interwar period, they were subsequently reused when the East Asian library of KU Leuven was moved from the Faculty of Arts into the KU Leuven University Library in the academic year 1980-1981.[91] Here Mullie's donation also found its final destination. The vase, donated by Crown Prince and later Emperor Hirohito, now belongs to the artistic heritage of KU Leuven, as does the writing set that Baron Ōkura had donated. There is no trace of the tea set, but its gold lacquer box is still extant.

The Satsuma Chair had also been divided and, at Louvain-la-Neuve, continued to be filled by Professor J. Masson, who had held it since 1955. On the Dutch-speaking side the Satsuma Chair was filled irregularly. In 1974 the Orientalist Institute of KU Leuven expanded its programme to a four-year curriculum. In 1978 it gained the full status of a department within the Faculty of Letters and started a four-year programme in Far Eastern Studies, with an emphasis on Chinese Studies, offering courses in Classical Chinese, modern Chinese, and modern Japanese, in addition to a number of courses dealing with the history, art history, and literary history of the Far East. In 1981 a chair of Japanese Studies was founded, to which the author of this essay was appointed, and in 1986 a fully-fledged four-year programme of Japanese Studies was launched, which over the years has attracted an increasing number of students. In 1995 a second chair was established to teach subjects related to present-day Japan.

The "Rediscovery" of the Japanese Donation

After its transfer to UCLouvain, the Japanese donation was stored in the closed stacks room of its huge underground book silos, in the 'Réserve précieuse' there. In the early 1980s, Harry Dewit, then catalographer at UCLouvain, invited me to have a look at the collection. Although I had obviously heard about it from KU Leuven's Head Librarian Prof. Jan Roegiers (1944-2013), among others, this was the first time I set eyes upon it myself.

Around the same time, Japanese bibliographers, having largely exhausted the prospective pool of collections that could be discovered, explored, catalogued, and classified in Japan, started turning their eyes abroad. That sparked a spate of explorations and visits by Japanese scholars of Japanese book collections, especially repositories of pre-Meiji documents, abroad. Thus a number of Japanese bibliographic 'explorers' visited the UCLouvain collection, among them: Koyama Noboru from the Japanese library of Cambridge University; Yamazaki Makoto from the National Institute of Japanese Literature, whom I already mentioned above in conjunction with the catalogue he published in 2000; and Yamaguchi Yōji, as research assistant for the project *Union Catalogue of Early Japanese Books in Europe*, coordinated by Hayashi Nozomu (then assistant professor at Toyoko Gakuen Women's College) as

well as Peter Kornicki (then lecturer of Japanese Studies, Cambridge University).[92] Koyama Noboru made a presentation about the donation at the Annual Conference of the European Association of Japanese Resource Specialists of 1994, held at the Japanologisches Seminar of Germany's Bonn University.[93] He later published the text in *Shibusawa Kenkyū*.[94] I myself made a presentation about the collection to the EAJRS conference, mainly drawing on the KU Leuven archives and my own experience, and published a digest of my findings in *EAJRS Newsletter* no. 8 (2001).[95]

Already quite some time before Yamazaki's visit, however, in the early 1990s Yamaguchi Yōji had spent about one year carefully drawing up index cards for the books and documents of the Japanese donation in UCLouvain, as well as the Japanese collection in the Royal Library, i.e. the Winiwarter Collection. His appointment as assistant to the *Union Catalogue of Early Japanese Books in Europe* being limited to four years, Yamaguchi, after the completion of his contract, transferred the index cards he had made of French, Belgian and other collections to Cambridge, with a view to entering them into the database of the *Union Catalogue*. According to the website of the *Union Catalogue*, the inputting of the data into the database was first carried out by Kornicki in Cambridge, but discontinued in 2001. Since then the National Institute of Japanese Literature, Tokyo, has taken over the data entry under the direction of Professor Itō Tetsuya. In November 2001 the *Union Catalogue* became freely accessible on the web. The data retrieval systems were created by Mr Ōuchi Hidenori.

Data input and revision are continuing.[96] It would appear that, as I write these lines (February 2020), this data entry process has not been completed yet. A sampling test yielded the following result. Of 108 items, including ninety-nine items selected in an initial stage for this exhibition catalogue, forty-three did not return a hit. For eight of them, UCLouvain turned out to be the unique holding location in Europe. Allowing for possible no-hits due to variations in the title, this result would at least seem to bear out not only that the entry of the UCLouvain data is still far from complete, but at the same time that these forty-three items are nowhere else in European collections, in the unlikely assumption of course that the *Union Catalogue* covers exhaustively all other relevant collections. If that assumption were correct, it would effectively mean that for these forty-three

items, plus the eight items that returned a unique UCLouvain location, mentioned above, UCLouvain is the unique holding location in Europe, which would come down to about one half of our total sample.

As the heirs of the former unitary university, the universities of Leuven and Louvain-la-Neuve celebrated their 575th anniversary during the academic year 2000-2001. One of the events marking this anniversary was a joint exhibition, held between February 1 and March 31, 2001, and entitled "Orientalia". It featured a selection of ninety-seven precious works from the various 'Oriental' collections held in the two university libraries. I acted as one of the editors of the catalogue for the exhibition (Dutch and French versions), which includes descriptions of all exhibited items, photographs of one or two pages of each exhibit, and four essays covering different

episodes in the history of 'Oriental Studies' at Louvain/Leuven. I contributed one of these essays, dealing with the historical circumstances and the actual execution of the Japanese donation, and selected forty-seven items from the Japanese donation. It was the first time that the Japanese donation was presented to the European public. According to the preface of the catalogue, in an environment where contacts with China and Japan seem completely dominated by commercial considerations, it is of paramount importance that the universities draw attention to the cultural aspects of the East-West relations. The purpose was to provide a real encounter with the specific of the other culture, regardless of everything that we take for granted based on our own. The exhibition was described as a stepping stone on an adventurous journey of discovery. We hope that this new exhibition will mark another stepping stone in that journey of mutual discovery and recognition.

65

▲ **15. Lacquer box donated by Baron Ōkura.** Source: Collection Kunstpatrimonium KU Leuven.

妙法蓮華經譬喩品第三　金字銀界紺紙寫經　一卷

Willy Vande Walle

Selected Books from the 1920s Japanese Donation

Introduction to the Selection from the Japanese Donation

It is an almost impossible task to select some sixty odd items from a collection of about 3,000 titles in almost 14,000 volumes. In the selection process, we have not only been motivated by an antiquarian perspective (rarity of the item) or from the viewpoint of the book historian, but also by the significance of the item for the cultural history of Japan, its visual attractiveness, and the uncommon aspects the item in question offers. Our main goal was to provide a general overview of the depth and breadth of the Japanese donation, of what the Japanese donors – and, in particular, the bibliographers and librarians who actually picked it out – considered to be representative of classical Japanese culture as they saw it (see list p. 291).

A Representative Selection

To provide such a global overview, we had to base our selection on the twenty-six divisions that the donors themselves used to categorize the donation. They were defined in the catalogue that was compiled at the time of the donation, and which was published in a limited edition. Some divisions have been left out due to their limited relevance, such as the division on education, while others are also less than evident to us. The division "philosophy", for instance, includes many books on fortune-telling and divination because these are often linked to the ancient Chinese *Yijing* (*Book of Changes*, Jap. *Ekikyō* 易経), which for many centuries has functioned both as a divination manual and as a book of wisdom. This classification reflects an interpretation of the definition of "philosophy" different from what we are used to. The donors used bibliographical concepts that,

to some extent, differed from contemporary Western ones. One conspicuous example is that Shintō, the indigenous religion of Japan, earned its own division alongside that of "religion", whereas nowadays it is subsumed into the division of "philosophy and religion". This former designation obviously reflects the special status Shintō had enjoyed in Japan since the Meiji period (1868-1912). In the division "religion", we come across both doctrinal essays and edifying folktales, mostly of a Buddhist signature. Although we have selected only one item from "religion", this category, at least as far as Buddhism is concerned, is largely represented in the division "precious and rare works".

The proportion of illustrated books in our selection is relatively large, since we assumed that this type of book was likely to interest a broader public. This decision means, for example, that books that constitute a minor genre and are known as "illustrated topographical descriptions" (the division "topography and travelogues") figure rather prominently in the selection. It also holds for the "scientific" books, which we come across in the divisions "natural sciences" and "medicine", as well as the books in the division "arts and crafts". Books in these divisions are usually more richly and more artistically illustrated. The books on 'scientific' subjects are also fascinating because they bear witness to the first stirrings of the scientific mind in Japan. In the view of many historians of the book, these works paved the way for the later rapid development of the modern sciences in the country, while Japanese arts and crafts have been more familiar and favourite aspects of Japanese culture in the West since the nineteenth century.

▸ Scroll of the *Lotus Sutra of the Marvellous Doctrine: The Parable Chapter*, illustrated manuscript, probably from the Kamakura period (1185-1333), and its wooden box (of later date). See selected books no. 62.

As mentioned in the preceding essay, a new catalogue on the Japanese donation was published in 2000, compiled by Yamazaki Makoto. He replicated the arrangement of the aforementioned original catalogue, with one difference: he has added a twenty-seventh division to the pre-existing twenty-six, so as to accommodate later additions to the collection, which were not part of the original donation but have since been integrated into it. While replicating the original arrangement, he expanded on the very scant information contained in the original catalogue by adding bibliographical data retrieved from the vast electronic database of the Kokubungaku kenkyū shiryōkan (National Research and Documentation Center for Japanese Literature in Tokyo) and from the database of the National Diet Library. In some cases, this augmented information has led to discrepancies between the physical item at UCLouvain and the bibliographic description derived from a union catalogue.

The donation consisted and still consists of five main categories: manuscripts, antiquarian books (generally from before 1868), maps (mostly from before 1868), scientific and scholarly works from the Meiji (1868-1912) and Taishō periods (1912-1925), and contemporary reproductions of classical works of art. The reproductions were made with the best means available at the time and, as such, represent the epitome of the surprisingly advanced Japanese reproduction techniques of the 1920s. Nevertheless, we have not selected any of them, because they are no match to contemporary reproduction techniques. Of the maps and other large-sized one-page documents, we could only make a limited selection in view of space limitations for the exhibition. We did not select any items from the scholarly and literary works from the Meiji and Taishō periods, either. Consequently, our selection is primarily focused on two categories, namely the manuscripts and what we have called antiquarian books. In the vast majority of cases, the latter are woodblock-printed editions, although we have also included so-called "old movable-type editions" (*kokatsujiban* 古活字版) and even one or two "early modern movable-type editions". Whatever the printing technique, all are bound in a Japanese style (*wasōbon* 和装本).

It follows, naturally, that nearly all selected books antedate 1868. Nevertheless, we have chosen a limited number of items of a more recent date. They include a pair of exquisite scrolls related to the enthronement and thanksgiving ceremonies of the Taishō emperor in 1915. They represent the finest of traditional Japanese painting techniques in the Taishō period. Notably, they are not categorized under the division "arts and crafts" but, rather, under division "laws and institutions". The copy of *Honzō zufu*, 本草図譜 a botanical album, dates from the Taishō period as well. It is a woodblock reprint of a work consisting of many fascicles, originally published between 1830 and 1844. The reprint is of extraordinary quality, and the copy in the UCLouvain is in mint condition. This superb colour print (*mokuhan no irozuri* 木版の色刷り) represents the pinnacle of woodblock printing (*mokuhan gijutsu* 木版技術). Until the Taishō period, the technique of woodblock printing was passed on from generation to generation perfectly, and that outstanding art could still be used in this *Honzō zufu*. After that, it was gradually lost. Whether book makers today are still capable of such consummate technical prowess on a similar scale is doubtful.

The layout and conventions of the Japanese-bound book are very different from those of a Western book. They come in various formats, all conspicuously different from traditional Western binding. One of the oldest formats on paper is the hand scroll (*kansubon* 巻子本), which is scrolled around a spindle, and which is also a traditional format for paintings. This is rather unhandy. Therefore, at one point, to make for easier handling, people started folding the long scroll in equal sections, not unlike a concertina. This type of book is called the folded book (*orihon* 折本). It is often found in Buddhist scriptures. The most commonly encountered format, however, is that of the *sensōbon* 線装本, the 'book bound with thread,' also called *fukurotojibon* 袋綴じ本, the 'book bound as a bag'. Each printed leaf that will make up the book is folded in two with the printing on the outside. The two edges of each leaf (on the opposite side of the fold) are aligned on top of one another. When the leaves thus folded and aligned reach a certain thickness, they are stitched together with a thread forming the back of the bound book. Since the stitching with a thread is not very robust, a 'book' is usually a thin fascicle, probably best comparable to what in French is called '*cahier*', so that one 'title' usually consists of a multiple of fascicles. The fascicles were sometimes wrapped in a jacket (*sotobukuro*

外袋), which had the same imprint as the *mikaeshi* 見返し, i.e. the page stuck on the inside or reverse of the front cover (*hyōshi* 表紙). The Edo period books that still have their jacket are rare. These paper jackets are not to be confused with the *chitsu* 帙, a wrapper or protective book case. The latter is basically a carton board wrapped in indigo cloth, such as those the National Committee had fashioned for the books. *Chitsu* are custom-made and are not provided by the bookseller. The *mikaeshi* is often made of coloured paper.

Apart from the fact that our selection not only strives to be as varied in content or genre as possible, it also offers a panoply of the variety that characterized the Japanese language before 1868, as well as of the many formats in which these manuscripts and books were produced. The variety in language is also noticeable in the graphic appearance of the writing. There are Japanese editions or reprints of Chinese books, written in Classical Chinese. The Chinese woodblock typefaces are generally 'squarer' than the Japanese ones. In addition, a great number of works written by Japanese authors were written in *kanbun* 漢文. *Kanbun* is a variety of Classical Chinese used by Japanese. It follows the grammar of Classical Chinese and uses the Chinese characters, but it is read in a meta-language based on Japanese syntax. Before 1868 very few Japanese spoke Chinese, so they had to read the written Chinese in a Japanese way. The writing and reading of such texts, where the reader has to constantly 'oscillate' between the two language systems, was and is a strenuous form of mental exercise. To help the reader, texts in *kanbun* were and are often supplemented with syntactical marks (*kaeriten* 返り点) indicating the Japanese syntactical order of the sentence, as well as with syllabic characters suggesting verb endings of Japanese verbs and particles (*okurigana* 送り仮名). Because Classical Chinese was the language of Buddhist doctrine and of Confucian learning, it enjoyed enormous prestige, much like Latin enjoyed in European cultural history. Conversely, we can also discern a parallel in the increasing use of vernacular, and of so-called national languages in Europe since the early Renaissance, and the increasing use of Japanese for various categories of the written language in early modern Japan. Japanese was and is written with a syllabic writing system developed by Japanese (*kana* 仮名), or in a mixture of Chinese charac-

ters and the *kana* syllabary (called *kanamajiri* 仮名交じり). There are two kinds of syllabic writing: *hiragana* and *katakana*. Both can be combined with Chinese characters.

Central to the production of the written word during the Edo period were not literary or theatrical genres. For Japanese of the Edo period or, rather, for the elite – admittedly a minority of the population – not Moto'ori Norinaga 本居宣長 (1730-1801), the great philologist of Japanese classics, who wrote in Japanese, but Ogyū Sorai 荻生徂徠 (1666-1728), one of Japan's most prominent scholars of Chinese Confucian classics, was arguably the greatest thinker. Among the poets, Kan Sazan 菅茶山 (1748-1827), who composed verse in Classical Chinese, was probably better known than Matsuo Bashō 松尾芭蕉 (1644-1694), who wrote poetry in Japanese. In prose, Rai San'yō 頼山陽 (1781-1832), who wrote in Classical Chinese, was definitely more famous than Kyokutei Bakin 曲亭馬琴 (1767-1848), who published in Japanese. The cultural elite of the Edo period held firmly onto the old tradition which revered Classical Chinese, a language which in its written form was shared by the elites in East Asia who used the Chinese characters, much like Latin once used to be a vehicle of communication among the elites in various European countries and regions. In sum, in China as well as in Japan, Korea, and Vietnam, literary production in the vernacular had a secondary status.

In the modern histories of Japanese literature, however, Japanese-language works take centre stage, somewhat at the cost of downplaying the importance of Classical Chinese. This 'distortion' was the result of the rising consciousness of national identity, which was strongly articulated starting with the Meiji Restoration, and which favoured the 'popular language'. This development was not unique to Japan. A similar evolution occurred in Western Europe. Who remembers the works of 'our national' scholars writing difficult and erudite treatises in Latin in the seventeenth century? It does mean, though, that works on which most of the intellectual energy was spent at that time have now partially or completely disappeared behind the cultural horizon. A small group of specialized academics may study them, but the fruits of their diligent work are not enjoyed by a wider audience.

Following the Western example, modern Japanese academics wrote literary histories which similarly marginalized *kanbun* works. In modern Japanese literary history, the Edo period is portrayed as the *chōnin bungaku* 町人文学, literature by and for the townspeople, as represented in the early phase by writers like Chikamatsu Monzaemon 近松門左衛門 (1653-1725) and Ihara Saikaku 井原西鶴 (1642-1693) and, in the later phase, by writers like Shikitei Sanba 式亭三馬 (1776-1822). This shift would have been hard to accept for intellectuals in the late Edo period. To them, Chikamatsu was a pleasant diversion, Saikaku was probably unknown to them, and they would have spurned the *gesakusha* 戯作者- the 'dime novelists' of the so-called *tenpō rokkasen* 天保六花撰 – since that was 'entertainment for women and children'. They were convinced that only literary and philosophical writings of the seventeenth-century Confucianists were must-reads.

The books selected by us mostly date back to the Edo period and provide us a glance at the vibrant culture of the time. Despite the country being largely closed off from the outside world, it experienced a period of great creativity. Or was it *because* of the isolation and imposed limitations? In such circumstances, the human mind can twist and turn itself in all kinds of ways to get around the limitations imposed. Such creative contortions sometimes resulted in intellectual or artistic achievements of epic proportions. One need only think of the Buddhist monk Jiun Sonja 慈雲尊者 (1718-1804), who aspired to return to the origins of his faith, but was cut off from direct contacts of this source, both in terms of distance and time. Not to be deterred, he set about reconstructing the grammar of Sanskrit relying on ancient Chinese and Japanese sources, including the *Honyaku myōgi-shū* 翻譯名義集, featured among the works selected here.

The explanations that accompany each of the selected items contain as a minimum a limited uniform set of bibliographical data, in addition to some explanation about its contents and its author(s). In many cases, though not uniformly so, they also include data about other particularities that are specific to the selected item in question: data given in the colophon, interspersed notes in the text, author's seals, collector's seals, Ex Libris stamps, as well as, in some cases, remarks on the physical aspects of the book, such as damage, wear, traces of restoration, quality of the paper, of the print or the illustrations.

Besides, within each description, we have included a reference to one or more reproduced illustrations taken from the described item, also briefly adding a description of the content or significance of the selected illustrations. The explanatory notes are concluded at the end of each entry with one or a few references to germane research literature on the subject dealt with in the explanatory text. There are several reasons for the lack of strict uniformity in the description: the varying importance of the title under review for the cultural history of Japan, its rarity, its history, its value, features specific to the copy in the UCLouvain, space limitations imposed by the publisher, and so on.

In many of the contributed articles one will come across Chinese characters inserted in the running text. We hope that the readers who are not familiar with these logograms (called *kanji* in Japanese) do not experience their presence as an unnecessary impediment to the smooth reading of the text. We have purposely included them following the names of Japanese persons, lesser-known place names, titles of Japanese books, institutions, important concepts and notions, or typically Japanese phenomena. All logographs that are included in the official list of the *Jōyō kanji* are consistently given in their simplified form. It is common practice in the field of Japanese studies to reproduce the *kanji*, and since this catalogue is also intended as a work of reference, we assume that both the students of Japanese studies, as well as Japanese readers, will appreciate the original renderings of the aforesaid word categories.

Within each catalogue division of those represented here, the books are ordered alphabetically per title. We have translated the Japanese title literally, where possible, or else paraphrased it. Many titles often include far-flung allusions or refer to other titles and so remain puzzling even in translation, unless a sufficient explanation is added. We hope the description following each title will adequately explain what the book, manuscript or scroll in question is about. All items exhibited here belong to the UCLouvain - Libraries Heritage Collections, Japanese donation. To avoid repetitiveness each item is identified in the catalogue descriptions by the abbreviation "UCLouvain Libraries," followed by its shelf number (e.g., RES JAP 15G12).

1. Kottō-shū 骨董集
('Collection of Curios [part one]')

3 chapters in 4 fascicles; 26.2 x 18 cm; black-and-white illustrations
Authors: Santō Kyōden 三東京伝; illustrators: Kita Busei

喜田武清, Utagawa Toyohiro 歌川豊弘, Santō Kyōzan 三東京山
Date: preface dated Bunka 文化 10 (1813), printed in Bunka 11-12 (1814-1815)

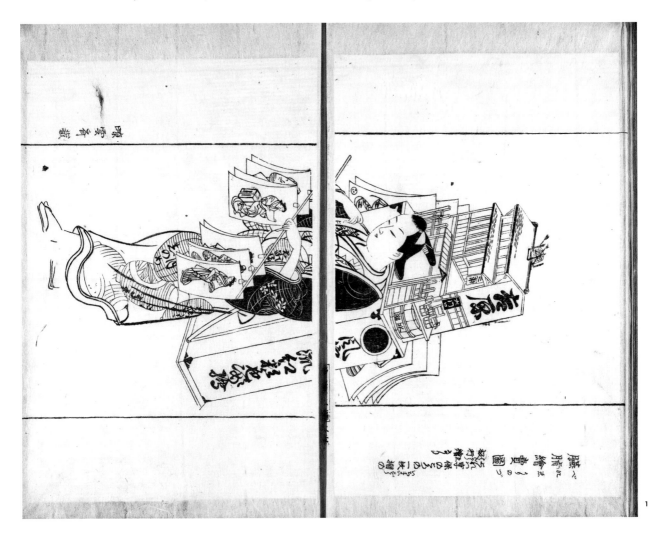

This is an essay by *ukiyo-e* 浮世絵 (woodblock print) artist and author of popular literature Santō Kyōden (1761-1816), with illustrations by Kita Busei, Utagawa Toyohiro, and Kyōden's brother, Santō Kyōzan. There were apparently also a second and third part scheduled, but only the first part was ever published. It is a study of habits, customs, clothing, games, toys, furniture, food, decorations, and so on, of the Edo period (1600-1868). The author investigates their origin and evolution in 111 sections. He does this with a certain scientific precision, drawing on some 350 sources and enriching his discourse with numerous illustrations.

Ill. 1: a young peddler plying the streets with a case on his back (illustration to section 21 of fascicle I, 上編上, 20b-21a). This print is of the *beni-e* 紅絵 type, and dates from the Kyōhō period (1716-1736). In the case the peddler is carrying single-sheet prints. Dangling from a bamboo stick in his hand are likewise a number of *beni-e* prints, all rep-

resenting 'portraits' of female beauties (*sugata-e* 姿絵). On the side of the chest we read the characters Yoshiwara 吉原 and *fūryū beni saishiki sugata-e* 風流紅彩色姿絵. Yoshiwara refers to Edo's officially certified 'pleasure' district, while the longer inscription translates as "fashionable red-coloured portraits", evidently of courtesans of the Yoshiwara district.

In the text that goes with the illustration, Santō Kyōden briefly retraces the development of the *ukiyo-e* print. Illustrated books had been around before, but beginning with the Enpō-Tenna period (1673-1684), printers started to print and sell single-sheet prints, [not unlike the posters of today]. The *beni-e* ('prints in red') were first put onto the market by a printer from the area of Asakusa gomon in Edo, at the beginning of the Kyōhō period (1716-1736). When glue was mixed into the ink, the colours took on a glossy shine. This kind of prints was called *urushi-e* 漆絵 ('lacquered prints'). Okumura Masanobu was an important artist in this genre. Incidentally,

▲ A young peddler plying the streets with a case on his back. The figure, which incidentally supplied the inspiration for the

cover of the present book, is drawn across a two-page spread, and has to be turned ninety degrees to be viewed properly.

2

it was not until the 1760s that the highly prized polychrome prints made their appearance.

Ill. 2: two travelling Buddhist nuns (Kumano Bikuni 熊野比丘尼), who spread the Buddhist message among the common people (illustration to section 1 of fascicle IV, 上編下之後 2b). They are holding an illustrated scroll in their hand, on which the terrors of hell are depicted. The illustrations serve to heighten the impact of their story.

The first page of each of the four fascicles bears the collector's seal of "Okuda & Inoue" and another of "Inoue Tsurumatsu".

Santō Kyōden (1761–1816) is the pseudonym of Iwase Samuru 岩瀬醒, also known as Kyōya Denzō

京屋伝蔵, a poet, writer, and *ukiyo-e* artist. As an *ukiyo-e* artist, he is known as Kitao Masanobu 北尾政寅 after his master Kitao Shigemasa 北尾重政. He began his career as an illustrator of a genre of novels known as *kibyōshi* 黄表紙 (see page 99), though he soon tried his hand at writing them himself under the pseudonym Santō Kyōden. Churning out *kibyōshi* 黄表紙, *sharebon* 洒落本 (novelettes about life in the red-light districts), *yomihon* 読本, and historical essays in great numbers, he garnered a wide readership and was one of the first fiction writers in the Edo period to be able to live by his pen.

Literature: Tsukamoto 1915

▲ Travelling Buddhist nuns, who spread the Buddhist message among the common people.

Collector's Seals

A remarkable feature of antique books in East Asia is that they often bear traces of their previous owners, either in the form of inscriptions and notes, or in the form of collector's seals (*zōshoin* 蔵書印). This usage was already known in China, during the Han Dynasty (202 BC-220 AD), and from there spread to other countries influenced by the Chinese culture.

In Japan, the practice of pressing seals in books is attested as early as the Nara period (710-784), but it is only much later that it became widespread, even beyond what was known in China and Korea. Seals were originally used to validate a document or certify its authenticity, but gradually their use shifted to marking one's ownership of a book. In the Edo and Meiji periods the pressing of collector's seals became a common practice. They were used by feudal lords (*daimyō*), official domain academies, schools, authors, and intellectuals. The library of the *shōgun* used a collector's seal from its founding in 1639. *Kashihon-ya* 貸本屋 or 'booklenders' also used them to mark their ownership of their books and in so doing limit theft.

Seals are hard to remove. They are usually pressed on the first page of the preface or of the corpus of the text and are commonly vermillion or black in colour. Most have a frame and a rectangular shape, although there are also round or elliptical ones. Certain intellectuals even used ones in the shape of an elephant or gourd.

Many books also contain marginal comments, notes, or remarks. In *kanbun* texts (in Classical Chinese), one often finds all manner of punctuation marks, such as lines along or through proper names in vermillion (*shubiki* 朱引).

Literature: Ono 1988.

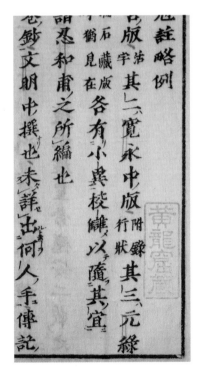

73

▲ Examples of collector's seals found in various books in the collection.

2. Semete wagusa 責而者草
('The Very Least We Should Remember')

Alternative title: *Semete wagusa* 勢免天話草 /
慙遺草 / 責而者草 / 責而話草

42 chapters in 12 fascicles; 18.5 x 12.7 cm
Author: Shibui Tokushō 渋井徳章
Date: unknown

74

In the *Kokusho sōmokuroku* 国書総目録, the title is given as 勢免天話草, albeit with the same pronunciation. These at first sight enigmatic characters are simply the *Manyōgana* 万葉仮名 style equivalents of the *kana* syllabary. The mimicry of *Manyōgana* style, transcribing even the morphological elements *te* て and *wa* は in *kanji*, resonates with the intention of the author to hark back to past times. He has gleaned testimonies about virtuous conduct and noble acts by *shōguns*, their relatives, feudal lords, ministers, councilors, down to virtuous women, from no less than thirty-six books. After careful investigation and collation - fact-checking we would say nowadays - he has retained only the most reliable and commendable data, those that at the very least should be remembered and cherished by posterity, hence the title. The books he excerpted include, among others, *Kyūsō shōsetsu* 鳩巣小説, a collection of essays by Muro Kyūsō 室鳩巣 (1658-1734), *Hankanfu* 藩翰譜, a repertory of *daimyō* families and their achievements by the Confucianist Arai Hakuseki 新井白石 (1657-1725), and *Buya shokudan* 武野蜀談 - each and every one of them reliable and authoritative sources, according to the author.

The author Shibui Tokushō was a Confucian scholar in the service of the lord of Sakura 佐倉. His

biography is included in *Sentetsu sōdan kōhan* 先哲叢談後編, chapter 7.

The UCLouvain copy is remarkable because it is a case of early modern wooden movable type (*kinsei mokkatsuji-ban* 近世木活字版, in contradistinction to the old movable type). There are several editions of this work, the number of chapters varying. There are copies that are datable to 1842 and 1866, but most extant copies lack a colophon, and so does the copy in UCLouvain. Since a colophon is lacking, the publisher of this wooden movable-type edition is not known, but since it comprises forty-two chapters in eleven fascicles, it is probably the Tenpō 天保 13 (1842) edition. The last page bears the seal of the Isobeya 磯部屋 bookstore in Tokyo, where the UCLouvain copy was presumably purchased by the National Committee.

During the Taishō period (1912-1926), the work was reprinted as part of the series *Nihon ijin genkō shiryō* 日本偉人言行資料 (Documents about Words and Deeds of Eminent Japanese), under the general editorship of Hagino Yoshiyuki 萩野由之 (1860-1924). This reprint in metal movable type, published by Kokushi kenkyūkai 國史研究会 in Taishō 6 (1917), was edited by Hotta Shōzō 堀田璋左右 and Kawakami Tasuke 川上多助 (1884-1959).

▲ First page of the table of contents, giving pride of place to the clan of the *shōgun* and its major branches (fascicle I, preface, p. 6b).

▲ Cover of *Semete wagusa*, with *daisen* mentioning: first instalment, chapters 1-3.

3. Ekigaku kaibutsu 易学開物
('The Exploration of Things Based on the Book of Changes')

3 chapters in 2 fascicles; 26 x 35 cm
Author: Minagawa Gen (Kien) 皆川愿 (淇園)
Date: manuscript copy dated 1828

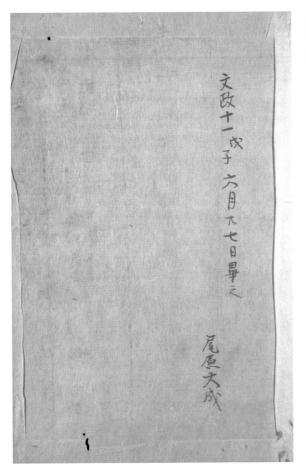
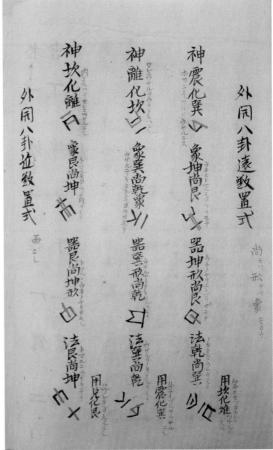

Minagawa Kien 皆川淇園 (1735-1807) was a Confucianist, painter, and writer born and active in Kyoto. He was invited to serve as teacher of Confucian classics by various feudal lords, including Matsudaira Nobumine 松平信岑 (1696-1763). His literary and pictorial skills made him an outstanding figure in the literati circles of the imperial capital. More than three thousand students from all rungs of society are said to have taken his lessons. With the support of various feudal lords, he opened his own private school named Kōdōkan 弘道館 in 1805, but he did not outlive its establishment very long.

Among other subjects, he studied the *Yi Jing* a.k.a. *The Book of Changes* (Jap.: *Ekikyō* 易経), developing an original linguistic theory, in which he explored the relationship between 'words' (*na* 名) and 'phenomena' (*mono* 物). In addition he authored commentaries on various Chinese classics, including the *Lunyü*, *Laozi*, *Zhuangzi*, and *Liezi*.

The term *kaibutsu* 開物 ('opening, exploring things'), an expression taken from *The Book of Changes*, refers to his philosophical method of exploring phenomena through the study of words (*na*). The phenomena cannot be directly experienced; their exploration has to be mediated by the analysis of sound and meaning enshrined in words. However, in his ethico-political approach, 'phenomena' are first and foremost human affairs, and their 'exploration' is relevant in view of wise government.

For him *The Book of Changes* is not a book of divination, as it was traditionally considered to be, but a book of wisdom. Despite its abstruse nature this classic stimulated Minagawa and other Confucianists in his wake to turn to the study of celestial phenomena as well. In recent times Minagawa has been re-appraised as a philosopher because of his positivist approach to Confucian studies, which made him a kind of forerunner of Western philosophy in Japan.

The UCLouvain copy is an unpaged handwritten copy of *Ekigaku kaibutsu* by Obara Taisei 尾原大成.

Literature: Saigusa 1957, pp. 109-119; Saigusa 1956, pp. 95-107.

75

▲ Hand-written colophon page in red ink by Obara Taisei, bearing date Bunsei 文政 11 (1828).

◀ Page from *Ekigaku kaibutsu*, demonstrating how the pronunciations arranged in the *Yunjing* 韻鏡 ('Mirror of Rhymes', oldest editions of 1161 and 1203 published by Zhang Linzhi 張麟之) must be related to the deeper meaning of notions of *The Book of Changes*. Current versions of the *Yunjing* date to AD 1161 and 1203, and were published by Zhang Linzhi.

4. Kōgiroku narabini furoku 孝義録並附録
('A Record about Filial Piety and Righteousness, with Supplement')

Alternative title: *Kankoku*官刻 / *Kōgiroku* 孝義録
50 chapters in 50 fascicles; 26.5 x 18 cm

Author: unknown
Date: Kyōwa 享和 1 (1801)

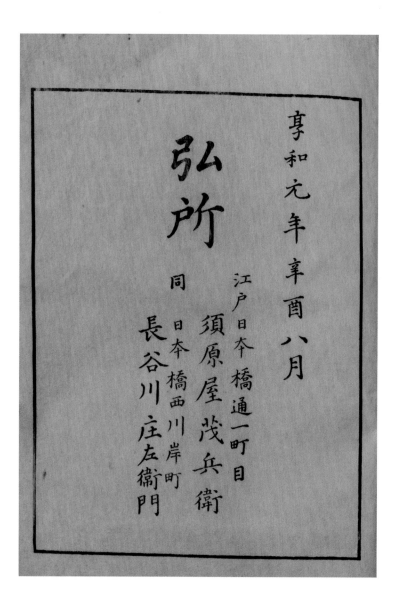

The spectacular development of publishing from the middle of the Tokugawa era onwards was generally looked upon by the shogunate with a certain degree of suspicion or caution. Mass publishing was viewed as an issue directly concerning social stability. Keen to control the flow of information, the authorities issued orders controlling publication and set up a system of publication censorship. Admittedly, the shogunate generally took a negative stance towards the circulation and spread of information, yet it also actively engaged in promoting desirable information through means of official publications.

The Kansei 寛政 period (1789-1801) witnessed a conspicuous case of this new and pro-active attitude of the government towards the media, an early case of politically manipulating information through these media: the compilation and publication of *Kōgiroku*. The *Kōgiroku* has been regarded as part of the implementation of the shogunate's policy of reform and popular edification, the so-called Kansei Reforms, but conversely, it may also be construed as a subtle way of advertising the virtues of the shogunate's righteous and benevolent policies, thus reinforcing the legitimacy of its rule.

The *Kōgiroku* project almost perfectly coincided with the beginning and end of this Kansei period, an era, moreover, of Confucianist revival. In Kansei 1 (1789), the shogunate, in the person of the chief senior councilor (*rōjū shuza* 老中首座) Matsudaira Sadanobu 松平定信 (1759-1829), ordered a nationwide survey of recorded cases of outstanding filial piety and righteousness. Since it is a government edition (*kankoku* 官刻 or *kanpan* 官版), the colophon does not mention any editors, only 'Hiromedokoro'

▲ Colophon page, mentioning the two bookshops that act as distribution centers for the books.

弘所 (distribution centres), followed by a few addresses. We know, though, that the versatile scholar and man of letters Ōta Nanpo 太田南畝 (1749-1823) was involved in the compiling and editing. Undertaken at the Shōheizaka gakumonjo 昌平坂学問所, the recently established official school of the shogunate, the work was completed in Kansei 12 (1800). The following year, the published book was officially presented to the shogunate, who gave permission for its public sale before the end of that same year.

While similar books extolling the (Confucian) virtues of people and published during the Edo period are believed to have numbered at least around a hundred, *Kōgiroku* is exceptional for its government sponsorship and its sheer volume, consisting of no less than fifty chapters. No less than 8,611 - numbers slightly vary according to the author: Van Steenpaal's figure is 8,611; Suzuki Rie's figure, 8,614 - of virtuous subjects from all over the country are mentioned, having been commended for their conduct, spanning a time frame between 1602 and 1798. 81 percent of them, that is, 6,985 individuals, belong to the second half of the eighteenth century. Those rated outstanding, 755 (Van Steenpaal's figure; Suzuki Rie's figure: 759) in all, are honoured with an individual biographical (hagiographical) notice. While the longest biographical notice runs up to 5,050 characters and the shortest counts a mere 196 characters, most have a length that varies between 400 to 2,000 characters.

This to all intents and purposes impressive number of individuals is subdivided in eleven categories, including filial piety, loyalty, devotion, chastity, brotherly love, and so forth - needless to say, all good commendable Confucian virtues. The overwhelming majority of the individuals included are ordinary people. There are only 78 members of the samurai class, in addition to a pitiful 15 members of the *eta* 穢多 and *hinin* 非人 class (Japan's equivalent of outcasts). This Confucian-inspired social bias towards the 'commoners' does however add to the relevance of the work as a source of social history.

Literature: Van Steenpaal 2009, pp. 35-52; Suzuki 2004, pp. 19-34; Sugano 1999.

77

▲ A few fascicles from *Kōgiroku*.

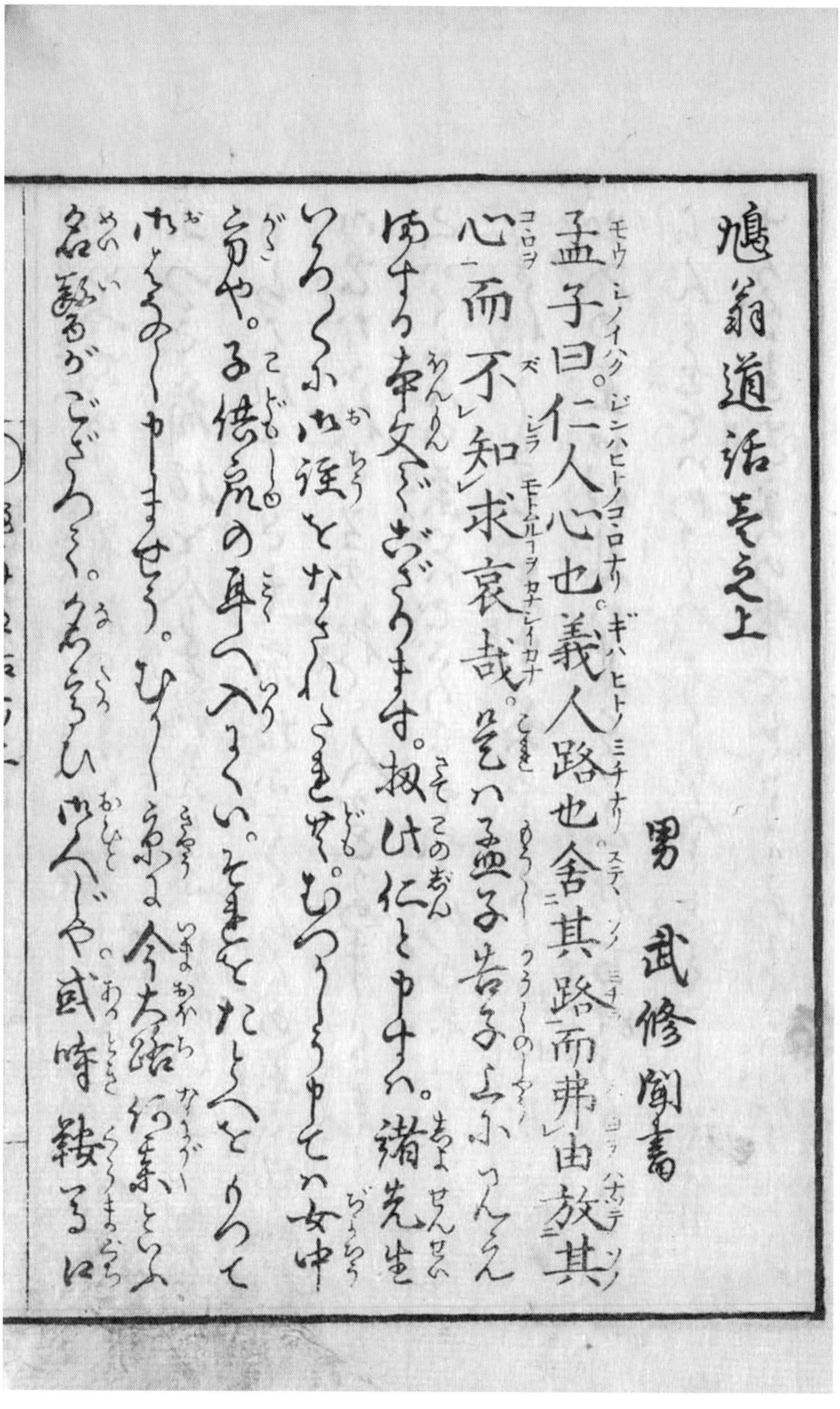

78

鳩翁道話 巻之上

男 武修 閲書

孟子曰。仁人心也。義人路也舍其路而弗由放其心而不知求哀哉。

心而不知求哀哉。此孟子が告子上に不んるん

はす孔孟ぐざります。扨此仁とやらへ。諸先生

いろくふ小径となれとまびつりましてぞ女中

方や。子供衆の年へ入くいとりて

れくのかますらう。びくふうる今大路行業とふ

名誉るがござつく。ねくしいくくじや武時

▲ First page of the first chapter of *Kyūōdōwa*, mentioning
that the sermons were written down as he spoke by Kyūō's son
Takeyoshi 武修 (Fasc.I/chapter 1, p. 1).

5. Kyūōdōwa fu zokuhen oyobi Ōsaka zokuzokuhen
鳩翁道話附続編及大阪続々篇
('Moral Discourses by Kyūō, first sequel and second sequel, published in Ōsaka')

Alternative title: *Kyūōdōwa* 鳩翁道話
Total of 9 chapters in 18 fascicles, each part consisting
of 3 chapters in 6 fascicles; 21 x 15.3 cm

Author: Shibata Kyūō 柴田鳩翁; editor: Shibata Gaiken
柴田艾軒
Date: published between Tenpō 天保 5 and 10 (1834-1839)

Shibata Kyūō 柴田鳩翁 (1783-1839) descended from a family of couriers, townspeople in Kyoto. He is especially known as the author of *Kyūō dōwa*, a collection of episodes taken from daily life and narrated in the colloquial style, meant to inculcate the simple ethics of "Heart Learning" (*Shingaku* 心学, or *Sekimon-shingaku* 石門心学). This particular school of moral philosophy was founded by Ishida Baigan 石田梅岩 (1685-1744), and it commanded a considerable following in its heyday. Its simple tenets were rooted in Neo-Confucianism, mixed with principles from Zen Buddhism and Shintō.

His family having fallen on hard times in the wake of the Great Fire of Tenmei (1788), which devastated major parts of Kyoto, Shibata began serving as an apprentice in a kimono store from the age of eleven (1793). After having lost both his father and mother in succession, and with his sister and her husband having taken over the family business, at the age of nineteen he went to Edo to try his luck there (1801). However, after seven years in Edo, he returned to Kyoto, now earning his living with a side job as painter. At age 28, he started giving performances of oral storytelling about historical events, military feats, and other sensational incidents. He garnered so much success that he decided to make a living out of this practice, honing his art by reading poetry and the classics.

One day he hit upon a work of Ishida Baigan and was greatly moved by the philosophy of Heart Learning expounded in it. He set about studying this doctrine in earnest, eventually earning a licence from one of the proponents of the doctrine. Subsequently, he practised Zen at a temple of the Ōbaku school of Zen Buddhism. Around 1825, coming to the conclusion that there were many commonalities between Heart Learning and Zen Buddhism, he said goodbye to his profession of telling stories and started a career preaching his newly found doctrine to the common people. He made a name for himself as the most prominent preacher of Heart Learning in the land. Benefitting from his experience, he interspersed his lectures with salient episodes and anecdotes taken from real life, the better to drive his moral message home with his audience. Unfortunately, his eyesight started to decline, before long leading to complete blindness. He took the Buddhist tonsure and henceforth styled himself Kyūō. This challenge did not stop him from continuing his lecturing tours in and around Kyoto, now sprinkling his narrative with episodes taken from his own adverse luck. His son recorded his lectures in the colloquial language of his father's delivery, publishing them under the title 鳩翁道話、続鳩翁道話、続々鳩翁道話 (Moral Discourses by Kyūō, First Sequel and Second Sequel). It has been speculated that Heart Learning was one of the cultural foundations for Japan's industrialization.

The UCLouvain copy has a collector's seal of a certain Watanabe.

In 1878, Comte Charles de Montblanc published a French translation of a part of this book. Although a French citizen, he was also Baron of Ingelmunster. As such, he may be considered the first "Belgian" to have translated (part of) a Japanese classic.

Literature: Shibata 1970, pp. 315ff.; Kracht 1974; Montblanc 1878, pp. 135-153.

6. Sekishinkō fuzokuhen 釈親考附続編 ('A Study of Kinship Terminology, and Sequel')

Alternative title: *Shakushinkō fuzokuhen* 釈親考附続編, 2 chapters in 2 fascicles; main title 1 chapter, sequel 1 chapter; 22.5 x 17.8 cm
Author: Itō Tōgai 伊藤東涯

Date: preface by Yasuhara Sadahira 安原貞平, dated Kyōhō 享保 12 (1735), published in Genbun 元文 1 (1736), later reprinted in Kansei 寛政 8 (1796)

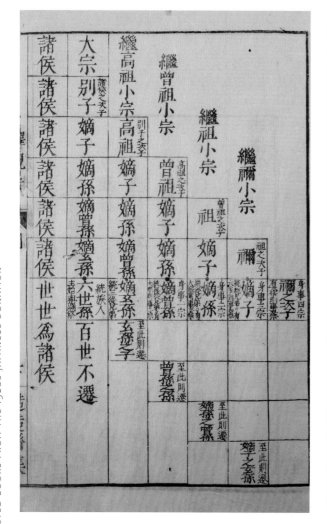
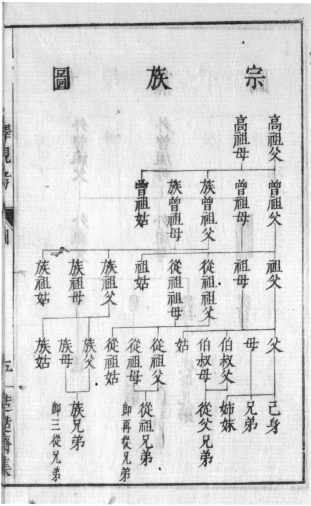

Itō Tōgai (1670-1736) was a prominent Confucian scholar, the eldest son of the even more famous Confucian scholar Itō Jinsai 伊藤仁斎 (1627-1705). He inherited from his father his private school Kogidō 古義堂. His given name was Nagatane, his courtesy name Genzō, his sobriquet Tōgai.

In biographical sources he is portrayed as a gentle person, supportive of his father and younger brothers, carrying on the legacy of his father by laying the foundations for the success of Kogigaku 古義学, the school of Confucian exegesis founded by his father. Besides devoting himself to editing and publishing his father's books, he also published a number of erudite studies of his own. His interests were in Chinese language, Chinese institutional history, and Confucian history. He befriended other outstanding Confucian scholars including Arai Hakuseki 新井白石 (1657-1725) and Ogyū Sorai 荻生徂徠 (1666-1728).

'A Study of Kinship Terminology, and sequel,' is one of Itō's lesser known works, and there are not many copies extant in public collections. It is a good example of his learning and philological meticulousness. Based on Chinese sources, it is a study of the complex kinship relations in Chinese history, defining the various kinds of relationships within the genealogical structure of the extended family (*kyūzoku* 九族) and the multitude of terms that are used in this context.

The book includes an original preface by Tōgai himself, dated Genroku 14 (1701), but the book was actually not published until the year of his death. It was his disciple Yasuhara Sadahira (1698-1780) who edited the book, including his own preface, and had it published in 1736. The copy of the UCLouvain is the reprint of 1796.

▲ Two pages showing the various kinship relations of the Chinese clan.

7. Teihan kokuji kai 帝範国字解
('Mirrors for Emperors, Explained in Japanese')

2 chapters in 2 fascicles; 22.6 x 16.3 cm
Author: Ichikawa Kakumei 市川鶴鳴
Date: Tenmei 天明 9 (1789)

This work is the Japanese version of *Di fan* 帝範, a Chinese equivalent of what is known in the West as 'Mirrors for Princes' (*specula principum*), a manual of statecraft. The book was allegedly compiled in 648 by Emperor Taizong 太宗 (r. 626-649), who consolidated the Tang dynasty and is considered one of the greatest monarchs of all time in Chinese history. He intended it as an introduction to the art of governing and leadership, serving as a mirror of good conduct and wise judgment for his son and successor Gaozong 高宗 (r. 649-683) - unfortunately to no avail, as it would later turn out.

The Chinese original consists of two parts in two chapters each and is divided into 12 topics. Since it reflected the ideas and inner thoughts about politics and leadership by an extremely successful monarch, it has always been considered the premier handbook of statecraft, or *Teiōgaku* 帝王学 (Instruction of rulers on rule and behaviour), in East Asia. There are two other books about Emperor Taizong's art of governing. Best known is *Zhen-guan zheng-yao* 貞観政要 (The Essence of the

Government of the Zhen-guan Era). It is a record of the pronouncements and acts of Taizong during the Zhen-guan period (627-649). This book, too, was revered as a 'speculum' for emperors. It was not only used in Korea and Japan, but also translated into the Tangut language for the rulers of the Xi-xia, into the Khitan language for the emperors of the Liao, into the Jürchen language for the emperors of the Jin, as well as into Mongolian and Manchu. The third book related to Taizong's art of governing is *Qunshu zhiyao* 群書治要 (The Essence of Government Culled from a Multitude of Books), a compilation of wise words and commendable policies excerpted from the classics, the official histories, and various other ancient writings, collected by Wei Zheng 魏徴 at the behest of Taizong (631). Of these three, *Di fan* is considered to be the most direct reflection of Taizong's vision on statecraft. Since it is mentioned in *Nihonkoku genzaisho mokuroku* 日本国見在書目録, Japan's oldest known catalogue of Chinese books, compiled by Fujiwara no Sukeyo 藤原佐世 (847-898) around 891, it must

81

▲ Fascicle with prescriptions for the ruler, and fascicle with prescriptions for the ministers.

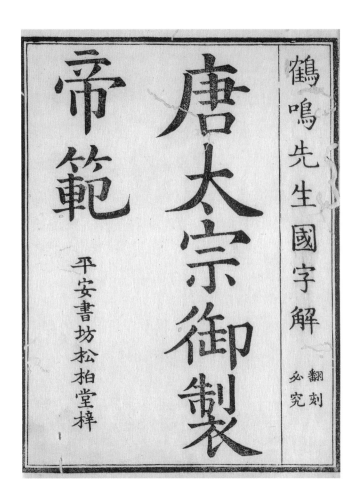

have been transmitted to Japan before the Kanpyō era (889-898).

The compiler Ichikawa Kakumei (1740-1795) was a Confucian scholar. He vehemently opposed the Kansei Edict (*Kansei igaku no kin* 寛政異学の禁) of 1790, which enforced teaching of Zhu Xi's version of Neo-Confucianism as the official Confu-cian doctrine in Japan. The decree banned certain publications and enjoined strict observance of Neo-Confucian doctrine, especially with regard to the curriculum of the official Hayashi school. He is also known as the first Confucian critic of the *Kodōron* 古道論 by Moto'ori Norinaga 本居宣長 (1730-1801).

Literature: Sakamoto 1964; Fumoto 1984.

▲ Title page, with mention 'reproductions will be prosecuted' (fascicle I).

8. Nakatomi no harae kotoba kokun 中臣祓辞古訓
('The Ancient Reading of the Nakatomi Liturgical Formulae of Purification')

Alternative title: *Shinka jōyō sekkyō hikkei* 神家常用説教必携 / *Ōharae kokun chūshō* 大祓古訓註鈔 / *Shinka hiyō* 神家秘要 / *Nakatomi no harae kokun chūshō* 中臣祓古訓註鈔
2 chapters in 2 fascicles; 27.5 x 18.6 cm
Author: Hashimura Masanobu 橋村正身

Revised by his disciples: Ono Fusakichi 小野房吉, Hashisako Koresada 橋迫是定, Kawasaki Masayo 川崎正世
Date: Hōreki 宝暦 11 (1761), preface by Arakida Morimi 荒木田盛箕 dated Hōreki 7 (1757)

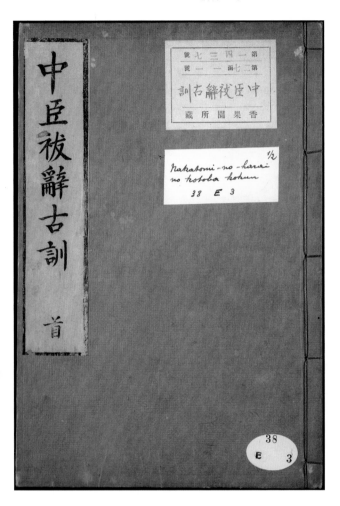
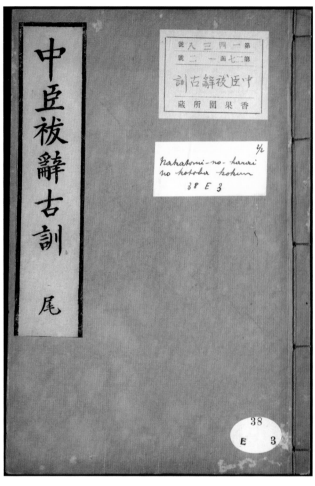

This is a philological study by Hashimura Masanobu (1714-1771), a Shintō priest connected to the Grand Shrine of Ise, about the correct, ancient reading of the liturgical invocation (*norito* 祝詞) recited in the *Ōharae* 大祓 or Great Purification Ceremony. In ancient times, the recitation was a monopoly of the Nakatomi clan, and ever since it has been called the "liturgical formulae of the Nakatomi". The ceremony that includes the incantation is performed on the last day of the sixth and of the twelfth month of the lunar calendar. The oldest extant version of these formulae is found in the *Engi-shiki* 延喜式, a compendium of rules and procedures for implementing *ritsu* 律 (penal codes), *ryō* 令 (administrative codes), and *kyaku* 格 (supplementary laws). Compilation was begun at imperial behest in 905

and completed in 927. Because one third of it deals with Shintō-related matters, the work has been revered as a Shintō classic since the middle ages, spawning numerous commentaries on it throughout the centuries.

According to the standards of the National Diet Library of Japan, this edition of the book is classified as 準貴重書 ("semi-precious book"), one of only 799 titles in its holdings as per March 2020. The library has 1310 titles in the category 貴重書 ('precious book'). The UCLouvain copy appears to be a reprint from the same woodblocks (*atozuri* 後刷り) of the original edition.

Literature: *Maison franco-japonaise* 1990, vol. 16, no. 1, p. 90, s.v. «Ōharae.»

83

▲ Covers of the two fascicles. Judging from the shelf number label on the cover of the UCLouvain copy, the book once belonged to a collection named Kōka-en 香果園. Its identity is unclear.

9. Kōbō daishi gyōjōki 弘法大師行状記
('The Life and Works of Kōbō Daishi')

Alternative title: *Kōbō daishi gyōjō ekotoba* 弘法大師行状絵詞, *Kōbō daishi gyōjō ki zue* 弘法大師行状記図会 (*A Biography of Kōbō Daishi, Illustrated*).
6 fascicles, 12 chapters; 25.7 x 18.4 cm
Author: Shinshu Shinnō 深守親王; preface by Shimizudani

Kinkatsu 清水谷公勝; illustrator: Tosa Mitsunobu 土佐光信 (attributed to)
Edition dated in the eighth year of Hōreki 宝暦 (1758, *atozuri* of 1877), originally written in the Nanboku-chō 南北朝 (Southern and Northern Courts) period (1336-1392)

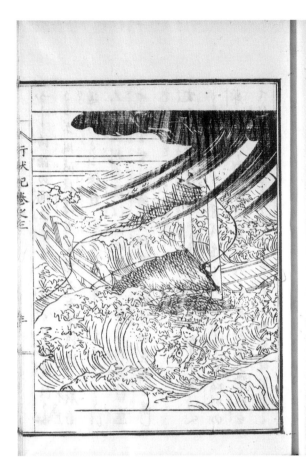

84

This is a hagiography, written in the vernacular (*kanamajiri* 仮名交じり) and richly illustrated, of Kūkai 空海 (774-835), also known posthumously as Kōbō-Daishi 弘法大師. Kūkai was one of the greatest Buddhist monks in Japanese history, and founder of the school of Esoteric Buddhism, known as Shingon 真言. In his youth he travelled to China to study the latest developments of Buddhism. There in the Chinese capital Chang-an, his training included the study of Sanskrit - under the guidance of an Indian pandit Prajñā (734-810?), who had been educated at the Indian Buddhist university of Nalanda - and also entailed practice in the arts of calligraphy and poetry - again, all with recognized masters. Most important of all, Huiguo 恵果 (746-805), the seventh patriarch of Esoteric Buddhism,

initiated him into the abstruse tenets of his doctrine at the Qinglong-si Monastery 青龍寺. He led him through the various stages of initiation, up to the final one, in a matter of months, making him a master of the esoteric lineage. Before dying, Huiguo instructed Kūkai to return to Japan to spread the esoteric gospel in his home country. Thus, according to tradition, Kūkai arrived back in Japan as the eighth patriarch of Esoteric Buddhism, with a large number of texts, many of which were new to Japan, and cultic images. His subsequent contributions to Japanese culture, not just in the field of religion and thought but also in many other fields, are immense, so great indeed that in the course of time he became the stuff of many legends.

Literature: Nishi 2018, pp. 1-225.

▲ 渡海入唐, Kōbō Daishi braving the waves on his journey to the capital of the Tang dynasty (fascicle II, chapter 3, pp. 2b-3a).

Note the two dragon heads among the waves, left and right in the foreground.

▲ 図像写経 Painting images and copying Holy Scriptures: Kōbō Daishi, sitting to the right in monk's garments, looks on while Chinese draughtsmen are drawing *maṇḍalas* and images for him to take back to Japan (fascicle II, chapter 4, pp. 7b-8a).

▲ Jichie (786-847), eminent disciple and relative of Kūkai, having petitioned for imperial sanction, performs the consecration ceremony at the temple Tōji (fascicle VI, chapter 11, pp. 4b-5a).

10. Asaina shimameguri no ki 朝夷巡島記
('The Story of Asaina's Wanderings around the Isles')

Alternative title: *Asaina shimameguri no ki zenshū* 朝夷巡島記全集
8 instalments in 40 chapters; 22.5 x 15.5 cm

Author (instalments 1-6): Kyokutei Bakin 曲亭馬琴,
illustrator (instalments 1-6): Utagawa Toyohiro 歌川豊広;
author (instalments 7-8): Shōtei Kinsui 松亭金水,
illustrator (instalments 7-8): Katsushika Isai 葛飾爲斎

86

This is a *yomihon* 読本 in eight instalments and 40 chapters (*maki*). The first six books are by Kyoku-tei (Takizawa) Bakin (1767-1848), the seventh and eighth are by Shōtei Kinsui. Its plot is based on the legends surrounding Asaina Saburō Yoshihide 朝夷奈三朗義秀 (1176-?). The work was written from the period Bunka 12 until Ansei 5 (1815-1858).

In 1213 Yoshihide's father, Wada Yoshimori 和田義盛 (1147-1213), made an abortive attempt to attack the Hōjō clan (regents of the *shōgun*, who ruled de facto over Japan with an iron fist), but Wada was defeated and killed. Yoshihide fled to the province

of Awa and settled in Asaina. From that moment on he adopted this toponym as his personal name. Although this is the last that was officially heard of him, legends about him gradually began to spread. They usually portrayed the incredible power and courage attributed to him. His mother Tomoe Gozen 巴御前, by the way, was also a valiant woman of legendary renown.

The illustrations show various scenes from the life of Asaina.

Literature: Hakubunkan 1902.

▲ Asaina on horseback goes to meet Ichizō and listen to his tales of old (chapter 33, pp. 5b-6a).

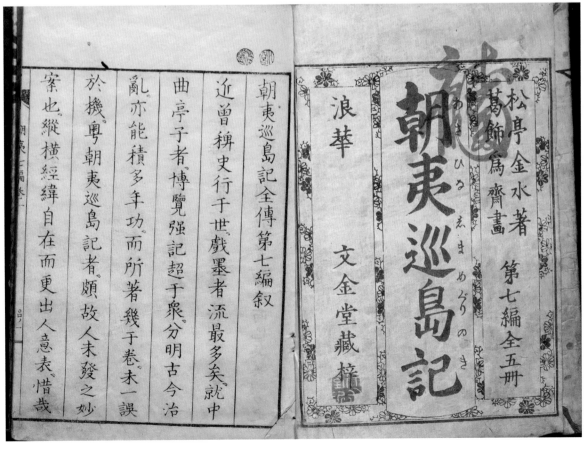

▲ A courtesan tries in vain to ensnare Asaina (Instalment 7, chapter 4, pp. 4b-5a).

▲ The *mikaeshi* (reverse of cover) of the seventh instalment.

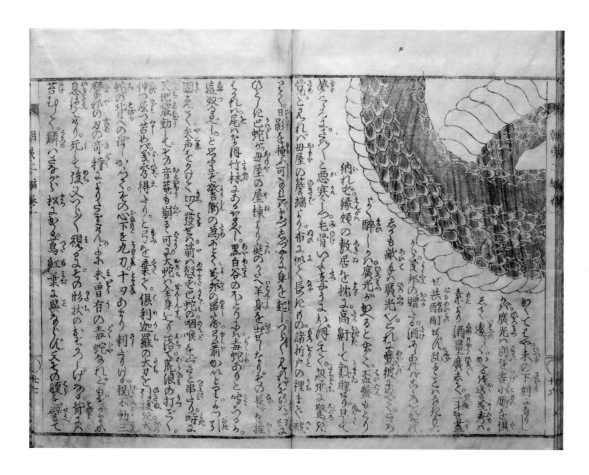

▲ ▲ Yoshihide shoots the gargantuan serpent Uwabami with his arrow and finishes her off with his sword. Note how the tail of the monster extends into the preceding page (2nd instalment, chapter 1, pp. 16b-18a).

11. Chiyo-ni kushū 千代尼句集
('A Collection of Haiku Poems by Chiyo-ni')

Date: parts 1-6 published in Bunka 文化 12 – Bunsei 文政 10 (1815-1827); parts 7-8 published in Ansei 安政 2-5 (1855-1858)

2 fascicles; 22.5 x 15.5 cm
Author: Chiyo-ni 千代尼; editor: Kihaku 既白
Date: Hōreki 宝暦 14 /Meiwa 明和 1 (1764)

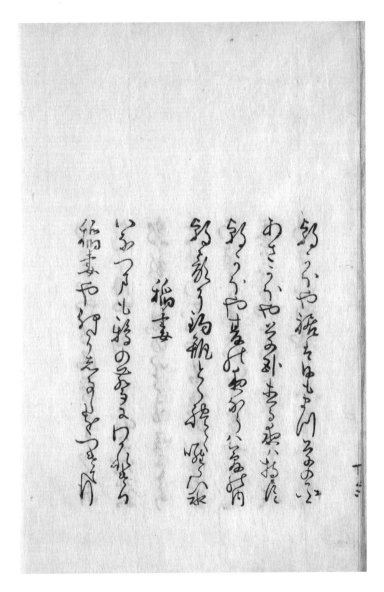

89

Kaga no Chiyo-jo 加賀千代女, a.k.a. Fukuda Chiyo-ni 福田千代尼 (1703-1775), was one of the few acclaimed women *haiku* (then called *haikai*) poets of the Edo period. Although in recent years, American and, in their wake, European authors have tended to overstate her stature among her peers, she was nevertheless an accepted member of a group of poets writing in the style of the great Master Matsuo Bashō 松尾芭蕉 (1644-1694). Despite being born into a family of scroll mounters (i.e., commoners), she is said to have started writing *haikai* from the age of seven. At the age of seventeen her talent was recognized by Kagami Shikō 各務支考 (1665-1731), one of Bashō's ten chief disciples. According to some, she married around 1720, but was widowed two years later. She thereupon returned home to take care of her parents, never remarrying. At the age of thirty she

took lessons in painting from a painter in Kyoto. In 1754, at the age of fifty-two (by Japanese reckoning), Chiyo-jo chose to become a Buddhist nun, hence the suffix *-ni* to her first name. At the age of seventy-two she wrote the preface to *Tamamo-shū* 玉藻集 (1774), a collection of *haikai* by women *haiku* poets, collected and edited by the great poet and painter Yosa Buson 与謝蕪村 (1716-1784), an unmistakable sign of the high esteem she was held in by her fellow poets. She is best known for this *haiku*:

朝顔に釣瓶とられてもらい水

A morning glory
entangled around my well bucket –
I will borrow water from the neighbour

Literature: Donegan and Ishibashi 1996, p. 256; Sato 2007, pp. 166 ff.

▲ The quoted *haiku* (fourth from the right) (fascicle II, p. 3b).

12. Datezome tazuna 伊達染手綱
Tanba Yosaku matsuyo no komurobushi 丹波与作待夜の小室節
('The Fancy Chequered Bridle of Yosaku from Tanba')

Alternative title: *Tanba yosaku* 丹波与作 / *Tanba yosaku datezome tazuna* 丹波与作 伊達染手綱
1 fascicles; 22.2 x 17 cm

Author: Chikamatsu Monzaemon 近松門左衛門
Date: premiere (*shoen* 初演) in Hōei 宝永 5 (1708)

Libretto of a *jōruri* play by Chikamatsu Monzaemon 近松門左衛門 (real name Sugimori Nobumori 杉森信盛, 1653-1725). He was a prolific playwright, writing libretti for *jōruri* 浄瑠璃, the form of puppet theatre now known as *bunraku* 文楽, and for live-actor drama, known as *kabuki* 歌舞伎. Of his puppet plays, around nine are *jidaimono* 時代物 (historical romances) and twenty-four are *sewamono* 世話物 (domestic tragedies), while around forty *kabuki* plays are credited to him. His most famous plays deal with double suicides of honour-bound lovers.

In the contemporary perception *jōruri* and *kabuki* libretti were not considered high literature. Many original libretti were lost in the course of time. In the Meiji and Taishō periods, however, these genres were reappraised as fine literature and hailed as a centrepiece of the literary canon. As a result many libretti were reprinted in movable type. The original ones had been published as woodblock editions.

This title is a fine example of such original woodblock-printed libretti. One will note the typical curly calligraphic style of the characters, called *Kanteiryū* 勘亭流, after Okazakiya Kantei 岡崎屋勘亭 (1746-1805), who initiated the style in 1779, a style still visible today in *Kabuki* posters and advertisements. It is just one variety of so-called *Edomoji* 江戸文字, i.e., Japanese lettering styles designed for advertising in the Edo period. These libretti were subjected to intense wear and tear during the recitation on stage. The National Committee has ostensibly been prompted to do some repair on this copy: reinforcing the folds of the pages and replacing the cover.

The plot runs as follows: The princess Shirabe of the Yurugi family in the country of Tanba is departing to marry the son of the Iruma family in the East, but she loathes to travel all the way to Edo. Her retinue, desperate to distract her, order a young groom named Sankichi to play backgammon with the princess to while away the time. After this ploy has succeeded, Shigenoi, the princess's wet nurse, is about to reward Sankichi for helping to distract the princess. Just before doing so, she realizes that the young groom is actually the child she had with her now estranged husband, Yosaku. Fearing that she might thus reveal that the groom and the princess are nursing siblings, she breaks down in tears and says goodbye to her son, without letting him know she is his mother. The "bridle" (*tazuna*) in the title is an allusion to the profession of the groom, who happens to be at the same time an enduring bond (*tazuna*) between the nurse and her former husband Yosaku.

Literature: Suwa 1981, pp. 173-207; Schönbein 1994, pp. 46, 310.

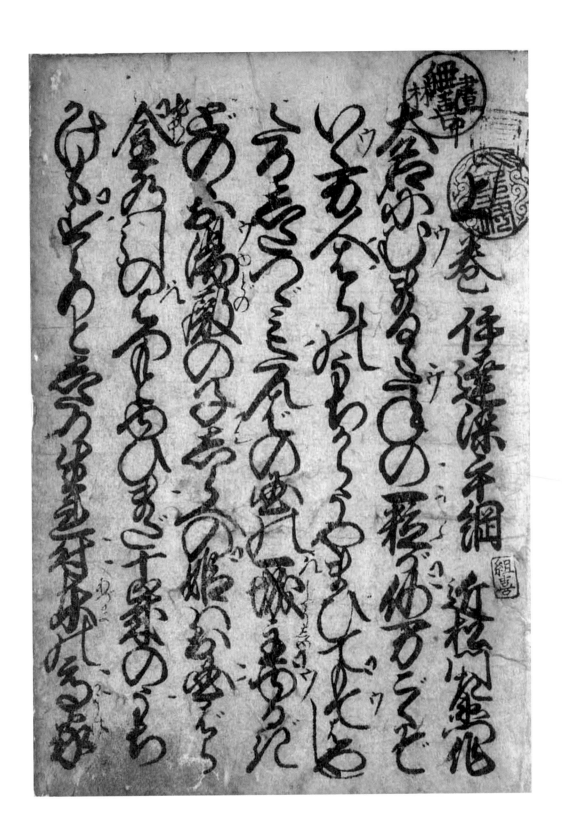

▲ The first page of the libretto.

13. Ehon baisō gundan 絵本黴瘡軍談
('An Illustrated Syphilis War Tale')

Alternative title: *Baisō gundan* 黴瘡軍談
5 chapters in 3 fascicles; 21.9 x 15.5 cm
Author: Funakoshi Kinkai 船越錦海

Illustrator: Ryūsai Shigeharu 柳斎重春
Date: Tenpō 天保 9 (1838)
(Entry contributed by Angelika Koch)

The samurai warrior is a defining image of Japan that has inspired some of the most enduring icons of its popular and literary culture since medieval times. Yet Funakoshi Kinkai's *Ehon baisō gundan* is a warrior tale of an entirely different kind; while blades are crossed and valiant deeds extolled in the narrative, its battleground is the human body, its warriors are under attack from the miasma of disease, and the insidious assailant is a scourge that was terribly familiar in early modern Japan: syphilis (see Ill. 1).

Such mock battles were in fact a prolific trope in Edo-period (1600-1868) literature and arts, which humorously pitted all kinds of inanimate objects against each other; these could range from rice wine and *mochi* rice cakes to different genres of popular literature and types of Kyoto textiles. Armed feuds between various medicines and diseases, such as measles and smallpox, were a particularly successful motif across a variety of media, from narrative fic-

tion to visual arts and commercial advertising. This type of military metaphor for the 'battle' against disease was not unique to early modern Japan, and even at the dawn of the twenty-first century we still regularly 'declare war' on cancer and 'combat' new epidemics.

If cultural theorist Susan Sontag is correct that deadly, widespread, and incurable diseases attract popular mythologization, then syphilis certainly fulfilled all these preconditions in early modern Japan. Modern science has proven the viral extent of its transmission - with Edo-period bone samples suggesting infection rates of between forty and seventy percent of the adult population - and contemporary accounts bear witness to a growing awareness of the rampant spread of the disease among all walks of life. Sugita Genpaku 杉田玄白 (1733-1817), one of the pioneers of Western-style medicine at the turn of the eighteenth century, claimed that no less

▲ The army of medications assailed by the toxic miasma of disease (fascicle. I, chapter 2, pp. 19b-20a)

than seven or eight hundred in a thousand patients he treated every year suffered from syphilis. Treatment was often ineffectual and unpleasant; apart from Chinese herbal medication and hot spring bathing, doctors swore by mercury-based medicines that caused serious side effects due to their toxicity.

Despite its prevalence, syphilis was in fact a comparably new disease in most of the early modern world. After appearing in Europe at the end of the fifteenth century, it subsequently swept across the continent at a breathtaking speed and reached the shores of Japan a mere two decades later at the beginning of the sixteenth century, presumably via the Asian mainland. The Japanese first referred to the skin eruptions of syphilis as 'Chinese boils' (*tōgasa* 唐瘡) due to their perceived geographic origin, applying a naming strategy similar to that in Europe, where the new malady was variously known as the 'French disease', 'Spanish disease', and 'Neapolitan disease'.

Medical opinions concerning this devastating illness changed throughout the Edo period – as did social attitudes towards it. Late sixteenth- and seventeenth-century Japanese physicians mainly interpreted its ulcers as the visible manifestation of stagnating sexual desires that had manifested physically under the skin's surface. Viewed as arising from the sufferer's body itself, initially no connection was drawn with another contaminated body or with the specific social context of prostitution. Indeed, manifold explanations existed in the Edo-period medical mind to make sense of syphilis: Some sources blamed environmental and climactic factors, others hereditary factors or the emerging urban *modus vivendi* of luxury and conspicuous consumption.

It was not long, however, before the notion appeared in both medical writings and popular conceptions of the disease that one possible source of syphilis was transmission through intercourse, particularly with prostitutes. One late eighteenth-century doctor, for example, complained:

> The prostitute should be called a storehouse for syphilis. A long time ago I was asked for help by a bordello and treated many cases of this disease. In every brothel seven or eight out of every ten prostitutes were secretly infected, but they made up their faces with rouge and white powder, covering up the signs of disease. They should truly be called monsters.

Needless to say, such rhetoric demonized professional sex workers as the source of syphilis infection and the flourishing early modern culture of the pleasure quarters as a cesspool of disease. Nevertheless, this vilification failed to produce any sustained public discourse questioning the institution of prostitution *per se* in early modern Japan, much less any detectable governmental attempts to prevent the spread of the disease. Only once Japan opened its ports to Western ships in the second half of the nineteenth century did such measures become a matter of debate, as a result of foreign intervention.

Until that point, dealing with the disease was largely left to the unfortunate sufferers, their families, and at times doctors with varying degrees of knowledge. In the course of the eighteenth century, the number of syphilis treatises published both for experts and lay people increased, and medical practitioners specializing in its treatment appeared, along with a booming market for commercial patent medicines. It is within this context that we have to place the appearance of a work such as *Ehon baisō gundan*.

Its author, Funakoshi Kinkai, was in fact one of the doctors who began to specialize in syphilis treatment. More precisely, he straddled the categories of both patient and practitioner. If we are to believe his own account of events, both of his parents were infected with the disease, while he himself "suffered from it for several years in his youth and sought relief with all kinds of remedies" – yet to no avail. The quest for a cure ultimately motivated him to become a doctor and to spend many years developing his own treatments. He later set up his practice in Osaka and dedicated himself to enlightening common people about the disease, penning several compendia on the topic in accessible vernacular before writing *Ehon baisō gundan*.

His first-hand experience in battling the affliction is perhaps nowhere more palpable than in the medical case studies he published, which paint a devastating picture of the horrors of the disease. His patients included men and women of all ages, prostitutes as well as the sons and daughters of merchant families, and those who had contracted the disease congenitally as young children as well as those infected later in life. Their symptoms are described in gruesomely graphic detail:

> Patient: the son of Hinoya Chōshichi, aged 26, from Osaka Shinsaibashi. His left leg had been eaten away by syphilis from the knee joint to two-thirds down his calf. The sores gaped like caverns in a rocky landscape - some deep, some shallow - up to about one *sun* (ca. three centimetres) in depth.

In *Ehon baisō gundan*, however, Funakoshi strikes a very different tone in order to disseminate his teachings. His self-confessed strategy in this work is "to compare the interactions between medications and disease to a military conflict, in order to convey information in an easily accessible manner." Adopting the "standard format of playful writings", he mimics the style and contents of contemporary popular

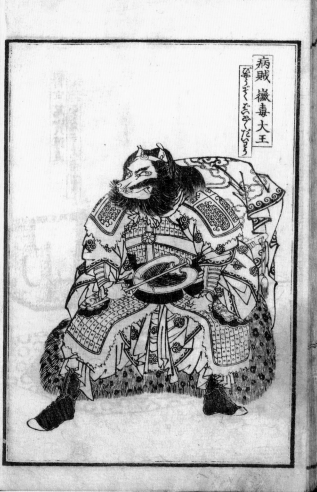

藥將 延壽丸

藥將 治瘡丸

病賊 黴毒大王

literature, including the "fervour of the battlefield" and supernatural elements such as spirits and deities – "without whom one can hardly hope to please readers these days". The narrative revolves around an attack by the evil 'King Syphilis' (*baidoku daiō* 梅毒大王), portrayed as a malevolent fox spirit (see ill. 2), who invades the "lands of the human body". His first port of call is the "country of the female body" in Nagasaki's Maruyama 丸山 district – the pleasure quarters in Japan's only harbour open to foreigners until the 1850s, where Chinese and Dutch ships regularly arrived to trade. From there, the villain rapidly advances into the "provinces of the male body", though soon meets resistance from the army of medications led by the deadly efficient General Long-Life Concoction (Enjugan 延壽丸) – none other than a personification of the patent medication that Funakoshi himself was selling. After a drawn-out war over five volumes which witnesses gains and losses on both sides, the medications predictably emerge victorious.

The changing fortunes of the prolonged struggle in the tale were a fitting representation of the vicis-situdes of syphilis and must have been all too painfully familiar to Funakoshi. Just as King Syphilis's soldiers, even when seemingly defeated, regroup once again and lay waste to one province after another, syphilis would recur repeatedly after periods of latency that lulled sufferers into the mistaken security of thinking themselves healed. It attacked new regions of the body over the years and in its terminal stages would not only disfigure the infected but might also render them blind, deaf, and mad. The varied symptoms of the disease appear in *Ehon baisō gundan* as the fiendish minions of King Syphilis's invading army, sporting humorous names such as Aching-bones Can't-move (Honeitami Ugokazu 骨痛動須), Ulcers Quick-sprout (Gekan Hayanari 下疳早成), and Poisons Hard-to-Kill (Idoku Nukekane 遺毒抜兼). Visually represented as grotesque demonic figures (see Ill. 3), the evildoers also display sores, ulcers, and boils on their bodies reminiscent of those affecting syphilis sufferers.

The choice of Nagasaki, Edo-era Japan's window on the world and, particularly, the Maruyama pleasure quarters as the site of King Syphilis's invasion

▲ King Syphilis of the Disease Army (right) and General Long-Life Concoction, the commander of the Medical Army (left) (fascicle I, *jutsui* 述意, pp. 5b–6a)

clearly reflects common perceptions of how the disease was propagated. As mentioned above, it was a widespread belief that the 'Chinese boils' had been introduced to Japan from abroad and hence inevitably via Nagasaki. Yet while Funakoshi mirrors this popular conception in his narrative, his postscript provides a more global view of the disease that is remarkable for its awareness of contemporary Western knowledge: "In the year 1494 according to the Dutch calendar, the French discovered America. [...] They attacked the Antilles Islands, looting treasure and women. When they brought these women onboard their ship and had sex with them, the crew developed syphilis. Following this, the disease spread in the lands of the Red-haired Barbarians [i.e., the Netherlands and by extension Europe]." Despite obvious mistakes in his account, Funakoshi was clearly aware of the European notion that syphilis was brought to Europe from the New World by Columbus's ships.

As mentioned previously, Funakoshi's reason for adopting a novel and dramatic style in his text was not merely to provide entertainment but also "to convey information in an easily accessible manner". This intention is most clearly seen in the final volume of the work, which consists entirely of a short treatise detailing the origins, symptoms, and treatments of the disease. Some editions of the book even include a note on the last page stating that the publication was not for sale and that it would be printed and distributed for free, as long as the person wishing to obtain the book brought their own paper (this generally being the most expensive part of the printing process) "since it was written with the aim of saving the sick people in our realm". The UCLouvain copy, however, like others currently in Japanese collections, lacks this magnanimous note and was clearly distributed on a commercial basis by the Osaka publisher Harimaya Gorōbei 播磨屋 五郎兵衛, who appended advertisements for his own goods and services at the back of the book. This variation suggests that the work was initially distributed free of charge but was probably sold to a commercial publisher at a later stage.

Yet Funakoshi's self-proclaimed lofty goal of 'saving the people' merely masks the deeply com-

▲ King Syphilis surrounded by his minions representing the diverse symptoms of the disease (fascicle I/chapter 1, pp. 11b–12a).

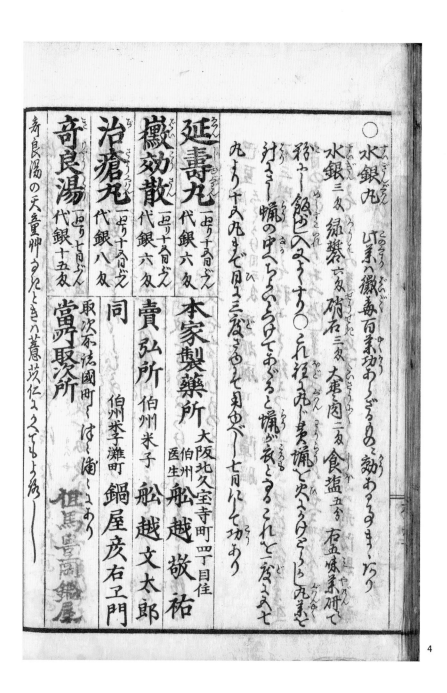

4

96

mercial and promotional character of the work, which also acted as an extended advertisement in narrative guise for Funakoshi's own medications, such as Long-Life Concoction (Enjugan), which were promoted in the book's back matter (see Ill. 4). Although this medication was produced at Funakoshi's shop in Osaka, the advertisement claims, possibly with a touch of hyperbole, that it could also be obtained from distributors in all the towns and provinces throughout Japan. The Louvain copy has a rare handwritten entry that identifies its distributor as "the Nabeya shop in Toyooka City, Tajima Province" (present-day Hyōgo Prefecture), suggesting that the book was circulated there, potentially together with the various medications. Funakoshi's business-oriented thinking is also evident in his

treatise on syphilis in the final volume, in which he instructs his readers how they can make a range of remedies for the disease – the formulas for his own prescriptions, however, are omitted with the curt statement that these are "commercially available medications".

Ultimately, *Ehon baisō gundan* is a multi-faceted work that was designed not only to entertain but also to circulate medical knowledge about the disease and act as an advertisement for commercial medications. Perhaps most importantly, though, it promised sick readers what the narrative acted out for them on the page: a victory over King Syphilis and a happy ending to their own story.

Literature: Funakoshi 1831; Fukuda and Suzuki 2005.

▲ Advertisement for Funakoshi Kinkai's syphilis medications at the back of *Ehon baisō gundan* (fascicle III, chapter 6, p. 22b).

14. Haikai saijiki 俳諧歳時記
('A Seasonal Almanac for Haiku Poetry')

2 chapters in 6 fascicles; 18.8 x 12.5 cm
Editors: Takizawa 滝沢 (Kyokutei) Bakin 曲亭馬琴
Date: printed in Kyōwa享和 3 (1803)

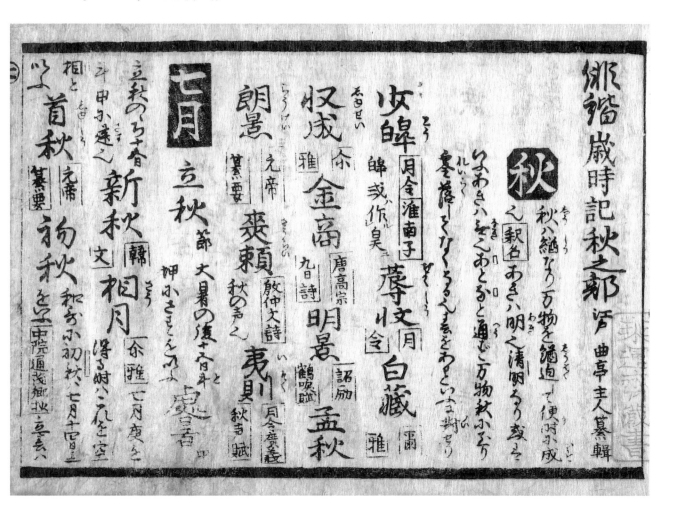

A *saijiki* 歳時記, literally a 'seasonal almanac', is a compendium of '*kigo* 季語' (seasonal terms) used in *haiku* and related forms of poetry. An entry in a *saijiki* usually includes a description of the 'seasonal term' itself, in addition to a list of similar or related words, and some examples of *haiku* that include that specific 'seasonal term'. Kyokutei Bakin's (1767-1848) compilation includes more than 2,600 entries, distributed over the four seasons, arranged in the order of the lunar months, and supplied with com-mentary. It also includes instructions about rules of composition and keeping score in a composition contest.

Traditionally, these almanacs were geared to the progression of seasons as experienced in Kyoto, but Bakin's commentaries and instructions are more in line with the seasons in Edo. His almanac is the first to do so.

Literature: Funakoshi 1831; Fukuda and Suzuki 2005.

97

▲ The first page of the section on autumn, bearing the collector's seal of *Jōunsai* 乗運斎 (Fascicle II/chapter 2, p. 7).

15. Hito wa bushi chūgi no isaoshi 人武忠儀功（板東七英士後編）
('It Takes a Samurai: Tales of Loyalty and Gallantry')

= Sequel to *Bandō shichi eishi* 坂東七英士 ('Seven Valiant
Warriors of the East')
2 chapters in 2 fascicles; 17.2 x 12.1 cm
Author: Jippensha Ikku I 十返舎一九 (一世)

Illustrator: Katsukawa Shuntei 勝川春亭
Date: Kansei 寛政 13/Kyōwa 享和 1 (1801) by Enomotoya
Kichibee 榎本屋吉兵衛

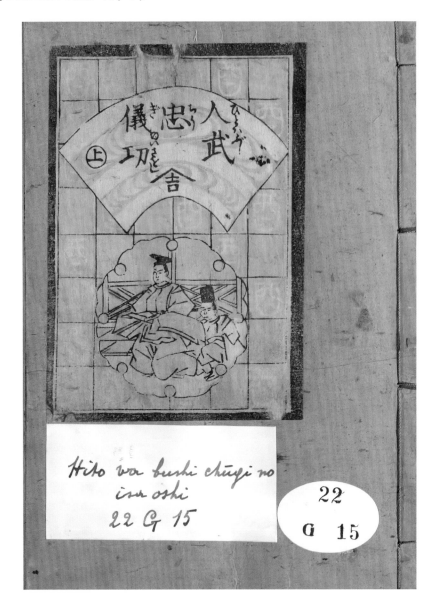

Jippensha Ikku (1765-1831) was the pen name of
Shigeta Sadakazu 重田貞一. He lived primarily in
Edo in the service of samurai but also spent some
time in Osaka as a townsman. He was among the
most prolific yellow-backed novel (*kibyōshi* 黄表紙)
writers of the late Edo period. Between 1795 and
1801, he churned out a minimum of twenty novels a
year, thereafter writing *sharebon* 洒落本, *kokkeibon*
滑稽本, and over 360 illustrated stories (*gōkan* 合
巻) (see also the text on *kibyōshi* and *gōkan* in this
volume, p. 99).

As often in this exquisite kind of 'pulp' literature, the title is a little gem of recreational linguistics. By reading a syntactic structure into the string
of characters, the title resonates with the saying

"Hana wa sakuragi, hito wa bushi"(Cherry blossoms
are foremost among flowers; samurai are foremost
among men). The expression also features in *jōruri*
and *kabuki* (e.g., *Kanadehon chūshingura* 仮名手本忠
臣蔵). The title thus takes on the ring of a proverb
or an exhortation. No need to add that the book tells
the story of valiant samurai, staunch to the bone.

We reproduce here the cover of the first fascicle,
unfortunately disfigured by the white label with
the transcription and shelf number. The book was
published in the year of the rooster 酉, whose corresponding character, visible as a watermark, is repeated in the rectangular checkerboard design.

Literature: Mizutani 1973. Nakayama 2002.

▲ Cover of the first fascicle.

Kibyōshi 黄表紙 and Gōkan 合巻

Kusazōshi 草双紙 (lit. "pulp picture books") is the generic term for a number of successive types of illustrated novels in the vernacular from the second half of the seventeenth century to the first decade of the Meiji period.

Having evolved one out of the other, they share some conspicuous traits in terms of format. They typically come in the size of a *chūbon* 中本 or *shirokuban* 四六判 (duodecimo, 18 cm high, 13 cm wide). One chapter (*maki* 巻) equals one fascicle, one fascicle comprises five leaves folded once and stitched at the opposite side of the fold into the back (thus making ten pages), while a single complete book title comprises between one and three fascicles (except for the last type, which may run into 100 fascicles). The first type to make its appearance around 1662 was the so-called "red cover" (*akahon* 赤本), a cheap picture book aimed at children, telling in simple words and crude pictures fairy tales and ghost stories. On its red cover was pasted a decorative slip (*edaisen* 絵題簽) mentioning the title.

With the passage of time, the story line grew more complex, featuring the plots of theatre plays and shifting its target to an adult readership. During the 1740s, due to a price rise in dyes, the red covers were replaced by black ones (*kurohon* 黒本), in addition to blue ones (*aohon* 青本). "Black cover" books and "blue cover" books took their material from drama scripts, historical chronicles, legends, and miracle stories. Initially, most of these books were published anonymously, but before long, gifted artists and painters of the early Ukiyo-e school – such as Okumura Masanobu 奥村政信 (1686-1764), Torii Kiyomitsu 鳥居清満 (1735-1785), Tomikawa Fusanobu 富川房信 (active about 1750–1780) – ventured into the field, providing both the story and the illustrations. Gradually, they would

associate with specialized authors in a more efficient division of labour, whereby both illustrations and text benefitted. Eventually, the blue colour was replaced by the cheaper and more colour-fast yellow.

The first "yellow cover" book (*kibyōshi*) was published in 1775, by Koikawa Harumachi 恋川春町 (1744-1789). Owing to its pointed and witty characterizations, it looked like an illustrated parody of the *sharebon* 洒落本 ("books about fashionistas"). Although set in the licensed red-light district in Edo, *sharebon* are lacking in overt descriptions of erotic scenes and rather concentrate on the analysis of the 'good taste' of the customers: taste in matters of clothing, manners, language, conversational skills, sensitivity for the feelings of the courtesans, and familiarity with the rules of etiquette. Whereas *sharebon* have few illustrations and contain mainly conversations between protagonists, *kibyōshi* combine comic text with pictures. Pictures are set in a frame spanning the entire surface of each pair of opened pages. The text is written vertically into the blank spaces between the figures, creating an overall impression of heavily crowded pages.

The popularity of the yellow covers attracted talented writers with a samurai background – such as Harumachi – as well as townsmen – such as Santō Kyōden 山東京伝 (1761-1816) and Shiba Zenkō 芝全交 (1750-1793) – and outstanding artists of the Ukiyo-e school – such as Kitao Shigemasa 北尾重政 (1739-1820), Torii Kiyonaga 鳥居清長 (1752-1815), and Kitagawa Utamaro 喜多川歌麿 (c.1753-1806). The genre enjoyed its heyday during the 1780s. At their best these works are full of light-hearted satire and subtle parody; at their worst they are marred by ludicrously implausible

situations, grotesque characters, and pedantic descriptions.

The authors' imagination was given relatively free rein during the time that the *shōgun's* chief senior councillor, Tanuma Okitsugu 田沼意次 (1719-1788), held the reins of power. After his death, the conservative chief councillor, Matsudaira Sadanobu 松平定信 (1759-1829), introduced a policy of austerity known as the Kansei Reforms (1787-1793), prohibiting the publication of frivolous books. The authors of samurai background discontinued writing, while those who did go on, changed tack, by henceforth imbuing their stories with moral lessons in the spirit of "Heart Learning" (*Shingaku* 心学), or by churning out stories of vendettas. The plot lines became increasingly long-winding and complicated, eventually necessitating a change of format. Theretofore, a *kibyōshi* had typically comprised one to three chapters/fascicles of five sheets (ten pages) each; from 1807 on, however, publishers adopted a new format: that of the *gōkan* 合巻 ('bound-together volumes'), in which one fascicle henceforth contained five chapters (*maki*). This format would be maintained until the end of the nineteenth century. They vary greatly in length, but some run into several tens, even close to several hundreds of chapters in several tens of instalments. Their plots are complicated, often implausible, with a penchant for grotesque and gory scenes. They often include portraits of popular actors, a feature suggesting their close affinity with Kabuki plays.

The presence of *kibyōshi*, as well as other varieties of what still may have been considered "pulp fiction" by other serious historians of literature, is another salient feature of the donation and testifies to Wada Mankichi's view on Japanese literature and culture in general, giving a broader scope to popular traditions.

16. Hokusetsu bidan jidai kagami 北雪美談時代鏡
('Mirror of the Age: An Edifying Story About a Handsome Lad in the Northern Snow')

Alternative title: *Jidai kagami* 時代鑑 ('Mirror of the Age')
74 chapters in 18 fascicles, incomplete set of a *gōkan*.
The complete set comprises in total 48 instalments in 192
chapters; instalments 1-16 in 8 fascicles, 17.5 x 11.5 cm;
instalments 17-37 in 10 fascicles, 18 x 12 cm, remaining
eleven instalments missing.

Authors: (instalments 1-44) Tamenaga Shunshō 為永春笑;
(instalments 45-48) Ryūsuitei Tanekiyo 柳水亭種清
Illustrators: (instalments 1-41) Utagawa Kunisada II
歌川国貞 (二世); (instalments 42-44) Utagawa Kunisada II
歌川国貞 (二世); (instalment 45) Utagawa Kuniaki
歌川国明; (instalments 46-48) Adachi Ginkō 安達吟光
Date: 1855-1883

100

An illustrated saga novel (*gōkan* 合巻), including coloured illustrations, in 48 instalments published between 1855 and 1883, by the Edo publisher Wakasaya
Yoichi 若狭屋與市 (dates unknown). The title varies
depending on the cover title, the preface title, the
mikaeshi title, and so on. The plot is vaguely based on
a historical family feud known as the Kaga Sōdō 加
賀騒動 (erupted in 1746, settled in 1754), an incident
of presumed intrigue, murder, and illicit love, which
rocked the prestigious house of the lord of Kaga. The
main plot of the novel narrates the amorous and
fantastic adventures of a handsome but morally un-
stable young man Yukari no Jō 由縁之丞, who was,
to make matters worse, an accomplished magician.
The word '*bidan*' in the title is written with the char-

acters for 'edifying story', but underneath resonate
the homonymous characters for 'handsome lad'. The
story was adapted and produced for the Kabuki stage
in March 1876, in the Nakaza 中座 in Osaka, under
the title *Keisei jidai kagami* けいせい時代鏡 ('Mirror
of the Age for Courtesans'), and in February 1881, in
the Harugiza 春木座 in Tokyo, under the title *Hoku-
setsu bidan jidai kagami* 北雪美談時代鏡. According
to Nojima (1990) the premiere took place in the Matsushima theatre 松島芝居 in March 1876.

The illustration here is the combined title print
for the two parts of the first instalment, designed by
Utagawa Toyokuni (the third), also known as Utagawa Kunisada (the second) (1786-1865).

Literature: Marks 2012, p. 222; Markus 1992, p. 255.

▲ Combined title print for the two parts of the first instalment.

17. Hyakunin isshu hitoyo-gatari 百人一首一夕話
('One Poem of One Hundred Poets' Told in One Night)

Alternative title: *Hyakunin isshu hitoyo-gatari* 百人一首比登与俄瑷里
9 chapters in 9 fascicles; 25.4 x 18.1 cm

Author: Ozaki Masayoshi 尾崎雅嘉; illustrator: Ōishi Matora 大石真虎
Date: Tenpō 天保 4 (1833)

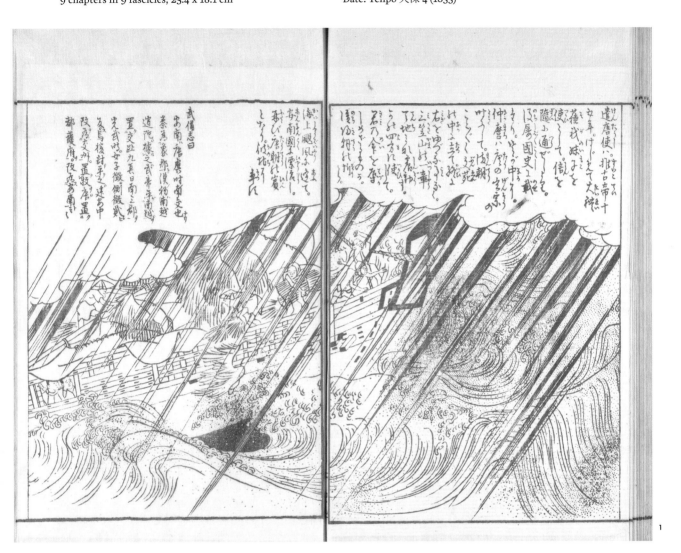

1

(*Ogura*) *Hyakunin isshu* (小倉)百人一首 is an anthology of one hundred classical *waka* poems by as many poets compiled by the preeminent classical poet Fujiwara Teika 藤原定家 (1162-1241). This work was reprinted countless times and served as a kind of catechism of classical Japanese poetry. During the Edo period (1600-1868), numerous commentaries on the anthology *Hyakunin isshu* appeared. Particularly well known are the *Hyakunin isshu kaikan-shō* 百人一首改観抄 by Keichū 契沖 (1640-1710), *Hyakunin isshu uimanabi* 百人一首初学 by Kamo Mabuchi 賀茂 真淵 (1697-1769), and *Hyakushu iken* 百首異見 by Kagawa Kageki 香川景樹 (1768-1843).

More unusual, however, is a work such as this *Hyakunin isshu hitoyo-gatari* by Ozaki Masayoshi (1755-1827). While it likewise offers commentaries on the poems of the famed anthology - mostly borrowed from Keichū as well as from Shimokōbe Chōryu 下河邊長流 (whose name can also be read as

'Shimokawabe Nagaru', 1627-1686) - the bulk of the work consists of biographies and anecdotes about the authors of the poems included in the anthology. In this respect it differs markedly from other commentaries. Moreover, it was written with a clearly educational purpose and with a scholarly approach. According to the preface, the author has assembled information from all quarters so as to inform the reader in one night about each of the hundred poets. The arrangement and order of the biographies and the anecdotes seem to be inspired by the format of the *yomihon*. Likewise, the illustrations are informed by the format of three different genres: (1) some are in the style of illustrated topographical accounts (*meisho-zue*), (2) others are in the style of the illustrations typical of the *yomihon* (a genre of historical fiction influenced by Chinese vernacular early modern novels), and (3) still others are inspired by the style of illustrations typical of the *Yūsoku ko-*

101

▲ After a stay of many years in the Chinese capital as a bureaucrat Abe no Nakamaru 阿倍仲麻呂 sails back to Japan.

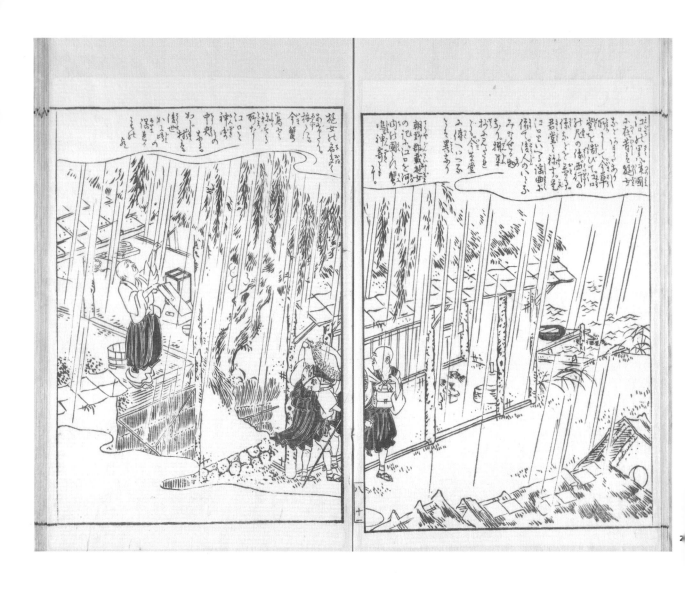

jitsu 有職故実 genre (transmitting precedents and customs at court and among the aristocracy). The illustrations are first and foremost intended to help in understanding the text, but they also have an autonomous artistic value.

The edition published in Osaka in Tenpō 4 (1833) by Tsurugaya Kyūbē 敦賀屋九兵衛 enjoyed a wide readership, and it was always assumed that it faithfully and integrally reproduced the text as it had been left by its deceased author Ozaki Masayoshi. In 1993, however, an autograph manuscript by the author was discovered, and many differences between the manuscript and the printed edition came to light. During the nineteenth and twentieth centuries, numerous xylographical and typographical reprints of this book appeared. Ozaki Masayoshi excelled in the writing of small characters. He made his own block copy (*hanshita* 版下, the copy which was pasted upside down upon the woodblock to be carved out) and, as it happened, the block copy for this book was nearly completed when he passed away. The work was subsequently finished by Tani-

kawa Ukyō 谷川右京, but it was not published until six years after Ozaki's death.

The UCLouvain copy once belonged to a collector, whose seal was ostensibly blotted out when the book was donated to the National Committee.

Ill. 1: after a stay of many years in the Chinese capital as a bureaucrat (described a.o. in *Ishō Nihonden* 異称日本伝), Abe no Nakamaru 阿倍仲麻呂 sails back to Japan. His ship runs into a storm and goes adrift. It eventually washes ashore on the coasts of Vietnam, whence he travels back to the Chinese capital, where he will eventually also die without ever seeing his home country again (Fascicle I/chapter 1, pp. 49b-50a);

Ill. 2: the hamlet Eguchi no sato 江口の里. The commentary by the author goes as follows: "The hamlet of Eguchi is located in Tsu Province. In olden days there used to be many prostitutes here. Now a paltry shrine stands here, housing statues of the nun of Eguchi and the wandering priest-poet Saigyō 西行 (1118-1190). People call this small shrine 'Kimidō' 君堂. It was built by people of later genera-

 The hamlet Eguchi no sato 江口の里.

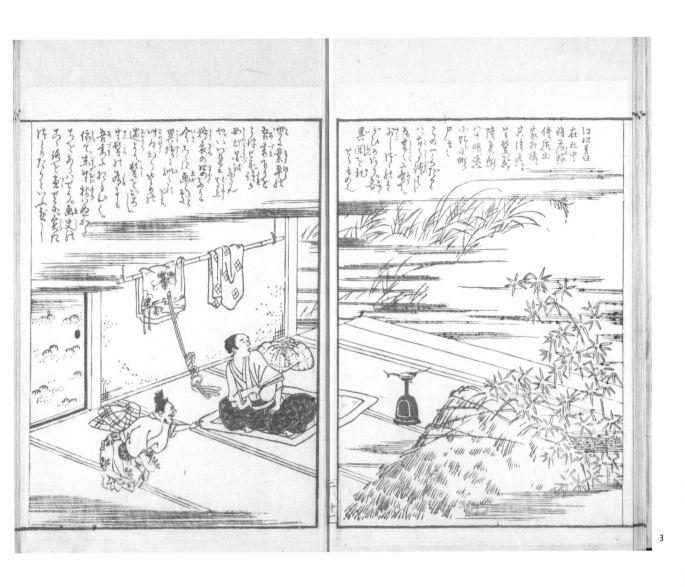

tions who took their inspiration from the Nō play *Eguchi*. I have checked the *Senjūshō* 撰集抄 [a collection of stories related to Saigyō], but the story differs from what is told in the little shrine." (Fascicles I/ chapter 1, pp. 12b-13a).

The story alluded to is that of the famous itinerant priest and poet Saigyō, who is surprised by a rain shower and is forced to beg for shelter in the house of a prostitute. Seeing he is a monk, she is at first unwelcoming, but when he sends her a poem reproving her lack of hospitality, she at once sends a smart repartee, one that outdoes the subtle critique of his own poem.

Ill. 3: the poet and courtier Ariwara no Narihira's 在原業平 (825-880) journey to Azuma 東 (Eastern Japan) (Fascicle II/chapter 2, pp. 11b-12a).

Léon de Rosny (1837-1914), France's first university professor of Japanese Studies, made the first translations in French of the *Hyakunin isshu* published in his *Si-ka-zen-yō Anthologie japonaise* on the basis of *Hyakunin isshu hitoyo-gatari*.

Literature: *Nihon koten bungaku daijiten* 1984, vol. 5, p. 192; Ozaki 1993.

18. Jiraiya gōketsu monogatari 児雷也豪傑物語
('The Tale of the Gallant Jiraiya')

Alternative title: *Jiraiya gōketsu monogatari* 児雷也豪傑譚 and various other variants.
Incomplete set, 86 chapters in 14 fascicles; 18 x 12 cm
Author: Mizugaki Egao 美図垣笑顔 et al.

Illustrators: Utagawa Kunisada 歌川国貞 et al.
Date: Ka'ei 嘉永 6 - Keiō 慶応 2 (1852-1866)
Adapted for *kabuki* by Kawatake Shinshichi II 河竹新七 (二世)
premiere (*shoen* 初演) in Ka'ei 5 (1852)

This is an incomplete set of a serial novel that runs up to 173 fascicles in 43 instalments and was published between 1839 and 1868. Writing involved, besides Mizugaki Egao (1789-1846), Ippitsuan Shujin 一筆庵主人 (1791-1848), Ryūkatei Tanekazu 柳下亭種員 (1807-1858), and Ryūsuitei Tanekiyo 柳水亭種清. Involved illustrators were, besides Utagawa Kunisada I (1786-1865), Utagawa Kuniteru 歌川国輝 (dates unknown), Utagawa Kunimori 国盛, Utagawa Kunisada II (1823-1880), Utagawa Kuniyoshi 歌川国芳 (1797-1861), Utagawa Yoshifusa 歌川芳房 (1837-1860), and Utagawa Yoshiiku 歌川芳幾 (1833-1904).

"The Tale of the Gallant Jiraiya" is a traditional Japanese tale that recounts the story of Ogata Shūma Hiroyuki 尾形周馬弘行, a marauding yet chivalrous ninja, subsequently known as Jiraiya (lit. "Young Thunder"). This sobriquet was a pun on the homophonous characters 自来也 ("It is me who was here"). The contemporary Japanese audience would no doubt have understood this pun, for they would have been familiar with the latter three characters as the name of a noble-minded robber who had appeared as the hero in a so-called reading book (*yomihon*) with the title *Jiraiya monogatari* 自来也説話 ('The Story of Jiraiya'), written by Kanwatei Onitake 感和亭鬼武 (1760-1818), published in 1806, and adapted for the Kabuki theatre stage in 1807. This *yomihon* story tells the tale, too, of a chivalrous robber, an accomplished ninja, whose habit of leaving the words "It is me who was here", namely, on the walls of the houses where he had intruded, was the origin of his sobriquet.

The story's success prompted its subsequent expansion into the voluminous serial novel (*gōkan*), 'The Tale of the Gallant Jiraiya.' Written by multiple authors and illustrated by seven print artists over nearly three decades, the plot lacks coherence, and the novel never reached its *dénouement*.

In this serial novel, the hero Jiraiya, now written in characters meaning "Young Thunder", was the scion of a powerful clan in Kyūshū. When his family fell into ruin, he went to the province of Echigo, where he was successful as a marauder, becoming the leader of a "chivalrous" band of thieves. He was initiated into the "magic of the toad" by an immortal who lived on Mount Myōkōzan 妙香山. Around that time he fell in love and married Tsunade 綱手, a beautiful young woman who was well versed in the "magical art of the snail". When he felt confident enough, he left to take revenge on the man who had been the cause of the ruin of his family, an old man named Sarashina, but he was unable to defeat him.

Sometime later, Yashagorō 夜叉五郎, one of his followers, was enchanted by the "magical art of the snake". By dint of hard study and practice, he acquired the ability to transform himself into a huge serpent. Changing his name to Orochimaru 大蛇丸, after the name of the mythical eight-headed snake Orochi 大蛇, he challenged Jiraiya and Tsunade. He managed to poison them with his serpent venom, and they fell unconscious to the ground. Fortunately, another of Jiraiya's followers, whose life he had once saved, came to his rescue. At this point, without conclusion, the tale abruptly ends.

The playwright Kawatake Shinshichi II (二代 1816-1893) adapted it for the kabuki theatre, basing himself on the first ten instalments of the novel. It was first staged, under the same title, at the Kawarasaki 河原崎座 Theatre in Edo in the seventh month of 1852, with the acclaimed actor Ichikawa Danjūrō VIII 八代目市川團十郎 (1823-1854) in the leading role. In 1881, Kawatake changed his first name to Mokuami 黙阿弥, the name by which he is best known.

On p. 105 we reproduce the combined title print by Kunisada (Toyokuni III) for the two parts of the second instalment.

Literature: Koike 1994; Markus 1992, p. 255; Okamoto 2002.

▲ Combined title print by Kunisada.

19. Kamado shōgun kanryaku no maki 竈将軍勘略之巻
('The Assault on the Castle of the General of the Kitchen Range')

3 chapters in 1 fascicle; 18 x 13 cm
Author and illustrator: Katsushika Hokusai I 葛飾北斎
(一世)

Date: printed in Ka'nsei 寛政 12 (1800) by Tsuruya
Jūsaburō 蔦屋重三郎

SELECTED BOOKS FROM THE 1920S JAPANESE DONATION

This is a typical *kibyōshi* 黄表紙 with a typical jestful title. Text and illustrations are by Katsushika Hokusai I, a famous printmaker, painter, and draughtsman (1760-1849), who signs here with one of his numerous other names Tokitarō Kakō 時太郎可候.

It is the story of a merchant's family, living a life of luxury and dissipation, whose members fall on hard times and are being hounded by creditors. When they are on the verge of bankruptcy, their branch family comes to the rescue. The story portrays the protagonists as rivalling lords of the Warring States era, but it is in fact a parody on Hoku-

sai's own time, the Kansei 寛政 period (1789-1801). The hero is Dadara Daijin Hiromune ダダラ大尽ひろむね, a man who squanders his money among the courtesans of the red-light district Yoshiwara 吉原, while his wife too maintains an extravagant lifestyle. Seeing that the household is inevitably heading for bankruptcy, one of the servants, acting the role of the typical traitor in a Warring States tale, goes to tip the creditor off. The latter, an implacable miser, is portrayed here as the enemy lord. The scene of the creditor laying siege to the castle of Dadara Daijin metaphorically means that he refuses to extend his credit, demanding the immedi-

▲ The maid is washing the lady of the house with gold and silver coins (p. 2b).

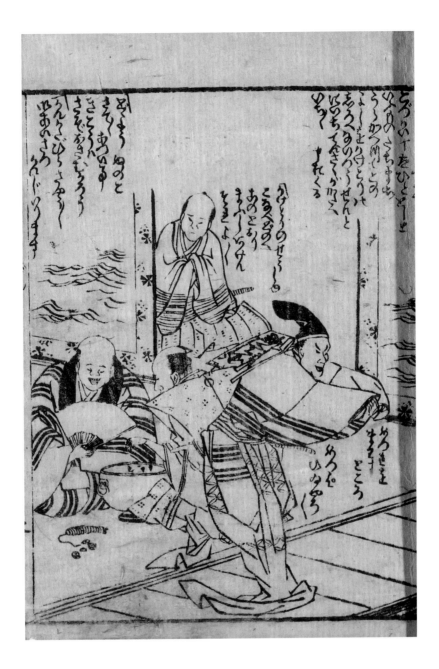

ate repayment of his loans. Dadara Daijin ignores the demands of the creditor and pawns some of his belongings in the pawnshop. His wife, too, pawns a few of her tortoiseshell hair ornaments.

Still, this is not enough. The wife flees in the company of the wet nurse, while Hiromune abandons his shop and goes into hiding in his country house. He puts his shop up for sale. Here the stage suddenly changes from the setting of the Warring States to a shop-lined street in Edo. Hiromune is now all of a sudden given shelter by a servant of the teahouse in the red-light district, which he used to patronize. A band of servants chases the army of the creditor off. At this point a subordinate retainer, who has remained loyal to his lord, enters the scene. He is actually a former shop assistant of Hiromune, who has started his own business and has become a wealthy merchant in his own right. He rescues his former boss, pays off the creditor, and the servant of the teahouse gets some reward as well. The story ends with a moral lesson both for the debtor and the creditor. This will surely have pleased the censor, who was supposed to enforce the edict of the Kansei period.

Literature: Hillier 1980, p. 245; Hioki 2009, pp. 79-101.

▲ The servant is setting off to tip the creditor (p. 2a).

20. Kanamajiri musume setsuyō 仮名文章娘節用
('A Handbook for Girls in the Vernacular', or:
'The Temperance of the Girl of Kana[ya] Bun[nojō]')

3 instalments, 9 chapters in 3 fascicles, 17.5 x 12 cm
Author: Kyokusanjin 曲山人, illustrator: Kyokusanjin,
Utagawa Kuninao 歌川国直 (1793-1854)

Date: instalments 1-2: Tenpō 天保 2 (1831); instalment 3:
Tenpō 5 (1834), preface: 1830

A melodrama, known as *ninjōbon* 人情本, in three parts and nine chapters (*maki*). It is believed that it was not created by Kyokusanjin (?-1836), but that he rearranged and refined an anonymous manuscript by an amateur writer. The name of the heroes are Kosan 小三 and Kingorō 金五郎, who have been stock protagonists in love stories of double suicide since the Genroku 元禄 period (1688-1704), but the novel does not portray a stereotypical love double suicide. Although it ends with the suicide of the woman, its main focus is on the opposition between *giri* 義理 and *ninjō* 人情, that is, social obligation opposed to personal inclination and desire.

Kingorō is the love child of Kanaya Bunnojō 仮名屋文之丞 and the chambermaid Tamazusa 玉章, who have eloped from the house of the Shiba 斯波 family. As fate would have it, Bunnojō also happened to have adopted Okame, the daughter of an old ironmonger, who was in dire straits and could not raise her himself. She later became the *geisha* Kosan and fell in love with Kingorō. Having been raised as brother and sister, their love posed a serious problem in samurai society, and, sure enough, it ends with the suicide of Kosan. The novel owed its popularity to its delicate drawing of the tender sentiments between the star-struck lovers, steering clear from the traditional moral lesson that the novels usually were supposed to inculcate. The novel was first published with illustrations by Utagawa Kunitsugu 歌川国次 (1800-1861), but later reprinted with illustrations by Utagawa Kuninao 歌川国直 (1793-1854), and it is this version that garnered great popularity. It is one of the representative examples of the genre *ninjōbon*.

As often in these kinds of books, the title suggests a pun. On the surface it is a neutral, even dull title, but some of the characters (logograms) also occur in the name of one of the protagonists. Thus on the underlying level the title adumbrates what the book is really about.

Publisher and place of publication are unknown.

Literature: Suzuki 1979; Suzuki 1957, pp. 2-5; Mutō 1994.

▲ Tamazusa playing with her child, as Bunnojō, sporting fashionable spectacles, is looking on (fascicle II, pp. 2b-3a).

21. Mukashi-gatari inazuma-byōshi 昔語稲妻表紙
('The Story of the Lightning: An Old Tale') & Inazuma-byōshi kōhen 稲妻表紙後編
('The Story of the Lightning: An Old Tale, Sequel')

Alternative title: *Inazuma-byōshi* 稲妻表紙
Title prefix: Fuwa Banzaemon Nagoya Sanzaburō 不破伴左
衛門名古屋山三郎.
5 chapters in 6 fascicles; 22.8 x 15.9 cm

Author: Santō Kyōden 山東京伝; illustrator: Utagawa
Toyokuni I 歌川豊国（一世）
Date: Bunka 文化 3 (1806)

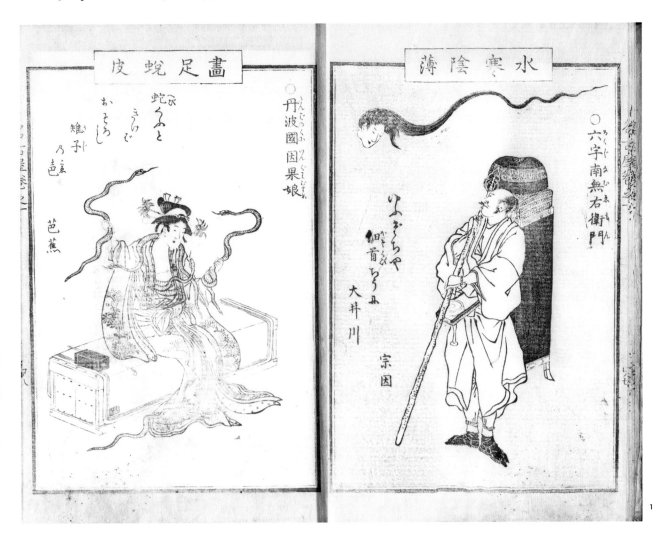

A *yomihon* by Santō Kyōden (1761-1816), with illustrations by Utagawa Toyokuni I (1769-1825). Loosely based on a play by Chikamatsu Monzaemon 近松門左衛門, it relates an internecine feud about the succession to the estate of a family of consequence, set in the Japanese Middle Ages, and pitting the loyal retainer Nagoya Sansaburō against the villainous retainer Fuwa Banzaemon. The latter sides with a concubine who tries to secure the succession for her son, but Nagoya, protector of the rightful heir, stymies their scheme, eliminates them, and causes righteousness to prevail. Owing to its huge success, this 'novel' was adapted for the theatre two years after its publication and staged in Osaka. The "lightning" in the title refers to the pattern on the clothing of the main character Fuwa Banzaemon. The actor Ichikawa Saigyū 市川才牛 (1660-1704) was the first to have this pattern dyed onto the fabric of

his costume. He was inspired to do so by a *haiku* by Kasui:

"The first lightning strike	稲妻の
I have seen over the pass	はじまり見てり
Of Fuwa"	不破の関

It was undoubtedly the fact that the family name of his character in the play was Fuwa, which suggested this link with the *haiku*.

Kyōden wrote a sequel to this book with a title that was not very ingenious, namely, *Inazuma-byōshi kōhen* 稲妻表紙後編 (lit. *Inazuma byōshi Sequel*). Because he wanted to stress the independent character of his book in relation to its predecessor, he also gave it its own title: *Honchō suibodai* 本朝酔菩提 ('A Japanese Version of Suibodai').

The hero in *Honchō suibodai* is the eccentric monk Ikkyū 一休 (1394-1481), and it is written from

109

▲ The karmic girl (*inga musume* 因果娘) of Tanba Province (left) and Rokuji namu'emon (right), both with a haiku.

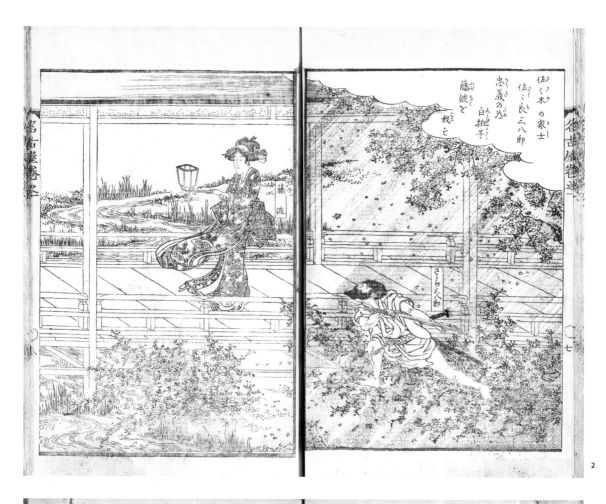

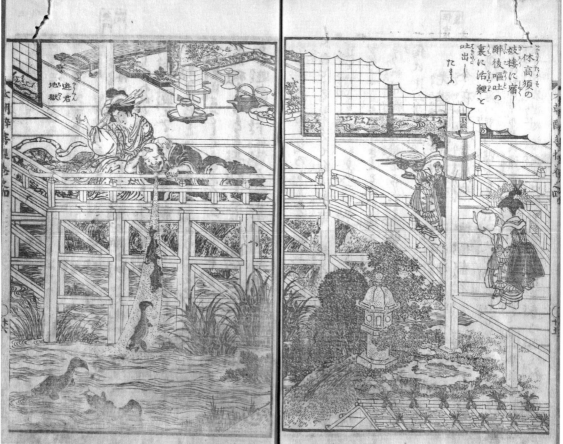

☙ Sasara Sanpachirō, retainer of the house of Sasaki, about to
kill the courtesan Fujinami out of loyalty.

▲ Ikkyū spends the night in the brothel.

the point of view of the Buddhist *upaya* (*hōben* 方便); all means are good as long as they lead people to the right path. Ikkyū's favourite 'means' is *yuge-zanmai* 遊戯三昧. This is an expression borrowed from Zen Buddhism, where it denotes a state of liberation of the trammels of ignorance and delusion. However, here Ikkyū, in his legendary eccentric manner, interprets the term in a more mundane sense, as "revelling in one's freedom", "unrestrained pleasure and gaiety". Embracing this freedom, our hero makes himself - only seemingly - guilty of all kinds of behaviour which in Buddhism would normally at once be condemned as "mortal sin". He behaves like a madman, visits brothels, gets involved in the most impossible situations, but it is all for a good cause: teaching people about the transience of life and converting them to Buddha's teachings.

Ill. 1: the karmic girl (*inga musume* 因果娘) of Tanba Province; next to the image of the girl, a fitting *haiku* by Bashō is quoted (Fascicle I, chapter 1, p. 8a):

> "The call of the pheasant,   蛇くふときけば
> When you hear it eats snakes, おそろし雉子の声
>   Sounds terrifying"

The point of the verse is that the call of the pheasant, while traditionally considered poetic and melancholy, suddenly sounds quite different when one learns that this bird actually eats snakes. The same sentiment applies to the girls of easy virtue, who may be very charming but actually lead one to a bad rebirth.

Ill. 2: Sasara Sanpachirō, retainer of the house of Sasaki, sneaking up to the unwitting courtesan Fujinami and about to kill her out of loyalty to his master (Fascicle I/chapter 1, pp. 7b-8a).

Ill. 4: final showdown between Nagoya and Fuwa, Nagoya avenging himself on his father's killer (Fascicle VI, chapter 5b, p. 16a).

From *Honchō suibodai*, the following scenes are reproduced:

Ill. 3: Ikkyū spends the night in the brothel (Fascicle IV/chapter 4, pp. 25b-26a). After getting drunk, he throws up the carp he has eaten, alive, thus respecting the Buddhist precept of not killing living beings.

Ill. 5: Ikkyū is on the road with a skull in his hand to remind people of the impermanence and fragility of life (Fascicle I/chapter 1, p. 10b).

Literature: Keene 1978, pp. 404-409; Tsukamoto 1918.

▲ Final showdown between Nagoya and Fuwa.

▲ Ikkyū on the road with a skull in his hand.

22. Nansō Satomi hakkenden 南総里見八犬伝
('Biographies of the Eight 'Dogs' of the Satomi Clan in the Kazusa Province')

Alternative title: *Satomi hakkenden* 里見八犬伝
9 instalments, 98 chapters in 106 fascicles; 22.7 x 15.7 cm
Author: Kyokutei Bakin 曲亭馬琴; illustrators: (inst. 1-8) Yanagawa Shigenobu I 柳川重信（一世）; (inst. 9) Yanagawa

Shigenobu II 柳川重信（二世）; (inst. 5, 6, 9) Keisai Eisen 渓斎英泉; (inst. 9) Utagawa Sadahide 歌川貞秀
Date: published between Bunka 文化 11 - Tenpō 天保 13 (1814-1842)

112

This is one of the most famous *yomihon* 読本. *Yomihon* or "reading books" are illustrated fictional stories where the text is more important than the illustrations, contrary to other genres where illustrations are central. They are interspersed with countless historical references to Japanese or Chinese history, and the reader is taught a moral lesson at the end of each episode. The portrayal of the characters is very schematic and stereotypical. The stories are set in a fantastic world of fairies, princesses, brave warriors, and villains. At its best the genre could be considered the epitome of the traditional art of storytelling.

Kyokutei (Takizawa) Bakin (1767-1848) is by far the foremost master of the *yomihon*. The work with the rather bizarre title *Nansō satomi hakkenden* (Biographies of the Eight 'Dogs' of the Satomi Clan in the Kazusa Province, 1814-41) may be considered his masterpiece. He began this *roman-fleuve* in 1814, when he was 47 years old. In total, he worked on it for 27 years, churning out no less than 106 volumes. The later instalments of the book were a true ordeal,

because the author was slowly but surely turning blind. In the end, he had to dictate his text to his daughter-in-law. It was no easy task for her to correctly write down his complicated sentences and formulations, and he often had to explain the more difficult characters (*kanji*) to her.

The story is set in the fifteenth century. General Satomi Yoshizane 里見義実 (1417-1488) is under siege in his castle. In despair, he declares that he will marry his daughter Fusehime 伏姫 to whoever will bring him the head of his enemy. His guard dog Yatsufusa 八房 hurriedly runs off only to return a short while later with the enemy's head. Fusehime, understanding the value of a promise made, absolutely wants to keep her father's vow and marries the dog. She goes to live with her canine groom in a cave in the mountains. One year later she is pregnant. Around the same time, a servant of her father comes to 'free' her. He aims at the dog but accidently hits the princess. She is mortally wounded, knows that she cannot be saved, and kills herself with a knife. A white cloud rises up from her wounds and

▲ Satomi Jibu no tayū Yoshizane 里見治部大輔義実 riding on a carp.

wraps around the crystal pearls around her neck. Eight of these pearls rise up into the air. On each of these pearls a character denoting one of the Confucian virtues is inscribed. Afterwards, each of these pearls is found in the hand of eight newly born sons of men who are all called "inu" (dog). Each of these so-called dogs turns out to be the incarnation of one of the Confucian virtues carved on the pearls. In the course of an endless series of adventures, the eight heroes encounter each other countless times, only to be separated again by the circumstances. Eventually, fate brings them together for their crowning feat of arms: the restoration of the Satomi clan to its former glory. Once the task is completed, the eight dogs retreat to Yatsufusa's cave and disappear from the face of the earth.

Bakin's *yomihon* were mostly read by the literate classes, particularly by the samurai class. The print runs for his books were about 300 copies per edition.

More than half of these were immediately sold to booklenders (*kashihon-ya* 貸本屋). Because he could not survive on that money alone, he additionally had to write a lot of 'pulp'. In his more serious works, he glorified the samurai virtues. His heroes refuse to be swayed from their supreme goal, neither by evil creatures nor by the stirrings of the heart. Even the love of the most beautiful woman is no match to their sense of duty. They will pursue their noble mission at all cost.

Ill. 1: Satomi Jibu no tayū Yoshizane 里見治部太夫義実 riding on a carp (instalment I, pp. 4a-5a prefatory section to chapter 1, pp. 4b-5a).

Ill. 2: Yatsufusa and Fusehime in the cave (instalment I, chapter 5, pp. 22b-23a). The accompanying text reads: "Keeping the promise made, Fusehime accompanies the animal (to the cave) deep in the mountains".

Literature: Keene 1978, pp. 424-428.

113

▲ Yatsufusa and Fusehime in the cave.

23. Tsugikase Kishō 月瀬記勝
('A Record of Scenic Spots in Tsukigase')

2 chapters in 2 fascicles; 25.4 x 17.2 cm
Author: Saitō Setsudō 斎藤拙堂
Date: preface dated Ka'ei 嘉永 4 (1851)

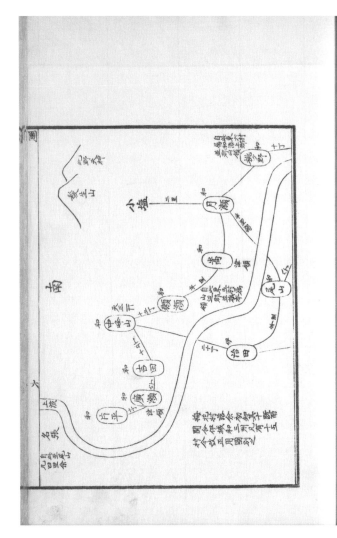
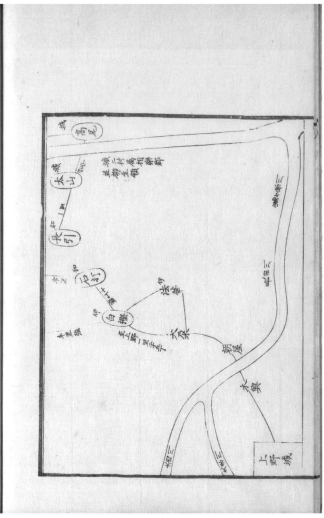

This is a travel account in poems, written in *kanbun*, about Tsukigase, the name of a village and a stretch of valley along the Nabarigawa River in Yamato Province. If Mount Yoshino counts as the most beautiful panorama of cherry blossoms in Japan, then Tsukigase is famed for its plum blossoms. The area was first celebrated in *kanbun*-poems by the literatus (*bunjin* 文人) and poet Yamaguchi Kanrengyoku 山口韓聯玉, who traveled through this area in Bunsei 2 (1819). He collected his poems, added works sent to him by scholarly friends, and published the whole as *Tsukigase baika-jō* 月瀬梅花帖 (A Notebook on the Plum Blossoms of Tsukigase) (1825). This was the first time that the area acquired a level of fame among certain groups of literati.

Saitō Setsudō (1797-1865), author of *Tsukigase kishō*, was born in Kansei 9 (1797) in Edo, in the residence of the lord (*daimyō*) of the Tsu domain in Ise Province. From an early age, he attended the school of the *Bakufu* (the Shōheikō 昌平黌), where he studied under Koga Seiri 古賀精里 (1750-1817). At the age of 24, he was summoned as a teacher to the school recently established by the lord of Tsu in his domain. Gradually he emerged as one of the foremost specialists of Confucianism in Tsu and, in his later years, even became political advisor to his *daimyō*.

Tsukigase Kishō is a travel account written by Setsudō in the wake of a trip to Tsukigase in the company of several friends. The work is divided into nine chapters, in which he describes the plum orchards in the Tsukigase valley from various points of view and under various circumstances. The text proper is preceded by eight landscapes in ink and light colour, no doubt intended as the Tsukigase version of the "Eight Views" in the style of *nanga* 南画 (literati painting). The "Eight Views" are a canonical

▲ A map showing the villages, including the village of Tsukigase, and hamlets where plum blossoms are worth viewing.

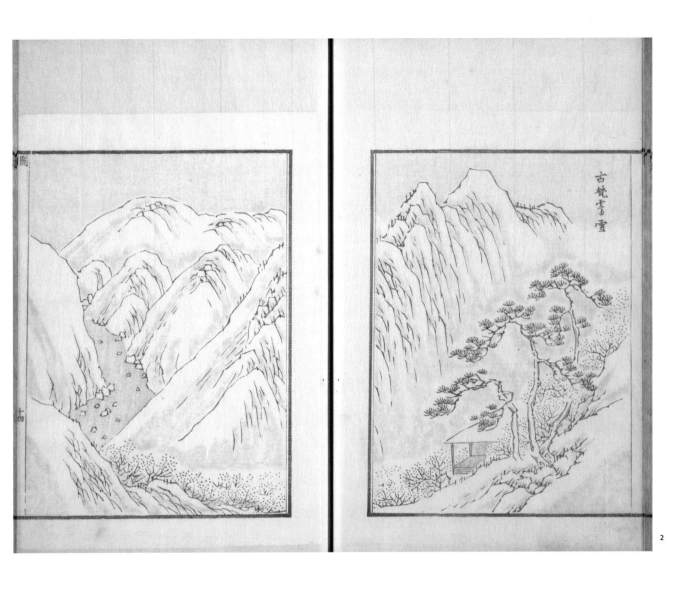

古梵書雪

set of landscapes in traditional painting, representing a scenic area under eight different meteorological or atmospheric conditions.

The first page of each fascicle bears the collector's seal "Tomita tosho 富田図書" and "Hoku ? kyū in Ōshima bunko 北?宮印大島文庫".

Ill. 1: a map showing the villages, including the village of Tsukigase, and hamlets where plum blossoms are worth viewing (chapter 1, pp. 5b-6a).

Ill. 2: view of a hermitage overlooking the valley of the Nabarigawa river with the inscription: "The old temple bell (echoes) in the clearing after snow." This solemn vignette embodies the detachment and unworldly lifestyle of the literary man (bunjin) (chapter 1, pp. 13b-14a).

Literature: Fujikawa 1991, pp. 19-20; Fujikawa 1992.

▲ View of a hermitage overlooking the valley of the Nabarigawa river.

24. Kinsei kijinden 近世畸人伝
('Lives of Remarkable People of Recent Times')

Alternative title: *Kijinden* 畸人伝
5 chapters in 5 fascicles; 25.7 x 18 cm
Author: Ban Kōkei 伴蒿蹊

Illustrator: Mikuma Shikō 三熊思孝
Date: preface dated Tenmei 天明 8 (1788), published in
Kansei 寛政2 (1790)

116

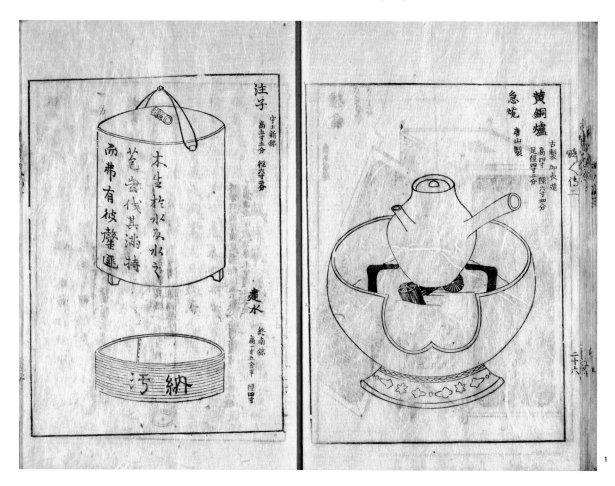

This work consists of five chapters (*maki*) and includes the biographies of about 100 persons from different walks of life - celebrities, eccentrics, madmen, and so on, as remarkable, outlandish, or exceptional characters - from the beginning of the Edo period down to the late eighteenth century. It includes, for instance, the Confucian scholar Nakae Tōju 中江藤樹; the monks Tōsui 桃水, Tetsugan 鉄眼, and Baisa-ō 売茶翁; the nun Hakyō 破鏡; the courtesan Ōhashi 大橋; and many others. The work was completed in 1788, and people still alive at that time were not included. It includes a foreword in *kanbun* by the monk Shaku Jishū 釈慈周 (1734-1801); a preface by the author himself; and a postscript by a friend of the author, Mikuma Shikō (Katen) (1730-1794), who also contributed forty illustrations to the book.

The author Ban Kōkei (1733-1806) was an erudite individual from Kyoto, who succeeded in gathering a host of stories and testimonies about monks, poets, scholars, hermits, and artists from various regions across Japan, though when writing the book he hardly ever left the capital. He was born in Kyoto

into a family of merchants. At the age of eight, he was adopted into the main branch of the Ban family. He eventually became the head of the family business and in that capacity often went on business trips to Edo, where the family owned a shop. When he was 36 years old, he passed the management of the business on to his adopted son and retired in Kyoto. From that point on, he adopted the name Kōkei. Although he did not belong to the court nobility, he was considered one of the great *waka* poets of his time. Moreover, he was a master of elegant Japanese prose and an eminent expert in Japanese and Chinese classics. Although he had a sickly constitution from childhood, he was blessed with a relatively long life for his time.

The term *kijin* 畸人 in the title needs some explanation. *Ki* 畸 here means "exceptional", "eccentric", or also "different". A *kijin* is therefore someone whose lifestyle and behaviour differ from that of the common person. In his preface Kōkei argues that the term has two meanings; the first is "remarkable", "extraordinary" in the sense of someone far exceeding the average, someone who is a consummate mas-

▲ Drawing of basket containing Baisa-ō's tea utensils.

ter in his profession or in his art. Examples of this are the scholars Nakae Tōju 中江藤樹 (1608-1648) and Kaibara Ekiken 貝原益軒 (1630-1714), who were allegedly exceptional paragons of Confucian virtues.

However, a second meaning is found in the Daoist classic *Zhuangzi* (Jap. *Sōshi*) 荘子, where we read that a *kijin* is someone who is different from others, and who lives in accord with heaven. Ban Kōkei's emphasis on this second meaning is understandably related to the success and popularity of the ideas of the Chinese philosophers Laozi (Jap. Rōshi) 老子 and Zhuangzi among intellectuals in eighteenth-century Japan. The compilation of the book *Kinsei kijinden* was also inspired by this intellectual trend. It is no ordinary collection of biographies.

Ban Kōkei describes Baisa-ō 売茶翁 as the epitome of eccentricity. Baisa-ō – his name means "tea-selling old man" – led an unusual existence. Around 1735 – when he was about 60 years old – he was known throughout Kyoto as an intellectual tea-peddler. He was a prominent intellectual, wrote excellent poems, and was also an excellent calligrapher. His style of life was an implicit yet sharp critique of the style of life of the contemporary clergy and intelligentsia. Even so, he attracted many like-minded people.

The illustrations in this work are of excellent quality; the text is considered to be written in an elegant and refined style.

Ill. 1: Baisa-ō in chapter II, pp. 25b-26a, drawing of basket containing his tea utensils.

Ill. 2: chapter II/fascicle II, p. 37a: the wandering monk Enkū (1632-1695). The description about Enkū in the *Kinsei kijinden* is the only biography about this legendary monk. He made various pilgrimages to holy places in Japan and set out to carve tens of thousands of little Buddha statues in order to accumulate spiritual merits. His biography in the Kinsei kijinden includes a passage where he is carving the faces of two colossal temple guardians out of the trunk of two withered trees. The illustration depicts two farmers watching, as Enkū 'tackles' the colossal tree with his chisel. We can already discern the contours of both legs and the face of one of the two giants. Afterwards, the tree started growing branches anew, a story about wondrous growth reminiscent of the Western legend of the Holy Cross (chapter II/fascicle II, p. 37a).

Ill. 3: the famous monk Tetsugen, handing out food to the poor (chapter II/fascicle II, p. 3b).

Literature: Van Alphen 1999, pp. 100-105; Munemasa 1972, pp. 501-512; Munemasa 1977.

▲ The wandering monk Enkū (1632-1695).

▲ The famous monk Tetsugen, handing out food to the poor.

Kashihon-ya 貸本屋 (Booklender Stores)

From the second half of the Edo period (1600-1868), a network of commercial 'booklenders' (*kashihon-ya*) spread throughout Japan. By the end of the seventeenth century, peddlers with packs of books on their backs were a familiar sight on the streets of the most important cities. It is mostly after the mid-eighteenth century, though, that *kashihon-ya* became the main suppliers of reading material for people living in the cities. Whenever new books appeared, the peddler went around visiting his clients to deliver the books to their

houses, or the customers came to his shop to borrow the books. It was mostly popular books, contemporary works of fiction, which were in high demand, especially when it concerned more voluminous books, too expensive for many to purchase. In such cases, the booklenders provided a more affordable alternative.

These itinerant bookshops were the pioneers of modern reading clubs or book clubs. They loaned from their collections on the honour system. To avoid books being

stolen, they marked them with seals. Books from the collections of these bookshops usually bore the signs of frequent use. One could often find notes or scribbling in them, too. The *kashihon-ya* strongly influenced society in the Edo period. They contributed to the reading culture and the "democratization" of knowledge. Among their clients were nobles, samurai, and citizens, as well as prostitutes. Through their home delivery system, the books were also accessible to a broad female readership.

Literature: Kornicki 1998, pp. 391-397.

118

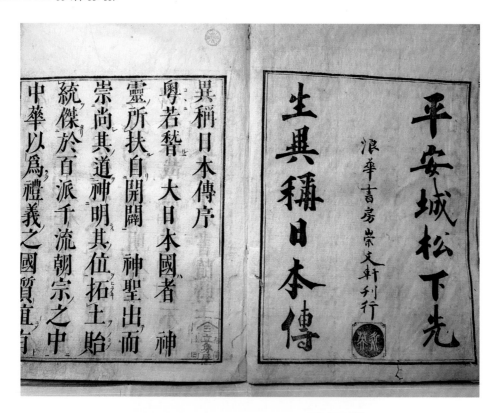

▲ First page of *Ishō Nihonden*, bearing the seal of the booklender store Risshin'ya, located in the district Uemachi in Fukushima.

25. (Zōho) Edo meisho-banashi (増補)江戸名所咄
('Stories About Famous Places in Edo', enlarged edition)

Alternative title: *Edo meisho banashi* 江戸名所はなし/
Edo-banashi 江戸咄
6 chapters in 8 fascicles; 27.2 x 18.5 cm

Author: unknown
Date: printed in Genroku 元禄 7 (1694)

This book is a partially revised and enlarged edition of *Kokyō-kaeri no Edobanashi* 古郷帰の江戸咄 (published in Jōkyō 貞享 4 (1687)). The original title is replaced in the newer edition by the present one.

On the first page we see the collector's seal 松平氏蔵書印. This is the seal of Matsudaira Naritsune 松平斉典 (1797-1850), fourth feudal lord of the fief Kawagoe 川越. He has gone down in history as a good ruler of his domain. He is also known for his promotion of education and learning. He set up a school for the education of samurai in his fiefdom as well as in Edo. In Tenpō 15 (1844), he gave orders to Yasuoka Reinan 保岡嶺南 (1801-1868), a Confucian scholar, to revise Rai Sanyō's 頼山陽 (1780-1832) famous *Nihon gaishi* 日本外史 (*Unofficial History of Japan*), originally published in 1829. The 1844 edition,

known as the Kawagoe edition, became a real bestseller going through no less than fourteen editions. Its woodblocks were kept in the Matsudaira clan's residence, until they were lost, along with other treasures, during an air raid in 1945.

If we assume this book was donated directly from the Matsudaira residence to the National Committee, then it escaped three disasters: the Kantō Earthquake and the ensuing conflagration, the German bombing of the Louvain library and, finally, the American air raid in 1945.

The copy in the UCLouvain bears the label "rare" 希購書. The colophon page bears the date Genroku 7 (1694), published by Sudareya Mataemon 簾屋又右衛門, located near Nihonbashi.

119

▲ The bridge Nihonbashi with samurai, *yakko* 奴 (footmen), and fishermen (fascicle I/chapter 1, pp. 19b-20a).

26. Edo-zu shōtaizen 江戸図正大全
('A Complete and Correct Map of Edo')

Woodcut hand-coloured map; 158.4 x 129.5 cm
Author (cartographer): Onseiken 温清軒 (?-?);

Publisher: Satō Shirōemon 佐藤四郎右衛門.
Date: Genroku 元禄 8 (1695)

▲ General view of the map.

This is a revised version of a map that was published in 1693, under the title *Edo-zu seihō kagami* 江戸図正方鑑, measuring 158.4 x 129.5 cm.

The top of the map represents the West. Edo castle, the residence of the *shōgun* is clearly indicated by the family crest of the Tokugawa clan, commonly known as the 'triple hollyhock,' but the privacy of the *shōgun* evidently being a matter of state interest, no lay-out of the buildings is given.

It offers a good impression of the lively city of Edo, today's Tokyo, during the Genroku era (1688-1704). On the map one can see temples and Shintō shrines, as well as the numerous mansions of feudal lords, marked by the respective badges of their clans. These badges are the same that are tied to spears and carried at the head of the processions in which a feudal lord travels in state to the castle of the *shōgun* or some other lofty destination. The map also features several separate columns with lists of temples and sanctuaries, and perhaps more unexpectedly for us fire brigade stations, which needless to say played a vital role in a wooden city like Edo. One also notices the many *kumiyashiki* 組屋敷, police stations, bearing witness to the police state that the shogunate maintained. Moreover, the names of the town districts are accompanied by the names

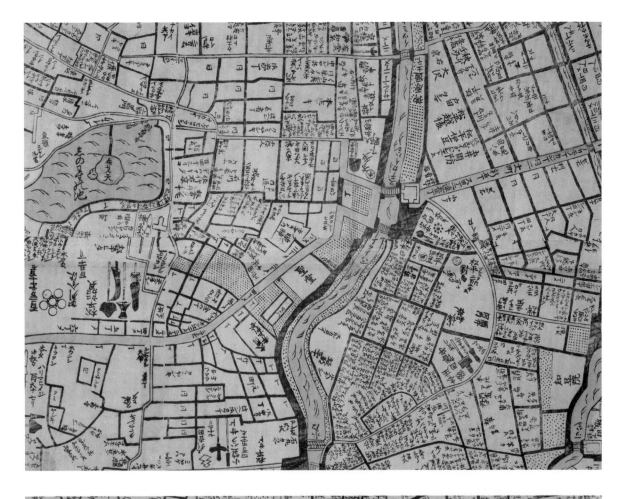

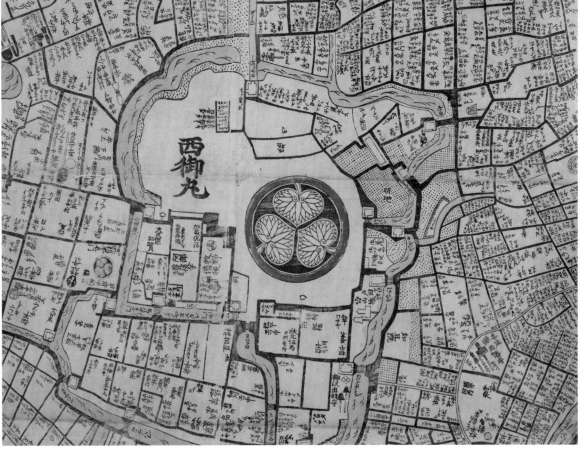

▲ The section of the city where the temple to Confucius (indicated here by the characters *seidō* 聖堂) is located.

▲ The Western section (Nishi omaru 西御丸) of Edo Castle where the retired *shōgun* and the designated *shōgun* resided.

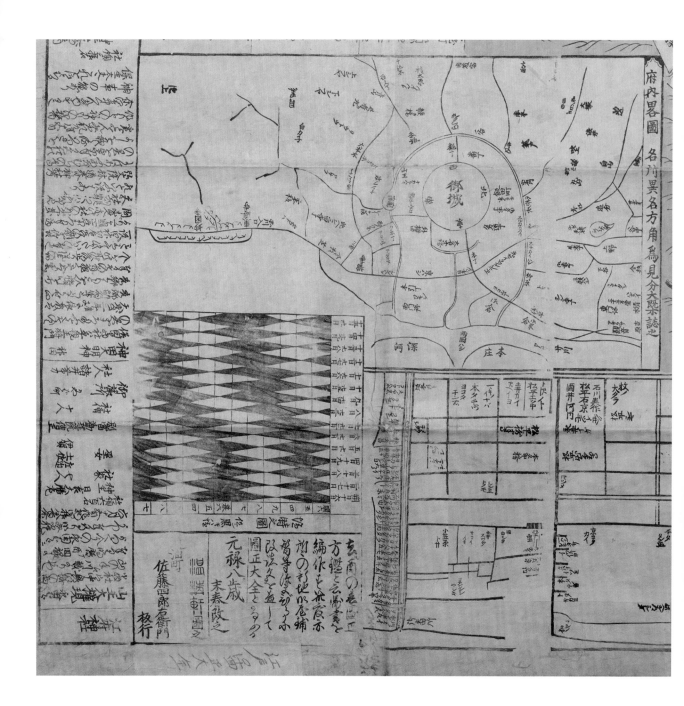

of the district heads (*machi-nanushi* 町名主), who act as go-betweens among the townspeople and the shogunate's administration. Yushima seidō 湯島聖堂, the temple dedicated to Confucius, is visible at its present location. It was relocated here from Ueno by order of the fifth *shōgun*, Tsunayoshi 綱吉 (1646-1709), in 1690-1691.

The map also includes inset tide tables, a feature missing in its 1693 predecessor. The UCLouvain copy has manifestly been backed with strong mulberry paper and slightly restored in some places, presumably as commissioned by the National Committee.

▲ The colophon of the map, mentioning the title of the map as '[Edo-]zu shōtaizen,' and the date 'late spring 1695'.

27. Konpira sankei meisho-zue 金毘羅参詣名所図会
('Famous Places on the Pilgrimage Road to the Sanctuary of Konpira, Illustrated')

6 chapters in 6 fascicles; 25.4 x 18.2 cm
Author: Akatsuki no Kanenari 暁金成; illustrator: Urakawa Kōsa 浦川公佐

Date: preface dated Kōka 弘化 3 (1846), published in Kōka 4 (1847)

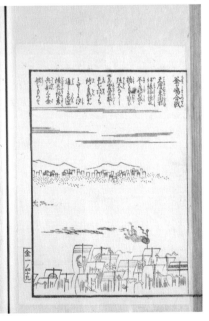

Illustrated topographical account of the pilgrim road to Konpira, with text by Akatsuki Kanenari (1793-1861) and illustrations by Urakawa Kōsa (active between 1830-1860), published in the year Kōka 4 (1847). The shrine of Konpira Daigongen 金比羅大権現 on Mount Zōzuzan in Sanuki Province (present-day Kagawa Prefecture) was considered the most important place of pilgrimage after that of Ise Jingū 伊勢神宮. This edition was meant as a sort of guide for the pilgrim. The descriptions are based on factual observation. Not unlike modern-day travel journalists, the author and illustrator spent two months in the province. Presumably the costs of this trip were paid for by the publisher. The signed preface is by the court official and *tanka* poet Uematsu Masataka 植松雅恭 (1825-1855).

According to the colophon, this is a "new print" (*shinkoku* 新刻), published by various bookstores in Edo, Kyoto, and Osaka. It is unclear if this means that it is also a first printing (*shozuri* 初刷り), but it is definitely a printing close to it. The first page of every fascicle bears the vermillion collector's seal 'Shōjidō 嘯而堂,' thus far unidentified.

Literature: Nagoya-shi hakubutsukan 1988.

⬆ The god of Sumiyoshi exorcises an evil spirit in the guise of an oxen (chapter 1, pp. 6b-7a).

▲ The site where the battle of Kamagashima was fought between the insurgent Fujiwara no Sumitomo 藤原 純友 (died 941) and the imperial armies (chapter 1, pp. 49b-50a).

28. Kyō warabe 京童
('Lads in the Capital')

6 chapters in 6 fascicles; 27 x 17.2 cm
Author: Nakagawa Kiun 中川喜雲
Date: printed in Meireki 明暦 4 (1658)

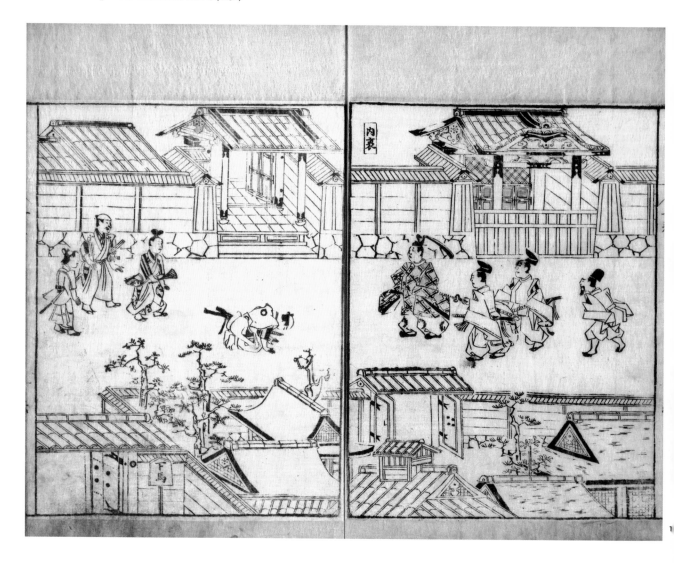

124

This title is the first *meisho-zue* about Kyoto (see also p. 127). The book is conceived as a narrative about two lads who take the reader (the visitor) on a tour of no less than eighty scenic spots in the imperial capital (ill. 1: fascicle I, pp. 5b-6a). The tour starts at the imperial palace. Each place is given a simple description by the author, concluded with one or more haiku or *kyōka* (comical poems), written by him, followed by an illustration.

The author, Nakagawa Kiun 中川喜雲 (1636-1705), came from Tanba Province and settled as a physician in Kyoto. He was a fervent haiku poet and writer of *kanazōshi* 仮名草子 (books of fiction or didactic intent), produced in the seventeenth century and composed mainly in the *kana* syllabaries.

Ill. 2: the shrine where the famous statue of the Buddha Amida looking over his shoulder is venerated (chapter IV/fascicle IV, pp. 5b-6a). It is in the temple Eikandō 永観堂 (Eikan's hall), named for the

famed monk Yōkan 永観. Worth noting is that the characters "永観" and "永観堂" were read as Yōkan and Yōkandō in the seventeenth century. Although the name of the temple is now read in the *kan'on* reading as Eikandō, the name of the monk is still pronounced Yōkan in the *go'on* reading.

The accompanying text reads: "This temple is officially called Zenrinji. Here the vinaya-master, a master in the rules of Buddhist monastic discipline, Yōkan (1032-1111), practiced a combination of three kinds of devotion: Zen meditation, the vinaya, and the Pure Land teaching. (...) The statue of the Buddha looking back dates from the time when Yōkan dedicated himself to intense religious exercises. The Buddha Amida was doing the same exercises at the time and looked behind him to see if (Yōkan) was following in his footsteps. Yōkan then made this statue of Amida in that pose so that it might be venerated for eternity. (...)."

▲ Start of the tour at the imperial palace.

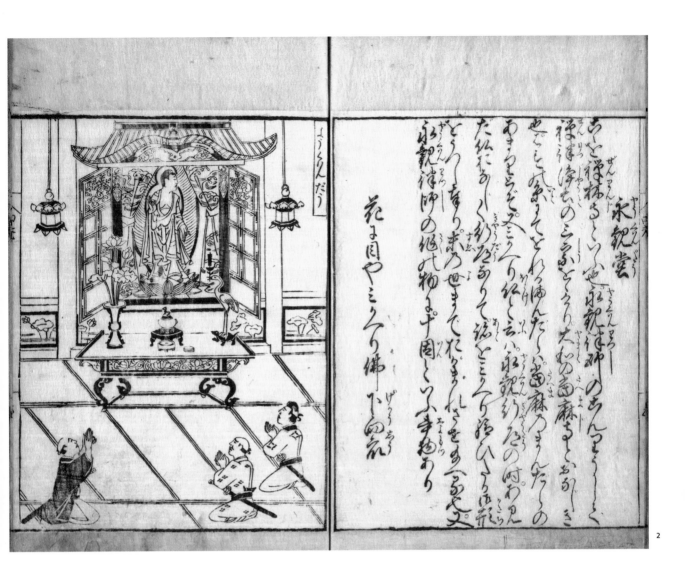

The illustration shown here comes with a haiku:

花にや
ミカヘリ
下向衆

While we look to the blossoms,
The buddha Amida looks back/after
'his' flock of sinners

The statue, known as the "mikaeri Amida", can even now be admired in the temple Eikandō. It was classified as an important cultural asset in 1999.

The first drawings in the first fascicle of this copy in the UCLouvain are faintly coloured by hand.

The rest are not. The date on the colophon is: 明暦四年七月吉日 (on an auspicious day in the seventh month of the fourth year of Meireiki (1658)), 八文字屋五兵衛新刊 (newly published by the Hachimonjiya Gohē). As such, it is a hachimonjiya-bon 八文字屋本, which makes this copy exceptionally valuable. The committee therefore rightly marked it as "rare". Hachimonjiya is the name of a publisher/bookseller in Kyoto, active from the late seventeenth century to 1767, and known for its publication of books in a number of popular genres, including novels and kabuki plays.

Literature: Nakagawa 1967; Nakagawa 1976.

▲ The shrine where the famous statue of the Buddha Amida looking over his shoulder is venerated.

Meisho-zue 名所図会: Illustrated Topographical Accounts

Meisho-zue are illustrated topographical accounts meant for a broader audience. Some classic examples of the genre include the works compiled by Akisato Ritō 秋里籬嶌. There is little to no biographical information on him, although he originally seems to have been a little-known *haiku* poet based in Kyoto. *Meisho-zue* contain illustrations of panoramas in bird's-eye view, although not in the strict sense of today's geographical methods. As a rule, they are in *daihon*-size 台本, i.e., a page of *Minogami*-paper 美濃紙 folded in half, which roughly corresponds to the current B5 size. The oldest topographical accounts focused on famous places and sights celebrated in classical poetry (*utamakura* 歌枕). A place that was not mentioned in any classical poem therefore did not originally qualify, no matter how stunning the view might have been. Conversely, someone who wanted to compose a classical poem would have needed to know about these famous places. This need fueled the publication of the earliest accounts, the *Utamakura-sho* 歌枕書 (Repertory of Utamakura) and the *Meisho-ki* 名所記 ('Tales of Famous Places'), which may be considered the forerunners of the *meisho-zue*.

The *meisho-ki* were structured as a story. The hero travelled from one famous place to another and described what he saw. The explanation was straightforward, the selection of famed places was rather arbitrary. This genre of books was illustrated, though the drawings were simple and unsophisticated and not drawn from the actual setting. Rather, they were imaginary landscapes.

The *meisho-zue* changed that practice. They are no longer stories but factual reports. They do not restrict themselves to *utamakura* but are methodical in their accounts. The author aimed to be exhaustive in covering all interesting and noteworthy places in a certain region or city. They come close to what we would call an illustrated trav-elogue. While there was already a topographical account on nearly every region before the advent of the *meisho-zue*, these were often written in *kanbun* 漢文 (Classical Chinese), tersely composed, and difficult to understand. Moreover, they barely included any drawings. The *meisho-zue* were a significant improvement: The description was in easy-to-understand Japanese, based on factual observations, and they were richly illustrated. These illustrations are generally realistic, although there was the occasional (imaginary) depiction of a historical event. They are depictions of temples, mountains, and rivers, usually from a bird's-eye view. As a rule, they describe the contemporary situation. Author and illustrator mean to report on the current look of the place based on factual observations. Even the poems (*tanka* and *haiku*) that are cited are not limited to classical examples.

The first authentic example of a *Meisho-zue* is *Miyako meisho-zue* 都名所図絵 (Famous Places of the Capital, Illustrated; 1780). The author was Akisato Ritō (?–1830), its illustrator Takehara Shunchōsai 竹原春朝斎 (1772-1801). When their partnership proved to be hugely successful, they produced a sequel: the *Jūi miyako meisho-zue* 拾遺都名所図会 (Famous Places of the Capital, Illustrated, supplement; 1787) and continued with similar books on different places in the Kinki and Tōkaidō regions.

The height of *Meisho-zue* occurred between the second half of the eighteenth century until the end of the Edo period (1600-1868), especially whenever the government subjected the publishing world to strict censorship. In such times, publishers were keen to tap the market potential of this politically and morally harmless genre.

The genre is dominated by two authors: the aforementioned Akisato Ritō in addition to Akatsuki Kanenari 暁鐘成 (1793-1861). While Ritō still attached much importance to *uta-makura*, Kanenari broke free from this convention. He also included sights and places that do not appear at all in classical poetry. One such example is his *Tenpōzan meisho-zue* 天保山名所図会 (Famous Places of Mount Tenpō Capital, Illustrated; 1780). This is a newly discovered area "without history". He also adopted an unusual format for this book, namely, that of the *chūbon* 中本, and it is very possible that he intended this book to be a parody of the genre. Ritō and Kanenari were also *haiku* poets (*haijin* 俳人) in their own right and wrote other books as well.

Ritō and Kanenari were true professionals in what we might call travel journalism. They received assignments from publishers who would also ensure that they were reimbursed for their travel expenses. After all, the book was a report of their journey. Such editions were of course intended as a profit-making enterprise. Not surprisingly, then, the topics were mainly chosen from popular 'tourist' spots such as Kyoto, Edo (now Tokyo), and major destinations of pilgrimage. Because mobility was on the rise at this time, and many people travelled under the guise of making a pilgrimage, the demand for a guide to such places was high. In less populated and less developed areas, local heritage experts or amateurs would produce a local topographical guide. They often published the book themselves, while in other cases the products of their pen never made it past the manuscript stage.

Meisho-zue are an ode to the varied landscapes and city views of Japan. The Japanese discovered the beauty of their country, and because they could never travel abroad, the archipelago was 'constructed' into a mini-world of its own. The varied ecological types and the vast climatological differences, in addition to the strongly defined local specialties, customs, and rituals, conjured up among the Japanese the illusion of '*dépaysement*', of travelling abroad.

Literature: Imai 1997; Nagoya-shi hakubutsukan 1988.

29. Miyako meisho-zue 都名所図会
('Famous Places of the Capital, Illustrated')

6 chapters in 6 fascicles; 25.7 x 18.2 cm
Author: Akisato Ritō 秋里離島;

illustrator: Takehara Shunchōsai 竹原春朝斎
Date: An'ei 安永 9 (1780)

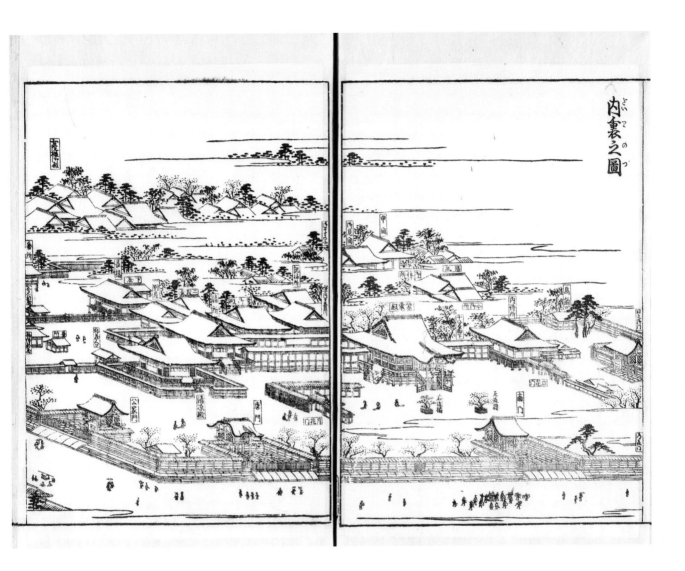

127

The first print of this work dates from An'ei 9 (1780). It was reprinted in Tenmei 天明 6 (1786). On the *daisen* 題簽 or *gedai* 外題 (the slip of paper on the outside of each fascicle bearing the title of the work) of the copy in UCLouvain *saikoku* 再刻 or 'reissue' is written. The colophon does indeed state that it is a new and enlarged edition of the year Tenmei 7 (1787). The book was clearly a great success.

This is the first topographical account to include the generic term '*Meisho-zue*' ('illustrated description of a famous place') in its title. The first two chapters are devoted to Heian-jō 平安城, the old centre of Kyoto. The third chapter is about the eastern part of the city, the fourth about the western part, the fifth about the south, and the sixth about the northern part of the city. A large proportion of the descriptions is devoted to Buddhist temples and Shintō shrines, not only famous institutions but also small chapels and hermitages, all written in simple language. That this did not turn out to be merely a touristic account is thanks to the occasional poems (*waka* and *haiku*) interspersed throughout the text. The *waka* are often classical, but the *haiku* are composed by contemporary poets and significantly enhance the text's vivacity.

Year of birth and death of the author are unknown, but based on indirect information we may assume that Akisato Ritō published the *Miyako meisho-zue* when he was about 45 years old. This was the first in a whole series of excellent illustrated topographical accounts he published in the same style. He published *Kisoji meisho-zue* 木曾路名所図会 - a topographical account of the mountainous Kiso region - in 1802, and since he would have been close to

▲ The imperial palace (fascicle I, pp. 6b-7a).

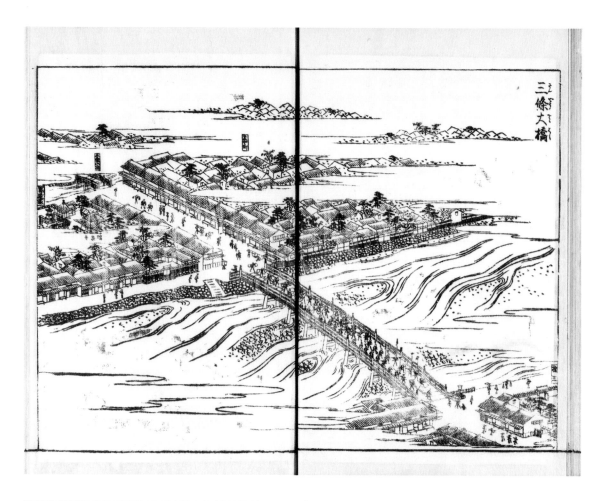

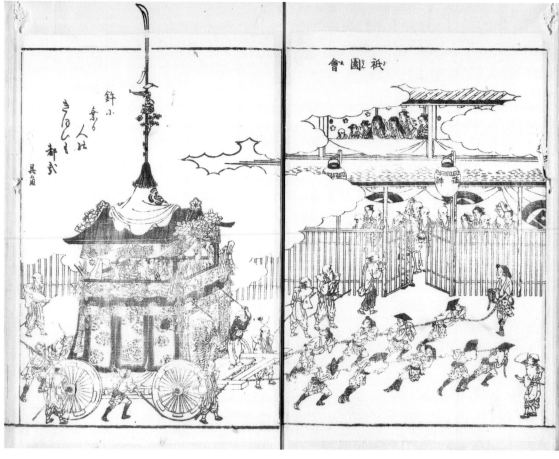

▲ The big bridge over the Kamo-river at the street Sanjō (fascicle I, pp. 31b-32a).

▲ The folk festival Gion 祇園祭 with its parade floats (fascicle II, pp. 6b-7a).

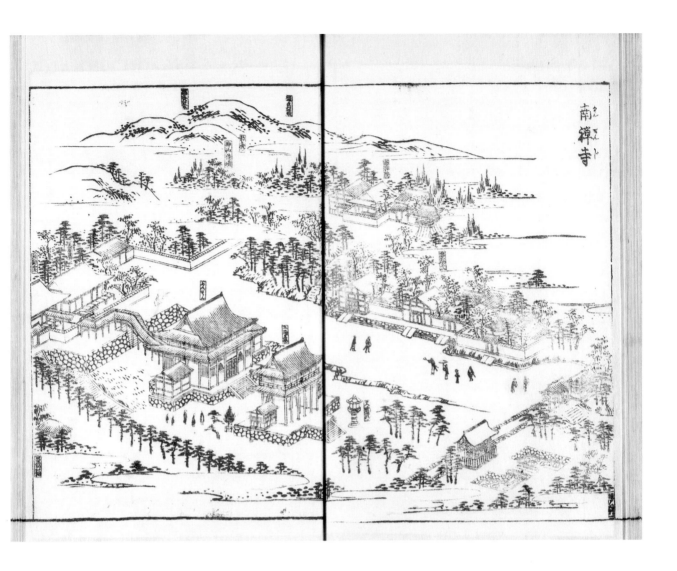

70 years old at the time, and he would have travelled the mountain paths and steep roads he described in the book himself, he must have enjoyed good health until an advanced age.

The real name of illustrator Takehara Shunchō-sai (?-1801) was Nobushige 信繁. He was a master of *ukiyo-e* prints and was active in Osaka. He also provided the illustrations for a few other *Meisho-zue* written by Ritō. They are the duo that largely defined and shaped the style of this genre. Shunchōsai draws the panoramic sights realistically and from a bird's-eye view. His illustrations are not only very refined and aesthetically attractive, but they also contain a wealth of information.

The preface states: "The great panoramas have been drawn with particular attention to detail. The small shrines and chapels have not been depicted smaller than they are. All illustrations feature human figures. If they have been drawn very small, it is because the surrounding panorama is vast. If the human figures are not small, it means they are represented in confined surroundings."

▲ The Zen temple Nanzenji 南禅寺 (fascicle III, pp. 51b-52a).

30. (Shinpan chizu) Nihon kaisan koriku-zu tsuki goki shichidō ekiro 新板地図日本海山湖陸図附五幾七道駅路
('Map of the Japanese Archipelago, Its Seas, Mountains, Tides and Land, including also the Five Home Provinces, the Seven Circuits, and Postal Roads (new edition)')

1 map, woodcut, hand-coloured; 106 x 124.6 cm
Illustrator: Ishikawa Tomonobu (Ryūsen) 石川流宣
Date: Genroku 元禄 7 (1694)

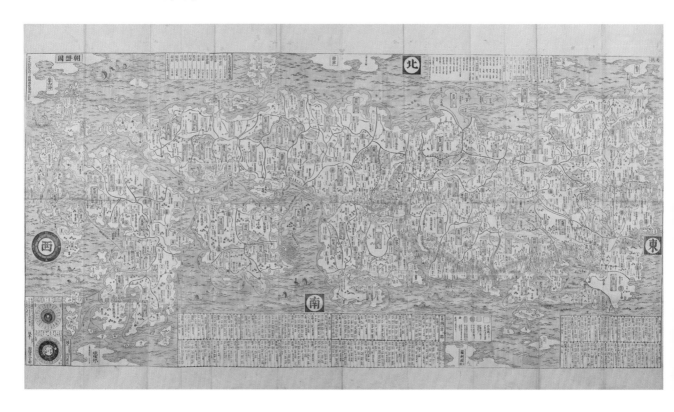

Ishikawa Tomonobu (alias Ryūsen, ?-?) was an *ukiyo-e* artist active in the late seventeenth and early eighteenth centuries. It is unclear who his teacher was, but his style seems to be close to that of Hishikawa Moronobu 菱川師宣 or Sugimura Jihee 杉村治兵衛. He was one of the prominent painters (*eshi* 絵師) of the Genroku era. In addition, he was active as draughtsman of woodblock-printed maps, which are eponymously known as Ryūsen maps (*Ryūsen-zu* 流宣図). Especially his maps of the Japanese archipelago, combining artistic execution with an abundance of practical information, enjoyed great popularity during the better part of the eighteenth century, right until the publication of the map by Nagakubo Sekisui 長久保赤水 in 1778.

In 1687, he drew the *Honchō zukan kōmoku* 本朝図鑑綱目, published by Sagamiya Tahē 相模屋太兵衛 in Edo, a small-scale map, reprinted from the same blocks two years later. He subsequently redesigned it into a large-scale map in 1691 (82 × 170 cm), under the title *Nihon kaisan chōriku-zu*. The UCLouvain copy belongs to the 1694 edition. As the title indicates, it was a new version, printed from newly carved blocks, probably the second edition of what eventually would turn out to be a series of about thirty in all, over a period of ninety years. Many copies were hand coloured. New versions were often given new titles, an alteration that required little adjustment, since these titles were not printed on the map itself but only on the *daisen* 題簽 or *gedai* 外題 (the slip of paper on the cover). The 1694 edition, which appears to be uncommon, has the binomen *koriku* 湖陸 in its title, whereas the 1691 edition had the binomen *chōriku* 潮陸. The 1703 version was published under the title *Nihon sankai-zu dōdaizen* 日本山海図道大全, though it was actually a reprint from the same blocks but with a new title. Like the 1691 edition, the UCLouvain copy has two small volvelles in the lower left corner, showing (above) the length of day and night in the 24 solar terms of the year and (below) the waxing and waning of the moon, as well as ebb and flow of the tide.

The 1691 map of Ishikawa served as the model for a map of Japan published by the Dutch Orientalist and cartographer Adrien Reland (1676-1718) in several editions, the first of which was published as *Le Japon divisé en soissante et six provinces*, in Amsterdam in 1715, not as a separate map but included in *Recueil des voyages au Nord*, vol. 3, édité par Jean Frederic Bernard, Amsterdam, 1716.[1]

Literature: Beans 1951-1955-1958-1963; Miyoshi 2004.

130

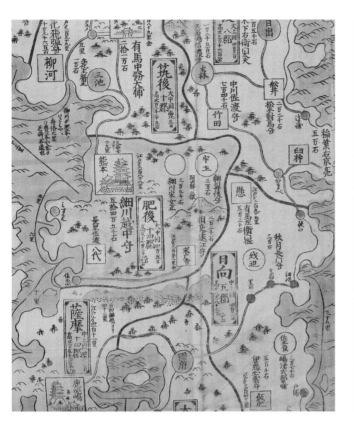

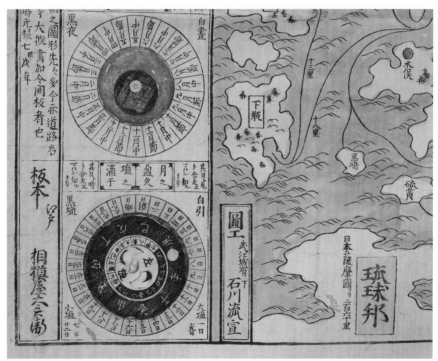

▲ Section of the map featuring major fiefs in Kyūshū.

▲ Section of the map featuring among others the Sanctuary of Nikkō in the province of Shimotsuke.

▲ Volvelles.

31. Washū Yoshinoyama shōkei-zu 和州芳野山勝景図
('Panoramas of Mount Yoshino in the Province Yamato')

1 *leporello*: 30.3 x 16.8 cm
Author: Kaibara Ekiken 貝原益軒
Date: preface dated Shōtoku 正徳 3 (1713)

132

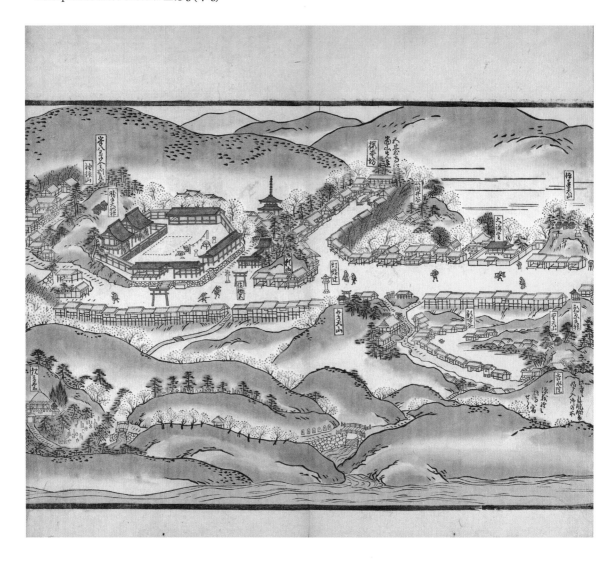

This item is a horizontal scroll which was mounted as a *leporello* book. It depicts, in continuous images, Mount Yoshino in spring when the cherry blossoms are in bloom. This mountain was famed for the beauty of its cherry blossoms. Even now it attracts great numbers of eager visitors each year in the blossoming period. The text is by Kaibara Ek(i)ken (Atsunobu 篤信, 1630-1714). He is known mainly as a Confucianist, although he was in fact a versatile scholar who published about a broad scope of subjects (see also no. 41, *Yamato honzō*). He signs his preface with the expression "text by Kaibara Atsunobu, at the age of 84" 八十四翁貝原篤信記.

A sheet glued in the back of the book has the following information: This book is the first in a series of five. The title of the series is: *Fusō meishō-zu* 扶桑名勝図 (Famous Places in Japan). The collection of rare Japanese books in the Royal Museums of Art and History, Brussels, includes a copy of another title in the series, titled *Itsukushima Sokei* 厳島麁景 (A General View of Itsukushima), likewise prefaced by Kaibara Ekiken (Atsunobu) and dated the second year of Genroku 元禄 (1689). However, the UCLouvain copy has no colophon.

The binding of *Washū Yoshinoyama shōkei-zu* is of a later date (*sōtei-naoshi* 装丁直し). The work itself is a good, though later impression from the original woodblocks. In the text section the line of the framing around the text is interrupted on a certain page, which tells us that the woodblock was repaired by inserting a new piece of wood (*umeki* 埋め木) here. The colophon reads:

京市六角通御幸町西入町
柳枝軒茨城多左衛門蔵版

Published by Ibaragi Tazaemon, Ryūshiken, residing in Kyoto, Rokkaku-dōri, Miyuki-chō nishi iru machi.

▲ The Shintō shrine of Katte daimyōjin 勝手大明神
(Katte jinja), 4th fold.

32. Edo meisho-zue 江戸名所図会
('Famous Places in Edo, Illustrated')

Alternative title: *Tōto meisho-zue* 東都名所図会
7 chapters in 20 fascicles; 25.8 x 18 cm
Author: Saitō Chōshū 斎藤長秋

Illustrator: Hasegawa Settan 長谷川雪旦
Date: preface dated Bunsei 文政 12 (1829), printed in
Tenpō 天保 5-7 (1834-1836)

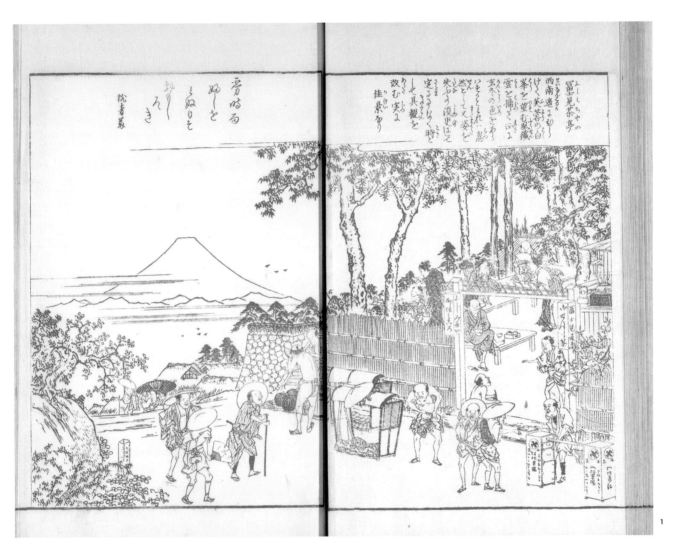

This particular copy is an original edition. The text is written by Saitō Chōshū (Yukio, 1737-1799), his son Agatamaro 縣麻呂 (Yukitaka), and Agatamaro's son Gesshin 斎藤月岑 (Yukishige 幸成). The illustrations are by Hasegawa Settan (1778-1843). This work includes prefaces by Matsudaira Kanzan 松平冠山 (1767-1833), Kameda Chōshi 亀田長梓 (1778-1853), Kataoka Kankō 片岡寛光 (?-1838), and one by Saitō himself dated Kansei 12 (1800).

Edo was originally a village, later chosen by Tokugawa Ieyasu 徳川家康 (1543-1616) to become the seat of his military government. In less than a hundred years' time, the place grew into a city of about one million inhabitants. At first, it resembled a kind of colony, where immigrants from all over Japan gathered to try their luck, and where thousands of male retainers resided together with their feudal lords every two years. A more conventional culture gradually developed, however, and people started to consider Edo their home. This book was compiled by such 'Edokko' 江戸っ子, as a typical inhabitant of Edo is called. It is an illustrated topographical account of Edo and its surroundings, which actually include large parts of the neighbouring Musashi Province. The description starts with the Castle of Edo and goes on to describe in clockwise fashion a long series of districts, quarters, and places of scenic interest. According to the author, he divided the city and its surrounding area into seven sections based on the seven stars of Ursa Major. The descriptions are detailed and based on personal observation. Settan has accurately portrayed the beautiful panoramas and scenic spots. This work is recognized as a masterpiece of its genre.

One scenic spot is a tea house with a view of Mount Fuji (ill. 1, fascicle VII, pp. 48b-49a). The ac-

133

▲ A tea house with a view of Mount Fuji.

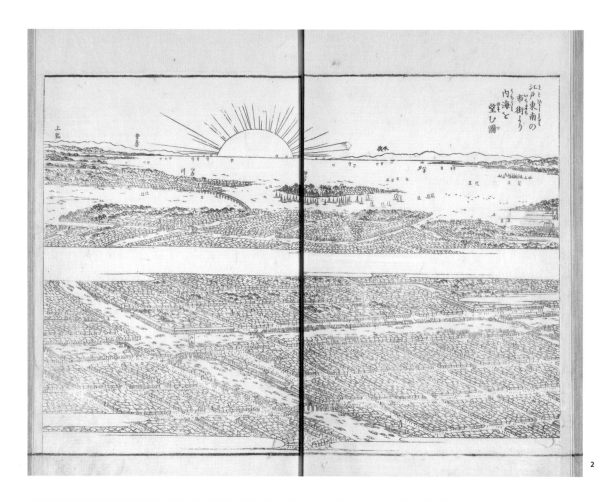

江戸東南の市街より内海を望む図

2

134

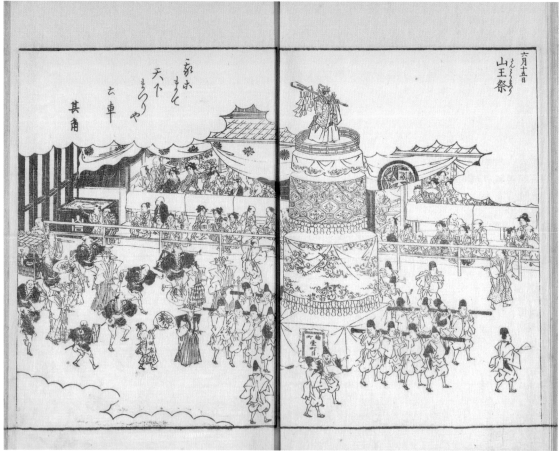

六月十五日
山王祭

家も天下まつりや其角
其角
之車

3

▲ Panoramic view of the South Easterly section of the city of
Edo, with in the background the sun rising over the bay (fascicle I,
pp. 23b-24a).

▲ The popular festival of Sannō 山王, a Shintō deity (fascicle II,
pp. 18b-19a).

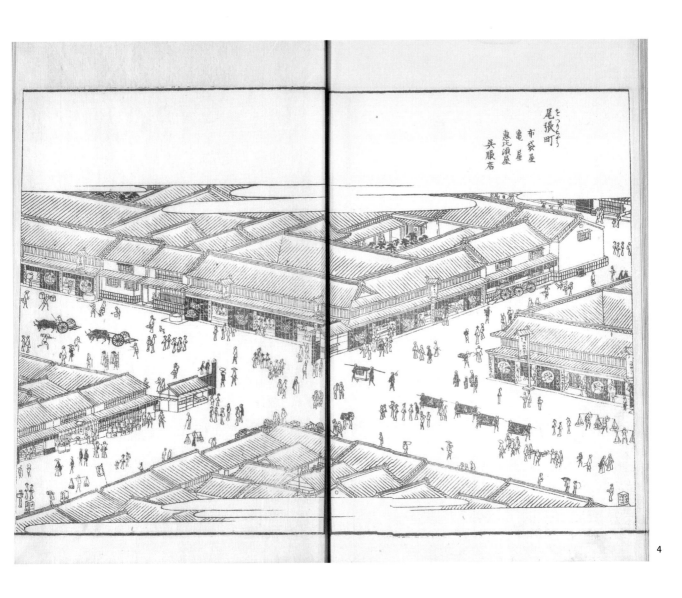

尾張町
市袋屋
亀屋
恵比須屋
呉服店

companying description above it includes, not with-out irony, a famous haiku by the poet Matsuo Bashō 松尾芭蕉 (1644-1694) (here under his pseudonym Tōsei 桃青):

"In the south-westerly direction, there is a vast panorama with a view on the white peak of Mount Fuji. When the wind blows away the light clouds, the wintry sight (of the mountain) sud-denly appears, only to disappear (as) suddenly. Ephemeral and ever-changing, and a different view each time! It is truly a wonderful panorama.

Through fog and rain	霧時雨
No Mount Fuji to be seen,	ふじをミぬ日そ
Now that's a true sight!	おもしろき
(Old Tōsei)"	桃青翁

▲ The shopping district Owari-chō 尾張町 (fascicle II, pp. 43b-44a).

33. Kinjō Tennō go-sokui-rei emaki 今上天皇御即位禮絵巻
('Illustrated Handscroll of the Enthronement Ceremony of the Present Emperor')
and

Kinjō Tennō daijōsai emaki 今上天皇大嘗祭絵巻
('Illustrated Handscroll of the Festival of Thanksgiving of the Present Emperor')

Pair of handscrolls in paulownia storage box; colour woodblock print.
Print by Urushibara Sanjirō 漆原三次郎

Text by Ikebe Yoshikata 池辺義象; illustrators: Yoshizaki Hokuryō 吉崎北陵 et al.
Date: Taishō 大正 4 (1915)

136

The first scroll *Kinjō Tennō gosokui-rei emaki* does not mention the author or any printing or publication data. At the end of the second scroll *Kinjō Tennō daijōsai emaki*, there is a notice dated November 10, Taishō 4 (1915), signed by Ikebe Yoshitaka. The colophon proper states the following:

> Revised (*kenkō* 検校) by:
> Commissioner for the Grand Ceremonies (of Enthronement and Thanksgiving) 大禮使事務官: Tada Kōmon 多田好問, noble of the fourth rank A, order of the third rank 勲三等.
> Text and calligraphy (*ekotoba narabi ni sho* 絵詞並書):
> Ikebe Yoshitaka, compiler in the Temporary Compilation Bureau of the Imperial Household Ministry 宮内省臨時編修局編修, noble of the sixth rank B.
> Painting (*tansei* 丹青):
> Yoshizaki Hokuryō 吉崎北陵, Kobori Tomone 小堀鞆音, Murata Tanryō 村田丹陵, Sekiyasu Koresuke 関安之輔, assistants, nobles of the fifth rank B.

This work is published by the Association for the Commemoration of the Imperial Enthronement 御即位記念協会. The head of this committee is Viscount Kiyo'oka Nagakoto 子爵 清岡長言 (1875-1963), a paramount specialist of court ceremonies and rituals. His delegate (*shuji* 主事) is Kimura Tadashi 木村正. The woodblock engraver (*chōkokusha* 彫刻者) is Katayama Kiseki 片山奇石; the printers (*insatsusha* 印刷者) are Urushibara Sanjirō and Urushibara Eijirō 漆原栄次郎; assistant (*hojo* 補助) is Takeda Katsunosuke 武田勝之助, and the mounter (*daikyōshi* 大経師) is Katō Tōju 加藤藤樹.

The enthronement is the most important ceremony at the imperial court. It is to be enacted meticulously and by following strict rules. Contrary to popular belief that they go back to times immemorial, these rules were actually often adapted and modified. The *Jōgan gishiki* 貞観儀式 (Procedures for Ceremonies of the Jōgan Period, compiled second half of the ninth century) provided a guiding framework, which, along with the tenth-century *Engi-shiki* 延喜式, codified the rituals of the imperial family and its attendant clans. This ceremony rather resembled the New Year Ceremony that used to be performed at the Chinese court during the Tang Dynasty (618-907). When Emperor Meiji succeeded to the throne in 1868, the ceremony was fundamentally changed and reshaped as a Shintō ritual. The garments were also adapted to reflect this change. The emperor no longer wore the *konben* 袞冕, a robe and cap in a Chinese-looking style, but the typically Japanese robe *sokutai* 束帯 and cap of the type *ryūei* 立纓. According to the ordinance of 1889, the ceremony of enthronement was supposed to be held in Kyoto, and according to the ordinance of 1909 (*tōkyokurei* 登極令), the ceremony of enthronement and that of thanksgiving had to be held in the same period, in the autumn or spring following the end of the mourning period for the previous emperor. The most important aspect of this ceremony is the ritual in the throne room (*shishinden no gi* 紫宸殿の儀). In this pair of scrolls, the most important moments in the ritual programme are illustrated with careful attention to detail.

Ikebe Yoshitaka (1861-1923) was a specialist in Japanese literature and history of law. He was the son of a samurai who served the feudal lord of the fiefdom of Kumamoto. His *gō* 号 (sobriquet) was *Tōen* 藤園. After the Seinan Rebellion (1877), he began his studies at the Jingū kyōin 神宮教院, a school of Shintō theology. In 1882, he enrolled in the Department of Classical Japanese Studies at the University of Tokyo. Starting in 1886, he successively became librarian at the Imperial Library, teacher at the First Higher Middle School, the Higher Pedagogical Institute for Girls, and member of the Historiographical Commission. From 1898 to 1901, he studied in France. After returning to Japan, he became lector at the Imperial University of Kyoto in 1903; in 1914, compiler in the Temporary Compilation Bureau of the Imperial Household Ministry; in 1917, a member of the Imperial Bureau for Poetry; and in 1918, an official in the Temporary Imperial Bureau for History. Ikebe is one of the earliest specialists in modern academia of legal and institutional history 法制史 in Japan. This may also explain why Wada Mankichi classified this illustrated scroll under the donation's division of Law and Institutions.

Copies of our pair of scrolls can also be found in the British Museum, Kōgakukan daigaku Shintō hakubutsukan 皇學館大学神道博物館 in Ise, and

the National Museum of Japanese History 国立歴史民俗博物館 in Sakura.

The pair of scrolls is a simplified pictorial survey of the salient moments in the various ceremonies, probably produced to be distributed as a souvenir among the important guests present at the ceremonies, or to be offered to important persons or prestigious institutions.

The first scroll *Kinjō Tennō gosokui-rei emaki* begins with three prefatory mottos (*daiji* 題字) in four-character lines by high officials in the imperial household. Each of the mottos (*daiji*) echoes a direct or indirect cosmological reference, meant as covert references to the emperor. They are redolent of the Confucian-inspired Classical Chinese texts extolling the greatness of the emperor, whose solemnity transcends space and time.

Literature: Murakami 1980, p. 148, s.v. "sokui no rei"; pp. 153-154, s.v. "daijōsai"; *Nihon jinmei daijiten* 1977, vol.1, p. 205, s.v. "Ikebe Yoshikata"; Tokoro 2018.

▲ *Kinjō Tennō gosokui-rei emaki* scroll: cabinet members, court officials, magistrates and guests lined up in front of the main hall of the palace.

▲ *Kinjō Tennō gosokui-rei emaki* scroll: the emperor proclaims his accession to the throne and receives the congratulations of those present. The emperor and empress are seated under the canopies (*takamikura* and *michōdai*) half visible behind the portico.

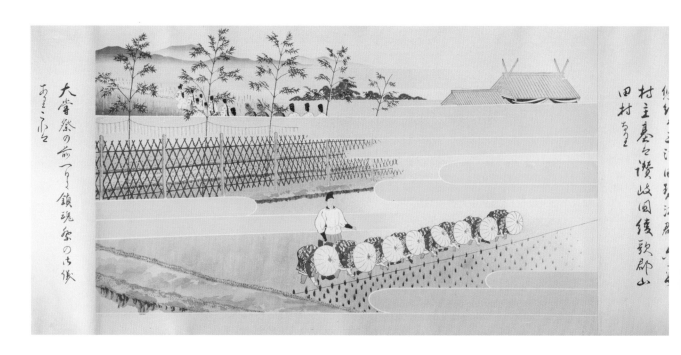

▲ *Kinjō Tennō daijōsai emaki* scroll: ceremonial rice planting.

▲ *Kinjō Tennō daijōsai emaki* scroll: performance of court dance and music.

34. Seiyō senpu 西洋銭譜
('Catalogue of Western Coins')

1 fascicle; 26 x 17.8 cm
Author: Kutsuki Masatsuna 朽木昌綱

Editor: Shōen Shujin 松園主人
Date: printed in Tenmei 天明 7 (1787)

139

Somewhat naively the Japanese National Committee put this numismatic study in the "economy" division. This book is a kind of *catalogue raisonné* for the collection of Western coins of Kutsuki Masatsuna (1750-1802), eighth generation of the Kutsuki clan, who ruled the fief Fukuchiyama 福知山 in Tanba 丹波 as feudal lord. Masatsuna, whose sobriquets (*gō*) included Ryūkyō 竜橋 was a man of learning. He was versed in Chinese and Japanese studies and was an excellent *waka*-poet. In addition, he was a prominent "Hollandologist" (*rangakusha* 蘭学者), who had studied under the famous Hollandologist Maeno Ryōtaku 前野良沢. He was also active as patron and sponsored the studies of the famous Hollandologist Ōtsuki Gentaku 大槻玄沢 (1757-1827), when

the latter was staying in Nagasaki to master Dutch studies. Kutsuki corresponded in Dutch with Isaac Titsingh (1745-1812), head of the Dutch factory on Deshima from 1781 to 1783. This correspondence in Dutch is now kept in the library of the University of Kyoto, where it is registered as 'Titsingh Isaak "Zes en veertig eigen handige brieven. 1785-1791"'. (Forty-six personally handwritten letters. 1785-1791).

Masatsuna was an avid collector of coins and published multiple numismatic essays, one of which is this *Seiyō senpu*. He even earned the nickname 'king of numismatics' 古銭家の王者. He later gave his collection of coins to Titsingh, who had helped him in building it. What happened to the collection after Titsingh's death is unclear, but what we do

▲ Image of a coin of Augustus the Strong.

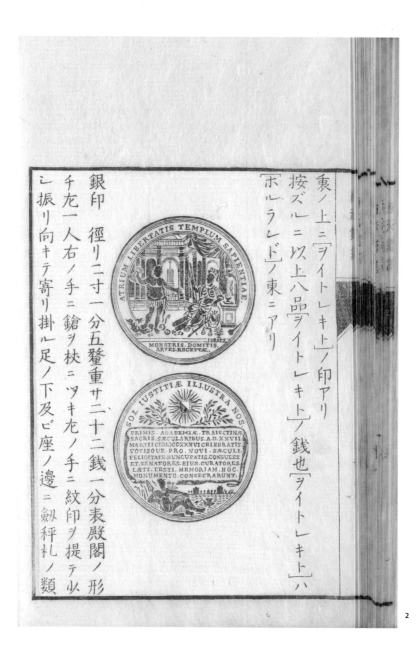

know is that in 1881, a German silk trader, Rudolph Frentzel, offered Masatsuna's collection, in total circa 9,000 coins, for sale to the British Museum. Before this institution had taken a decision, however, the German merchant sold the entire collection to Howel Wills (1854-1901), who subsequently sold 2,524 Japanese and other occidental coins to the British Museum in 1884. He donated the rest of his collection to the Indian Institute in Oxford. There are, however, no Western coins in this collection, so it is still unclear what happened to the coins featured in *Seiyō senpu*. Titsingh had no heirs. The story of his inheritance and its distribution is a complex and intriguing tale.

Ill. 1: image of a coin of Augustus the Strong (p. 14a). The obverse reads 'AUG USTI (sic) AUGUSTAM VIRTUTEM NAMA (sic) CORONAT.' The reverse states: 'A.M. 1666 AETA NAT X APR IP E', and in the centre of the coin, the motto "Alles mit Bedacht" (Everything

with prudence) is written. Wolfgang Leschhorn, *Braunschweigische Münzen und Medaillen: 1000 Jahre Münzkunst und Geldgeschichte in Stadt und Land Braunschweig*, Braunschweig: Appelhans, 2010, p. 85, has the transcription virtutem fama coronat Augusti Augustam ('Fame crowns Augustus' virtue').

Ill. 2: silver commemorative medal of the province of Utrecht (p. 28b). According to the text, the United Provinces draw up a closing balance of the budget of all provinces every one hundred years. As proof that the accounts have been closed, each official receives such a medal. There are gold, silver and copper versions, according to the Dutch informant of the *daimyō*.

Literature: Lequin 2003; Wang 2010; Lequin 2002; Lequin 1990; Lequin 1992a; Lequin 1992b; Yamazaki 2000, p. 498; Kokushi daijiten henshū iinkai 1979-1993, vol. 4, pp. 817-818 s.v. "Kutsuki Masatsuna"; vol. 12, p. 92, s.v. "Fukuchiyama-han".

▲ Silver commemorative medal of the province of Utrecht.

35. Setsuyō ryōri taizen 節用料理大全
('Summa of the Culinary Art of our School')

Alternative titles: *Tōryū setsuyō ryōri taizen* 当流節用料理
大全 / *Chūya banpō* 昼夜万宝 /
Title prefix (*tsunogaki* 角書き): Tōryū kaisei 当流改正
Revised by our school.

Tōryū setsuyō ryōri taizen 当流節用料理大全
5 chapters in 1 fascicle; 25.5 x 18.5 cm
Author: Takashima 高島
Date: Shōtoku 正徳 4 (1714)

The word "*setsuyō*" in the title suggests that this is a work of popular reference. The book is made up of five chapters (*maki*) bundled into one fascicle. The author is someone named Takashima, a member of the Shijō 四条 clan. Nothing else is known about him/her. The publishers are Sudō Gonbē 須藤権兵衛 of Edo and Yorozuya Hikotarō 万屋彦太郎 of Osaka. The name of Yorozuya Hikotarō's shop (*yagō* 屋号) was Shōjudō 松寿堂 (Hall of Pine Longevity), and he was the owner of the woodblocks. The book includes twenty-six illustrations in the text itself and another thirty-six in the introduction. The book consists of eighty-five folios. The pagination, however, continues until page 107, because the numbering skips in several places. This work contains recipes for banquets, for the menu of each of the twelve months, methods of preparation, as well as information on the toxicity of certain ingredients.

It is one of the earliest cookbooks that manages masterfully to include illustrations in its text. This book is a compilation of data the author has found in cookbooks of the Shijō school, supplemented with information from other cookbooks and herbals. According to the findings of Shinosaki Kazuko 篠崎和子, this work is based in large part on some five earlier works. There are at least three editions in existence, the first being from the year 1700. The National Diet Library owns one copy of that edition. Most of the remaining copies date from Shōtoku 4 (1714). Of this edition, there is also a reprint from the same year with an identical colophon (*kanki* 刊記). Finally, there is a reprint by Kikuya Shichirobē 菊屋七良兵衛, who bought the woodblocks from the original publisher.

With this book, the author attempted to provide a kind of reference work about the art of cooking in

▲ The *mikaeshi* 見返し (reverse of the cover) and the
frontispiece of *Setsuyō ryōri taizen*.

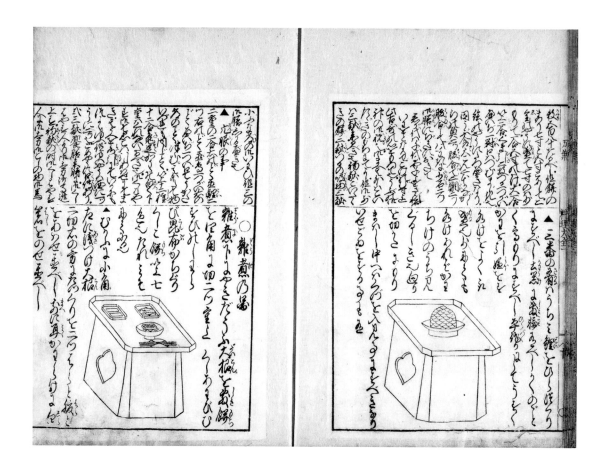

142

the *Shijō* style. It was meant as a sort of household encyclopaedia or dictionary. Numerous Japanese collections include examples of passages copied from this book. It was not just intended for professional chefs but also for the higher classes in general. Most of the preserved copies are later prints of the same woodblocks (*atozuri* 後刷り).

The existence of this kind of book confirms that already during the Edo period (1600-1868), there were various niche markets for printed books such as cookbooks, books on flower arrangement, medical books, etc.

The illustration on the frontispiece (p. 141) depicts a wedding party. Japanese mythology (recorded in the Kojiki 古事記) describes how Watatsumi's 綿津見 daughter Otohime 乙姫 married the human

Ho'ori 火折尊. After Ho'ori had lost his brother Hoderi's 火照命 fishhook, he went searching for it at the bottom of the sea. There he met and married the dragon goddess Otohime and stayed there to live in the sea god's underwater palace, Ryūgū-jō 竜宮城. After three years however, Ho'ori started feeling homesick and wanted to return to the land, which he eventually did. In the illustration we see the groom Ho'ori sitting on a dais, at his right-hand side his bride, and obliquely to her right-hand side her father the dragon king. The platform where the ceremony is taking place is surrounded by the waters of the sea. Not surprisingly, the fare consists of fish.

Literature: *Kinsei joshi kyōiku shisō* 1980; Shinozaki 1968a; Shinozaki 1968b; Shinozaki 1969; Shinozaki 1971; Yoshii 1978-1981, vol. 3.

▲ Instruction on how to prepare *ozôni*, a dish associated with the Japanese New Year (fascicle I, chapter 1, pp. 10b-11a).

36. Genroku nananen itaru Meiji ninenreki [*Ise-goyomi*]
元禄七年至明治二年暦 [伊勢暦]
('Popular Calendars of Ise from the Year of Genroku 7 until Meiji 2')

123 *leporello* books; dimensions varying between 25 x 8 cm
and 25 x 9.3 cm
Edited at Ise Yamada

Date: printed between Genroku 元禄 7 and Meiji 明治 2
(1694-1869)

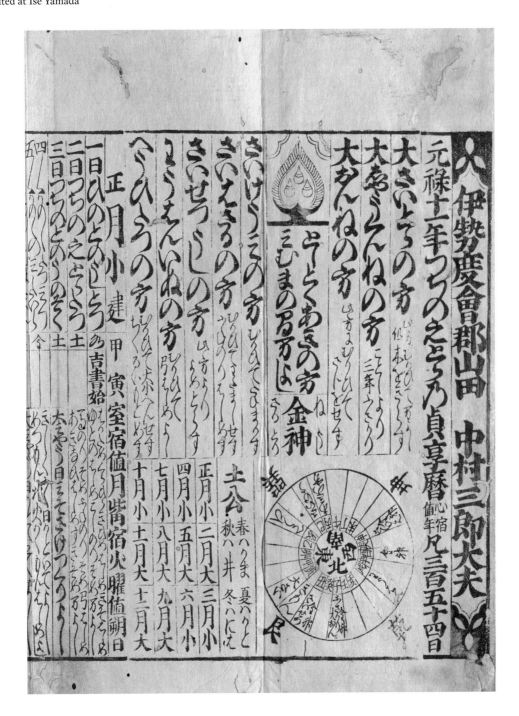

In China, one of the most important tasks of the emperor was to draw up the calendar. He ruled time, and he received his legitimacy from it. That is why it was one of his most sacred duties to publish an accurate calendar each year. The Japanese emperor, on the other hand, derived his legitimacy from the myths about his being a descendant of the gods and was no ruler of time. The regulation of the calendar

was therefore less vital to him. Just like China, however, Japan was an agrarian state, which meant it needed a calendar that predicted the turn of the seasons. It was an important duty for the government, which entrusted the task to a few noble families who turned it into a hereditary monopoly.

Similar to China, calendars in Japan belong to the oldest printed works. The oldest mention of a

▲ The calendar of the year Genroku 11 (1698) (first and second fold).

(xylographic) printed calendar in Japan is dated Kenkyū 建久 9 (1198). The oldest existing calendar in the syllabic writing system of *hiragana* dates back to Genkō 元弘 2 (1332), while the oldest calendar in the syllabic writing system of *katakana* is from the year Shitoku 至徳 4 (1387).

The calendars known as *Guchūreki* 具注歴, written in Classical Chinese, also already existed in the Nara (710-794) and Heian periods (794-1185). They contained detailed explanations for the signs of the zodiac, auspicious and unlucky days, celestial bodies, and so on. Manuscript copies of this kind of calendar from the Heian period have been preserved. The oldest preserved printed *guchūreki* dates back to the Kamakura period (1185-1333).

Calendars in Japanese syllabic writing (*hiragana* and *katakana*), whether they are handwritten or printed, differ little in form and appearance across the centuries. The format has been more or less fixed since the Kamakura period. In medieval times, calendars were published in *hiragana* as well as *katakana*. From the Keichō period (1596-1615) onward, however, they are mostly only *hiragana*-calendars. Scarce are the woodblock-printed calendars dating from the Keichō until the Genroku period (1688-1704) that have been preserved. This dearth must presumably be owing to the boom of the typographical (*kokatsuji-ban*) technique. Whether or not these typographical calendars completely supplanted the xylographic ones for a while – and if so, how long - is not clear. In any case, the xylographic print reclaims its monopoly from the second half of the Kan'ei period (1624-1630) onward. In the early Edo period (1600-1868), many calendars were published by publishers in Edo, Kyoto, and Osaka, and from the second half of the period onward, sundry varieties and formats of calendars emerged in various places across the country. It was however the priests (*onshi/oshi* 御師) of the Shintō sanctuary in Ise who are truly to thank for the large-scale spread of printed calendars.

Four calendrical reforms were enacted during the Edo period. Any reform of the calendar was announced in the heading (*kantō* 巻頭) of the calendar for the following year. Calendars were always printed in the preceding year. This is always mentioned at the end of the calendar. As a result, when the era name (*nengō* 年号) changed, it was not yet mentioned in the calendar of the era's first year. The previous era name is still used in the calendar of the first year of a new era (*kaigen* 改元).

The format of the *Ise-goyomi* remains practically unchanged. It is cut on one woodblock: from the year's beginning to the fifth month on the front side, and from the sixth until the twelfth month on the back side. The frame containing the first five months is often of a different format than the one framing the other months.

The calendar was printed on sheets of *minogami* paper, which were glued together horizontally. Thus glued together, the pages then formed a long horizontal strip which was then folded as a *leporello* book (*orihon* 折本). In most cases, it was wrapped in an indigo, blue, or black cover, although there are also copies without any cover. The vertical paper slip on which the title is written (*gedaigami* 外題紙 or *daisen* 題簽) is yellow, pale red, or white. The title is stereotypical, for example: "Calendar for Hōreki 14, (Year of the) Monkey".

No one contributed more to the popularity of the calendar than the *onshi* of the Shintō sanctuary of Ise. They welcomed the pilgrims, provided them with calendars and amulets, guided them through the sanctuary, and arranged lodgings for them. On occasion, one and the same *onshi* distributed both a large-sized and a small-sized type of calendar, but usually one person only published one calendar, commonly over a period of multiple years.

The *onshi* also travelled through the entire country to distribute the amulets of Ise among the devotees, and as a bonus they would give an Ise calendar as a souvenir. This is why this type of calendar is called Ise-goyomi (Ise calendar). It is the precursor of the current Jingūreki 神宮暦 (Calendar of the Sanctuary), sold to pilgrims and visitors in the Ise Sanctuary to this day.

The copy in the UCLouvain collection is valuable because of its completeness. Many copies of Ise-calendars can be found, but sets as complete as this one are rather rare.

Literature: Kawase 1943, pp. 1752-1766; Nakamura and Itō 2006, p. 309.

37. Heitengi zukai 平天儀図解
('Explanation of Heitengi with Illustrations')

Alternate title: *Tenmon shōkei* 天文捷経 / *Heitengi zukai* 平天儀図解
1 fascicle; 26.2 x 18 cm

Author: Iwahashi Yoshitaka 岩橋嘉孝
Date: Kyōwa 享和 2 (1802)

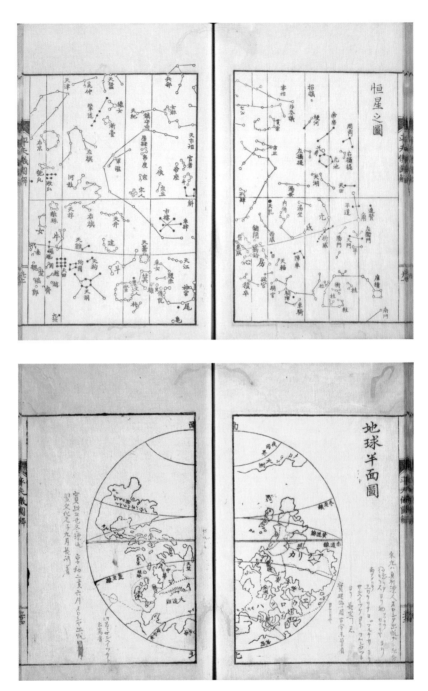

The word *heitengi* 平天儀 originally refers to a celestial map. The spherical celestial sky is projected onto a flat surface. Around the year 1800, Iwahashi Yoshitaka – also known as Iwahashi Zenbē 岩橋善兵衛 (1756-1811, sobriquet (*gō* 号) Kōryūdō 耕玗堂), a craftsman from a village in the south of Izumi Province (present-day Osaka) – came up with a device to represent the spherical sky in a somewhat three-dimensional way. Five concentric discs were placed on top of each other and fixed at their centre to a

common axis. The discs could rotate freely in both directions. The smallest disc represented the earth, then came the disc with sun, moon, and ecliptic, followed by the disc representing the sky with the twenty-eight constellations (*shuku*, Chinese: *xiu* 宿). Next came the disc with the twelve directions and, finally, the disc with the twelve double-hours of the day. From these discs, one could easily read the orbit of the sun and the position of the moon, the tides, and so on, for every region on the earth. In his work

▲ Firmament with the fixed stars (pp. 91b–92a).

▲ One of two hemispheres of the globe, apparently on paper of different quality and colour than the rest of the book, suggesting these leaves were inserted later (pp. 33b–34a).

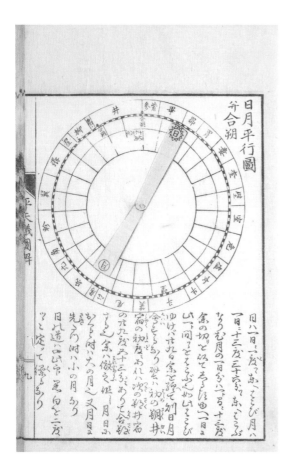

146

Heitengi zukai, Iwahashi explained the workings of this simple yet ingenious system and expanded on the astronomical knowledge he had gained during the course of his research.

Moreover, this book was written in *kanamajiri* 仮名交じり, that is, easy-to-understand vernacular Japanese. It was meant as an educational book on astronomy, as is indicated by its *tsunogaki* 角書き (title prefix): 'a shortcut to astronomy'.

Among other things, this book includes a preface with an explanation on the use of the concentric discs, a map with the earth at its centre (*chishin no zu* 地心の図), a map of the geocentric system of the Danish astronomer Tycho Brahe (1546-1601) (*sōten no zu* 宗天の図), a map of the positions of the moon, and more.

Iwahashi Zenbē is mostly known for his construction of a telescope, called *kitenkyō* 窺天鏡. It was made of wood. According to Suzuki Kazuyoshi 鈴木一義, there were quite a number of these wooden telescopes in the late Edo period. Even more remarkable is the telescope built by Kunitomo Ikkansai 国友一貫斎 (1778-1840). This man, who was employed by the shogunal government as a gunsmith (*teppō kaji* 鉄砲鍛冶), is credited with the construction of the first Japanese reflecting telescope (*hansha bōenkyō* 反射望遠鏡). It was built in 1834 and is presently preserved in the Municipal Museum of Ueda City 上田市立博物館.

On this map, a later hand marked in vermillion (shu 朱) a route while adding some other data, all of which seem to be linked to the voyage of Daikokuya Kōdaiyu 大黒屋光太夫 (1751-1828), though the man is not called by name here. He was a Japanese castaway who spent nine years in Russia. His drifting ship made landfall at Amchitka, in the Aleutian Islands. With his surviving crew he managed to travel all the way to Saint Petersburg and was given an audience by Catherine the Great. He requested to be sent back to Japan and his wish was granted by Catherine, who ordered he be escorted back to Japan by Adam Laxman (1766-1806?). In the end, only three of the original crew made it back to Japan, one of them dying soon after landing. Kōdaiyu and his only surviving companion Isokichi 磯吉 were sent to Edo. Of the original crew, two had converted to Christianity and stayed in Irkutsk, and eleven others had died. After his return to Japan, he came under the suspicion of the shogunal government as a possible spy, as would have happened to any returnee in those days. Kōdaiyu had to spend the rest of his life in Edo, where surveillance of his movements and contacts by the authorities was much easier. However, he was not treated as a prisoner and had relative freedom of movement in Edo, where he could mingle with *rangaku* (Dutch learning) scholars.

Literature: *Kokushi daijiten* 1979-1993, vol. 1, p. 865; vol. 12, p. 470.

▲ The orbits of the sun and moon and their conjunction (p. 9a).　　▲ The telescope built by Iwahashi Zenbē (p. 98).

Honzōgaku 本草学: The Study of Materia Medica

Honzōgaku is the name for the collection and study of plants, animals, and minerals that can be used as ingredients for medicine, in other words, for pharmacology.

Honzōgaku originated in China. It was already mentioned in the Hanshu 漢書, the annals of the Western Han Dynasty (202 BC – 8 AD). During the Eastern Han Dynasty (25 – 220), the work *Shennong bencao jing* 神農本草経 is said to have been compiled. When Sino-Japanese relations took a more formal turn in the sixth century, knowledge of Chinese materia medica also entered Japan. In order to be useful for the Japanese, it was essential to compare the Chinese and the Japanese names of the plants, herbs, fauna, and minerals and identify which plant, herb, animal, and mineral corresponded with which name. The first book on pharmacology compiled by a Japanese person dates from 918. It is known by the title *Honzō wamyō* 本草和名 (Japanese Terminology of Materia Medica). It includes 1,025 types of useable ingredients, divided into nine categories, and for each product both the Chinese and the Japanese name are given.

During the Edo period (1600-1868) *honzōgaku* developed into its own discipline in new ways. In 1607 the Confucian scholar Hayashi Razan 林羅山 (1583-1657) acquired a copy of the 1596 edition of Li Shizhen's 李時珍 (1518-1593) *Bencao gangmu* 本草綱目 (*Honzō kōmoku*) in Nagasaki, and presented it to the military government (*Bakufu*). From 1638 onward, the *Bakufu* had gardens for medicinal herbs (*yakuen* 薬園) laid out in two places in the city of Edo: one in Shinagawa 品川 and one in Ushigome 牛込. This undertaking marked the beginning of a type of pharmacology based increasingly on observation and experiment. Its sphere of interest also expanded constantly and gradually evolved into natural history (historia naturalis). The Confucian scholar Kaibara Ekiken 貝原益軒 (1630-1714) compiled *Yamato honzō* 大和本草 (Japanese Materia Medica), a book consisting of 16 chapters of text, 2 chapters of appendices, and 1 chapter of illustrations, which includes no less than 1,366 products. This book, printed in 1709, is based largely on field observations. Kaibara did for Japanese pharmacopeia what the German herbalists and the herbalists in the Low Countries, such as Rembert Dodoens (1517-1585), did for European pharmacology. Another Confucian, Inō Jakusui 稲生若水 (1655-1715), compiled *Shobutsu ruisan* 庶物類纂 (A Systematic Classification of All Things [in the natural world]), by which he attempted to create a kind of summa of the materia medica. His pupil Niwa Shōhaku 丹羽正伯 (1691-1756) researched useful plants and products throughout Japan as part of the policy of the eighth *shōgun*, Tokugawa Yoshimune 徳川吉宗 (1684-1751), who wanted to stimulate domestic production. Niwa continued the compilation his master had started and published the resulting amalgamation as *Shobutsu ruisan* (1747), a truly monumental work comprising one thousand chapters (*maki*). The feudal fiefdoms followed the *bakufu's* example and launched similar initiatives to stimulate the production of useful substances through *honzōgaku*.

In the second half of the eighteenth century, *honzōgaku* achieved new heights in Edo and Osaka. In Edo, Hiraga Gennai 平賀源内 (1728-1780) and Tamura Ransui 田村藍水 (1718-1776) organized exhibitions of medicinal and useful products. This marked a huge step forward. They were no longer satisfied with what was written down in books. Instead, they aimed to enlarge their knowledge through direct observation. We may call this trend the first stirrings of a modern scientific approach in Japan. Gennai compiled a catalogue of his exhibitions under the title *Butsurui hinshitsu* 物類品隲 (An Examination into Natural Products), in which he also expanded on the cultivation of Korean ginseng and sugarcane, as well as on methods of sugar production. Gennai was a prodigy and an original thinker, who aimed to realize a synthesis of natural history on the basis of Japanese, Chinese, and Western knowledge (so-called Hollandology). Another of Inō Jakusui's pupils, Ono Ranzan 小野蘭山 (1729-1810), was an eminent hollandologist and author of *Honzō kōmoku keimō* 本草綱目啓蒙 (Commentaries on Materia Medica), a synthesis of the state of the art of Japanese materia medica and natural history at the time.

Still, all these were essentially developments of a science based on the Chinese materia medica. In the beginning of the nineteenth century, though, Philip Franz von Siebold (1796-1866), a German scholar in the service of the Dutch government, brought Carl Peter Thunberg's (1743-1828) *Flora Japonica* to Japan, a description of Japan's flora based on the taxonomy of Linnaeus. It confronted Japanese scholars with an entirely different scientific approach. Siebold's talented pupil Itō Keisuke 伊藤圭介 (1803-1901) adapted Linnaeus' method in his work *Taisei honzō meiso* 泰西本草名疏 (The Nomenclature of the Western Herbal, 1829), which became the foundation of modern botany in Japan. At the same time, it ushered in the gradual marginalization of the traditional *honzōgaku*. In the second half of the nineteenth century, *honzōgaku* and medicine in the Chinese style were largely displaced by their Western counterparts in the system of education that the Meiji government established from 1868 onward.

Literature: Yamada 1995.

38. Honzō kōmoku 本草綱目
('Compendium of Materia Medica')

53 chapters, appendices 10 chapters, in 45 fascicles.;
25.2 x 17.4 cm
Author: Inō Jakusui 稲生若水

Date: printed in Shōtoku 正徳 4 (1714), in Edo, Kyoto,
and Osaka.

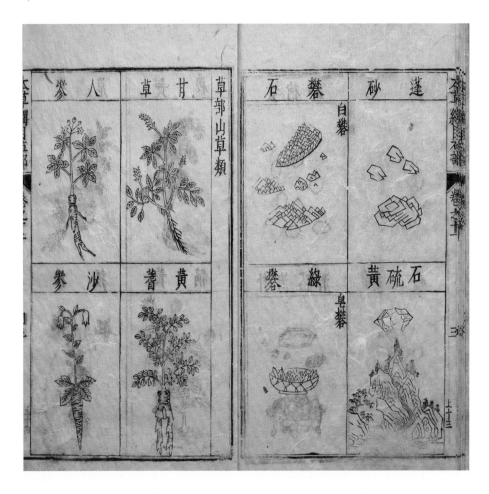

148

Honzō kōmoku, compiled by Inō Jakusui is the Japanese adaptation of the Chinese Compendium of Materia Medica *Bencao gangmu* 本草綱目. The book includes an introduction (*reigen* 例言) in *kanbun* by Hirose Genpaku Tōkei 広瀬元白東啓, an early practitioner of Western medicine, as well as a preface in *kanbun* by Itō Nagatane 伊藤長胤, a Japanese Confucian scholar. In addition, it reproduces the Chinese prefaces written by Wang Shizhen 王世貞, a poet and writer from the Wanli period 万暦 (1573-1620), as well as those written by the mandarins Xia Liangxin 夏良心 and Zhang Dingsi 張鼎思. *Kaeriten* 返り点 and *okurigana* 送り仮名 have been added to all five prefaces as well as the main text for the benefit of the Japanese reader. By this creolization process the text is made accessible to Japanese readers in some semblance of the original. In the margins above the texts of these prefaces, some erudite Japanese reader has added glosses in ink. Most of them are about the Sino-Japanese pronunciation and the meaning of rare characters. The Japanese preface and the introduction show elevations (*taitō* 擡頭) jutting out above the printed frame (*kyōkaku* 匡郭)

to accommodate characters referring to the emperor or to Japan.

On the last page of every fascicle, we notice an oval collector's seal in vermillion with the mention "逸身氏所持 property of Mr. Hayami" (unidentified). The book has no *okugaki* 奥書; the colophon is printed on the *mikaeshi* 見返し. A leaf from the gingko tree can be found between the pages of this copy to ward off bookworms.

The text of the *mikaeshi* in translation reads as following:

"*Honzō kōmoku*, revised edition in 53 chapters. This is the book of which master Inō Jakusui revised the characters and corrected the mistakes. For example, the coltsfoot in the section on herbs and the 'molili' in the section of fruits had all disappeared from the old edition and have now been added again. If the names of categories of insects, fish, herbs, and trees have been passed on inaccurately, then the damage is not insignificant. This is why they have been corrected. All [corrections] are based on the daily experiences and observations of the master,

▲ 本草綱目新校正図経乾 **Illustrations, fascicle** 乾 **p. 14a: first page of the section on mountain herbs** 山草.

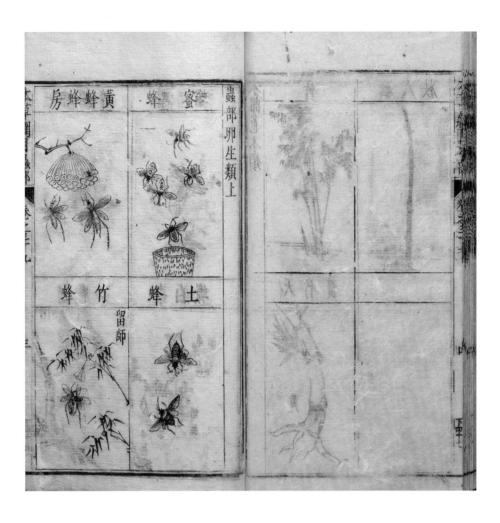

and on books that circulate among the people. [The book] contains much useful information and constitutes truly the essence of medicine. Moreover, it is also a contribution to a general overview of natural history."

The original book with the same title, *Bencao gangmu*, was written by the Chinese scholar Li Shizhen (1518-1593), who lived during the Ming Dynasty (1368-1644). The compilation process took 27 years. The text consists of 1,892 entries on plants, animals, minerals, and other items that were believed to have medicinal properties. The British historian of Chinese science Joseph Needham has called this book "undoubtedly the greatest scientific achievement of the Ming". The first draft was completed in 1578, but its first edition dates from 1596 and is known as the Jinling edition, named after the place of publication Jinling 金陵 (present-day Nanjing 南京). The first edition is considered very rare, there are only seven complete copies known to be extant in the world, of which four can be found in Japan. The first reprint is dated Wanli 31 (1603) and is known as the Jiangxi edition. Still other editions were published during the Ming Dynasty, and even during the Qing Dynasty (1644-1911) numerous reprints were made. The compendium is generally recognized as the first early modern book on traditional Asian medicine and is said to have heralded the dawning of modern pharmacological studies. The illustrations, however, are rather crude. The book was submitted by China and recommended for inclusion in the UNESCO "Memory of the World Register" in 2010 and included in the Register in 2011.

This book first came to Japan in the year 1604. The descriptions are fairly detailed and especially those on fauna are markedly better than the earlier compendia. As a result, it was not only used in Japan as a compendium of medicines, but it gradually evolved into a handbook on natural history. It provided the *honzōka* 本草家 (specialists in the materia medica) of the Edo period with the necessary knowledge for collecting and identifying medicinal herbs and was one of the factors that fueled the boom of *hakubutsugaku* 博物学 (historia naturalis). Fourteen Japanese editions (*wakokubon* 和刻本) are known, which can be divided into three lineages. The Jakusui-version (1714) is considered to be the best of the Japanese editions. For the main text (*honbun* 本文) the same woodblocks were used as for the Kan'ei 寛永 edition (1637), the first Japanese edition of the *Honzō kōmoku*.

This book must not be confused with *Yamato honzō* 大和本草, as Yamazaki 2000 does.

Literature: Needham 1954, p. 147.

149

▲ 本草綱目新校正図経乾 Illustrations, fascicle 坤, p. 48a: first page on ovarian insects 蟲部卵生類上.

39. Honzō zufu 本草図譜
('Album of Pharmacopoeia')

96 chapters; 25.5 x 17.1 cm
Author: Iwasaki Kan'en 岩崎灌園

Date: preface dated Bunsei 文政11 (1828), published
between 1916 and 1921

150

Despite its title, this work is not so much a work on pharmacopoeia than a botanical album, a monumental work compiled by Iwasaki Kan'en (1786-1842) over a period of twenty years. It consists of 96 chapters which were published between 1830 and 1844. It is the first Japanese botanical album to be illustrated in colour. It includes some 2,000 plants, which are provided with explanations based on the classification of the *Honzō kōmoku* (hence its title), that is, the classification into herbs, grains, tubers, fruits, and trees. Kan'en not only included wild varieties but cultivars as well. Moreover, he also included plants and products of foreign origin. A few minerals and animals are included, too.

Most of the illustrations were drawn by Kan'en himself, but some are copies of images in the *Taalrijk register der plaat- ofte figuur-beschrijvingen der bloemdragende gewassen* (1748). This is the Dutch translation by Johannes Burmannus of the florile-gium *Phytanthoza iconographia* by the Regensburg pharmacist Johann Wilhelm Weinmann (1683-1741), compiled between 1737 and 1745. The Hollandologist Udagawa Yōan 宇田川榕菴 (1798-1846) owned a copy of this Dutch translation, whose title Japanese authors translated as *Kenka shokubutsu zufu* 顕花植物図譜 (Album of Flowering Plants).

Honzō zufu is the first pictorial album of Japanese flora in the modern sense, but at the same time it marks the apogee of *honzōgaku* (study of materia medica) in the Edo period, along with the *Honzō kōmoku keimō* 本草綱目啓蒙 (Clarifications on Honzō Kōmoku) by Ono Ranzan 小野蘭山 (1729-1810), who had been Kan'en's teacher. The first chapters (*maki*) were printed from woodblocks, but the majority of them were copied by hand and distributed through personal networks. Therefore, the extant copies from the Edo period are of varied quality and degree of completeness, yet many of these hand-

▲ The *Kichikō* 桔梗, the Platycodon grandiflorum (chapter 1, pp. 14b-15a).

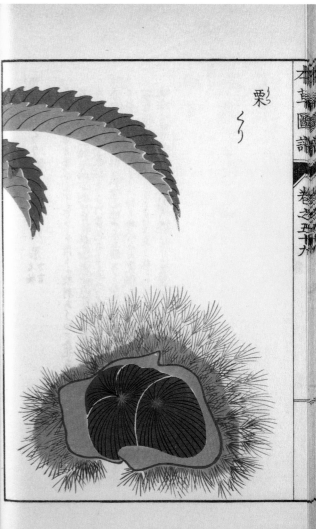

written copies have been preserved. A large number of them were also coloured by hand. In the Taishō period (1912-1926), a complete xylographic edition of the book was printed and published between 1916 and 1921. It comprised a run of 600 copies of superb quality. One of these copies figures in the collection of the UCLouvain and is still in mint condition.

The personal name of Iwasaki Kan'en was Tsunema-sa 常正. He originated from Mikawa 三河. He also authored the *Honzō sodate-gusa* 草木育種 as well as *Bukō sanbutsu-shi* 武江産物志.

Literature: Kitamura et al. 1986; *Kokushi daijiten* 1979-1993, vol. 12, pp. 824-826; Sugimoto/Swain 1978, pp. 387-392.

▲ The *kuri* 栗, the chestnut (chapter 59, pp. 14b-15a).

40. Tenmon zukai 天文図解
('Illustrated Expostulation about Astronomy')

5 chapters in 5 fascicles; 26.9 x 19 cm
Author: Iguchi Tsunenori 井口常範
Date: Genroku 元禄 2 (1689)

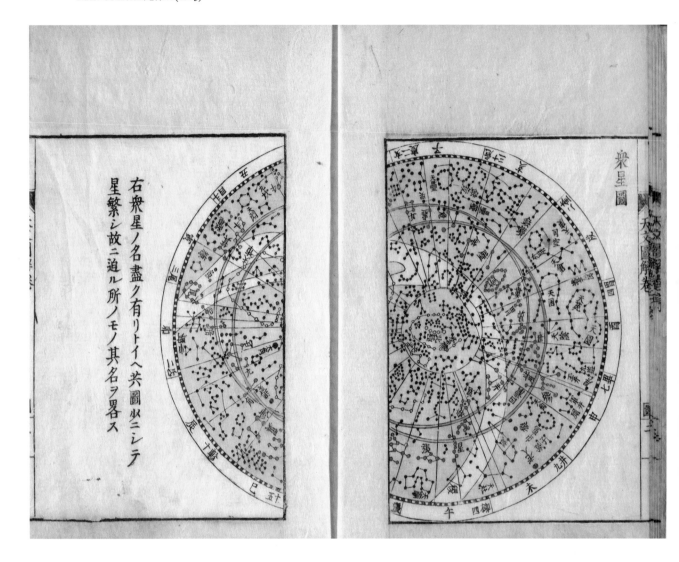

▲ A map of the stars (fascicle I, map 2b-3a).

152

This work is the oldest and most famous astronomical treatise published during the Edo period (1600-1868). About the author Inokuchi Tsunenori, however, nothing is known. It is even unclear whether the characters of his surname should be read as 'Inokuchi' or as 'Iguchi'.

The work consists of 5 chapters. Chapters 1 to 3 discuss the celestial bodies, in addition to the position of the five planets, the sun, and the moon. Chapter 1 includes seven illustrations: an equatorial armillary sphere of the old type and one of the new type, the central world-mountain (Sumeru) as it is portrayed in Buddhism, a celestial map, an ecliptic armillary sphere, and the nine celestial spheres. According to the preface, the author excerpted the data from various books perused in the course of many years. The equatorial armillary sphere of the old type is, judging from the drawing, a kind of conflation of the armillary sphere of the Chinese astronomer Su Song 蘇頌 (1020-1101), built in 1090, and that of Guo Shou-jing 郭守敬 (1231-1316), who designed a new armillary sphere in 1276 by order of Kublai Khan. An exact copy of Guo Shou-jing's instrument was in place in the observatory of Nanjing around 1600, where it was seen by Jesuits. The armillary sphere of the new type appears to be meant for demonstrations rather than for factual observations.

The concept of the nine heavens has existed in China since ancient times. The number nine in this combination actually referred to the heaven in the four cardinal directions, the regions between the four points of the compass and the centre. The scheme of concentric heavens shown here, however, is of Western inspiration. The author had learned of it through Chinese books that dealt with Western astronomy.

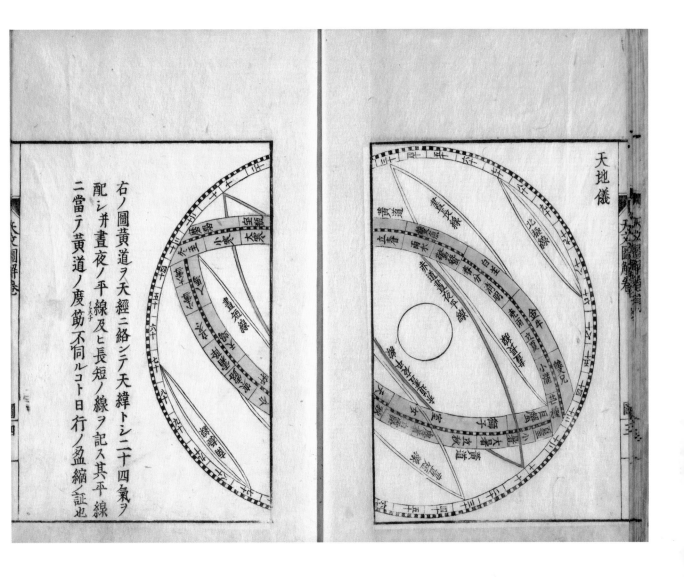

In chapter 2, the moon, the positions of the moon, and the 28 *xiu* 宿 or lunar mansions are discussed. Chapters 3 and 4 deal with, among other topics, eclipses and the lunar calendar. In chapter 5, the author once again discusses the lunar mansions. The illustrations are coloured by hand.

This copy bears on the first page of each fascicle the vermillion oval relief collector's seal 'Futsukaya tosho' 両日屋図書 and the vermillion square relief collector's seal Jōsuitei kazō 穠翠亭家蔵. I have not been able to identify the collectors yet, but their seals appear in other known book collections as well.

Literature: *China hemel en aarde* 1988, pp. 22-45; Iguchi and Ōya 1980.

153

▲ Drawing of an armillary sphere (fascicle I, map 3b-4a).

41. Yamato honzō 大和本草
('Japanese Materia Medica')

Alternative title: *Yamato honzō kōmoku* 大和本草綱目
19 chapters: 16 chapters of text, 2 chapters of appendices
and 1 chapter with illustrations, in total 10 fascicles;
22.2 x 15.6 cm

Author: compiled by Kaibara Ekiken 貝原益軒, published
by Yamanaka Zuikindō 瑞錦堂, Kyoto.
Date: published in Hōei 宝永 6 (1709), appendices and
illustrations in Shōtoku 正徳 5 (1715)

154

The book includes a preface written by Tsuruhara
Osamu 鶴原韜 (?-?), a student of Ekiken, as well as a
preface by the author himself. Both are dated 1708.
Kaibara Ek(i)ken (1630-1714) wanted to compile a
book that was based on his own observations and
study of native specimens, and which would rival
Li Shizhen's *Bencao kangmu* (Jap. *Honzō kōmoku*).
He records 1,362 specimens in the compendium
and discusses both Chinese and Japanese medicinal
herbs, fauna, and minerals, comparing them and
pointing out their similarities and differences. He
also includes many varieties that cannot be found
in the work of his Chinese predecessor. His descriptions of plants are thorough and instructive. Because he does not only cover a wide range of edible
and otherwise useful plants, but also includes ani-

mals and minerals that can be found in Japan, the
book is more than just a pharmacopeia and instead
bears much resemblance to a *summa* of natural history. Kaibara Ekiken was a polymath, who wrote
about the most varied topics. He was the son of a
samurai in the service of the *daimyō* of Fukuoka. His
given name was Atsunobu 篤信, his courtesy name
was Shisei 子誠. His sobriquet was initially Sonken
損軒 (literally 'House of Loss'), but, bespeaking a
fondness of wordplay, was later changed to Ekiken
(Ekken) 益軒 ('House of Gain').

In the chapter with illustrations, both animals
and plants are depicted but no materia medica are
included.

Literature: Kosoto 1999, p. 386; Tucker 1989.

▲ First page of section on water fowl (chapter 15, p. 1a) also
featuring unidentified collector's seal.

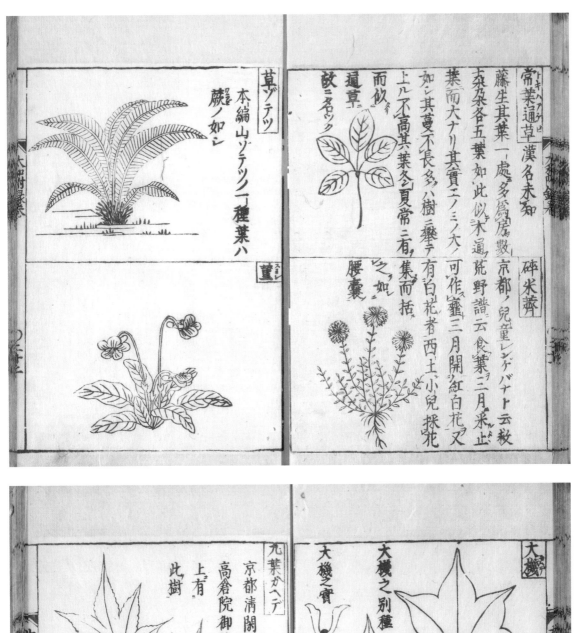

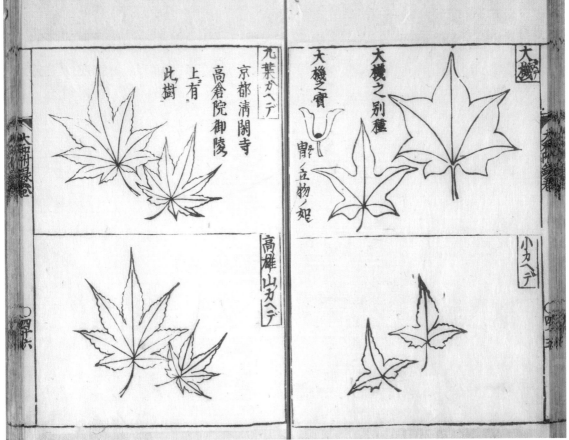

▲ A fern (fascicle IX, pp. 21b–22a); the accompanying text reads:
"*kusa-zotetsu* 草蘇鉄 (ostrich fern): a kind of *yama sotetsu* 山蘇
鉄. The leaves resemble those of the fern."

▲ Types of maples (fascicle IX, pp. 45b–46a).

42. Anpuku zukai 按服図解
('Massage of the Abdomen, Explained Through Illustrations')

1 fascicle; 25.3 x 17.9 cm
Author: Ōta Shinsai 太田晋斎;

Illustrator: Murata Yoshikoto 村田義言
Date: preface dated Bunsei 文政 10 (1827)

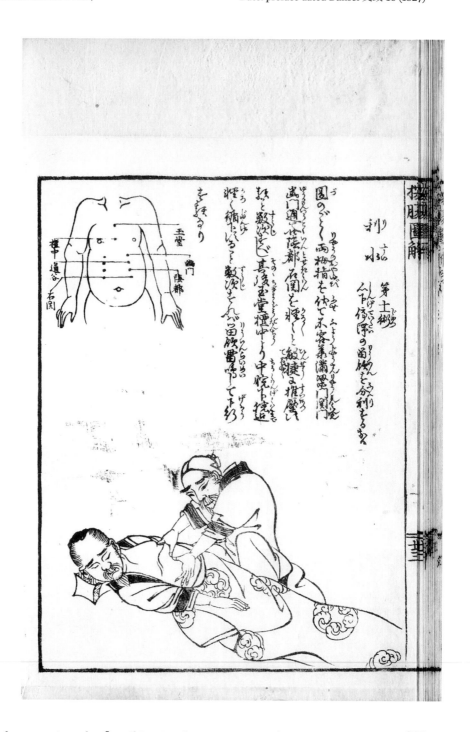

This work was written by Ōta Shinsai and comprises one volume, which is not divided into further chapters. It deals with massage, particularly that of the abdomen. This work is the most famous book about massage from the Edo period. It provides a physiological description of the beneficial effects of massage and recommends it as a manner of treatment for nerve pain and colic.

The author Ōta Shinsai came from Osaka. His personal name was Taketsune 武経 and his court rank was that of *hokkyō* 法橋.

According to the colophon, the book was published by Yamashiroya Sahei 山城屋佐兵衛, a Kyoto publisher, the name of whose shop was Bunseidō 文政堂. In the colophon he describes himself as specialized in publications of Shintō, Confucian, or Buddhist content, besides texts for preaching, Buddhist scriptures, illustrated books, and the like.

Literature: Kosoto 1999, p. 3; Ōta 2011.

▲ Depicted here is *risui* 利水, the draining of fluids from the body (p. 23b).

43. Fukushō kiran Fukushō kiran kōhen 腹証奇覧 附後編
('An Extraordinary Look into Abdominal Diagnostics, and Sequel to An Extraordinary Look into Abdominal Diagnostics')

2 chapters in 2 fascicles (both the principal book and its sequel); 23 x 15.6 cm
Author: Inaba Katsu (Bunrei) 稲葉克 (文礼)

Date: principal book printed between Kansei 寛政 11 and Kyōwa 享和 1 (1799-1801), sequel printed between Kyōwa 1 and Bunka 文化 6 (1801-1809)

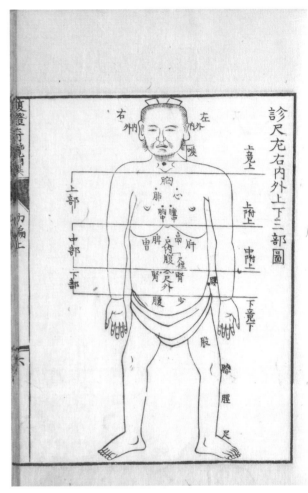

Inaba Katsu (?-1805, sobriquet: Konan 湖南) was an adherent of the so-called ancient medicine (ko-ihō 古医方), a movement within traditional Asian medicine of the Edo period, which aspired to resurrect the medical knowledge of the Ancients in the contemporary age. Proponents of this approach tended to take a critical stance towards Chinese medicine as it had evolved after the Song 宋 period (960-1279), and insisted on reconnecting with *Shōkanron* (Chinese: *Shānghán Lùn*) 傷寒論, known in English as the *Treatise on Cold Damage Disorders*, and with *Kinki yōryaku* (Chinese: *Jīnguì Yàolüè*) 金匱要略, translated in English as *Essential Prescriptions from the Golden Cabinet*. Both are traditional Chinese medicine treatises compiled by Zhāng Zhòngjǐng

(Japanese: *Chō Chūkei*) 張仲景 (150-219) at the end of the Eastern Han Dynasty.

Typical for this branch of medicine in the Edo period was the practice of so-called abdominal diagnostics, the *fukushō* 腹証 of the title. The diagnosis of symptoms is made by palpations of the abdomen. Based on his findings the doctor would then prescribe the appropriate medicine. This book teaches the reader or student through illustrations how the physician should perform the various types of palpations. Inaba did not write the book himself but dictated it to his students. The principal book was written in 1799 and published in 1801, while two sequels were written in 1801 and published in 1809.

Literature: Hattori 1978; Kosoto 1999, p. 330.

157

▲ Prescription to relieve a feeling of a hard lump choking the stomach (first *Sequel*, chapter 2, pp. 1 ff).

▲ Chart showing the location of the various organs (second *Sequel*, chapter 1, p. 6a).

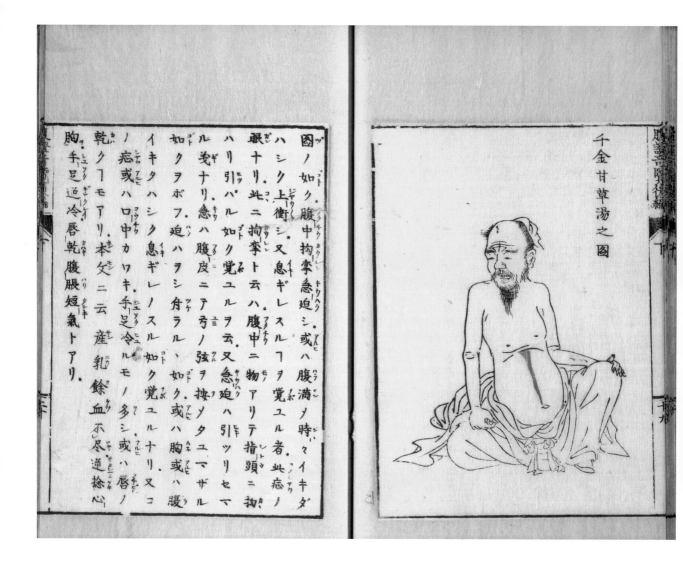

千金甘草湯之図

圖ノ如ク腹中拘攣急迫シ、或ハ腹満ノ時々イキダ
ハシク上衝シ、又急ギレスルヲ覚ユル者此症ノ
眼目ナリ、此ニ拘攣ト云ハ腹中ニ物アリテ指頭ニ拘
ハリ引バル如ク覚ユルヲ云、又急迫ハ引ツリセマ
ル如ク覚ユルヲ云、又腹皮ニテ弓ノ弦ヲ按ユマザル
如クボヲ覚ユル、如ク、或ハ胸或ハ臍
イキタハシク息ギレノスルヲ云、ゴトク覚ユルナリ又コ
ノ症或ハ口中カワキ、手足冷ユルモノ多シ、或ハ唇ノ
乾クコモアリ、本父ニ云、産乳餘血不尽逆搶心
胸・手足逆冷唇乾腹脹短氣トアリ。

44. Naika hiroku 内科秘録
('The Secrets of Internal Medicine')

14 chapters in 14 fascicles; 25.6 x 16.7 cm
Author: Honma Sōken 本間棗軒
Date: Genji 元治 1 (1864)

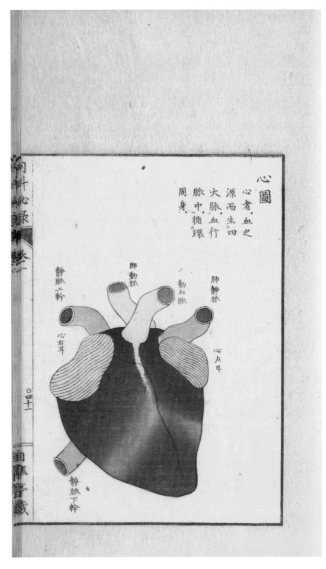

This is a book on clinical medicine by Honma Sōken (1804-1872). Sōken was a scion of a family of famous physicians. His courtesy name (*azana* 字) was Wakei or Wakyō 和卿. He studied Chinese medicine under Hara Nan'yō 原南陽 (1753-1820), Dutch medicine under Sugita Ryūkei 杉田立卿 (1787-1846), and the Confucian classics under Ōta Kinjō 大田錦城 (1765-1825). He travelled to Nagasaki to study with Philip Franz von Siebold (1796-1866), the famous German physician employed by the Netherlands Trading Society (Nederlandsche Handel-Maatschappij). In Kyoto he took lessons with Takashina Kien 高階枳園 (1773-1844), in Wakayama 和歌山 at the school founded by the famous surgeon Hanaoka Seishū 華岡青洲 (1760-1835). He settled as a physician in Edo and practiced surgery in the style of Hanaoka. He is considered the most talented surgeon of Hanaoka's school, but because he divulged a secret technique he had learned from Hanaoka in one of his books, he was 'excommunicated' from the school.

He was the first surgeon to successfully amputate a femur. Later he took up a position as personal physician of the lord of the Mitō domain, and finally he became professor of medicine in the same fiefdom. *Naika hiroku* is inspired by one of the works of his mentor Hara Nan'yō. It starts with a general introduction into medicine, diagnostics, and the principles of internal medicine. The subsequent chapters discuss the various fields of medicine and their many syndromes, illustrated with copious examples from his rich experience as physician.

Literature: Hattori 1978; Kosoto 1999, p. 303.

▲ Portrait of the physician Sōken (fascicle I, chapter 1, p. 10a).

▲ Illustration of the heart (fascicle I, chapter 2, p. 41a).

45. Yōka hiroku 瘍科秘録
('The Secrets of Ulcer Treatment'; Zoku yōka hiroku 続瘍科秘録 ('The Secrets of Ulcer Treatment, Sequel')

15 chapters in 17 fascicles; 25.6 x 16.5 cm
Author: Honma Genchō (Sōken) 本間玄調 (棗軒)

Date: preface dated Tenpō 天保 8 (1837), printed in Kōka
弘化 4 (1847)

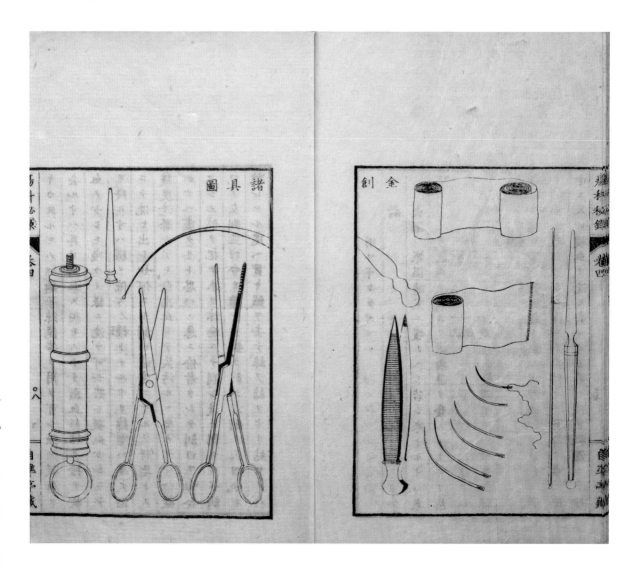

This work comprises a treatise about dermatology by Honma Sōken (1804-1872). The preface is dated Tenpō 8 (1837), but the book was not printed and published until 1847. In 1859, a sequel appeared entitled *Zoku yōka hiroku* 続瘍科秘録 ('The Secrets of Ulcer Treatment, Sequel'), which includes the oral teachings of Sōken, penned down by one of his pupils. Sōken was versed in both Chinese and 'Dutch' (i.e. Western) medicine. Dermatology was his forte, and in this work he reveals both his theoretical knowledge and his specific methods of treatment. At the time of their publication, his books represented the state of the art in their discipline. The book is written in *kanamajiri* 仮名交じり (Japanese written in both characters and *katakana*) - in other words, in the vernacular - thus being accessible to less learned practitioners as well.

Yōka hiroku includes the description of a syndrome called *shokuto chūdoku* 食兎中毒 (poison from eating rabbit) by Sōken. This entry has been alleged to be the very first mention in medical history of rabbit fever (*yatobyō* 野兎病) or tularemia. *Zoku yōka hiroku* includes a description and illustration in colour of the amputation of a thigh in a patient suffering from gangrene. Sōken performed this operation under general anaesthesia using the procedure invented by his mentor Hanaoka Seishū 華岡青洲. This was the first amputation under general anaesthesia performed in Japan. Hanaoka Seishū is generally recognized to have been the first surgeon in the world to successfully apply general anaesthesia. He used it for the first time in an operation for breast cancer in 1805. In the West, general anaesthesia was not applied until 1846.

This copy bears the collector's seal of a certain Yoshida 吉田.

Literature: Hattori 1978; Kosoto 1999, p. 388; Sugimoto/Swain 1978, pp. 387-392.

▲ Surgical instruments (*Yōka hiroku*, chapter 4a, pp. 7b-8a).

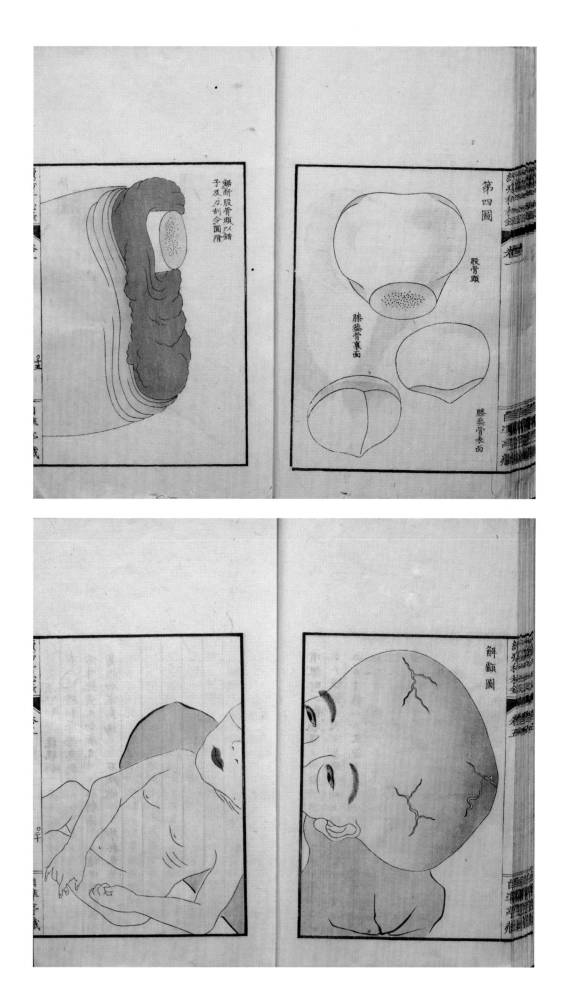

鋸断股骨顥以錯
子及刀刮令圓滑

第四圖

股骨顥

膝葢骨裏面

膝葢骨表面

解顱圖

▲ A leg amputated because of gangrene (*Zoku yōka hiroku*, chapter 1, pp. 14a–15b).

▲ Child with fractured skull (*Zoku Yōka hiroku*, chapter 5, pp. 19b–20a).

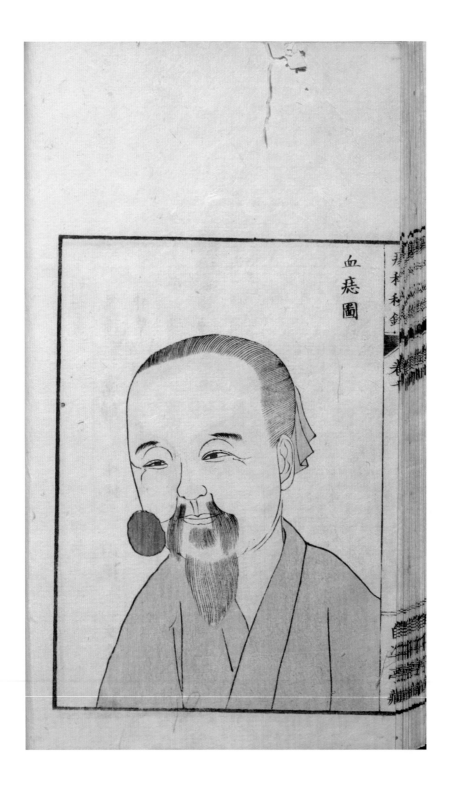

▲ Blood clot on the cheek (*Yōka hiroku*, chapter 10, p. 24b).

46. Ehon noyama-gusa 絵本野山草
('Picture Book of Plants in Fields and Mountains')

Alternative title: *Noyama-gusa* 野山草
5 chapters in 5 fascicles; 22.2 x 15.5 cm
Illustrator: Tachibana Yasukuni 橘保国

Date: printed in Hōreki 宝暦 5 (1755), reprinted from the same blocks by other publishers (*kyūhan* 求版) in Bunka 文化 3 (1806)

Tachibana Yasukuni (1715-1792) was born in Osaka, the son of the painter (*eshi* 絵師) Tachibana Morikuni 橘守国 (1679-1748), whose sobriquet (*gō* 号) was Soken 素軒. Morikuni first studied painting under Tsuruzawa Tanzan 鶴沢探山 (1655-1729), a painter of the Kanō school 狩野派. Afterwards, he changed his vocation and earned his livelihood by printing and publishing model books (*ehon* 絵本). The cause for this change was his expulsion from the school. He had dared to publish allegedly proprietary sketches (*funpon* 粉本) of the Kanō school, thus divulging a professional secret of his master. Yasukuni then learned painting from his father. After his father's death, he succeeded to the family business and adopted the sobriquet Kō-soken 後素軒 (the second Soken).

The target audience for model books in the Edo period (1600-1868) were people aspiring to become professional painters. Morikuni is said to have published over 20 painting books. The famous *Hokusai manga* 北斎漫画, too, were not meant as a simple collection of comic strips but as a model book for the draughtsman and painter. Morikuni earned a measure of renown with the publication of his model books, which were drawn with great accuracy and refinement. His style was a source of inspiration for many *ukiyo-e* artists in the Kamigata area (the region of Kyoto, Osaka, and Nara). His books included 'studies' of natural phenomena, of buildings, customs, traditional festivities, fauna, and flora.

In 1740 he published the work *Ehon Ōshukubai* 絵本鶯宿梅 ('*My Plum Tree Where the Bush Warbler Used to Roost*, Illustrated'). In the fifth chapter, 37 varieties of plants were illustrated. What is re-

▲ *Ran* 蘭, orchid (fascicle II, p. 11b).

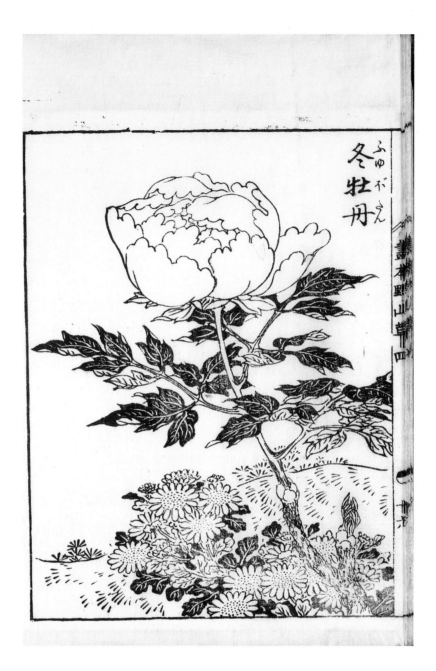

ふゆぼたん
冬牡丹

markable about this work is that, in addition to the sketches, glosses are added about the use of pigments and colours. His model books were used by students of the major traditional painting schools (the Kanō school and the Tosa school 土佐派), as well as by the masters of *ukiyo-e*, who used them when making their compositions.

Yasukuni continued in the style of his father. Intending to extend the range of subjects covered in the earlier *Ehon Ōshukubai*, he published the work *Ehon Noyama-gusa* 絵本野山草 in 1755. It included detailed sketches of trees, 21 wild plants and garden varieties, and 144 herbs, accompanied with guidance for the pigments and colours, as well as quotes from Chinese and Japanese works to detail the names and features of the illustrated plants. He also included imported varieties such as the marigold (*tagetes*), the hollyhock, and the poppy. In some

copies, the illustrations have been heightened with colour, though not in the copy of the UCLouvain. The drawings are very detailed and precise, and the author shows a thorough knowledge of trees, plants, and herbs. In the Edo period, horticulture reached unseen heights, spawning a whole array of remarkable plant varieties and colourful picture books on horticulture. Although *Ehon Noyama-gusa* is not a book on horticulture, it testifies to the highly developed knowledge in this field in the mid-Edo period.

Besides the original date of publication (1755), the colophon page also mentions the woodblocks were purchased from Narahara Kihee 楢原喜兵衛, who was apparently a descendant of the illustrator, for 'Narahara' was the real family name of Tachibana Yasukuni.

Literature: *Shinchō sekai bijutsu jiten* 1985, p. 889; Iwasa 1982, pp. 261-262.

▲ *Fuyu-botan* 冬牡丹, winter peony i.e. Paeonia suffrutticosa or tree peony (fascicle IV, chapter 4, 16b).

47. Nantei gafu 楠亭画譜
('Album with Drawings by Nantei')

3 chapters in 3 fascicles; 26.4 x 18 cm
Illustrator: Nishimura Nantei 西村楠亭
Date: Kyōwa 享和4 (1804)

165

Nishimura Nantei (1755-1834) was a painter active in the circle of Maruyama Ōkyo 円山応挙 (1733-1795), one of Japan's greatest painters. Nantei excelled in drawing the human figure, and this album, a collection of genre scenes, eminently illustrates his talent in this respect. They are executed with the brush in an exuberant and comical style, and left uncoloured, all the more stressing the flourish of his brush. They are accompanied by *kyōka* 狂歌 (comical *waka*). The first page of the book bears a seal with the words: 'Ine no ya zō' 稲廼舎蔵, the collector's seal of the *kokugakusha* 国学者 (a scholar of native Japanese classics) Kusakada Taruho 日下田足穂 (1814-1890).

Literature: Chibbett 1977, pp. 219-220.

▲ Taking the baby for a walk with the nursemaid (fascicle II, pp. 6b-7a).

▲ *Kōshin-machi* (庚申待 – Kōshin Waiting), a type of religious folklore, involving nightly festivities (fascicle II, pp. 8b-9a).

48. Seirō bijin awase 青楼美人合
('Beauties from the Blue Pavilion Compared in Pairs')

Alternative title: *Ehon seirō bijin awase* 絵本青楼美人合
4 chapters in 4 fascicles, bibliographical info: 5 fascicles;
25.9 x 18 cm

Illustrator: Suzuki Harunobu 鈴木春信
Date: Meiwa 明和 7 (1770)

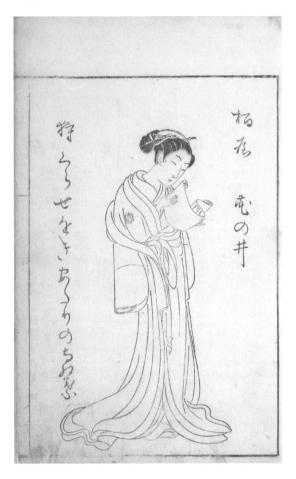

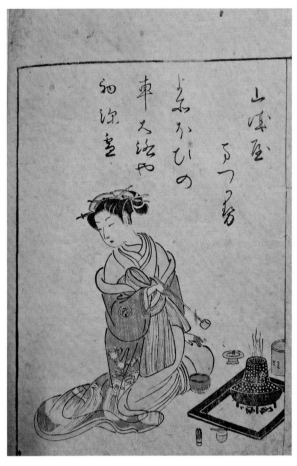

The comparison of things in pairs is an old pastime in Japan. During the Heian period (794-1185), aristocrats amused themselves with the comparison of paired *waka*-poems. Later on, this custom was extended to other forms of artistic expression, and during the Edo period (1600-1868) even to female beauty. The "blue pavilion" of the title is a euphemistic reference to the licensed red-light district Yoshiwara 吉原. There was unlicensed prostitution in many places, but Yoshiwara had been designated by the military government as the place where prostitution was authorized. This protection, albeit under severe constraints, created the conditions for the district to develop into a microcosm ruled by its own laws and conventions, rituals, and festivals. Knowing all the rules was absolutely vital if one wanted to enjoy any respect in the district. There was a ranking system in place among the women, and the highest rank of women (*oiran* 花魁) were sometimes true celebrities. They were versed in the arts and often started new fashion trends. For this reason, they often drew the attention of artists and became a favourite subject of the *ukiyo-e* 浮世絵 or 'prints of the floating world'.

This book therefore offers a series of compari-

sons in pairs of the beauties at the time in the pleasure district Yoshiwara. The drawings are by the famous print artist Suzuki Harunobu (1725-1770). His style is immediately apparent from his ideal of beauty so typical to his work: All women are represented as ethereal, day-dreaming girls. Only one of the drawings is coloured by hand. For each woman, the name of the teahouse she belongs to as well as a *haiku* are given.

The first page of this copy bears the collector's seal in vermillion of Kurokawa Mamichi 黒川真道 (1866-1925). The Kurokawa family is known for its tradition of classical Japanese studies and its collection of books. The most famous head of the family was Kurokawa Mayori 黒川真頼 (1829-1906). Mamichi was his son. The style of the characters in the seal of Mamichi strongly resembles that of Mayori. According to the colophon, the woodblock cutter is Endō Shōgorō 遠藤松五郎 (?-?). On the final page (inside the back cover), Kurokawa Mamichi has added a note in ink in fluid handwriting, extolling the art of the illustrator Suzuki Harunobu. The note is dated October of the fourth year of Taishō (1915).

Literature: Suzuki 1981, Fujisawa 2003.

▲ The courtesan Hana-no-i 花の井 of the House Hinokiya 柏屋 (fascicle III, p. 12a).

▲ The courtesan Matsukaze of the House Yamashiroya (fascicle IV, p. 61b). This is the only image that is coloured.

49. Teito gakei ichiran 帝都雅景一覧
('Elegant Views of the Imperial Capital at a Glance')

2 parts: 4 chapters in 4 fascicles; 25.6 x 16.7 cm
Authors: Tatsukawa Seikun 竜川清勲 (part 1), Rai San'yō 頼山陽 (part 2); illustrator: Kawamura Bunpō 河邑文鳳

Date: part 1: printed in Bunka 文化 6 (1809), part 2: printed in Bunka 12 (1815)

Each of the four fascicles bears the collector's seal "Tomo" 鞆. The four fascicles are respectively titled *higashi(-yama)* (Eastern (mountains)), *nishi(-yama)* (Western (mountains)), *minami(-yama)* (Southern (mountains)), and *kita(-yama)* (Northern (mountains)). "East" and "West" form a set and were published first. "South" and "North", also a set, were published subsequently.

"East" is the first part of the first set. It includes a preface by Tatsukawa Seikun, with calligraphy by Kensai 研斎, dated winter, year of the hare Hinotō 丁卯冬 (winter 1807).

The second part "West" of the first set opens with a *gogon zekku* 五言絶句, a Chinese poem of four lines with five characters to the line, written by and in the calligraphy of Kōtei Korehiro 栲亭之熙 – that is, Murase Kōtei 村瀬栲亭 (1744-1819), a famous sinologist and Confucianist. It is additionally accompanied by two seals (blank characters against a black background). The top seal includes his last and first name: Minamoto Korehiro 源之熙; the lower seal contains his sobriquet (*azana*字) Kunseki 君績.

On the last page, we read: 文鳳馬声図: drawings by Bunpō Basei (Kawamura Bunpō 河村文鳳), with a gourd-shaped seal containing the characters Nanzan'ō 南山翁; in a column separated by a vertical line, the calligraphic inscription states:

丁卯小春題于観海詩楼 Written in the Kankai shirō in the early spring of 1807
十州小栗光胤 by Tōshū Oguri Kōin.

On the colophon page, advertisements by the publisher announcing future publications, including the second part (i.e., "South" and "North") of *Teito gakei ichiran* 帝都雅景一覧 with drawings by 文鳳山人. Also written on the colophon page are the date 'early spring' of Bunka 6 (1809) and the printers/publishers: Morimoto Taisuke 森本太助, residing in Shinsaibashi 心斎橋 in Osaka; Teishiya Genjirō 丁子屋源治郎, residing in Rokkaku-machi 六角街 in Kyoto; and Yoshida Shinbē 吉田新兵衛, residing in Sankyō-machi 三橋街.

"South", the first part of the second set, includes a preface by San'yō Gaishi, namely, the famous scholar Rai San'yō, accompanied by his seals, dated sixth month of the year of the dog 甲戌秋六月 (autumn 1814).

"North", on the other hand, has a preface written with calligraphy by Kōtei Korehiro, dated autumn, seventh month of the year of the dog 甲戌秋

七月 (autumn 1814). On the last page of "North", we find:

甲戌甲戌孟春 (first month of spring of the year of the dog, 1814)
文鳳馬声図: drawings by Bunpō Basei (i.e., Kawamura Bunpō), with a gourd-shaped seal containing the characters Nanzan'ō 南山翁

and, in a column separated by a vertical line, the calligraphic inscription:

woodblock cutter 彫工 Inoue Jihei 井上治兵衛
printer 摺工 Hori Kisaburō 堀喜三郎

The colophon page reads: publisher/printer, bookshop: Teishiya Genjirō 丁子屋源治郎, of the bookstore Fukui Shōbōdō 福井正宝堂 across from the Rokkaku-dō 六角堂 in Kyoto.

The book provides an overview of the sights of the imperial capital Kyoto. This work, however, is not classified in the catalogue as a *Meisho-zue* but, rather, in the division 'arts and crafts'. This division is owing to the style of the illustrations being entirely different from those of the *Meisho-zue*, as the number of illustrations far outweigh the text, and since what little text can be found is not informative but, rather, meditative in nature. As a rule, they are short poems celebrating the sights in Classical Chinese (*kanshi* 漢詩). The book is in no way intended as a guidebook. It belongs to the ethereal cultural sphere of the eighteenth-century literati, while the *Meisho-zue* targeted a different, more popular audience. This difference is also apparent from the title, which includes the word *gakei* 雅景 (stylish, elegant, courtly places), a reference to a more courtly tradition.

Be that as it may, it would be highly interesting to compare a place in *Kyo warabe* to the same one in *Teito gakei ichiran* and see how it had changed over a century's time or how differently it is portrayed. In the volume "Eastern (mountains)" on page *Jō* fourteen 上十四, "Evening sun above (the temple) Shin'nyodō 真如堂" is depicted, which may be compared to *Kyo warabe*'s volume 3, page 19 recto. The drawing in *Teito gakei ichiran* simply depicts the temple's main building, with a copse of trees on both sides of the path leading to the building. No human presence, simple, but topographically correct. *Kyo warabe*, on the other hand, offers a sketchy depiction of the main building and the pagoda, without backdrop or décor. Three figures also appear prominently in the scene, lending the scene an anecdotal

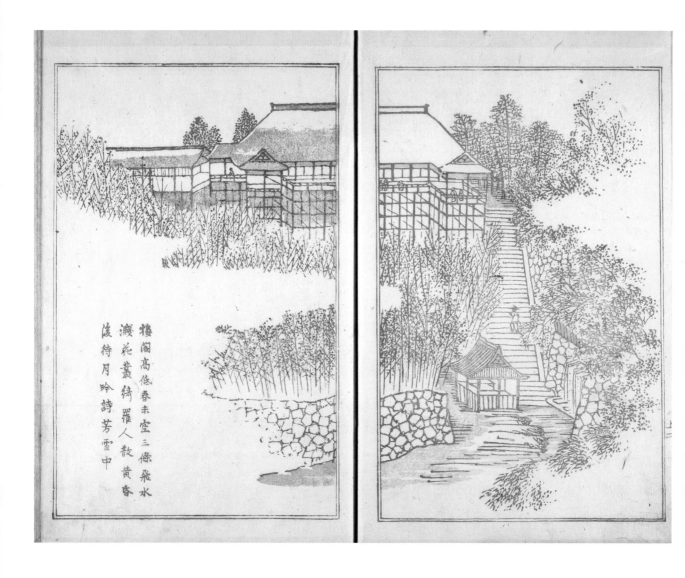

樓閣高低春未空三條飛水
濺花叢繞羅人散黄昏
後待月吟詩芳雪中

appearance, contrary to *Teito gaikei ichiran*'s more poetic and dreamier atmosphere.

The illustrator Kawamura Bunpō (1779-1821) blended the style of various painting schools, but in this case the influences of *nanga* and the Maruyama school are striking.

Shown here is the famous temple Kiyomizu-dera. The meditative and intimate atmosphere as well as the soft colours are typical of the literary painting style (*nanga*). The poem is a shichigon zekku 七言絶句, a four-line verse with seven characters to the line:

> Temple buildings high and low, no spring yet in
>   the air,
> In three streamlets, the waterfall flows down,
>   spattering on a bunch of flowers
> A dressed-up wanderer, sauntering after dusk,
> Is waiting for the moon to write a poem about
>   blossoms in the snow.

A poem, although consisting of four lines of seven characters to the line, does not necessarily have to be written as calligraphy in four lines. Not the visual, typographical representation but, rather, the rhyme and grammatical structure of the calligraphic text indicate the type of poem.

Another copy of *Teito gakei ichiran* belongs to the 'Fonds Hans de Winiwarter' in the Royal Library Albertina, no. H.W. 896.

Literature: Chibbett 1977, p. 222; Kozyreff 1992, pp. 66-67.

 The famous temple Kiyomizu-dera in Kyoto (fascicle I, pp. 2b-3a).

50. Tōto shōkei ichiran 東都勝景一覧
('Fine Views of the Eastern Capital at a Glance')

2 chapters in 2 fascicles; 24.2 x 17.9 cm
Illustrator: Katsushika Hokusai I
Date: printed in Kansei 寛政 12 (1800)

This collection comprises *kyōka* 狂歌 ('comical poems' in *tanka* format), illustrated with images of famous sights in Edo, drawn by the famous print artist Hokusai (1760-1849) and published in Kansei 12 (1800). It is clear that the images are of more importance than the poems. The design is conceived as a rolling landscape. The book starts off in Shinagawa in early spring, and as the reader turns the pages, the panorama and seasons change.

This is the popular version of *Tōto meisho ichiran*. There was also a more exclusive, luxury version. Both versions were published at almost the same time. The first edition appeared in Edo, and the second in Nagoya in 1815. Of the second version, Philip Franz von Siebold (1796-1866) brought a copy back to the Netherlands. In 1840 a third edition appeared in Osaka. The present item belongs to that edition. At the end of the nineteenth century, the woodblocks of this book ended up in the Boston Museum of Fine Arts.

The copy in the collection of UCLouvain bears the collector's seal of Hayashi Tadamasa 林忠正 (1853-1906), the famous Paris-based antiquarian and art expert, whose clientele included nearly all French impressionists.

Incidentally, in the sales catalogue of Hayashi Tadamasa's collection, we find the luxury edition of this work under number 1714:

"Tōto meicho ichiran – Coup de'oeil [*sic*] sur les endroits célèbres de Tōto (Edo).
Signatures-Dessinateur: Hok'sai Tokimasa [*sic*]
Graveur: Andō Yenchi
Quarante pages de gravures
Tirage en couleurs, 2 vol. 25 cm x 17 cm".

▲ A scene at Shinagawa (fascicle I, pp. 2b-3a).

A copy of the sales catalogue of the Hayashi collection is included in the UCLouvain's Japanese donation (*Collection* Hayashi 1902). This copy is marked with the collector's seal 'Nagasaki' 長崎蔵書之印, the seal of Nagasaki Shōgo 長崎省吾 (1850-1937), high ranking official and advisor to the Imperial Household.

With the exception of the last page of fascicle I and the first page of fascicle II, each view is spread across two pages. In the empty 'sky' above the pictured scene, the name of the depicted place and four germane *kyōka* are reproduced, two per page.

Shown in ill. 1 is a view of Shinagawa. A child is playing with a kite, while three adults are seemingly peering at something on the ground near the riverside. The sitting man, smoking a pipe, is a boatswain; the woman runs a tea stall along the river; above the image, calligraphy with *kyōka*. In fascicle II above the first print (one page), the following *kyōka* is reproduced:

湯島天満宮
座巳登々丸
きのふまで
つづきしうごの
ミはらしハ
愛宕にまけぬ
ゆしま天神

The (shrine of) Yushima Tenjin:
    until yesterday
The rain dragged on,
    but now the view is no less
than that at the shrine of Atago (Zashi Todomaru)

In the colophon (*kanki* 刊記) we read:

画工北斎辰政
彫工安藤円紫

寛政十二年
江戸日本橋通一丁目
須原屋茂兵衛
天保十一年九月求版
大阪心斎橋通伝(博)労町角
河内屋茂兵衛版

Illustrator: Hokusai Tatsumasa
Engraver: Andō Enshi
Suwaraya Mohei [1756 – 1820; active], residing in Edo, Nihonbashi-dōri itchōme, printed and published this work in Kansei 12 (1800). In Tenpō 11 (1840) Kawachiya Mohei, residing in Osaka, on the corner of Shinsaibashi-dōri denrōchō, bought the woodblocks and [re]published [this book].

In Japan, publishing as a commercial enterprise took root around the middle of the seventeenth century, and publishers could claim publishing rights to their own publications. This right, called *hankabu* 版株, meant that woodblocks could be bought and sold between publishers, a practice known as *kyūhan* 求版. In this case the Osaka printer Kawachiya Mohei purchased the woodblocks from his Edo colleague Suwaraya Mohei, as is evidenced by the colophon.
Literature: Nagoya-shi hakubutsukan 1988.

▲ **The Shrine of Yushima Tenjin (fascicle II, p. 1a).**

51. Ryōchi shinan 量地指南
('Lessons in Land Surveying')

Alternative title: *Zukai ryōchi shinan zenpen kōhen* 図解量地指南前編後編

Part I: 3 chapters in 3 fascicles; Part II: 5 chapters in 5 fascicles; 27 x 18.7 cm

Author: Murai Masahiro 村井昌弘

Date: Part I: foreword dated Kyōhō 享保 17 (1732), author's preface dated Kyōhō 15 (1730); Part II: author's postscript dated Hōreki 宝暦 4 (1755)

▲ Figure dressed in samurai attire, looking at a point of reference using an alidade (*mikomi* 見込み) (fascicle I, chapter 1, p. 6b).

Land surveying (*sokuryō* 測量) has two intended purposes: measuring distances and measuring surface areas. People used to measure distances with a rope, but since this did not require any kind of mathematical knowledge, traditionally books of mathematics make no mention of it. Yet some Chinese treatises do refer to the method of measuring distances by using the proportionality of a right-angled triangle. Japanese disquisitions from the Edo period, such as

the *Warisansho* 割算書 and the *Jinkōki* 塵劫記, also refer to this method.

The surface area was measured by stringing a rope in the form of a rectangle around a plot. One had to make sure that the part of the plot that fell outside the rectangle was equal to the surface size of the part that fell inside it. The surface area of the rectangle yielded the surface size of the plot that had to be measured. Another method consisted of dividing the plot into a number of triangles, and then adding up the various surface areas of these triangles. This seems to have been the most commonly used method in seventeenth-century Japan.

The making of maps took things one step further. Originally, maps, such as cadastral maps, covered only a very limited area. The rectangular shape was used here as well. Around the area to be measured, a rope was strung in the shape of a rectangle. Using ropes, the rectangle was divided into a grid of many small squares. The grid was then copied onto a piece of paper. A conspicuous feature on the terrain was chosen as point of reference and was likewise copied onto the paper. For the contours of the area, the lines of the ropes forming the grid were also noted. Because the use of the grid was not very precise, here, too, people eventually switched to using the method of the sum of the triangles instead. The benefit of the triangle method was that not everything had to be measured. Certain parts of the terrain which were hard to access were difficult to measure anyway. The triangle was drawn onto a piece of paper and, from there on, it sufficed to measure only two sides and one inside corner angle, or one side and two inside angles.

Dividing the plot into a grid and the use of the triangle were methods used in China, which were also known in Japan. Onto this traditional know-how Western surveying techniques were then applied.

Triangulation, the method developed by the Dutch mathematician and astronomer Snellius (1580-1626), was the first form of Western land surveying used in Japan. It is said to have been introduced in Japan around the 1640s in the form of what we call the *planchet*. This method, too, divides the plot into triangles. Once the three points of the triangle have been marked on the terrain, the grades/degrees of the inside corners of that triangle are plotted on a plane table with the help of an alidade, a device that uses the line of sight to view a distant object (see ill. 1). Then it suffices to actually measure only one side in order to calculate the length of the two other sides. This instrument, or at least its principles, were allegedly introduced in Japan by the German surgeon Caspar Schamberger (1623-1706), who in fact stayed in Japan from 1649 to 1651, employed by the Dutch East India Company (VOC). He allegedly passed the know-how about its use on to the Japanese Higuchi Gon'emon 樋口権右衛門 (1601-1684). Higuchi was a scholar from Nagasaki, an astronomer more commonly known by the name Kobayashi Kanesada 小林謙貞 (also read as Kobayashi Kentei).

Thus, Higuchi Gon'emon became the heir to this new kind of know-how, which he in turn passed on to his students. His school became the most influential approach in land surveying during the Edo period. One of his students, Shimizu Teitoku 清水貞徳 (1645-1717), perfected the technique and lent his name to the school: Shimizu-ryū 清水流. Its method, known as the *kiku genpō* 規矩元法, was passed on as secret knowledge. Although the principles were noted, the resulting records were only kept as manuscripts and were deliberately not printed or published for many years. Many of the surveying permits from the Edo period, which are still preserved today as archival material, were issued by this school.

In the first half of the eighteenth century, against the background of growing demand, many books on land surveying were compiled. The eighth *shōgun*, Tokugawa Yoshimune 徳川吉宗 (lived 1684-1751), promoted a vigorous policy of economic development, leading to massive clearance of arable land throughout the country. The failed harvest and ensuing famine of 1732 only strengthened his resolve. During the same period, he relaxed the embargo on the import of foreign books, allowing more books from China to enter the country. In the Kyōhō period - more specifically, in the year 1733 - the Chinese compilation *Chongzhen lishu* 崇禎曆書 (Jap. *Sūtei rekisho*: 'Astronomical Treatises of the Chongzhen Reign') arrived in Japan. This work is a Chinese compilation by Jesuits active in China, including Giacomo Rho (1592-1638), Adam Schall von Bell (1591-1666), and others. It incorporates content of various European astronomical treatises with scant citation, making it hard to identify its European sources. At any rate, it also included tables with trigonometric functions. Similar tables were found in Dutch books on navigation. These tables were copied by hand and spread throughout Japan. The mathematician Nakane Genkei 中根元圭 (1662-1773) wrote a brief commentary on their use, but it took considerable time before they were actually used in the practice of land surveying. It was not until the 1830s, when the demand rose once again, that the use of trigonometric tables became widespread. By now, however, land surveying was no longer the province of surveyors but of mathematicians. Understandably, their publications pay less attention to actual surveying and more to explaining the method of calculation.

To successfully make use of these tables, more sophisticated instruments than the *planchet* are needed. The few octants and sextants imported by the Dutch were soon copied by the Japanese, but even so the demand exceeded the supply. It did not take long before DIY books appeared, explaining how people could make simple surveying instruments themselves. Thus land surveying know-how became widespread. When the sweeping land reform was enacted in the early Meiji period, this knowledge came in handy.

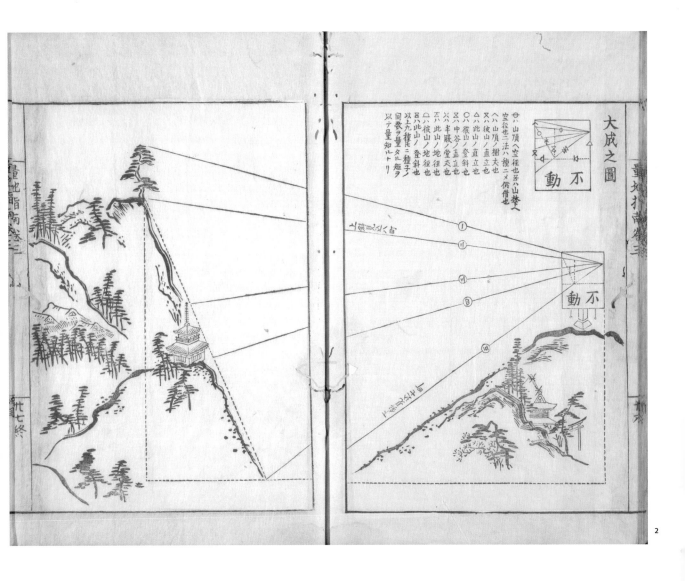

Biographical information on the author, Murai Masahiro is scanty. He inherited his expertise indirectly from Higuchi Gon'emon, although he did not belong to the Shimizu school. His sobriquet (*gō*) was Sodō 蘇道 or Sodōshi 蘇道子. He hailed from Ise, but moved to Edo at an early age. Most likely, he was a masterless samurai (*rōnin* 浪人) and a specialist in military science. In Edo, he opened a private school. He appears to have been the author of various treatises on military science, including strategy and tactics, many of which probably only existed as manuscripts at the time of his death. According to the preface and the postscript of the first part, his grandfather Murai Masami 村井昌躬 had learnt the art of surveying from Higuchi Gon'emon and passed it on to his son, Masahiro's father. The second part was written by Masahiro with the help of his son. From the preface of the first part we learn that the manuscript was completed in Kyōhō 15 (1730), while the colophon (*kanki* 刊記) informs us that printing by Noda Yahee 野田弥兵衛 in Kyoto and by Noda Tahee 野田太兵衛 in Edo was completed in Kyōhō 18 (1733). The preface of the second part mentions the date Hōreki 4 (1754),

but the colophon gives the date Kansei 寛政 6 (1794) instead. The book includes another preface, this one dated Kansei 9 (1797), which is presumably the year in which the second part was actually printed. It was the grandson of Masahiro who saw this second part of the book through the press.

In the first part, Murai explains triangulation, referred to in Japan at the time as "the Dutch method". This is the crucial part of his treatise. In the second part, he discusses various topics, including the use of the compass, and records various data he has culled from other books or has learnt from informants.

Ill. 2: a description with illustration of the method used to measure from the top of a mountain the height, incline, and diameter of another mountain, as well as the height, incline, and diameter of the mountain one is standing on, in addition to the height of the tree on top of the other mountain, the height of the temple on the slope of the other mountain, and the depth of the valley between both mountains (chapter 3, pp. 26b-27a).

Literature: Murai/Ōya 1978; Horiuchi 1994.

▲ A measuring description (chapter 3, pp. 26b-27a).

52. Wakan sen'yō-shū 和漢舩用集
('Collection of Japanese and Chinese Ships and Their Use')

Alternative title: *Gazu wakan sen'yō-shū* 画図和漢舩用集
12 chapters in 12 fascicles; 22.6 x 15.6 cm
Author: Kanazawa Kanemitsu 金沢金光

Date: preface dated Hōreki 宝暦 11 (1761), printed in Meiji 明治 3 (1870)

174

This work is a study of the typology, construction, and use of vessels in Japan and China. The overview of the Japanese and Chinese ships is particularly impressive. In addition, it goes on to discuss – albeit to a much lesser extent – ships of Korea, the Ryūkyū Archipelago, Portugal, the Netherlands, the Philippines, and so forth. The abundance of sloops used by the Japanese for river navigation is illustrated appropriately.

Birth and death dates for the author are unknown. He was a shipwright (*funadaiku* 船大工) from Osaka. For many generations, his family practiced the ship-building profession in the district Dōjima funadaiku-machi 堂島船大工町 in Osaka. The book is a distillation of their secret know-how, handed down over a period of two centuries for seven generations in the author's family.

Literature: Ichiko 1995-1996, vol. 1, p. 494, s.v. Kanazawa Kanemitsu 金沢兼光.

▲ A Dutch ship, here called *kōmō-sen* (ship of the red-haired). This illustration was selected because of its recognizability

(fascicle IV, pp. 44b-45a). Note the four-legged creature on the ship's bow.

53. Shokuba kō 飾馬考
('Study on Horse Tack')

Alternative title: *Kazari uma-kō* 飾馬考
2 fascicles; 25.3 x 18.2 cm

Author: Matoba Katsuyoshi 的場勝美
Date: Ansei 安政 4 (1857)

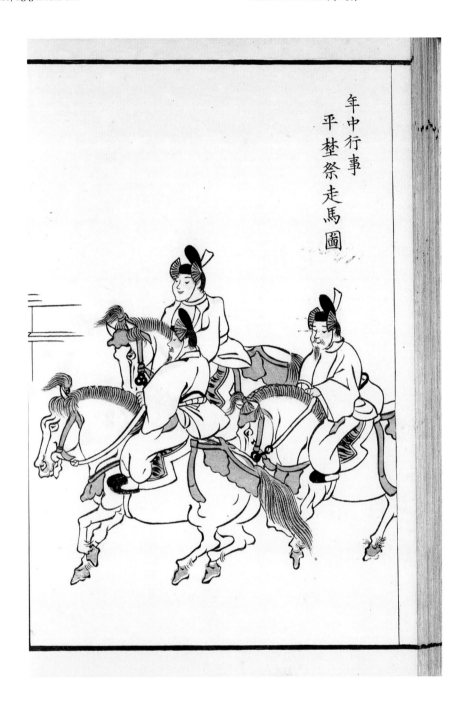

年中行事
平埜祭走馬
圖

The foreword is dated Ka'ei 嘉永 3 (1850) and was written in *kanbun* by the nobleman Kiyohara Nobuaki (also read as 'Senmei') 清原宣明 (1790-1863). The epilogue, also in *kanbun*, is by Arai Kimihiro 荒井公廣 (?-?).

According to the author's preface (*hanrei* 凡例), the book is a historical study of the horse saddle. His aim is to codify the various types and to 'immortalise' them. As a nobleman, who is usually far-removed from any and all military operations, he is not so much interested in their practical use as he is in their decorative and historical character. The codification of objects, usages, customs, techniques, and instruments belonging to the living environment of the aristocratic and warrior classes grew into a true pseudo-science called *yūsoku kojitsu* 有職故実.

On the first page of the preface, the book bears a seal printed in relief with the words "Taika sanbō zōsho" 太華山房蔵書, the collector's seal of novelist Takahashi Taika 高橋太華 (1863-1947), also famous for his young adult literature.

▲ A ritual horse race held yearly in the Shintō shrine Hirano jinja 平野神社 in Kyoto (fascicle II, p. 30b).

176

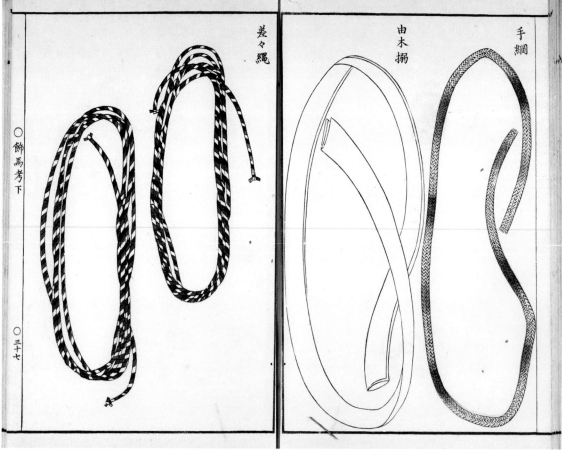

▲ A noblewoman on horseback, an illustration borrowed from an old masterpiece, known as the *Illustrated history of the temple Ishiyamadera* 石山寺 (fascicle II, pp. 31b-32a).

▲ Bridles and lassos (fascicle II, pp. 36b-37a).

54. Jokōroku 除蝗録
('An Account on the Control of Locusts')

Alternative title: *Nōka chōkoki furoku* 農家調宝記付録
1 fascicle; black-and-white ill.; 22.8 x 16 cm

Author: Ōkura Nagatsune 大蔵永常
Date: Bunsei 文政 9 (1826)

For the biographical background on the author, see the description about *Kōeki kokusan-kō* 広益国産考 (pp. 179-181). This work is a treatise on the control of locusts. Insects damaging the crops were a scourge for farmers. During the course of the seventeenth century, a farmer in the Chikuzen 筑前 Province (present-day Fukuoka Prefecture) discovered an effective method. It consisted of sprinkling whale oil over the paddies, which would form a greasy layer over their entire surface. The insects were then shaken off the rice stalks so that they fell onto the layer of oil in which they remained stuck and eventually suffocated.

Whether Ōkura Nagatsune came up with this technique all on his own, is a matter of debate. The fact that insects get stuck in oil is likely to have been observed everywhere. A Chinese source from the Qing Dynasty mentions the sprinkling of a mixture of vegetable oil and water over the crops.

Incidentally, in the West, too, there are cases where whale oil was used as a pest control. This was first recorded in the American state of Massachusetts, where whale oil was mixed with soapy water and sprayed on roses. The experiment in Chikuzen was apparently effective enough for it to spread to other parts of Japan. Even the government lent a hand. The *shōgun* informed his officials that this method was to be recommended.

The book *Jōkoroku* (1826) played a considerable role in the spread and use of this method. During his travels through the country, Nagatsune had managed to amass a wealth of practical knowledge and experience on the subject, which he organized and compiled into his book. Japanese farmers continued using this method until the end of the Second World War.

In the introductory chapter of his book, Nagatsune states that he is writing this work to introduce

177

▲ Driving out the locusts (fascicle I, p. 11a).

▲ Burning torches and lighting fires in the paddies to attract locusts (fascicle I, p. 24a).

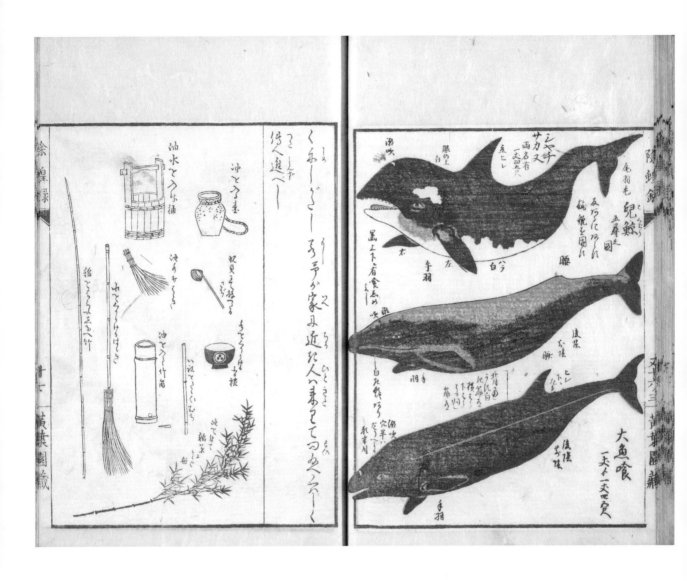

the method in the Tōhoku region, an important agricultural area in northeastern Japan, where it was not yet known. In 1844 he published a sequel (kōhen 後編). In it, he discusses other types of animal, vegetable, and mineral oils as replacements for whale oil. The sequel was apparently far less widely distributed and, as such, now has much more value as an antiquarian work than the first volume. Both volumes were reprinted in the Meiji period (first volume 1886, sequel 1887), not as a reprint of a classic but as a practical guide for farmers.

Literature: Ōkura et al. 1977, pp. 108-118; Konishi and Ōkura 1978, pp. 413-437.

▲ Whales and tools to spread the whale oil over the crops (fascicle I, pp. 16b-17a).

55. Kōeki kokusan-kō 広益国産考
('An Inquiry into Domestic Production for the Greater Public Good')

Title: *Kokusan-kō* 国産; alternative title: *Kōeki kokusan-kō*
広益國産考
8 chapters in 8 fascicles; black-and-white illustrations;

22.4 x 15.2 cm
Author: Ōkura Nagatsune 大蔵永常
Date: Tenpō 天保 13 (1842)

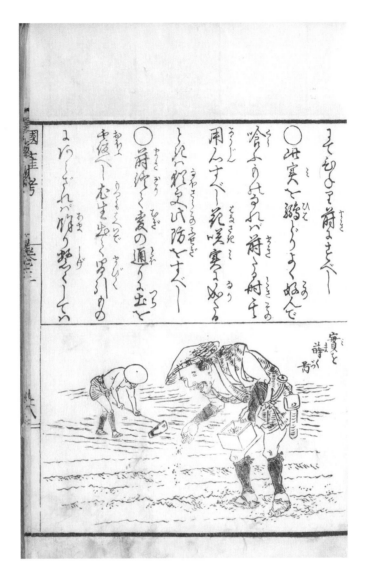

▲ Sowing (fascicle III, p. 18a).

Ōkura Nagatsune was born in Meiwa 明和 5 (1768) in the Bungo 豊後 Province (today's Ōita Prefecture). He passed away possibly in 1861. He was the fourth child in a farmer's family of eleven. His parents were middle-class farmers. The life of a farmer was relentless and dreary. Becoming a scholar or a monk were the only two possible routes of escape from the societal constraints of class. As a boy, Nagatsune dreamt of becoming a Confucian scholar, but his father opposed the idea. He then turned to the study of agriculture and apprenticed to a wholesaler specializing in wax.

When he was in his twenties, he left the region of his birth and worked as an agricultural worker in various places in Kyūshū. At the age of 29, he went to Osaka, where he first found employment as a journeyman and then as a teacher of calligraphy. After a few years, he started to make his living by trading in

seedlings, shoots from the wax tree (*hazenoki* 櫨木, Rhus succedanea), and other plants. For his work, he travelled often through the Kinai region, the most advanced farming region of Japan, and, in so doing, learnt much about farming techniques and management. He became an expert in the field of growing wax trees, the production of wax and sugar, as well as the manufacturing of farming equipment.

He became friends with a publisher in Osaka, who offered him the opportunity to turn his vast knowledge and experience into a book. Thus, seven years after he moved to Osaka, he could publish his first book, *Nōka eki* 農家益 (For the Benefit of the Farmer), in three chapters. He came very close to committing plagiarism, however, for his book was almost identical to *Kyūmin yakō no tama* 窮民夜光 の玉 (The Shining Pearl in the Night that Rescues the People), a work published by Takahashi Zenzō

179

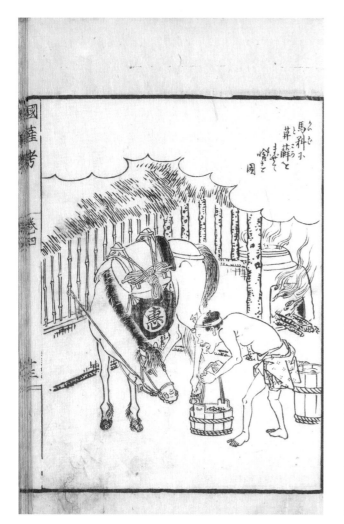

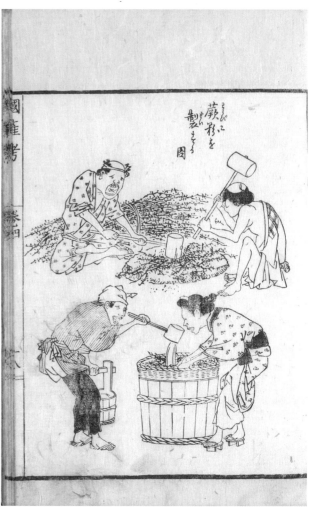

高橋善蔵 (1684-1761) some fifty years earlier. He did not stop there, instead publishing one book after another, making him one of the three foremost agricultural experts of the Edo period (1600-1868).

After having lived in Osaka for 29 years, he moved to Edo. From now on, he would only live from his expertise and by his pen. In 1834, he was officially appointed as advisor of economic affairs (*kōsankata* 興産方) in the service of the feudal lord of the Tawara 田原 domain in the Mikawa 三河 Province. Thus this farmer's son joined the samurai class, albeit at a lower rank. Nobody less than the famous scholar and painter Watanabe Kazan 渡辺崋山 (1793-1841), advisor to the same domain, had recommended him for the position. At the time, Nagatsune was already 67 years old. His salary was the equivalent of the stipend (*fuchi* 扶持) of six men, a status comparable to that of an *ashigaru* 足軽 (samurai of low rank). Now he would finally have the opportunity to put his theories in practice. However, he was denied the time to reap the rewards of his know-how. When his protector Watanabe Kazan first landed in jail and was then put under house arrest for criticizing the *Bakufu*, Japan's military government, Nagatsune, guilty by association, was fired.

He found temporary residence in Okazaki. His wife was ill, and his daughter had passed the age of marriage. In Okazaki, life must have been very bleak. In Tenpō 13 (1842), he was appointed as advisor of economic affairs (*kōsankata*) of the Hamamatsu 浜松 domain. He was given a fairly large residence with a garden, the allowance (*fuchi*) of five men and ten *ryō* 両.[2] Three years later, however, his lord was fired as advisor of the *Bakufu* and had no choice but to change domains. This also meant the end of Nagatsune's tenure. In these three years, he published *Kokusan-kō*, which was later incorporated into his *magnum opus Kōeki kokusan-kō* 広益国産考, and he also completed the manuscript of this latter work. This book, counting eight chapters, was published in 1860, the year of his death.

Nearly all agricultural treatises (*nōsho* 農書) written in the Edo period were penned by farmers who lived in their region of birth all their life, and who wanted to pass on the rich experience and know-how they had acquired while farming to their children and descendants. There are only two exceptions to this pattern: Miyazaki Yasusada 宮崎安貞 (1623-1697) and Ōkura Nagatsune (1768-1860). These two authors travelled through farming villages in

 Mixing yams (*tokoro* 野老, Discorea japonica) into horse feed (fascicle IV, p. 13a).

 Making bracken starch (fascicle IV, p. 18a).

180

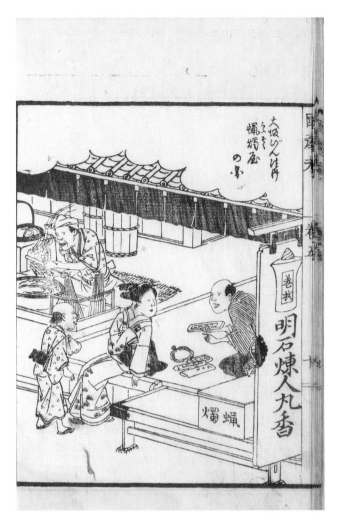

various agricultural areas, especially the Kinai region, and systematically observed their customs and techniques. After his travels, Miyazaki retired to his village of birth, and during the ensuing 40 years put into practice all he had learnt, while at the same time recording it for posterity. The result of his labour is the *Nōgyō zensho* 農業全書 in ten chapters.

Ōkura Nagatsune, on the other hand, did not stay in his native village, nor did he return to it. He settled first in Osaka, then in Edo, and devoted himself entirely to writing books on agriculture as practised in the most advanced areas, intending them as guidebooks for farmers in less advanced regions. During his lifetime, Nagatsune published 30 books in 70 fascicles. Iinuma Jirō 飯沼二郎 (1918-2005), a prominent agrarian historian, has called him the only agricultural journalist of the Edo period.

The techniques and farming equipment Ōkura Nagatsune describes in his books were all tried out by him first. His descriptions are detailed and accurate, so that they might benefit the reader who wants to put his advice and instructions into practice. He did not write for his children or descendants, nor for the farmers of his native region, but for the farm-

ers in all of Japan. For this reason, his descriptions are more elaborate and systematic and require less prior knowledge. Moreover, his writings are always accompanied by detailed and accurate illustrations, based on sketches which Nagatsune himself drew from life. While Miyazaki's scholarship was limited to the cultivation of rice, Ōkura Nagatsune's main focus lies on profitable specialty crops.

Traditionally, taxes were collected in rice, but by the end of the Edo period, these levies no longer sufficed to keep up the high living standards the samurai class wanted to maintain. Samurai and farmers alike looked for other specialty crops that would yield a higher return. A commercial monopoly on specialty crops could potentially constitute an important source of income. In the beginning of the nineteenth century, a vibrant nightlife began to develop in the three main cities, Edo, Osaka, and Kyoto. The use of candles increased spectacularly, stimulating the cultivation of wax trees (*haze* 櫨), which provided the raw material for the candles. One of the intended purposes of Ōkura Nagatsune's books was to serve as a manual for the cultivation and trade of specialty crops, such as wax trees.

Literature: Aoki 1997, pp. 59-88; Ōkura 1999.

▲ A candle shop in Osaka (fascicle V, p. 10b).

▲ Clearing brushwood, cultivating the fields, and sowing (fascicle VIII, p. 19a).

56. Seikei zusetsu 成形圖説
('Explanation on the Natural World with Illustrations')

30 chapters in 30 fascicles; 26.6 x 18 cm
Authors: Shimazu Shigehide 島津重豪, Sō 曽 Han 槃

(Senshun 占春), Shirao Kunihashira 白尾国柱
Date: preface dated Bunka 文化 1 (1804)

182

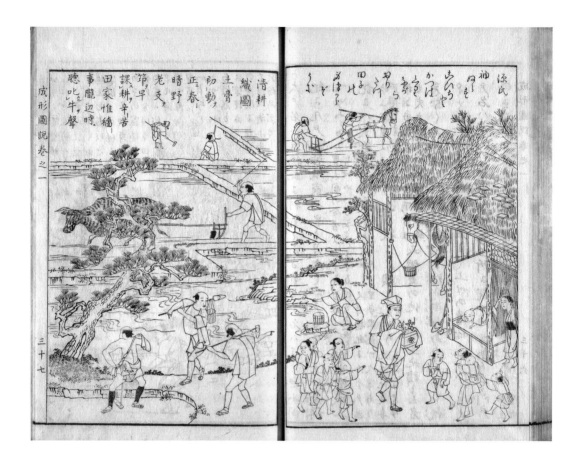

Shimazu Shigehide (1745-1833), the feudal lord of Satsuma, was an enlightened and progressive ruler. As part of his policy to stimulate agriculture and industry in his domain, he set out to compile a *summa* of all available knowledge on the products of nature. He assigned this work to Sō Han (common name: Senshun) (1758-1834), a great *honzōgaku* specialist. He was assisted by Shirao Kunihashira (1762-1821), a specialist in *kokugaku* 国学, the school of 'national learning' (a school of Japanese philology and philosophy). In a workshop specially dedicated for that enterprise in the lord's residence in Edo, the two men completed this work, which eventually consisted of 100 chapters. In 1806, when only thirty chapters had been printed, a fire destroyed all manuscript drafts and woodblocks. Undeterred, Sō Han continued his work, but in 1829 all manuscripts drafts and woodblocks once again went up in flames. Even then he continued his work, and it is from this work that the manuscript drafts have been preserved. The thirty chapters that survived the 1806 fire were printed again in Tenpō 天保 2 (1831). The manuscripts of the drafts which Sō Han delivered after the fire of 1829, and which were preserved, were typographically printed and published in the twentieth century.

The copy of the UCLouvain is not the original edition (*motohan* 元版) of 1806 but the reprint of 1831.

For the standards of the time, Shimazu Shigehide enjoyed a long life. His most active years, however, were those between 1780 and 1790. When the Dutchman Jan Cock Blomhoff (1779-1853), the "opperhoofd" (*kapitan*) of the Dutch factory on the artificial island Dejima in Nagasaki Bay, made the obligatory courtesy trip to the Edo court (the so-called 'hofreis naar Edo') in 1818, he was greeted by Shigehide upon reaching Shinagawa, a suburban district of Edo. Shigehide was very much into everything Dutch. Blomhoff says about Shigehide that he greeted him in Dutch and "enige onverschillige discoursen voerde" (addressed to him a few discourses on sundry topics). *Seikei zusetsu* does indeed include (in Japanese transcription) quite a number of Dutch words such as the names for the months and names for various types of scholarly fields, and so forth.

Sō Han descended from Chinese in the Fujian province, who had settled in Nagasaki many generations ago, running a medical practice and working as Chinese-Japanese interpreters. He was born in Edo and entered the service of the lord of Shōnai 庄内 in 1776. After one year, he resigned from his position

▲ Work on the rice fields (chapter 1, pp. 36b–37a).

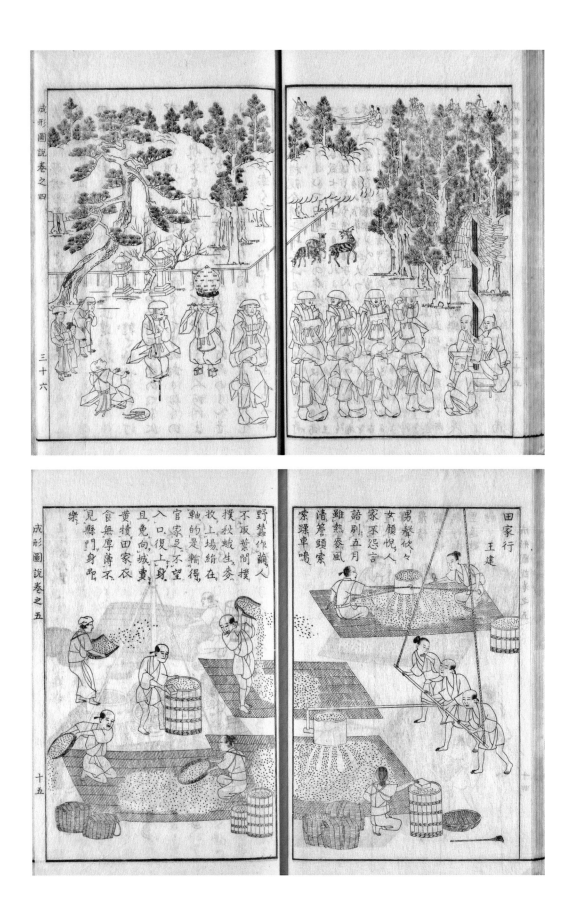

there to study medicine under Taki Rankei 多紀藍渓 (1732-1801), in addition to *materia medica* (pharmacology) under Tamura Ransui 田村藍水 (1718-

1776). In 1792, he became the personal physician to Shimazu Shigehide, who greatly admired him.

Literature: Forrer and Effert 2000, p. 78; Needham 1954, vol. 4, pt. 2, pp. 171-172; Nichiran gakkai/Numata 1984, p. 377.

⬆ The religious dances honouring the god of Mount Kanasa (chapter 4, pp. 35b-36a).

▲ Winnowing the rice (chapter 5, pp. 14b-15a).

57. Sumō kumogakure-ge 相撲隠雲解
('The Secret Pages on Wrestling Sumō Explained')

1 chapter; 27 x 17.8 cm
Author: Shikimori Kagyū 式守蝸牛
Date: preface dated Kansei 寛政 5 (1793)

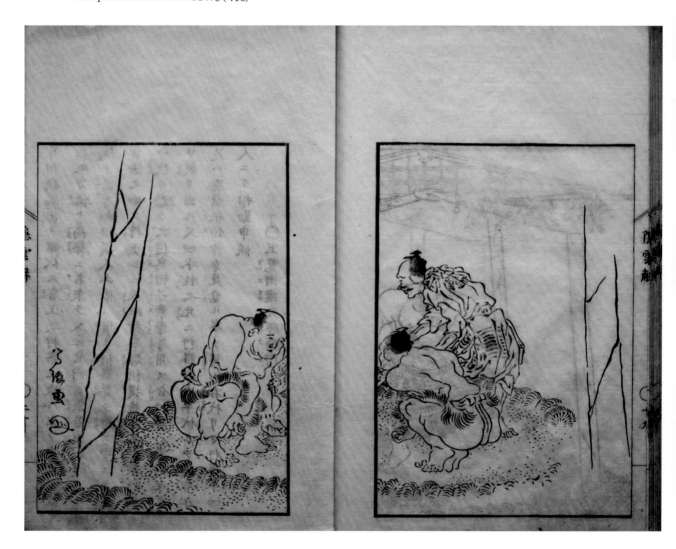

184

This is a treatise on the origins of *sumo* wrestling and the customs surrounding it, supplemented with a description of a ritual sumo bout organized at the behest and for the pleasure of the *shōgun*.

The author Shikimori Inosuke 伊之助 (1740-1822, alternative dates 1743-1823) was a famed chief referee (*tate-gyōji* 立行司) of sumo in Edo, and the first incumbent of the rank of chief referee with the hereditary stage name Shikimori Inosuke. He began his career in 1767 and ended it in 1793. The bearer of the stage name Shikimori Inosuke (the current one is the 41st in line) is one of only two chief referees, the other one being the bearer of the hereditary stage name Kimura Shōnosuke 木村庄之助, who has precedence over Shikimori. The latter is associated with the champion of the west, whereas Kimura is associated with the champion of the east. In Sumo,

east has precedence over west. The chief referees enter the arena together with their associated champion. After his retirement as head referee, Shikimori Inosuke adopted the sobriquet (*gō*) 'kagyū', meaning 'snail'. The shape of the snail can be observed in his stylized autograph (*kaō* 花押). It is under this name that he published this book.

On the *mikaeshi* 見返し (inside of the front cover) is mentioned: 不許数外千部必絶 'circulation may not exceed 1000 copies.' The work also includes a preface by Senjintei Sunchō 千尋亭寸鳥, not mentioned by Yamazaki. On the inside of the back page, the following notice is written by hand: 禁売 'may not be sold' and 白木家蔵書 'collection of the Shiragi family'. The book bears some three collector's seals, one with the text 'Ogura bunko'.

▲ A sumo bout (chapter 1, pp. 19b.-20a).

58. Bukka Engo zenji hekigan-roku 佛果圜悟禪師碧巖録
('*The Blue Cliff Record* by Zen master Bukka Engo')

Alternative titles: *Bukka engo zenji Hekigan-roku shudenshō* 仏果圜悟禅師碧巌録種電鈔 / *Hekigan-shū shudenshō* 碧巌集種電鈔

12 chapters in 5 fascicles, 27 x 15.3 cm
Author: Taichi Jittō 大智実統
Date: preface dated Kyōhō 享保21 (1736), printed Genbun 元文4 (1739)

Bukka Engo zenji hekigan-roku, or *Hekigan-roku* (Ch.: *Bi yan lu*), is the Japanese edition of a Zen classic that was compiled in China in 1125, during the reign of Emperor Huizong 徽宗 of the Song Dynasty (960-1279). It is a collection of so-called *kōan* 公案, to which two commentators have added verses and comments of various kinds.

The term *kōan* (Ch. *Gong-an*) literally means 'public case,' suggesting a likeness between law cases and the one hundred anecdotes of sayings and doings, mainly from traditional accounts of Zen masters and acolytes, included in this book. *Kōan* serve as precedents to judge whether or not a student has correctly grasped a certain aspect of the teachings. Later, *kōan* simply meant a problem of the Zen doctrine which was phrased as a riddle or a paradox. *Kōan* are a remarkable aspect of religious literature of Zen Buddhism, which probably does not have an equal in any other religious tradition. They make up part of the training of Zen acolytes. Especially the Rinzai 臨済 school sets great stock by this aspect of training. The master gives the novice a *kōan*. The latter has to come up with a sufficient answer, only then will he be given another one. As he succeeds in formulating answers that are approved by his master, he advances in his religious development.

The text we now know as the *Hekigan-roku* originally consisted of a collection of one hundred *kōan* selected from old Zen records by Xuedou Chongxian (Jap. Setchō Jūken 雪竇重顕, 980-1052), an exceptional Zen master and poet. To each *kōan* he added verses (*geju* 偈頌) and remarks to elucidate the meaning. This expanded text was titled *Setchō juko hyakusoku* 雪竇頌古百則 (Setchō's One Hundred Verses about Old [*Kōan*]). The book was very popular. Some sixty years later, the Zen master Yuanwu Keqin (Jap. Engo 圜悟克勤, 1063-1135) added glosses (so called 'capping phrases', *chakugo* 着語) to each sentence or saying in the *kōan* text and each accompanying poem by Setchō, in addition to synthetic commentaries (*hyōshō* 評唱) on the context of each *kōan*. Moreover, he added a short introduction (*suiji* 垂示) to most cases. Together, the original anecdotes, Xuedou's verses, Yuanwu's introductions, remarks, and commentaries all form the book *Hekigan-roku*. The title is allegedly inspired by the name of the abode on Mount Jia 夾山 in Hunan in China, where Yuanwu originally delivered his explanations of the *kōan*. In another version, Yuanwu's abode displayed calligraphy for the two characters *bi* 碧 (azure) and *yan* 巌 (rock); *lu* (Jap. *roku*) 録 means 'record, note, document'.

Although the commentaries of Yuanwu were certainly no superfluous luxury for understanding the paradoxes and hidden allusions of this text, some masters in the Zen school deemed them to be too intellectual and believed that they hampered the immediate and direct experience. For that reason, Dahui Zonggao 大慧宗杲 (Jap. Daie Sōkō, 1089-1163), the successor of Yuanwu and also a great Zen master, so tradition alleges, destroyed the woodblocks of Yuanwu's edition. The version of the *Bi yan lu* (*Hekigan roku*) known to us today is the work of the layman Zhang Mingyuan (Jap. Chō Mei'en 張明遠), who around 1300 supposedly recovered whatever copies remained of the text and, based on those, reconstructed the original book through emendation and collation. In the meantime, the text had already fallen prey to corruption and additions, especially Yuanwu's glosses and commentaries (ill. 2: fascicle I, p. 2b). The most important parts of the book, the actual *kōan*, Xuedou's verses, and Yuanwu's introductions were presumably left reasonably intact. All extant editions were indirectly based on this edition.

According to Zen tradition, the famous Japanese monk Eihei Dōgen 永平道元 (1200-1253) brought back to Japan a handwritten copy of this book in 1227, after a sojourn of four years in China, which in view of the date would mean that he copied a version that antedated Zhang Mingyuan's reconstituted text. This copy, known as the 'One Night Blue Cliff Record', because he allegedly copied the text in one night the night before his return to Japan, is preserved at present in the Daijōji Temple 大乗寺 in the city of Kanazawa 金沢市. If it was indeed transmitted to Japan in the course of the thirteenth century, by Dōgen or someone else, it represents the oldest version of the text extant.

In the 1920s the National Committee identified this book as *Bukka Engo zenji Hekigan-roku*, which is the complete title of *Hekigan-roku*. This title is kind of generic, however, since Zhang Mingyuan's version did not come down to us as an independent text but only as quoted in two Japanese editions. One of these is Taichi Jittō's 大智実統 *Bukka Engo zenji Hekigan-shū shudenshō* 佛果圜悟禪師碧巖録種電鈔 or *Hekigan-roku shudenshō* 碧巌録種電鈔 (12 *maki*) for short, the two titles given by Yamazaki as alternative titles. The other is Kiyō Hōshū's 岐陽方秀 (1361-1424) *Hekiganroku Funishō* 碧巌録不二鈔 (10 maki, published 1657). Both offer a detailed commentary on *Hekiganroku* in *kanbun*.

185

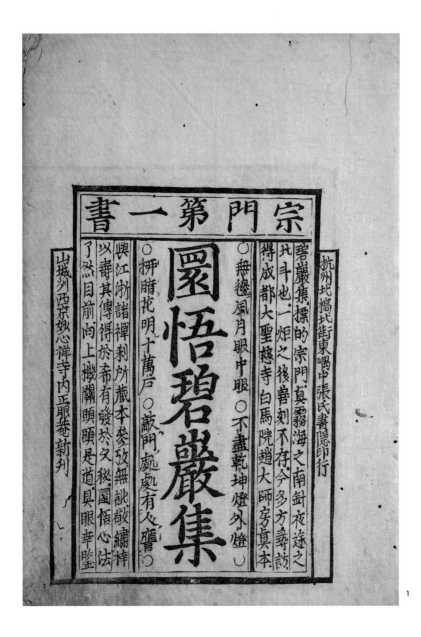

1

▲ The title page (fascicle I).

On the reverse of the cover the National Committee pasted a slip of paper on which it identified this copy as a movable type edition of the Myōshinji Temple 妙心寺 in the western district of Kyoto, dating from the Genna-Kan'ei period (1615-1644). This dating does not tally with the identification as Taichi Jittō's compilation. Taichi Jittō 大智実統 was a Zen monk of the Ōbaku 黄檗 school. His compilation, comprised of 12 chapters in 12 fascicles, has a preface dated Kyōhō 享保 21 (1736) and was printed in Genbun 元文 4 (1739), according to the colophon.

The typographic style of the title page in the UCLouvain copy is remarkably different from the main body of the text. It is a woodblock-printed page, ostensibly transferred from an older edition (*fukkoku-bon* 復刻本), presumably a *gozanban* 五山版 edition. The original frame (*kyōkaku* 匡郭) of the title page has ostensibly been extended by a column to the left and one to the right. In these two columns the publisher has added the colophon data

relating to the reprint at hand. The vertical column to the right states that the Chinese book *Bi yan lu* was printed in Hangzhou, the one to the left that it was reprinted in the Shōgan-an 正眼庵, a temple in the large Zen monastery Myōshinji 妙心寺, west of Kyoto (ill. 1). This woodblock-printed title page has been added to precede a movable type impression (*kokatsujiban* 古活字版). One may wonder whether it was the original page of this movable type impression. Maybe it was deliberately borrowed from an older (Chinese?) woodblock version to lend the book that extra Chinese flavour. Since this book is an old print in movable type, it is an edition dating from the early seventeenth century. The identification with Taichi's compilation is therefore erroneous.

At the conclusion of every chapter someone has pressed a seal mentioning 嶀中張氏書隱刻梓: 'published based on the hidden versions of Mr. Zhang [Mingyuan] from the [eastern] mountains',[3] as if to stress that it was a reprint of the oldest extant ver-

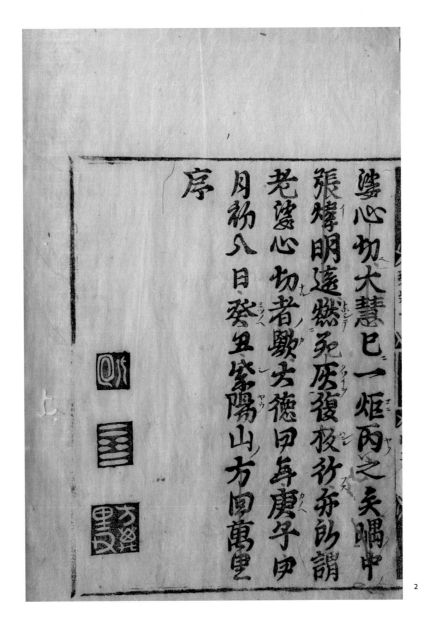

序

婆心切大慧巳一炬丙之矣囑中
張燼明遠然死灰復叛竹弄所謂
老婆心切者歟吉德甲午庚午伊
月初八日癸丑紫陽山方回萬里

2

sion. The title page suggests a *fukkoku-bon* 復刻本 of a Chinese edition, though this is not actually the case, since it is a reprint in movable type.

On the UCLouvain copy someone has added by hand in ink syntactic marks (*kaeriten* 返り点 and *furigana* 振り仮名), as well as strokes (*shubiki*) and points in vermillion (*shuten*). On the final page of volumes 1, 3, and 4, there is a handwritten note by a reader, presumably the person who added the syntactic marks. It says: 'Soryō 祖了 of the Kōshūji Temple 光周寺, in the village Sugawara 菅原, in the Kusu commandery 玖珠郡, in the province of Bungo 豊後. On a favourable day in the new year's month of Kyōhō 5, Year of the Rat.' Kyōhō 5 is the year 1720. This inscription too precedes the date of publication of Taichi Jittō's compilation. Consequently, the identification in Yamazaki's catalogue must be wrong. The original title slip (*daisen*) is missing. Someone has scribbled the title on the spot where the slip

once was. The same rather sloppy hand has scribbled on the cover of fascicle IV the characters: 養寿寺什物, "a treasure of the Yōjuji Temple". Whether there is any connection with the Yōjuji Temple in the town Nishio, in the Aichi Prefecture, is unclear.

Hekigan-roku has seen many editions and reprints and was frequently translated into various Western languages in the twentieth century.

Ill. 2: end of preface by Fanghui Wanli 方回萬里 (1227-1305), referring in a humorous pun to the burning by Dahui and the salvaging by Zheng Yuanming (fascicle I, preface, p. 2b): 大慧巳一炬丙之矣… "Dahui once burnt it, but Zhang Mingyuan from the [eastern] mountains breathed new life into the dead ashes and published it…"

Literature: Asahina 1982; *Zengaku jiten* 1974, p. 1271, s.v. "Hekiganshū"; p. 1272, s.v. "Hekiganshū shūdenshō"; Ono Gemmyō 1978, vol. 9, p. 359; Katō 1939; Nishitani and Yanagida 1974; Iriya 1981; Hirata 1982. Sekida 1977; Cleary/Cleary 1977; Heine 2016.

▲ **End of preface by Fanghui Wanli** 方回萬里 (1227-1305).

Movable Type Editions

The typographical printing technique was introduced in Japan when Alessandro Valignano (1539-1606), the Visitor of the Society of Jesus, imported a Western printing press into Japan in 1590. The press was first installed in the Jesuit college of Kazusa 加津佐 but was soon moved to Amakusa 天草 and finally to Nagasaki 長崎. Valignano was accompanied by a Japanese man, known only by his Western name Constantino Dourado (1566-1620), who had learnt the art of printing in Lisbon. He had already demonstrated his mastery of the printing technique in Goa and was likely the first to operate the printing press in Japan. Barely forty works of these so-called Jesuit editions have been preserved in Japan, and of some of them only one single copy. How many copies a single edition totalled is hard to ascertain, but it has been claimed that the number of copies for a single edition was in the range of 1,300-1,500.[4] A huge number of copies went up in flames or was otherwise destroyed as a result of the persecution of Christians in the seventeenth century. Several scholars have made an effort to identify and inventory the total output of the Jesuit press. The total tally of confirmed titles in the world stands at forty-one,[5] although the Jesuits may have printed around one hundred titles before they were silenced permanently.

Since it was a European printing press, the first editions were naturally produced in a European language, predominantly Latin. Very soon, however, Japanese dies and fonts were created as well, probably first *katakana*, followed by *hiragana* and some *kanji* (Chinese characters or logographs). Although it goes without saying that most editions had a religious, devotional, or educational intent, quite a few secular works were printed as well. A part of the thirteenth-century war tale *Heike monogatari* 平家物語, in an adapted version and transcribed into Roman script, was printed in Amakusa in 1592. This was the first work of Japanese literature (in the sense of 'belles-lettres') ever printed in Japan; before that, only handwritten copies had circulated. Many books about language study, intended as a tool to help Jesuits in their study of Japanese, were also printed. Of the *Rakuyōshū* 落葉集, a Chinese-Japanese dictionary, for example, an exceptionally fine edition was produced, a copy of which is kept in the Archivum Romanum Societatis Iesu in Rome. Whether the typographical editions of the Jesuits had any deep impact on the further development of printing in Japan, however, is doubtful.

More likely, this honour goes to the typographical technique developed in Korea. Although there are clues suggesting that a typographical technique with ceramic fonts, and later to a limited extent with wooden fonts, existed in China during the tenth century, this Chinese practice seems to have had no influence on the development of movable type in Japan. The independent Korean tradition of typography thus was that much more influential. It was transmitted to Japan at the end of the sixteenth century. It made use of metal fonts. Its origins date back to the early thirteenth century, but it became a matter of national interest when, in 1392, the Korean court set up a bureau for publishing, both for casting type and printing books. The oldest examples of this kind of movable type editions extant today date back to the end of the fourteenth century, half a century before Gutenberg's Bible (1453).

This marked the start of typography as a method of publishing books in East Asia. Why the technique caught on is unclear, since woodblock printing had been the preferred technique for many centuries. The Korean contribution consisted mainly in the invention of a method to cast metal type. From the end of the fourteenth century on, Korean printers also used wooden type. Both metal and wooden fonts were introduced in Japan in the wake of the military campaigns of Toyotomi Hideyoshi 豊臣秀吉 (1536-1598) on the peninsula. Both materials were used on a large scale in Japan during the seventeenth century.

The Korean bureau for publishing had been established by the Yi 李 Dynasty (1392-1910), when Confucianism held pride of place. Unsurprisingly, the books printed by the bureau were secular works in Classical Chinese, mainly Confucian texts. Naturally, when Korean typography entered Japan, it was strongly associated with secular works, in contrast to woodblock printing, which from its beginnings had had a strong association with Buddhism.

Korean movable type and printing equipment were taken to Japan as spoils of war and offered to Emperor Go-Yōzei 後陽成 (1586-1611). They were immediately put to use, and the first work printed with the Korean equipment was the Confucian classic *Xiao jing* 孝經 ('Classic of Filial Piety'), printed in 1593. It is not known whether Korean printers were taken to Japan as well.

Because the Korean technique was associated with the elite of Japanese society, it enjoyed great prestige and strongly influenced the ensuing history of printing in the country. For a period of about fifty years, Korean typography was adopted on a large scale for the production of books. These editions are known as *kokatsuji-ban* 古活字版 (old movable type editions). This does not imply, however, that typography completely supplanted woodblock printing, which continued to be used on a large scale, especially for editions that included illustrations. Moreover, facsimiles of Chinese editions were also still being printed using the *kabusebori* 被せ彫り[6] technique, as was the case with a Chinese *materia medica*, *Bencao gangmu* (*Honzō kōmoku*) 本草綱目 (Classification of Materia Medica), of which a late sixteenth-century Chinese edition was published in 1637.

Shortly after 1593, Emperor Go-Yōzei ordered the carving of wooden type. He and his successor, Emperor Go-Mizuno'o 後水尾 (1611-1629), ordered the printing of a number of so-called imperial prints using this type. Remarkably, all of these works – printed between 1595 and 1621 – were secular books. The majority were Chinese, such as the *Four Books* of Confucianism, but there were some Japanese works as well, for example, the *Nihon shoki* 日本書紀 (*The Chronicles of Japan*).

Although many secular works were being printed by now, the close traditional link between printing and Buddhist texts still had not entirely been broken. Even during the seventeenth century, Buddhist texts continued to occupy a sizeable part of the Japanese market. Temples even experimented with movable type for the printing of Buddhist texts. There are testimonies pointing to a budding cooperation between temples and local printers, run by laypeople on a commercial basis. These are the first signs heralding a new trend: the transition

from editions published under the protection of a powerful institution to commercial editions by private citizens.

Thus, private individuals started printing books. Very soon after the introduction of Korean type, wooden type had been cut, not only of the Chinese logographs but also of the Japanese syllabic script. This came at an opportune time, as printers started to publish more and more texts in Japanese. The most striking representative of this new category of movable type editions by individuals are the so-called *Saga-bon* 嵯峨本 (Saga editions), printed between 1599 and 1610, in Saga near Kyoto. They were the product of a unique cooperation between the versatile artist Hon'ami Kōetsu 本阿弥光悦 (1558-1637) and the intellectual merchant Suminokura Soan 角倉素庵 (1571-1632). Kōetsu no doubt provided the splendid calligraphy from which the type was carved, and perhaps also the layout, while Suminokura took care of financing and printing. The extensive use of ligatures, making it possible to reproduce in print the flowing calligraphic lines of the Japanese *hiragana* writing, as well as the incorporation of illustrations, and in certain cases the use of high-quality paper, resulted in the production of unsurpassed jewels of printing. The *Saga-bon* almost exclusively comprise texts written in Japanese, in particular *Ise monogatari* 伊勢物語 (*The Tale of Ise*). This is the first illustrated, secular Japanese book that has come down to us, in various editions indeed, a fact attesting to a wide circulation. Although these books may never have been intended for sale, and as such may not have been published in the commercial sense, the *Saga-bon* nevertheless exerted great influ-

ence because they used Japanese syllabic writing and paved the way for the routine publication of illustrated versions of texts written in the Japanese language (in contrast to Classical Chinese). Illustrated editions became the norm during the remainder of the Edo period (1600-1868).

Before long, in spite of this short-lived outburst of movable type editions, woodblock-printed editions (*seihan* 整版) recovered their erstwhile dominant position, although wooden movable type did continue on a modest scale. Here a few words on terminology are in order. Editions published up to the first half of the seventeenth century are specifically called 'old movable type editions' (*kokatsuji-ban*) in contradistinction to later editions, published after the heyday of movable type up to the early Meiji period, which are called 'early modern wooden movable type editions' (*kinsei mokkatsuji-ban* 近世木活字版). There is no unanimity among scholars about where the line has to be drawn between the 'old' editions and the early 'early modern' editions. For some the 'early modern' editions start from the second half of the seventeenth century, while others have them starting in the late eighteenth century (Tenmei and Kansei eras). Indeed, around this time a Chinese book on printing technology titled *Qinding Wuying dian juchenban chengshi* (Jap. *Kintei Bueiden shūchinban hōshiki*) 欽定武英殿聚珍版程式 ('Technique of movable type editions printed at the Wuying Hall, by Imperial Command) was introduced in Japan. Using some of the know-how contained in it, Japanese printers were able to reduce the production costs of the printing process, thus paving the way for publications with limited capital or in limited copies, privately printed books (*shikaban* 私家版), amateur editions, and so on. In addition, it now became economically viable to publish schoolbooks at educational institutions, ranging from the official schools of the Edo Shogunate to the local schools of the feudal fiefs down to the privately run schools of Confucian scholars.

In those days, the concept of 'copyright' was extremely vague. The owners of woodblocks came closest to what we would now consider to be the copyright holders. They were mostly concentrated in the three major publishing centres of Edo, Kyoto, and Osaka. They understandably looked askance at these 'infringements' on their near monopoly, but the trend could not be stopped.

Private presses were much harder to control by the censors of the Edo Shogunate or the authorities of the feudal domains, so it became the favourite channel to launch new-fangled ideas (including in the fields of politics, economics, and ideology) or to tap new kinds of readership. There are allegedly more than 1,000 titles of early modern wooden movable type editions extant.

Literature: Chibbett 1977, pp. 61-78; Kornicki 1998; Koakimoto 2010, pp. 221–237.

59. Eigen jakushitsu oshō-go 永源寂室和尚語
('The Sentences of Zen Master Eigen Jakushitsu')

Alternative titles: *En'ō zenji goroku* 円応禅師語録 /
Jakushitsu-roku 寂室録 / *En'ō roku* 円応録
2 chapters in 2 fascicles or 4 chapters in 4 fascicles;
23.4 x 14.3 cm

Author: Jakushitsu Genkō 寂室元光
Date: compiled circa Jōji 貞治 6 (1367), printed in Eiwa
永和 3 (1377)
Gozan edition

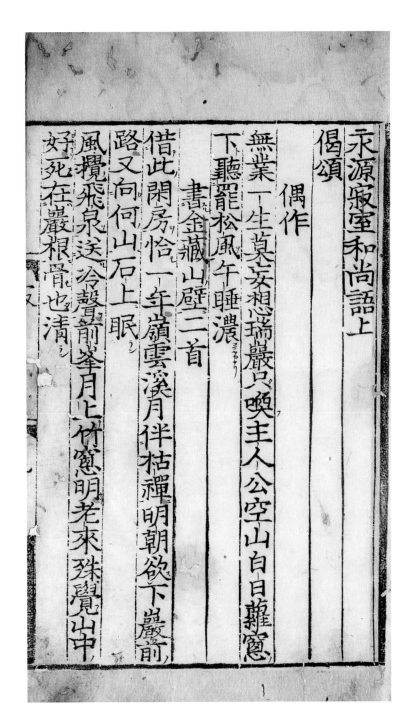

This book contains the sayings, sermons, essays, and poems by Zen master Eigen 永源 (1290-1367), written down by some of his disciples shortly after his death. He is called Eigen because he founded the Eigenji temple 永源寺. His monastic name (*dōgō* 道号) was Jakushitsu, and his taboo name (*imina* 諱), given to him by his teacher, was Genkō 元光. Eigen hailed from the province of Mimasaka. Already at a young age, he went to study under a Zen master of the famous Tōfukuji temple 東福寺 in Kyoto. In 1320, at the age of 31 years (according to Japanese count), he travelled in the company of Kaō Sōnen 可翁宗然, a Zen painter who later became famous, to China, which was ruled at the time by the Mongol Yuan Dynasty (1279-1368). There he visited several prominent Zen masters. After a stay of 6 years, he

▲ The first page of the first chapter (fascicle I/chapter 1, p. 1a).
The text starts off with *gāthās* (stanzas).

returned to Japan, to live a life of seclusion in various Zen temples for the next 25 years, systematically declining invitations from the imperial court or the military government, the shogunate. When he was 72 years old, he was granted some land by the provincial governor (*shugoshoku* 守護職) Sasaki Ujiyori 佐々木氏頼 (1326-1370), on which he was allowed to build a temple, which he called Eigenji. After his death, the emperor awarded him the posthumous sobriquet (*okurigō* 諡號) of En'ō Zenji. In November 1928, he was given the honorific title (*shōgō* 称号) Shōtō kokushi 正燈国師 by Hirohito, the young Shōwa emperor. The temple Eigenji is now the head temple of one of 15 autonomous branches of the Rinzai school of Japanese Zen Buddhism.

Chapter 1 of the book includes 269 Buddhist stanzas (called *geju* 偈頌, from the Sanskrit term *gāthā*: a poem usually of the *zekku* 絶句 sort, a so-called modern style poem in Classical Chinese, consisting of four lines, comprising a total of 20 or 28 characters, depending on whether the line length is of either five or seven characters). *Maki* 2 includes 34 essays on liturgical prescriptions and performance, 19 essays, 15 letters, 56 sermons, counsel for posterity, and posthumous gāthās. There is also an epilogue (*batsu* 跋) contributed by the monk Shōkin 性均 at the time of the book's publication in 1377. In the year Kan'ei 寛永 21 (1644), Isshi Bunshu 一糸文守 (posthumous sobriquet: Butchō kokushi 仏頂国師; 1608-1646), venerated as the second founder of Eigenji, wrote a hagiographic essay about Master Eigen, which was included in the Shōho 正保 2 (1645) reprint of the book. There is also an old typographical edition with wooden type consisting of 2 *maki*. In Genroku 元禄 10 (1697), an annotated version in 4 *maki* was published. Of this version, an enlarged edition with a critical apparatus was published in Kan'en 寛延 4 (1751). Of the version in two *maki*, a reprint appeared in the Kyōhō 享保 period (1716-1736). Another version appeared during the Kanbun 寛文 period (1661-1673), this one consisting of three chapters. The frequent reprints prove that this text was quite popular among Zen monks.

The *kanbun* text in this edition has been supplied with *kaeriten* (marks to indicate the order the characters should be read in) and *okurigana* (kana suffixes which follow the characters to inflect verbs and adjectives). This copy also has *shubiki* 朱引き (lines in red) and *shuten* 朱点 (dots in red), tools for marking and punctuation, added in the course of reading or study by a diligent student or reader.

In the UCLouvain collection the protective wrapper containing the Gozan version also contains a copy of the enlarged edition of 1751, which interestingly bears the collector's seal of the Ōryōkutsu 黄龍窟 (the Cave of the Yellow Dragon), the library of the famous Zen temple Kenninji 建仁寺 in Kyoto. It was no doubt the National Committee that put it with the original edition in the same wrapper.

Literature: Ono Gemmyō 1978, vol. 1, p. 249.

60. Hachikazuki はちかづき
('The Girl with the Bowl on her Head')

3 fascicles; colour illustrations; rare; 15.9 x 23.5 cm
Note inside the book: "Ancient manuscript avec des ill.

colorées dites 'Naraye' "
Date: 17th-18th century, no date in the book

This is a story about a Japanese Cinderella, Hachikazuki 鉢かづき (the girl with the bowl on her head), sometimes also called Hachikatsugi.

In Katano 交野 in the Kawachi 河内 Province, the Governor of Bichū 備中, Sanetaka 実高, lived with his wife. The married couple had no children. The couple prayed and prayed to the Bodhisattva Kannon of the Hasedera temple 長谷寺 and finally their prayers were heard: They would get a daughter. Then, when the girl was thirteen years old, the mother passed away.

Just before dying, the mother put a wooden bowl on the head of her daughter, so deep that it covered most of her face. To make matters worse, the bowl turns out to be stuck and impossible to remove. The girl is now forced to go through life with the bowl on her head. This offers the pretext for her stepmother – the father had remarried in the meantime – to expel

her from the house, with nothing but a thin dress to cover her body. She is doomed to roam around and, in utter despair, she decides to drown herself. The bowl on her head keeps her afloat, however, and she is saved by a fisherman.

Eventually she ends up in the residence of a lord, where she is given the task to stoke the fire in the bathhouse. The lord's son notices her beautiful hands and falls in love with her. Because the son's parents object to his intention to marry the servant girl, the two youngsters decide to elope. At that very moment the bowl drops off the head of the girl and breaks. Money, valuables, and fine clothing appear from the bowl. Now everyone can see the beautiful princess who was hidden under the bowl. She outshines all the other marriage candidates and is chosen to be the bride of the lord's successor.

Literature: Kosugi and Pigeot 1995; Nakano et al. 1988.

193

▲ Hachikazuki, the girl with the bowl on her head (fascicle I, p. 7b).

 ▲ The scene in which Hachikazuki outshines the other marriage
candidates (fascicle III, folio 6v).

Nara-ehon 奈良絵本

Nara-ehon 奈良絵本 (literally: printed books from Nara) is the name loosely given to a type of woodblock-printed picture book or illustrated handscroll produced in the late Muromachi period (1333-1573) and early Edo period (1600-1868). They often reproduce or adapt fairy tales and short (leg-endary) stories, which were known as *otogi-zōshi* 御伽草子, from these eras. Other material they adapt include *katarimono* 語り物 (nar-rative genres), such as *kōwaka* 幸若, *sekkyō* 説教, and *jōruri* 浄瑠璃. In some cases they take their inspiration from older masterpieces of prose literature, such as *Taiheiki* 太平記, *Ise monogatari* 伊勢物語, *Genji monogatari* 源氏物語, and so forth. The narrative episodes alter-nate with colourful hand-painted or printed illustrations.

During the Muromachi period, most *Nara-ehon* came in horizontal scrolls (*makimono* 巻物), but in the seventeenth century they were usu-ally bound as a booklet (*sasshibon* 冊子本).

These *sasshibon* were printed from woodblocks in one of three formats: a 'horizontal format' (*yokobon* 横本) of approximately 15-16 cm in height and 21-23 cm in width;

a vertical format measuring ap-proximately 21-23 cm in height and 15-16 cm in width; a grand format (*ōgata-bon* 大型本) of approxi-mately 24-28 cm in height and 17-19 cm in width. The really luxurious items may even be of a bigger for-mat, measuring 30 cm by 21 cm. The covers of the books are often decorated with mist and cloud shapes, sprinkled with flowers and grasses painted in gold (*kindei* 金泥). The titles were written on rect-angular slips and pasted onto the upper middle or upper left side of the covers. Gold foil (*kinpaku* 金箔) and gold dust (*sunago* 砂子) were used in high-end products, not only in the illustrations themselves but also on the bindings.

Nara-ehon are often printed on a special type of paper called *maniai-gami* 間似合紙. It is the same paper used for *byōbu* 屏風 (decorative, painted folding screens) and *fu-suma* 襖 (paper sliding doors which form the walls of rooms and hide deep shelves in traditional houses).

The illustrations of *Nara-ehon* are distinctly naïve, using a palette of bright, even colours, gold foil, and artless brushwork. The illustra-tions are anonymous, and their style ranges from *Yamato-e* 大和

絵 to *Tosa-e* 土佐絵 to *Kanō-ha* 狩野派. The calligraphy of the text, done by someone other than the illustrator, is similarly anonymous in most cases. Until the first quar-ter of the seventeenth century, the *Nara-ehon* were made to order, but from that point onward they were increasingly commercialized and 'mass-produced'. In a parallel de-velopment, in the early period they were handmade, but as demand in-creased in the seventeenth century, the number of woodblock-printed items rose accordingly.

A possible explanation for the name *Nara-ehon* (printed books of Nara) is that their creators were initially painters of Buddhist scenes working for the temple Kōfukuji 興福寺 in Nara, who, in their spare time, set about illustrating famous and beloved stories. According to another explanation, painters in the service of the Buddhist temples of Nara set up shop as commercial painters in Kyoto, where they took to making *Nara-ehon*, either made to order or mass-produced, for subsequent sale. There are other theories on the origin of the name, but in any case it gained coinage only much later, in the Meiji period, and the connection to the city of Nara remains unclear.

Literature: Ono Tadashige 1978, pp. 35-78; *Nara ehon-shū* 2018-2020; Yokoyama and Matsumoto 1983-1988.

61. Hon'yaku myōgi-shū 翻譯名義集
('Dictionary for Translations')

7 chapters in 7 fascicles; rare; 26.8 x 19.5 cm
Author: Shi Fayun 釈法雲

196

A note pasted on the inside of the cover by the donors states: "impression à caractères mobiles, au cours de l'époque Keichō-Genna". This coincides with the period 1596-1624. It is not clear on which data the donors based their decision regarding the date or period of time to which the printing of this work should be assigned. We know of a woodblock edition from the Muromachi period (1333-1573), as well as a typographical edition from the Kan'ei 寛永 period (1624-1644), the latter a reprint of the Ming edition. Of the latter edition, some sources provide the precise date as the year Kan'ei 5 (1628). The copy in UCLouvain probably belongs to that edition.

In the preface and various parts throughout the book, *shubiki* 朱引 can be found: vertical lines in vermillion (*shuzumi* 朱墨) that mark place names, proper names, and period names. There are *shuten* 朱点 as well: punctuation marks in vermillion. In certain parts of the book, *kaeriten* 返り点 (syntactic marks) and *okurigana* 送り仮名 (morphological marks) have been added in ink with a thin brush.

The pages of the preface count eight columns per page and fifteen characters per column. In the main body of the text, the entries are written in one single line per column, while the explanation of the entries is written in a double row per column with eighteen characters per column. On the *mikaeshi* 見返し of the fourth fascicle, we find the name 'Kan'yaku 観益', probably the name of a monk, in addition to his stylized autograph (*kaō* 花押), both written in ink. On the inside of the back cover, there is another handwritten addition in ink which is partially struck out. The book lacks a colophon.

The work *Hon'yaku myōgi-shū* is a compilation by the Chinese monk Fayun (1088-1158), who lived during the Song Dynasty (960-1279). He worked on it for twenty years before completing it in 1143. The preface was written by Zhou Dunyi 周敦頤 (1017-1073). It is a dictionary that explains Sanskrit words in Classical Chinese. The Sanskrit words themselves are not reproduced in an Indian alphabet or sylla-

bary, but are transcribed in Chinese characters, which at best approximate the genuine Indian pronunciation. The book was meant as a dictionary for translators of Buddhist texts.

The history of the translation of Indian Buddhist texts into Classical Chinese spans more than a thousand years, ranging from the first century CE to about the twelfth century. This period is often divided into two parts: the period up until the great translators and thinkers Xuan-zang 玄奘 (600-664) and Yijing 義淨 (635-713), and the period thereafter. These two masters criticized earlier translations (*kuyaku* 旧訳), claiming that they were often incorrect. As a result, many of the older translations were discarded, and the new translations provided by these masters became the only norm. Xuan-zang's criticism is however partially due to a lack of etymological knowledge. The older translations were not necessarily wrong, but their language was no longer adapted to the times. Fayun was aware of this and recognized the merits of the older translations. He collected a large number of Sanskrit words, illustrated them with passages from Buddhist scriptures, and explained their meaning in Classical Chinese.

The historian of the Japanese language, Sugimoto Tsutomu 杉本つとむ (1927-), surmises that the Japanese word *hon'yaku* 翻訳, now commonly used in modern Japanese to denote the notion of 'translation', may have been used for the first time by Fayun.[7]

Attached to a letter dated 'Bruxelles 9 octobre 1924', from Ambassador Adachi to Rector Monseigneur Ladeuze, is a translated excerpt from a letter of Furuichi Kimitake to Adachi. This excerpt includes a list of valuable works to be included in the first shipment to Leuven. One of them is *Hon'yaku myōgi-shū*, erroneously transcribed by Adachi in the *kan'on* reading as *Hon'yaku meigi-shuu*.

Literature: Mizuno et al. 1977, pp. 23, 53b, 309a; Ono Gemmyō 1978, vol. 10, p. 214; Sugimoto 1998, p. 28; Suzuki Gakujutsu zaidan 1916, p. 166.

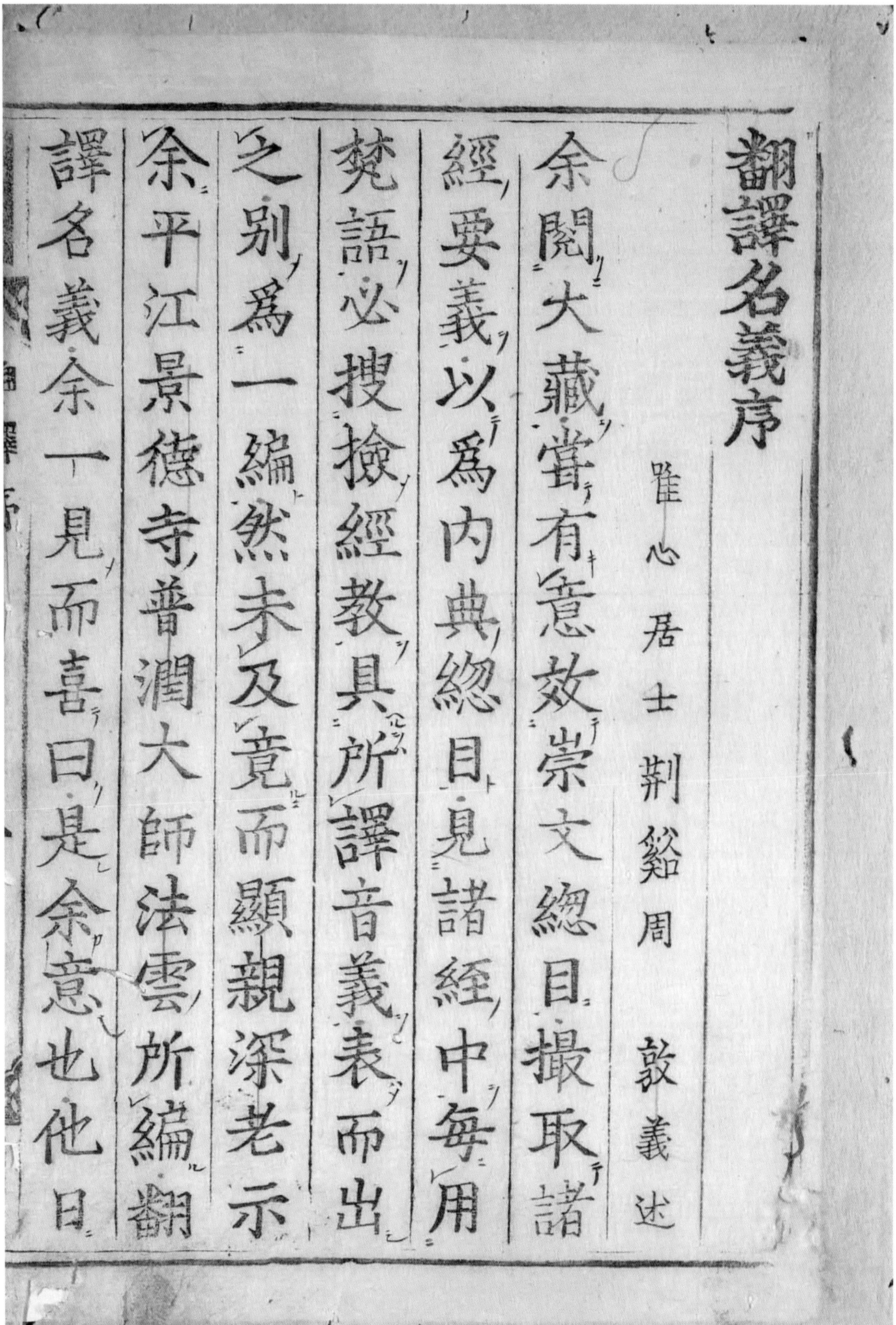

翻譯名義序

唯心居士荊谿周敦義述

余閱大藏嘗有意效崇文總目撮取諸
經要義以爲內典總目見諸經中每用
梵語必搜撿經教具所譯音義表而出
之別爲一編然未及竟而顯親深老示
余平江景德寺普潤大師法雲所編翻
譯名義余一見而喜曰是余意也他日

▲ First page of the preface (fascicle I).

62. Myōhō renge kyō hiyu-hon 妙法蓮華経譬喩品
('Lotus Sutra of the Marvellous Doctrine: Parable Chapter')

1 scroll; 25.4 cm x 11.04 m
Author: unknown
Date: unknown

The *mikaeshi* 見返し features an illustration of the Buddha preaching, ostensibly of a later date to substitute an original that had been damaged. The beginning of the scroll has been lightly restored in a few places. The scroll is rolled around a wooden spindle that is decorated on both ends with a brass button of later make. There is no colophon, but the florid pattern of the cover, the writing style of the text, and the material aspect of the scroll suggest that it is probably a Kamakura period (1185-1333) manuscript.

The Lotus Sūtra (Sanskrit: Saddharma Puṇḍarīka Sūtra, literally: Sūtra on the White Lotus of the Sublime Dharma) ranks among the most popular and most influential scriptures of Mahayana Buddhism. Originally written in a Prakrit language, and subsequently transposed into Sanskrit, it was translated for the first time into Chinese in 286 CE. This early translation was superseded by a translation by Kumārajīva in 406 CE. In 601, a revised version of Kumārajīva's text was published. Of high literary quality, Kumārajīva's translation became the classic Chinese edition for the scripture, and it is this version that also became hugely popular in Japan. The scripture is rich in content and full of intricate imagery. It consists of 28 chapters. The third chapter is the "Parable Chapter". A father promises his children various toy carts to lure them out of a burning house. Once they are outside, he gives them just one large cart. This is a metaphor for Buddha's teaching as a great vehicle on which all sentient beings can ride towards ultimate liberation. The various teachings of Buddhism, called 'vehicles', are ultimately all subsumed in the one great vehicle of Buddha's teaching.

Although the text represents the third chapter, the drawing on the frontispiece can best be understood as setting the stage as described in the first chapter of the scripture. During a gathering at Vulture Peak, Buddha Śākyamuni goes into a state of deep meditation, and he shines forth a ray of light which illuminates thousands of buddha-fields in the East. The Bodhisattva Mañjuśrī then states that the Buddha is about to expound his ultimate teaching.

The third chapter begins with the following words: "Thereupon Śāriputra stood up ecstatic and joyful, pressed his palms together and, gazing at the Buddha, the Bhagavat, said: 'Now, hearing the words of this Dharma from the Bhagavat, my heart is full of joy for I have experienced something unprecedented. What is the reason for this? In the past when I heard this Dharma from the Buddha and saw the bodhisattvas receive their predictions, I was not included. I grieved because I thought I had been deprived of the immeasurable wisdom and insight of the Tathāgata.'"[8]

Although woodblock printing had developed very early on in China and was also introduced in Japan in an early phase, the production of manuscripts in Japan persisted for a long time afterwards. It was not until the nineteenth century that manuscript culture began to fade as a result of the general spread of typographical printing technique. That the manuscript maintained such a prominent status may be attributed to multiple reasons. First of all, it was a time-hallowed practice for Japanese literary

▲ The frontispiece of the scroll, featuring the Buddha preaching the Lotus Sūtra, and the first page of the text.

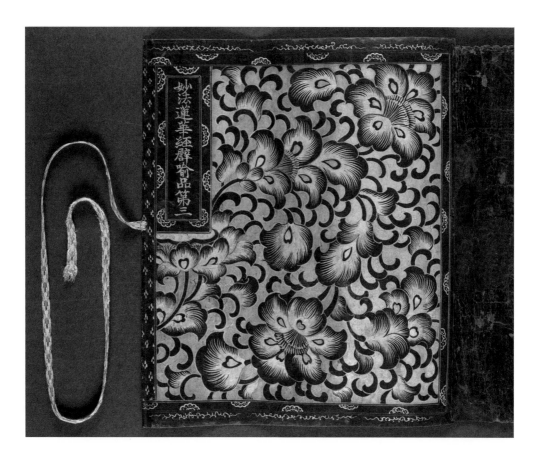

texts to be reproduced and passed on in manuscript form. Printing was, in view of its cost, reserved for Buddhist texts and secular Chinese texts for many centuries. Besides, the manuscript was a suitable means of controlling access to certain texts, either because they were politically sensitive and could not or were not allowed to be printed, or because they were meant for experts, as was the case for tea ceremony or flower arrangement, for example. Moreover, printing books was a laborious and expensive process, and copying was often the fastest way to acquire or reproduce a text. Another important reason was that copying sutras earned spiritual merits. Particularly copying the Lotus Sutra (*Hokekyō* 法華経, *Myōhō renge kyō* 妙法蓮華経) was considered of great merit.

Most specimens of these handwritten sutra copies take the form of the scroll (*kansubon* 巻子本), but some exist in the form of a bound book (*sasshibon* 冊子本) or concertina book (*orihon* 折本). The custom of copying sutras originated in India, whence it spread to China and thence to Korea and Japan.

In Japan, the copying of sutras peaked in the Nara period (710-784). The oldest extant specimen of a hand-copied sutra dates to 686. Copying was a state-run activity. In the capital there was a *scriptorium* (*shakyōjo* 写経所 or *hōsha issaikyōsho* 奉写一切経所), which was part of the civil service. One of the earliest sutras copied there and still preserved is a copy of the *Daihannyakyō* 大般若経 (*Mahāprajñāpāramitā sūtra*), which was copied out by order of Prince Nagaya 長屋 (684-729) in 728. No doubt the first copies were transcribed from imported Chinese manuscripts, but after official diplomatic relations between China and Japan had been discontinued in the Heian period (794-1185), most copies were likely transcribed from Japanese manuscripts.

Many copies include a colophon stating who commissioned the work and for which purpose the copy was made. As a rule, persons sponsoring the work did not make the copy themselves but outsourced it to professional copyists. Often the copy was made to pray for the health or salvation of the parents of the sponsors. They were almost always members of the imperial family, the upper aristocracy, or the higher echelons of the Buddhist clergy.

During the Nara period, at least some twenty cases are known of the entire Buddhist canon being hand-copied. Most sutras were copied in black ink on paper, seventeen characters to the line. The paper was, as was the case in China, dyed with a buff juice to fend off bookworms. Some copies, however, were copied out in gold or silver ink on indigo-dyed paper. This practice seems also to have existed in China and Korea, but very few Chinese examples have been preserved.

The custom of hand-copying sutras continued during the Heian period (794-1185) and subsequent eras, despite the growing number of available

199

▲ The cover of the scroll, featuring the typical flower motif known as *hōsōge-karakusa* 宝相華唐草, abundantly used in manuscripts of the Nara and Heian periods.

printed Buddhist texts, in addition to the Song editions of Buddhist writings that were brought to Japan at the end of the Heian period. By then, however, the practice lost its state-sponsored character. Temples copied sutras for their own use and, when individuals sought to earn religious merit, they copied the texts themselves.

No text was copied more often than the Lotus Sutra, owing to the exceptional powers ascribed to it. From the Heian period, more devotional copies of this sutra have been transmitted than from all other scriptures combined. Similar practices are known in the West. To name but one example, Thomas à Kempis (ca. 1380-1471) copied the Bible at least four times, of which one copy in five parts is preserved in Darmstadt, Germany.

The use of gold and silver ink on indigo-dyed paper gradually increased. From the eleventh century on, it became common practice to add the equivalent of a Western frontispiece to the sutras. This custom also existed in China, as can be seen from the frontispiece of the printed copy of the Diamond Sutra in the British Library, which was printed in 868. Fragments of a frontispiece that were discovered in Korea allegedly date back to the eighth century. They feature images in lines drawn in golden

ink on dark-blue paper and are allegedly inspired by a style of illustration typical of the Tang Dynasty (618-907). The oldest Japanese specimen of this kind of frontispiece is attached to a copy of the Lotus Sutra in silver ink dating from the ninth century. The representation is merely a stylized decoration, presumably based on a Chinese model. Later Japanese frontispieces usually depict the scene of the Buddha Śākyamuni preaching to his disciples on the Vulture Peak (Sanskrit: Gṛdhrakūṭa), also known as the Holy Eagle Peak, the Buddha's favourite retreat in Rājagṛha (now Rajgir) and the scene for many of his discourses.

During the Heian period, Japanese decorators developed various new forms of decoration for the sutras. Well known are the hanging scrolls onto which the text of the sutra was copied in gold ink in the shape of a pagoda. After the Heian period, the custom of copying sutras in a decorative manner continued, though it often lacked the beauty and splendour of the earlier copies. Thus, the copy in UCLouvain more than likely dates from the Kamakura period.

Literature: *Kokushi daijiten* 1979-1993, vol. 7, pp. 202-205; Kornicki 1998, pp. 78-99; *Shinchō sekai bijutsu jiten* 1985, p. 659; Nara kokuritsu hakubutsukan 1997, pp. 301-302.

▲ The end of the scroll.

63. Shoju senkai kobun shinpō kōshū 諸儒箋解古文真宝後集 ('The True Treasures of Antique Style Writing', the latter collection, with explanations by various scholars)

10 chapters in 2 fascicles
Author: unknown
Date: Meiō 明応 1 (1492)

Kobun Shinpō 古文真宝 (True Treasures of Antique Style Writing) is a digest of Classical Chinese texts, which includes ancient poems and prose writings spanning a time frame from the Han Dynasty (202 BCE-220 CE) to the Song Dynasty (960-1279). It is believed to have been completed at the end of the Song Dynasty or at the beginning of the Yuan period (1279-1368).

The compilation is attributed to Huang Jian 黄堅 (Jap. Kōken), or even to the great Song poet Huang Tingjian 黄庭堅, or the Ming emperor Shen-zong 神宗, these last two being quite unlikely authors. In any event, little is known of the compiler or the circumstances of the compilation. The book as it has been transmitted went through several editions, so that it is hard in fact to determine the date of its final version. In its transmitted version the compilation includes two "books", called respectively "former collection" (*zenshū* 前集) and "latter collection" (*kōshū* 後集), containing ten chapters each.

The compiler's aim was to make a sampling of poetry and prose written in the so-called antique style (*kobun* 古文), which claims to go back ultimately to the Chinese classic *The Book of Odes* (Shījīng 詩經), traditionally said to have been compiled by Confucius. *Kobun Shinpō* was supposed to embody a style that was in stark contrast to the new style of poetry, defined during the Six Dynasties period (220-589), and characterized by tone harmony, rhythmic patterns, antithetic parallelism, and ornate word usage to the detriment of depth and content.

The "former collection" includes 217 poems in 11 different styles or formats from the Han to the Song periods, while the "latter collection" contains 67 samples of prose, covering 17 different genres (12 types of unrhymed prose and 5 types of rhymed prose poems). Depending on the edition, however, there are variations in the number of selected items, their arrangement, the number of chapters, and the title.

It was conceived as a sample book introducing the learner to the various genres and styles. In China, it served as a handbook for the aspiring bureaucrats preparing for the state examinations, because in these great emphasis was put on the mastery of the various literary styles and genres. In Japan, which had no state examinations, it served as a primer for students aiming to acquire a basic understanding of classical culture.

The two fascicles in the Japanese donation are part of this "latter collection".

The first chapter of the "latter collection" contains samples of *jirui* 辭類 (lyrics) and *furui* 賦類 (rhapsodies), the only two lyrical genres (*genshi* 言志) in the entire collection, which otherwise includes no less than 12 genres that 'discourse on the Way' (*saidō* 載道), that is, genres of social or political relevance, or philosophical or moral character.

Kobun Shinpō was introduced to Japan at the beginning of the Muromachi period 室町時代 (1333-1573). It spread among the learned Zen monks of the Gozan temples establishment and was eventually published as a woodblock edition by them (*Gozanban* 五山版). Moreover, several Zen monks published commentaries on the book, so-called *senshaku no hon* 箋釈の本. The number of annotated editions or versions, both in China and Japan, is impressive.

During the Edo period (1600-1868), *Kobun Shinpō* went through numerous editions and was widely used as a reader of Classical Chinese, also spawning numerous commentaries. The great novelist Ihara Saikaku 井原西鶴 (1642-1693) as well as the famous poet Matsuo Bashō 松尾芭蕉 make references to *Kobun Shinpō*, a fact that testifies to its wide circulation as a style sample book. However, because of the variations between the various editions, the lack of cohesion in its selection, and the alleged lack of discernment of the compiler(s), it was rejected as a 'vulgarizing book' (*zokusho* 俗書) by the great Confucian scholar and sinologist Ogyū Sorai 荻生徂徠 (1666-1728) and his followers. Therefore, as a sample book for the proper style it was gradually supplanted by *Tōshisen* 唐詩選 (A Selection of Poetry from the Tang Era) for poetry composition and by *Bunshō kihan* 文章軌範 (Models for Prose Writing) for prose composition. The latter two compilations are basically focused on samples from the Tang and Song periods, whereas *Kobun Shinpō* also includes many samples of an earlier date, ranging from pre-Han times (202 BCE) up to the Song period (960-1279), including old style poetry (*koshi* 古詩), ballads (*gafu* 楽府), poetry of the Six Dynasties, and songs from the Three States (*Sankokuka* 三国歌). Despite its alleged deficiencies, it continued to go through reprints well into the Meiji period (1868-1912). The word *kobun shinpō* even made it into the parlance of the Japanese language as a quasi-adjective denoting 'with a solemn, grave look, ceremonious'.

The copy in the Japanese donation bears the mention 'rare' on its cover. It is not rare in the sense of the text being uncommon. Since the work went through countless editions and reprints, that could

hardly be the case. However, it *is* rare because this is an old manuscript. Yamazaki's catalogue, *Shoju senkai kobun shinpō kōshū* (Yamazaki 2000, p. 700, under number 55A08), mentions that it is an 'old manuscript', dated in the first year of Meiō 明応 元年 (1492). This was the period when the Gozan monasteries were at their height, and book printing was still in its infancy. Based on the title, we have to conclude that this manuscript is likely a copy of the annotated version of the *Kobun shinpō*, which is classified in the catalogues under the title *Kaihon daiji shoju senkai kobun shinpō zenshū jikkan kōshū jikkan* 魁本大字諸儒箋解古文真宝前集十巻後集十巻. Its compiler is unknown.

Since printed copies were still rare at the time, one or more copyists (Zen monks in circles of the Gozan monasteries) copied this text from a printed model at hand. The copying may also have been intended as an exercise. Until the 20th century, copying – even in Europe – was considered a good and adequate method to learn or memorize something. This manuscript is particularly interesting because the original Chinese text is interspersed with Japa-

nese translations, commentaries, or glosses. This book was used for study, still bearing the traces of a student hard at work, and it bears witness to the function the work held in Japan. It was an important book for learning Classical Chinese.

Classical Chinese fulfilled a role more or less equivalent to that of Latin and Greek in Europe, although the degree of indigenization of Classical Chinese (or literary creolization) may have been higher than that of Latin in Europe. After all, Chinese was read aloud, not in a Chinese pronunciation but in a meta-language which combines Sino-Japanese pronunciations, Japanese pronunciations, and Japanese syntax. It could be compared to seeing the Latin word 'tabula' written but reading it aloud as 'table', or seeing 'iustitia' written only to pronounce it aloud as 'justice'. The vast majority of Japanese did not know the Chinese pronunciation, only a corrupted pronunciation derived from Chinese. It should be noted in passing that we do not know the exact way Latin was read in Roman times, either, and that the pronunciation in Medieval times deviated from the original one. To the best of this author's knowledge,

▲ The folio shown here is folio six (六丁) of what should be chapter one.

however, nowhere else has there been a similar development of a systematic classical meta-language, incorporating the syntax of another living language.

The folio reproduced here is folio six (六丁) of what should be chapter one (the first four folios are apparently missing). To its right, on folio 5 verso, we read the following passage:

漢書儒林伝ニハ易、礼、周礼、毛詩、尚書、春秋ヲ六芸ト云や。("The biographies of Confucian scholars in the Book of Han defines the Book of Changes, the Book of Rites, the Rites of Zhou, the Book of Odes, the Book of Documents and the Spring and Autumn Annals as the six classics"...)

Folio 6 begins with the following words:

飯去来云々山谷云東坡在.... ("Going Back Home, etc., Huang Tingjian wrote: Su Dongpo was....")

Kikyorai 飯去来 or Kikyorai-ji 帰去来辭 ('Going Back Home') is the third text in chapter one of the *Kobun shinpō*. It is a lyrical prose poem by Tao Qian (365-427), better known by the courtesy name (azana 字) Yuanming 淵明. The poem describes how he suddenly resigns from his position in the bureaucracy and returns to the countryside to live as a gentleman farmer. The poem voices his aversion towards life as a career bureaucrat, which places great importance on appearances and is rife with flattery, and instead sings the simple pleasures of country life. He praises the authenticity of the rustic life, the honesty of simple country folk, devoid of artfulness and deceit. His dithyramb in fairly simple wording resonated with the aspiration of the aristocrat or gentleman, both in China and Japan, longing for a life in retirement dedicated to contemplation and the arts.

Tao Yuanming's poetry was only moderately successful among his contemporaries, but during the Tang Dynasty (618-907), his simple and authentic lyrics enjoyed greater success, and he became one of the most beloved poets. In Japan, too, he was one of the most appreciated Chinese poets.

Literature: Hoshikawa 1963; Hoshikawa 1967a; Hoshikawa 1967b; Sakakibara 1910; Hayashi and Ugai 1910; Hattori 1984.

64. Teikan zusetsu 帝鑑図説
('Illustrated Guidelines for a Good Monarch/Illustrated Mirror for Princes')

3 chapters in 6 fascicles; 26.7 x 18.1 cm
Author: unknown
Date: unknown

204

The work *Teikan zusetsu*, a 'mirror for princes', was compiled in the year Long-qing 隆慶 6 (1572) and published in 1573, by the scholars Zhang Juzhi 張居正 (1525-1582) and Lü Tiaoyang 呂調陽 (1516-1578). The compilation was undertaken in China at the behest of the Ming emperor Shen-zong 神宗 (1572-1619), who is better known by the name of his reign period Wan-li 万暦. It includes eighty-one cases of commendable behaviour (*zenkō* 善行) by Chinese emperors, worthy of emulation – starting with the legendary Emperor Yao 堯 (2357-2258 BC) down to Emperor Shen-zong 神宗 (1067-1085) of the Northern Song Dynasty (960-1125) – as well as thirty-six cases of objectionable behaviour (*akkō* 悪行) – from the semi-legendary Xia emperor Tai-kang 太康 (2188-2159 BC) down to the eccentric and last emperor of the Northern Song period, Hui-zong 徽宗 (1100-1125). Each case is represented by an illustra-

tion, the original quote describing the commendable or reprehensible behaviour, and an explanatory comment. The book may well originally have only existed in manuscript form, until it was printed and distributed in 1573. One or more copies from China also reached Japan.

In Japan, the book was first printed and published in 1606, at the order of Toyotomi Hideyori 豊臣秀頼 (1593-1615). This copy was a print in wooden movable type, one of the earliest typographical editions to include illustrations. The illustrations, however, were printed from woodblocks, with one illustration continuing from the recto to the verso side of the folio leaf (*chō* 丁). Hideyori may have decided to publish this mirror of princes out of a sense of rivalry with his archenemy Tokugawa Ieyasu 徳川家康 (1543-1616), who would eventually be the instrument of his undoing. A Japanese version of

▲ Soldiers at a gate. Above the illustration, the caption mentions the Treaty of the Eight Passes 入関約法 by Emperor Gaodi 高帝 (256-195 BC) of the Han Dynasty (fascicle II, p. 33b).

▲ Emperor Wu-di 武帝 (464-549) of the Liang Dynasty offering himself up to the Buddhist temple Tongtai-si and taking on the 'simple' life of a monk (fascicle VI, p. 55a).

this book was published in 1627, also a typographical edition. The fonts used here include types where four characters or characters with *furigana* 振り仮名 are combined on one font.

Later, the *kanbun*-version was reprinted multiple times. The book's illustrations inspired artists of the Kanō school, who adopted images of certain episodes to decorate the interiors of palaces and castles with edifying episodes of 'ancient' times. In the palace of the *shōgun* in Edo, there was even a 'mirror of princes room'.

The copy in UCLouvain is incomplete and lacks the last volume, which would normally have included the colophon or postscript. It is therefore hard to determine to which edition it belongs. As a matter of fact, many copies in public collections seem to be incomplete. The copies of the Hideyori edition (1606, five copies are known) have some typical type-setting errors in common. These errors are lacking in the copy of the UCLouvain, which means that it is of a later date. All fascicles of the UCLouvain copy show some traces of damage, but the four fascicles in part I have been restored by the National Committee.

On the inside of the fly page of fascicle I, someone has pasted a strip of paper with two lines in *kanbun* which, in view of the style of writing, must date from the nineteenth or twentieth century. It reads (in translation): "In the prefatory notes to *Nihon shoki tsūshō* 日本書記通証 (A Running Commentary on the *Nihon shoki*, 1762) it is said: 'Printing in Japan possibly started during the Genbun 元文[9] era, but it was exclusively typographical. The xylographical printing that we nowadays know started from the end of the Keichō 慶長 era ...'"

That this old Japanese typographical print (*kokatsuji-ban*) uses wooden fonts (*mokkatsuji-ban* 木活字版) can be deduced from the breaks in the printed frame in which the block of text was set. At the bottom, in the corners where the horizontal and vertical lines of the frame are supposed to connect, there are some places where they do not join. Moreover, some characters are out of alignment.

There are two kinds of old movable-type editions (*kokatsuji-ban*): *dōkatsuji-ban* 銅活字版 (with copper fonts) and *mokkatsuji-ban* (with wooden fonts). Suruga editions (*Suruga-ban* 駿河版) were printed with copper fonts, while Fushimi editions (*Fushimi-ban* 伏見版) were printed using wooden fonts. The famous and aesthetically refined Saga editions (*Saga-bon*) are *mokkatsuji-ban*. Although

Korean typography preferred copper fonts, Japanese preferred to cut them from wood, because this allowed them to cut elongated fonts which could accommodate ligatures of multiple characters, such as verbs ending in the auxiliary verb 'sōrō 候'. The type case with the copper fonts is nowadays preserved by the large publishing company Toppan Insatsu 凸版印刷. The type case with wooden fonts in the *kaisho* 楷書 style is now preserved in the temple Enkōji 圓光寺 in Kyoto. Both represent the oldest movable type sets in Japan.

It was Tokugawa Ieyasu, the founder of the Tokugawa Shogunate, who ordered the establishment of the temple Enkōji in Fushimi by Zen master Sanyō Genkitsu 三要元佶 (1548-1612). Here the approximately 100,000 wooden fonts brought back by the Japanese armies from their expeditions in Korea were stored. With these fonts, famous works in *kanbun* were (re-)printed, such as *Jōgan seiyō* 貞観政要, *Bukei shichisho* 武経七書, and *Kōshi kago* 孔子家語. This is why they are called Fushimi editions or Enkōji editions.

After Ieyasu had retired to Suruga, he ordered two more important books to be printed with copper movable type. They were *Daizō ichiranshū* 大蔵一覧集 and *Gunsho chiyō* 群書治要. The temple Enkōji, on the other hand, whose printing press had now run out of work, was moved from Fushimi to the temple Shōkokuji 相国寺 in Kyoto, and later moved once again to the district Ichijōji 一乗寺 in the northeastern part of Kyoto, where it has remained to this day. In the early Meiji period the temple was abandoned for some time, but it was later revived as a convent for Buddhist nuns. The type case with the wooden movable types is still preserved here.

The story of Emperor Wu-di 武帝 (464-549) of the Liang Dynasty offering himself up to the Buddhist monastery (*shashin butsuji* 捨身仏寺) Tongtai-si 同泰寺 and taking on the 'simple' life of a monk is emblematic. His ministers called at the monastery and beseeched him to return to the palace and take up the business of government again. After the third entreaty he finally acceded, but not without imposing a hefty ransom to be paid from the government treasury into the coffers of the monastery. He was a great patron of Buddhism but from the Confucian point of view, he was an abhorrently deluded ruler (fascicle VI, p. 55a).

Literature: *Kokushi daijiten* 1979-1993, vol. 9, pp. 842-843; Kondō 1978, p. 564; Ozaki, Chikusa, Togawa 2013, p. 880.

65. Urashima うらしま
('The Story of Urashima')

1 fascicle; manuscript; rare; 16.3 x 28.5 cm
Author: unknown
Date: 17th century (no date in book)

This *nara-ehon* tells the well-known tale of Urashima Tarō 浦島太郎. This man saved a sea turtle that was being badgered by children. After being saved from this cruelty, the animal turned into a beautiful princess who invited him to join her in the dragon's palace (ryūgū 竜宮, i.e., the palace of the sea-god under the sea). Here, he married her and spent three happy years. Eventually, however, homesickness got the better of him, and he returned to his home village. To his dismay he discovered that he no longer recognized anyone. At wit's end, he opened the box the princess had given him as a souvenir, although she had insisted he not open it. From the box rose a purple cloud, and he instantly turned into an old man (ill. 1: p. 2a). He had been away for seven hundred years.

This old folk tale, with numerous variations in the details, appears all over Japan. In one version, he does not become an old man but, rather, a crane, who is reunited on the isle of immortals with the princess, who had transformed back into a sea turtle. Finally he appears as the god Urashima no myōjin 浦島神. This is also the case in this particular copy.

The oldest traces of the story of Urashima (Tarō) go back to the Nihon shoki (720) and the Man'yōshū 万葉集 (760), but the narrative as we know it today originated during the Muromachi period. It belongs to the *otogi-zōshi* 御伽草子 (fairy tale) genre, a group of stories written between the Muromachi period and the beginning of the Edo period. In its narrow sense, this particular genre only includes twenty-three stories, published under the eponymous title *Otogi bunko* 御伽文庫 or *Otogi-zōshi* 御伽草紙 or 御伽草子 during the 1720s. The designation was later expanded to include about 400 anonymous illustrated prose narratives, most of them written in the Muromachi period (1392–1573). *Urashima (Tarō)* is one of the twenty-three stories in the stricter sense.

In *Otogi-zōshi*, the dragon's palace is not located under the sea but on an island or even on the mainland, and it is also represented like that in illustrated scrolls and picture books. This feature is also the case in the UCLouvain copy where, in one illustration, we see the couple sitting in an open room looking out onto the garden, with what looks like waves on a shore in the background.

206

▲ The scene in which the fisherman turns into an old man (folio 3 r).

▲ The scene in which the fisherman saves the turtle (folio 14 r).
The following illustration in the book (not reproduced here)
shows the transfiguration of the sea turtle into a beautiful
princess.

Freya Terryn[1]

Japanese Art in Belgium in the 1920s: Hidden Treasures and Public Celebrations

Introduction

The 1920s was an important decade for the celebration and appreciation of Japan, its culture, and its art in Belgium. It manifested itself, first of all, in the imperial visit of Prince Hirohito (1901-1989) in 1921 and in the donation of a collection of 13,862 books by the Japanese government to the University of Louvain, as KU Leuven was then called.[2] Other events that celebrated Japanese art and culture were exhibitions in Belgium introducing Japanese artists residing in Paris at that time. At its apex came the exhibition at the Kodak gallery in Brussels (14 June-13 July 1929), set up by the French Japanese Artists Association (*Furansu Nihon Bijutsuka Kyōkai* 仏蘭西日本美術家協会). On a more institutional level it was sustained through acquisitions and donations of Japanese paintings and woodblock prints, which were added to the collections of Japanese art of the Royal Museums of Fine Arts of Belgium (RMFAB) and Royal Museums of Art and History (RMAH), respectively.

When discussing the appreciation of Japanese art in Belgium at public and institutional levels, it should be noted that its groundwork had been laid several decades earlier and carefully curated by several key figures. A turning point in the spread of awareness of Japanese art among the general public was the 1889 exhibition of Japanese woodblock prints, the first of its kind in Belgium, organized by the Parisian art dealer Siegfried Bing (1838-1905) and Belgian art collector and composer Edmond Michotte (1831-1914).[3] The Belgian King Leopold II (1835-1909) also contributed significantly, as he commissioned the Parisian architect Alexandre Marcel (1860-1928) to build the so-called 'Japanese Tower'.[4] Other crucial contributions were the acquisition of Michotte's collection of Japanese art[5] by the Belgian government

for the RMAH in 1905, and the Royal Library of Belgium amassing roughly 500 Japanese prints between 1888 and the beginning of the twentieth century.[6]

Given the foregoing groundwork,[7] this essay explores the fascination for Japanese art in the interwar period. It explores how Japanese woodblock prints and modern paintings shared several similarities. More precisely it centres on a print series by the artist Tsukioka Yoshitoshi 月岡芳年 (1839-1892) preserved in the RMAH, and on paintings by the artist Fujita Tsuguharu 藤田嗣治 (1866-1968), well known in Europe as Léonard Foujita, in the RMFAB. In what follows, the print series is interpreted in the context of its acquisition, whereas the latter is framed in the context of a series of events leading up to the Kodak exhibition of 1929. The longstanding appreciation for Japanese prints in both Europe and Belgium not only contributed to the acquisition of the abovementioned woodcuts and paintings by Belgian institutions, but also influenced the Japanese donators to incorporate a high number of highly illustrated Edo period (1603-1868) books, such as the fifteen volumes of the *Hokusai Manga* 北斎漫画 (published 1814-1878), in the collection that was presented to the University of Louvain in the 1920s.

Yoshitoshi's hidden treasures

In the 1920s the Japanese woodblock print collection of the RMAH was expanded by several acquisitions, donations, and exchanges. Most interesting are the three exchanges taking place in 1921. Archival material indicates that a total of 200 Japanese woodblock prints entered the collection through exchanges on 20 April, 18 July, and 1 October 1921. Although the details on these

209

exchanges are scant, the archives confirm that a group of four people was involved in each exchange. It seems that the idea of a 'swap' originated with Jules Bommer (1872-1950), the curator of the then divisions of ethnography, folklore and the Far East. He reported the proposed swap to the chief curator of the museums, Eugène Van Overloop (1847-1926), who notified the Minister of Sciences and Arts, Jules Destrée (1863-1936)[8]. Finally, Destrée's chief of staff, Richard Dupierreux (1891-1957), was also a key figure in greenlighting these exchanges.[9]

The rationale behind the swaps was to get rid of some unwanted art objects from Michotte's collection. A certain number of these objects were considered by Bommer to be of no interest to the museums. At the time they could not be refused as the collection was purchased in one unit, even though these unwanted objects required much space, maintenance, and security.[10] Especially a certain number of *netsuke* 根付 - miniature sculptures tied to their respective containers holding medicine, tobacco, or other personal items - and *okimono* 置物 - decorative objects made

for display - were judged to belong to that group of unwanted art objects. Bommer had already expressed this impetus for exchange as early as November 1919 and again in January 1920, but it took until the spring of 1921 for the swap to come to fruition.[11] Ultimately, Bommer exchanged 67 *netsuke* and *okimono* in April, estimated at a value of 3,120 Belgian francs, for 123 woodblock prints, one *kakemono*, one painting, and five illustrated books.[12] Among the prints was a lot of 48 prints by Utagawa Hiroshige 歌川広重 (1797-1858) deemed highly desirable for the collection as it would complete some of his series.[13] In July another group of *netsuke* and *okimono*, with an estimated value of 1,550 Belgian francs, made room for a lot of 60 woodcuts.[14] Here, too, Hiroshige's prints were deemed most valuable for the museums. Finally, 117 woodcuts were inventoried on October 1.[15] Unfortunately, the lack of archival material on this last exchange makes it impossible to determine which objects left the collection, although it is certain that it also involved *netsuke* and *okimono* from Michotte's collection.[16]

It is interesting to note that a striking number of prints by artists of the Meiji period (1868-1912) were part of these swaps. From two in April to 22 in July, the total culminated in October with 51 prints. Bommer deemed these prints to be rare and believed that their value would increase over time.[17] Such a positive assessment of Meiji prints is uncommon, as they had always been placed

210

▲ 1. *Jingū, 15th Empress* (*Dai jūgodai Jingū kōgō* 第十五代神功皇后)
Ōban triptych, 37 x 71,5 cm
Publisher: Morimoto Junzaburō 森本順三郎
Date: April 1879
Signed: Taiso Yoshitoshi 大蘇芳年 (seal. Taiso 大蘇)
Engraver: Watanabe Eizō 渡辺栄蔵
Collection: ImageStudio © Royal Museums of Art and History, Brussels, JP.05312. Creative Commons CC BY – KMKG/RMAH/MRAH.
Literature: Keyes 1982, no.418; Ing and Schaap 1992, no.38; Kozyreff 1998, no.196; Uhlenbeck and Newland 2011, no.108

in stark contrast to the prints of the Edo period. This contrast between woodblock prints of both periods was underscored with the opening of Japanese ports in 1858 to international trade, when Japan left behind its feudal regime for modern nation-state building, a departure that came to be reflected in the woodcuts depicting the modernization and westernization of society. As a result, the Edo prints were revered for their natural coloration and treatment of traditional topics - landscapes, beautiful women, and *kabuki* actors -, whereas Meiji prints were ridiculed for their untraditional topics - such as foreigners and the modernization of society - as well as for their (often crude) application of imported Western aniline dyes. Or to put it in the words of Destrée himself: "The prints were in a state of decadence and artists had run out of inspiration, whereas we [Westerners] were to blame for precarious aniline dyes replacing the sumptuous vegetable colours."[18] Destrée was one of many in a sea of Western art collectors and critics who voiced his condemnation of Meiji prints, resulting in their exclusion from many collections.

▲ *2. Yūryaku, 22nd Emperor (Dai nijūnidai Yūryaku tennō* 第二十二代雄畧天皇)

Ōban triptych, 37 x 71 cm
Publisher: Tsujiokaya Kamekichi 辻岡屋亀吉
Date: 29 April 1879
Signed: Taiso Yoshitoshi 大蘇芳年 (seal. Taiso 大蘇)
Engraver: Horikame 彫亀
Collection: ImageStudio © Royal Museums of Art and History, Brussels, JP.05313. Creative Commons CC BY – KMKG/RMAH/MRAH.
Literature: Keyes 1982, no.418; Ing and Schaap 1992, no.38; Uhlenbeck and Newland 2011, no.108

Among the swapped prints there is an almost complete series entitled *Short Illustrated History of Great Japan (Dai Nihonshi ryaku zue* 大日本史略図会). Drawing on the talents of Yoshitoshi, one of today's most celebrated woodblock print artists of the Meiji period, this series consists out of ten confirmed triptychs issued in 1879 and 1880, while involving five different publishers.[19] Although once printed in large quantities, this series is considered relatively rare today. As the RMAH houses eight of its triptychs, it is therefore one of the museums' many hidden treasures.

For Yoshitoshi this series was issued at a time of steady productivity and public acknowledgement by his contemporaries, as between 1876 and 1880 he added more than 400 prints to his corpus of work and was perceived as an authority in warrior prints.[20] He stretches his drawings over three sheets to introduce personae connected to Japan's imperial history and frames them in partially unrolled *emaki* 絵巻 (scroll painting), allowing the viewer to scroll through the narrative from right to left. At the right side, the print title introduces its main character, while an explanatory text chronicles an important anecdote (Figure 2) or lists several accomplishments (Figure 1).[21] When put together, this print series supports the original intention of *emaki* spreading out a long story over several scrolls, which is here an illustrated history of "great Japan". In such a way, this series can be interpreted in the context of the Japanese government recognizing the importance of promoting a national history among the general public, and especially among young children, as schoolbooks were being published on Japan's imperial history. Although no direct link can be established between Yoshitoshi's prints and these schoolbooks, it is assumed that the publishers involved were responding to the demand for educational material created by the government throughout the 1870s.

Figure 1 unravels the story of the legendary Empress Jingū 神功皇后 (r. 201-269) who, after her husband Emperor Chūai 仲哀天皇 (r. 192-200) was killed by the resisting Kumaso 熊襲 tribe, successfully suppressed the rebels and conquered Silla, one of the three kingdoms of ancient Korea. According to the explanatory text on the print, she carved into a rock that "the king of Silla is the dog of Japan," for which the triptychs provides the setting. Hereafter she allegedly conquered the other kingdoms of Korea and returned home. It is said that she was pregnant with her husband's child before she took off and only gave birth to an imperial prince after her return, three years later.

Figure 2 introduces Emperor Yūryaku 雄畧天皇 (r. 456-479), who allegedly became emperor after successfully vanquishing the clan who killed his younger brother Emperor Ankō 安康天皇 (r. 453-456). The setting here depicts the encounter between the emperor, depicted in full military regalia, and a rampaging boar on Mt. Katsuragi 葛城. According to the explanatory text on the print, his footmen ran away, whereas the emperor, in a moment of fortitude, raised his leg and killed the boar with a kick.

The public celebration of Fujita

With Paris as its centre, Japanese woodcuts had saturated Western markets since the 1860s and continued to appeal to Western collectors and institutions throughout the interwar period, as is demonstrated above. Simultaneously, the city had also been a platform for Japanese painters to promote their artwork. Before the turn of the century, prolific painters such as Kuroda Seiki 黒田清輝 (1866-1924) and Yamamoto Hōsui 山本芳翠 (1850-1906) had come to master Western painting techniques. This cultural and artistic exchange continued in the interwar period when inspiration and training in the world's artistic capital was sought by subsequent Japanese artists like Fujita, Oka Shikanosuke 岡鹿之助 (1898-1978), and Yazawa Gengetsu 矢澤弦月 (1886-1952). In the early

summer of 1929, the works of these three artists, alongside other Japanese painters, were exhibited at the Kodak gallery in Brussels. It was the second exhibition organized by the French Japanese Artists Association and presented a total of 125 works by 33 artists. The association intended to spread Japanese culture and art via exhibitions in every major European city, but only managed to organize three exhibitions – two in Paris and one in Brussels – before disbanding already in 1929, the same year in which it had been established.[23] At the core of the association was the artist Fujita, as its president, and the philanthropist and writer Satsuma Jirohachi 薩摩治郎八 (1901-1976), as its founder and main benefactor. Using his family fortune that stemmed from cotton production, Satsuma purchased art works and sponsored – in addition to the association – the establishment of the Satsuma Chair to celebrate the 500th anniversary of the Catholic University of Louvain in 1925, although the chair was not inaugurated until the academic year of 1928-1929.[24]

The exhibition aroused enormous interest, for on 25 June, only a week after its opening, it was attended by the Belgian King Albert I (1875-1934) and Queen Elisabeth (1876-1965) (Figure 3). The exhibition was quite the success as it resulted in the purchase of several paintings by the queen herself, the RMFAB and the art collector Georges Hulin de Loo (1862-1945).[25] In contrast, the Belgian press painted a bleak picture of the exhibition. In general, newspapers lamented the loss of the "Japanese-ness" and "Oriental delicacy" in the paintings, for it left visitors wondering whether they had really attended a Japanese exhibition. Instead, they found themselves surrounded by an array of Western-style paintings "simply made by artists of Japanese nationality" and feared that the "Japanese artists living abroad had lost their originality and that the spirit of Paris subdued the spirit of Tokyo."[26] This fault finding was not unique to the 1929 exhibition, but had originated much earlier according to a journalist of the newspaper Le Peuple: "While Europe, following [Edmond de] Goncourt and [Claude] Monet, had barely discovered the old Japanese masters, we were sad to see that the sections of modern Japanese art in world's fairs were filled with paintings in the European style by artists from the Far East who settled in London or Paris."[27] As a result, the Belgian public harshly criticized the Japanese paintings that strayed from the Western-set assumptions and expectations.

One modern artist who did receive accolades for his works was the painter Fujita Tsuguharu, also known as Léonard Foujita.[28] Trained under Kuroda, he left for Paris in 1913 after being rejected from the Ministry of Education Art Exhibition (*Monbushō Bijutsu Tenrankai* 文部省美術展覧会), because he was considered not to have met the classical requirements of an official painter for the Fine Arts Reviewing Committee (*Bijutsu shinsa inkai* 美術審査員会). He settled in Montparnasse and became a modernist of the *École de Paris*, which in its broadest sense included all artists working in Paris during the first half of the twentieth century. His technique of combining Western oil painting and *sumi-e* 墨絵, (lit. water-ink painting) allowed him to rise to fame in the 1920s and sell his art across Europe.

In 1929 the Belgian press judged him to be the only Japanese painter on display who kept "his fundamental personality, native originality, and respect for the artistic traditions of his country".[29] Moreover, in contrast to other Japanese painters castigated for painting according to European stylistic conventions, Fujita was applauded for his portraits, nudes, Parisian landscapes in

the "pure and stripped-down style of Utamaro and Hokusai".[30] The sale of one of his landscape paintings and nude drawings to Hulin de Loo attests to his continuing appraisal amongst Belgian critics and art collectors.[31] Fujita's success in Belgium was no exception at that time, however, but was built up over the course of the 1920s. His official debut to the Belgian public occurred in the summer of 1920 in Antwerp, where he exhibited two oil paintings and three gouaches.[32] This debut inspired consecutive exhibitions, including a vernissage of eight paintings in Brussels in October of the same year, four more exhibitions and four solo-exhibitions in Brussels before the Kodak exhibition of 1929.[33]

The first testimony of an accolade of Fujita's art is the purchase of his self-portrait (Figure 4) by the RMFAB in 1922. This work was displayed at his solo-exhibition of 34 works at the gallery Le Centaure (13-29 January 1922), which was advertised at the time by three different newspapers.[34] Although as many as eight paintings were sold, only the acquisition by the museums was reported in the Belgian press.[35] In a newspaper review of this exhibition, Fujita was once more described as a "real" Japanese painter: "And here is one, Japanese from Japan … who came to Europe, saw the things of Europe with the eyes of a Japanese and interpreted them with the soul of a fellow Hokusai and Utamaro. … Here is a real *Nippon*."[36]

In this serious self-portrait, Fujita stands out with his bowl cut, round glasses, and moustache

213

▲ 3. The Belgian King and Queen awaiting a painting demonstration at the 1929 French Japanese Artists Association's exhibition
Photograph, 18,1 × 23, 9 cm
Date: 25 June 1929
Collection: Waseda University Library—Documents Relating to Satsuma Jirohachi 早稲田大学図書館―薩摩治郎八関連資料 (2011)
From left to right: the general director of the French Japanese Artists Association Yanagi Ryō 柳亮 (1903-1978), King Albert I, Viscount Motono Moriichi 本野盛一 (1895-1953), Queen Elizabeth, the wife of ambassador Nagai Matsuzō 永井松三 (1877-1957), and Yazawa Gengetsu.

cut into the shape of an *m*. It shows us a glimpse into his private life, as he is posing in his apartment. Surrounded by a hanging ceramic plate and two pipes, a canister of tobacco, a clock and matches, he introduces us to one of his vices: smoking tobacco.[37] This portrait also stands out when compared to his other self-portraits, for it is missing his pet cat and signature golden earrings.[38]

A second testimonial came from the activities of three figures who contributed to the awareness of his art in Belgium, namely Dupierreux, Destrée, and Satsuma. Dupierreux gave a lecture on the painter at the Modern Museum of the RMFAB on 14 November 1923.[39] Unfortunately, it is difficult to shed light on the content of his lecture given the dearth of contemporary documentation.[40] A year later, Destrée wrote an article on the painter, identifying Fujita as one of the "descendants of Hokusai and as an artist who

succeeded in keeping the traditions of his country alive without Europeanizing too much."[41] This article, which also featured a picture of Fujita's self-portrait acquired by the RMFAB in 1922, was published in relation to his solo exhibition at the Le Centaure gallery (25 October-5 November 1924). This exhibition proved to be another milestone in Fujita's Belgian career, for both the Japanese ambassador to Belgium Adachi Mineichirō 安達峰一郎 (1870-1934) - who also was one of the driving forces behind the Japanese book donation - and Queen Elisabeth attended the exhibition.[42] Fujita's final contributor was his friend and supporter Satsuma, as he donated one of his nude paintings (Figure 5) to the RMFAB in 1928. Unfortunately, any details regarding the donation are missing from the museums' archives.[43] And as Fujita produced a large number of nude paintings, it is impossible to determine in which exhibition it could have been featured.[44] Nevertheless, the donation was reported by two newspapers, both featuring its picture, making even the front page in one of them.[45]

▲ 4. Self-portrait 自画像
Oil on canvas, 100 x 80,5 cm
Date: 1921
Signed: T. Foujita 嗣治
Collection: Royal Museums of Fine Arts of Belgium, Brussels
1922 – no.4405 © Fondation Foujita/SABAM Belgium, 2022
Literature: Buisson and Buisson 2001, no.21.01

In this work, Fujita painted a nude supported by a pillow while lying on a bed draped in translucent white sheets. The muscular, voluptuous woman and her accompanying cat are posed against an all-white background. In such a way, this painting is an archetype of his famous 'milky-white' nudes. Reminiscent of odalisque paintings, Fujita replaced all accessories conjuring up exotic fantasies with his favourite animal: the cat.

Conclusion

In conclusion, two parallels can be drawn between the Meiji period prints and the modern paintings that found their way into Belgian collections in the 1920s. First of all, they are connected by way of Jules Destrée and Richard Dupierreux. In case of the Meiji prints, both figures were crucial for the approval of their exchange and consequently their existence in the RMAH's collection. For Fujita's paintings, they were essential in spreading appraisal for his art among the general public through a lecture and an article in one of Belgium's leading newspapers. Secondly, both the Meiji prints and modern paintings were condemned for their "un-Japanese-ness" and were expected to live up to Western expectations by treading in the footsteps of Hokusai and Utamaro in depicting the "real" Japan. This expectation that Japanese artists adhere to a traditional

representation of their country and apply conventional techniques needs to be interpreted in the reopening of Japanese ports to international trade in 1858. Ever since, Western critics and collectors lamented the loss of the "old" and "real" Japan, for which they blamed themselves, as Japan was rapidly westernising. Thus, the desire was born for Japanese artists to create art free from Western influence and, as a result, any art that deviated from its Western-appointed purpose was disdained. Although Hiroshige's prints were the main drive behind the swaps, Jules Bommer expressed hope that the prints would rise in value over time. In case of Fujita, despite being Europeanized to a certain degree, he was applauded for keeping up Japanese artistic traditions.

Finally, it should also be noted that the celebration and appreciation of Japanese art was not only sustained by several Belgian institutions and personae, but that Japan also played a decisive role. Satsuma Jirōhachi, who sponsored exhibitions on Japanese art and donated Fujita's nude to the RMAFB, and Adachi Mineichirō, who was involved with the Japanese book donation and attended Fujita's exhibition, were also driving forces behind the continuous Belgian interest in Japan, its art, and its culture. This particular interest in the visual aspects of Japanese culture did not go unnoticed by the Japanese book donators and is therefore also reflected in the extensive array of illustrated books in the collection donated to the University of Louvain in the 1920s.

▲ 5. Nude 裸婦
Oil on canvas, 63,5 x 98,5 cm
Date: 1927
Signed: Foujita 嗣治
Collection: Royal Museums of Fine Arts of Belgium, Brussels
1928 – no.4715 © Fondation Foujita/SABAM Belgium, 2022
Literature: Buisson and Buisson 2001, no.27.[23]

松竹キネマ超特選楽譜　NO.122
（ヴァイオリン.マンドリン.ハーモニカ用）

松竹映画主題歌　銀河の唄

（喜美子と繁の唄）

小モ三方編曲　仲谷定一
作曲　日暮六郎
作詞　一夫郎

松竹キネマ
蒲田レコード吹込
NO 3 B

松竹キネマ楽譜出版社發行

Aurel Baele[1]

Japan's Sonic Modernity: Popular Music and Culture in the 1920s

Introduction

"Jazz is the current mass music [in the 1920s]. It is our living and thinking that is being reflected here. [...] The urge for the present massification flowing through the world is being filled by jazz."[2] The contemporary critic Horiuchi Keizō illustrates how, here exemplified with jazz, Japan's society in the so-called Roaring Twenties was rapidly transforming into a mass society signified by mass consumption. Japan emerged from the First World War as one of the victors at the 1919 Paris Peace Conference.[3] As one of the world's great powers, it also contributed to the postwar reconstruction of the university library in Leuven.[4] The 1920s book donation might be seen as a reflection of Japan's postwar society. Parts of the Japanese cultural elite judged the effects of its transformation into a mass society as detrimental to an authentic Japan. Hence some of them believed a true cultural self was to be found in the Edo period (1600-1868), which explains the selection of many books for the donation to the University of Louvain.

Of course, the conception of such a past was rather imagined than real and, in itself, a very modern idea. In fact, in many ways ever since the Meiji Restoration in 1868 and the beginning of a construction of a modern nation state in the following decades, Japan experienced an identity conflict in which looking towards past, present, and future were all inherently modern.[5] Nonetheless, the donation mostly showed only the 'modern past' since most of the books were from the now glorified Edo period. At the same time the mass culture of 1920s Japan was as modern as in Europe and the US, advancing at a fast pace. It was consumed in a visual, material, and culinary way,[6] but - not to be underestimated - also sonically via the ubiquitous presence of new sounds that reverberated through society and literally set the tune for this new type of advanced modernity.[7] In this sonic modernity, jazz and jazzy popular music signified the tempo and energy by which change was taking place. To illustrate this transformation to mass culture, this essay briefly discusses the socio-economic context of the 1920s, followed by the places where popular music was consumed, and lastly both the role and influence of the culture industry.

Japan's Transformation to a Modern Mass Society

During the First World War, Japan profited from the power vacuum in East-Asia. As the region became cut off from European supplies, the demand for Japanese products from the Entente powers and the US soared. Japan's own industrial sector was stimulated because of the regional demand for not only chemicals, machinery, and heavy industrial products but also for liquor, toys, and other commodities that the European wartime economies could not deliver. After a burst of investment, the Japanese domestic market became less dependent on the importation of foreign goods. By 1920, as a result of its expanding heavy industry, Japan had finally completed its industrial revolution and had in many ways transformed into an economic state comparable to the United Kingdom, Germany, and the United States.

The industrialization process affected all of Japan, both urban centers and the rural areas alike. New infrastructural development connected and integrated cities within a broader domestic transportation network. Cities provided more work opportunities and commuting became

217

▸ 1. Cover of sheet music titled for the film 'The Milky Way' (*Ginga no uta*) of 1931 by Shōchiku. Private collection of Aurel Baele.

easier. Heavy urbanization made cities grow tremendously. By 1920 Tokyo had already doubled in size from around 1900 to over three million inhabitants; Osaka rose from 820,000 to about 1.25 million; Kobe went from 240,000 to 640,000; Kyoto grew from 350,000 to 700,000; Nagoya more than doubled from 240,000 to 610,000; Yokohama exploded from 190,000 to 570,000; and ten other cities reached more than 100,000. In addition to the work opportunities, urban centers had a broader array of choices for consumption and offered the comfort of technological progress. Department stores; new commodities like the radio; the colorful lightbulbs of the entertainment industry; the explosive expansion of the transportation network, including the first subways in East Asia; electrically driven machinery in bigger factories; the honking of cars and buses – all characterized the speed with which the future was arriving. Another potential factor was the creative effect of destruction: The Great Kantō Earthquake and the subsequent fires on 1 September 1923 razed most of Tokyo and Yokohama and killed almost 100,000 civilians. As a direct consequence, many in the entertainment sector moved to Osaka. Even so, the greater Tokyo area experienced an accelerated modernization during the reconstruction that followed, ultimately establishing itself as an ultramodern space. In the end, cities came to symbolize a future where possibilities seemed unlimited and growth endless.[8]

These drastic changes had consequences for Japan's society. The working class increased from roughly 20 million in the 1880s to about 27 million by 1910.[9] More prominent was the rise of the middle class, characterized by the salaryman. Their share increased from 1% around 1900 to about 10% in the beginning of the 1920s. Another fundamental change in Japanese society concerned the position of women. They filled about 30% of the blue-collar jobs in manufacturing, but in the 1920s became increasingly active in white-collar positions such as clerks, elevator girls, bus-girls, and teachers. Despite a gender inequality that manifested itself in lower wages, having their own income provided women the opportunity to become more financially and personally independent, and to cultivate the self before marriage.[10] Lastly, there were the *nouveaux riches* or *narikin* 成金 who profited immensely from the booming economy in the 1910s, and who were prominently portrayed in newspapers as decadent money spenders. Despite this general trend of social and economic progress, inflation and the volatility of the economy made for rising inequality.[11]

In the 1920s the masses in Japan enjoyed their access to new commodities and leisure activities like the dance hall, cafés, and travel resorts. The advent of mass media in Japan played a major part in this expanding consumerism. Although print media already flourished in the Meiji period (1868-1912), when the literacy level rose from 30% to 70%,[12] their sales boomed in the 1920s. However, the accessibility and dissemination of new media, like the cinema, records, and radio, offered the Japanese – as was the case worldwide – a new, different sensory experience. Together these media offered images about modern life, especially via iconic figures like the *moga* モガ (modern girls) and the *mobo* モボ (modern boys), who defied traditional gender roles through their habitus and avant-garde fashion styles. Even if these two figures were mostly fantasy, it was their medial representation that mattered. The Japanese intelligentsia heavily documented quotidian life with a mixed feeling of anxiety and intellectual curiosity, pointing to their influence on society. The *mobo* broke with typical ideas of Japanese masculinity, while the *moga* was as a "powerful symbol that represented the possibilities for what all women could become."[13] Breaking with the old and embracing the new was accompanied by exploring new frontiers. It was no wonder that a greater interest in discovering more about the erotic, the grotesque, and the nonsensical led to a phenomenon called *ero guro nansensu* エロ・グロ・ナンセンス. These concepts clearly contrasted with traditional ideas about gender, sexuality, the position as imperial subject, and cultural influences from outside. The nexus between consumerism and modern life had a profound impact on the discussion of Japanese identity.[14]

Popular Music and Modernity in Japan

Few music genres have characterized a global phenomenon so clearly as jazz in the so-called Roaring Twenties. While jazz is generally accepted to have begun in the United States in 1917, its syncopated notes reverberated in a synchronous moment over the entire world.[15] By the early 1920s the first articles on the American phenomenon appeared in Japanese newspapers.[16] Meanwhile, Japanese travelers to the US seemed to take quite an interest in acquiring records – even if only a minority had been able to travel intensively. On the other hand, "Jazz allowed Japan's self-styled modernites [sic] to experience an authentic and simultaneous modernity though they might never see or directly experience the rest of the world."[17]

Commercial dance halls and cafés were the main places that popularized jazz in Japan during the 1920s. The former boomed as social dancing had already taken off among urbanites in the previous decade. Moreover, several cafés even transformed into dance halls, like the Union in Osaka.[18] The floor of the dance hall was cramped with embracing couples who moved on the upbeat syncopations of live jazz performances. Part of the allure of these places came from how they tore down traditional gender barriers. Their exotic names hinted at a promise of experiencing the modern, with places such as *Paulista*, *Florida*, and *Parisien* in Tokyo and Osaka, while smaller cities emulated the metropoles by hosting their own dance halls, like *Venus* in Kanazawa.[19] The business was highly lucrative, not only significantly influencing the development of jazz but also the public perception of the music. Male customers could partner up with so-called "taxi dancers" 職業ダンサー for a limited amount of time by buying tickets. One method to increase the profits of the house was to let musicians play short songs so that "taxi dancers" could sell more tickets. Revenues could also be raised by testing the limits of the erotic as boundaries with outright prostitution were blurred. When "taxi dancers" with their Western style clothing and bobbed hairstyles became involved in scandals, the press and Japanese authors eagerly exploited the events. Mass media and literature presented the modern girl as lascivious, thereby further fanning the flames of the debates about Japanese collective identity, morality, and gender.[20] It was thus no surprise that in the 1920s many municipalities considered jazz and dance halls dangerous to public morality. Already by 1928 a national ordinance was implemented to regulate the sector.[21]

Jazz coffeehouses provided an alternative for the more expensive dance halls of the late 1920s. Its origins lay in the Meiji period, when the concept of coffeehouses came to Japan with the import of Western culture. These coffeehouses or *kissaten* 喫茶店 served as public spaces where people could socialize regardless of class or rank.[22] However, with the advent of the record and gramophones, a new combination was formed: specialized music coffeehouses, such as the classical music coffeehouse or *meikyoku kissaten* 名曲 喫茶店. Now a gramophone, such as the *Harmony* by Nipponophone ニッポノフォン displayed in our exhibition, offered background music for the visitors. In fact, the jazz coffeehouse was more an amalgam of different types of businesses from the early twentieth century, combining elements from the café, music coffeehouses, and milk halls. The *jazu kissaten*, however, built up a reputation for having an excellent sound installation boosted by a big record collection of foreign jazz, or in some cases via visual stimulation. The waitresses, who sometimes became celebrities, were also advertised outside the businesses with snapshots. Thus, besides jazz from the gramophone, one could enjoy food and drinks, or in some venues even receive "erotic services".[23]

The Commodification of Popular Sounds

In the 1920s popular music, in addition to music in general, was consumed both live and recorded. Though already active in Japan around the turn of the nineteenth century, record companies boomed after the war. The number of gramophones purchased increased more than tenfold in five years (1919-1924): from 125,000 imported and 260,000 domestically produced ones to almost 1.7 million and about 4.3 million ones, respectively.[24] In addition, the 1920s saw major technological improvements in the music industry, such as electrical recording. An important change came, however, after the Great Kantō Earthquake of 1923. To balance the budget for the reconstruction of the devastated areas and protect the economy, the Japanese government imposed a tariff of 100% on imported luxury goods, including records and gramophones. In order to circumvent this new tariff and be able to compete with national companies, three foreign record companies established their own subsidiaries in Japan in 1927: the Victor Talking Machine Company, Columbia, and the German Polydor thus created Nippon Victor 日本ビクター, Nippon Columbia 日本コロムビア and Nippon Polydor 日本ポリドール.[25]

Victor, Columbia, and Polydor brought in their own business concepts, thereby substantially changing how music was produced and sold in Japan. Until 1927, record companies waited for a song to become a hit before recording it to make profit. The archetypical example is *Kachyūsha's song* カチューシャの唄, which was composed for the actress Matsui Sumako 松井須磨子 to sing in the play *Resurrection*. After the play was

performed in the major Japanese cities, the score and record were sold. After 1927, though, the industry reversed that strategy in a Fordist way to record and sell as many hits in a row as possible.[26] Record companies introduced an exclusive contract system that bound performers, composers, and lyricists overseen by music directors in an assembly-line structure.[27]

What characterized Japan's popular music in the Interwar period – generally called *ryūkōka* 流行歌 – is its tendency for being highly cosmopolitan and having confusing categories. Various subgenres existed with the use of Western or Japanese instrumentation, or a mix of both, and a pentatonic scale. The so-called jazz songs or *jazu songu* ジャズソング offered translations of American Tin Pan Alley songs with a jazzy tune, yet were different from the jazz of Duke Ellington or Louis Armstrong. "New folk songs" (*shin min'yō* 新民謡) incorporated Japanese folk songs or themes with Western arrangements. The commonality for *ryūkōka* and jazz was often the absence of any

clear distinction, thereby blurring the boundaries. In fact, jazz referred to an amalgam of different Western popular music genres such as fox trot, tango, rumba, waltz, and symphonic jazz. Jazz musician Kami Kyōsuke 紙恭輔 (1902-1981) wrote in the film magazine *Kinema junpō* キネマ旬報 in 1935: "The word 'jazz' is a strange word and even if its origin lacks details, there is also no definition; and because nobody knows it, it has become a word that I don't know if it's good to tell anything when you immediately hear it and try to explain it."[28] The music industry played into this ambiguity, using the buzzword "jazz" as a nexus between other aspects of modern life for selling more records.

Record sleeves served to attract customers visually in a similar fashion to CDs or LPs and even continue today in a virtual setting like Spotify. They were sold with artistic designs that helped to create a certain idea of what one could expect from a record company and its music.

The beautiful designs on the sleeves displayed in our exhibition illustrate how they potentially reflect a 1920s sensibility. A remarkable example

▲ **2. 1920s records in sleeve with carrying box.** Collection Research Group Japanese Studies, KU Leuven Faculty of Arts.

is a sleeve from *Nipponophone*: it shows a gramo-phone with its typical flower-shaped horn, of which the melodious notes and the brand name succeed in even enticing a sitting Buddha away from his meditation.

It should be noted that the English text was not necessarily aimed at a foreign audience. Instead, it fitted the context of consumerism and interest in the exotic. Moreover, the English words connected to the dominance of Anglo-Saxon culture after the First World War and gave an aura of being modern. The front and back cover for *Tsuru rekōdo* ツルレコード or *Crane Records* is an example of how the use of electricity was breaking through in society.

This Nagoya-based company boasted being the first Japanese company to produce electri-cally recorded records, a development which is fittingly reflected by the lightning bolt that flash-es through their logo. In that way the company promoted itself as part of the modern future. The front sleeve shows a cabinet gramophone offering the experience of live performances of traditional

Japanese music styles and modern music. Simi-larly, the back cover depicts a record shooting a flash of lightning towards a radio. In both in-stances traditional and popular music come to life, as can be seen from the dancers and musi-cians in the middle. There could also be different references to the other wonders of the modern age people were living in. *Hikōki rekōdo* ヒコーキレコ ード, literally *Airplane Records*, honors its name by depicting biplanes on the back cover. While the airplane was already in military use during First World War, it symbolized the next frontier in transport technology in the 1920s, when civil aviation began to develop and became a major symbol of 1920s modernity.[29]

Development of a Dense Mass Media Mix

The consumption of popular music via the dis-semination of records was further encouraged by the collaboration of different mass media. Through a dense "media mix" of the Japanese na-tional radio-broadcasting company NHK with re-cord and film companies, the combination of each other's audience benefitted all parties in maxi-mizing their profits. Newspapers and magazines

▲ 3. Sleeve of a record issued by the Japanese company Nippon-phone, with a Buddha enticed by music from the gramophone. Part of a box of Japanese records of the 1920s, Collection Research Group Japanese Studies, KU Leuven Faculty of Arts.

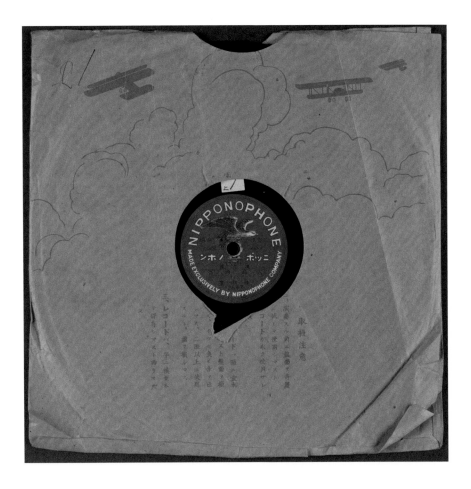

served as mass advertisement platforms, featuring articles that introduced the newest popular records and films, as well as listing the daily radio programs.

In 1925, the first radio broadcast was launched in Tokyo by the Tokyo Broadcasting Station, and a year later the fusion of three metropolitan radio companies (Tokyo, Osaka, and Nagoya) established the first nationwide radio company, the *Nihon Hōsō Kyōkai* 日本放送協会 (NHK). Japanese popular music was first considered a lowly, vulgar genre by government officials and metropolitan intellectuals, and thus unsuitable for broadcasts. Broadcasts were originally limited to classical music, Taishō period (1912-1926) educational songs, and some Western pop songs. However, the programs gradually changed by the beginning of the 1930s. As the price of radios sharply declined, they became increasingly accessible to Japanese citizens. Various radios were produced by Japanese firms such as the Matsushita Electric Industrial Company (currently Panasonic).

Some radio makers also produced records, like Nippon Victor – a prewar 'sonic empire' – which evolved after 1945 into the entertainment electronics giant JVC, best known for its postwar global success, the VHS.

The early radios had free-standing horns as speakers, but those soon became integrated in the radio itself and in some cases combined with the record player. It became clear that the new audience favored Japanese popular music, such that *ryūkōka* – though under government censorship – became programmed for the airwaves. Record companies saw an opportunity to collaborate with NHK, thereby directly promoting songs to a nationwide audience.[30]

The 1929 silent film *Tōkyō Kōshinkyoku* (Tokyo March) excellently exemplifies the cooperation between record and film companies. Famous director Mizoguchi Kenji 溝口健二 (1898-1956) adapted the original love story from author Kikuchi Kan 菊池寛 (1888-1948).[31] Despite the rather negative reviews in newspapers and movie magazines, this silent film performed well with the masses.

Its success was due to the popularity of the film's accompanying theme song (*eiga shudaika* 映画主題歌), which sold over 300,000 copies. Film company Nikkatsu 日活 had struck a deal

223

1931. Jazz played an essential role to the story and the main theme song reflected jazz's modern allure. While the theme song and the talkie movie profoundly impacted the cinema experience – relaying sound from film itself, often coupled with a contemporary story – they did not radically replace silent movies in Japan. The silent films accompanied by the *benshi* 弁士, the popular live narrators of 1920s cinema, only gradually lost terrain. The historical, sword-swinging samurai film genre called *chanbara* チャンバラ, for example, remained popular into the 1930s. Nonetheless, recorded sound heralded the future, and jazz saw its popularity skyrocket by the end of the 1920s and during the 1930s. Besides the availability of records, fans also had access to music sheets for playing and singing the *shudaika* themselves. The covers for these sheets are visually modernistic, conveying the atmosphere of the movie. Using elements of what signified modern Japan, real or imagined, was a way to attract consumers. Again, the image of the *moga* evoked such ideas (Figure 1). Even the erotic element was not shunned in regard of better sales, as is evidenced by the cover for the music of *Miss Nippon* (Figure 8).

Conclusion

Japan's transformation into a society of mass culture and mass consumption in the 1920s was on par with the West. Jazz, and popular music in general, represented this transformation as it made the modern audible to its audience. Additionally, jazz in Japan allowed anyone to experience another world without having to travel abroad. However, Japan's sonic modernity was far from limited to the audible. A trip to a dance hall meant an evening out to dance to live jazz, possibly with a partner from the other sex. A jazz coffeehouse offered recorded jazz with a glass of beer brought by a waitress, which was part of the gendered attraction at that time. The record sleeve, too, referred visually to technological progress. Furthermore, that same record was also music in a visually and materially compacted form. Thus, through its interconnectedness with other aspects of modernity in Japan, popular music represented the possibilities of what it meant to be modern.

The demand for such dreams was accommodated by the booming mass media that provided these images for consumption. Through cooperation via advertisements, sleeves, records, covers,

with Nippon Victor to record the *shudaika* and then distribute it strategically, timed with the movie's release, in cafés and in Nikkatsu-owned cinemas in and around Tokyo.[32] Furthermore, this jazzy hit – sung by Satō Chiyako 佐藤千夜子 (1897-1968), written by the renowned poet Saijō Yaso 西條八十 (1892-1970), and composed by Nakayama Shinpei 中山晋平 (1887-1952) – reached that hit status, particularly because it mirrored different aspects of modern life in Tokyo. The four stanzas reflected the four parts of the city, each with its own distinct characteristics. Ginza boasted the dance halls where men and women drank liquor and danced to the syncopated beats of jazz; Marunouchi had the business center, crowded with people during rush hour; Asakusa was where the first subway in East Asia operated; and, lastly, Shinjuku stood for cinema and teahouses to relax, department stores, and the newly opened Odakyū train, which connected the capital with the resort area Hakone, close to Mt. Fuji.[33]

The importance of the theme song continued into the 1930s and became even more prevalent with the arrival of the first talkie *The Neighbor's Wife and Mine* (*Madamu to Nyōbō* マダムと女房) by Gosho Heinosuke 五所平之助 (1902-1981) in

▲ 7. Japanese-made radio of the Interwar period.
Collection National Museum of Japanese History, H-686-46-1.

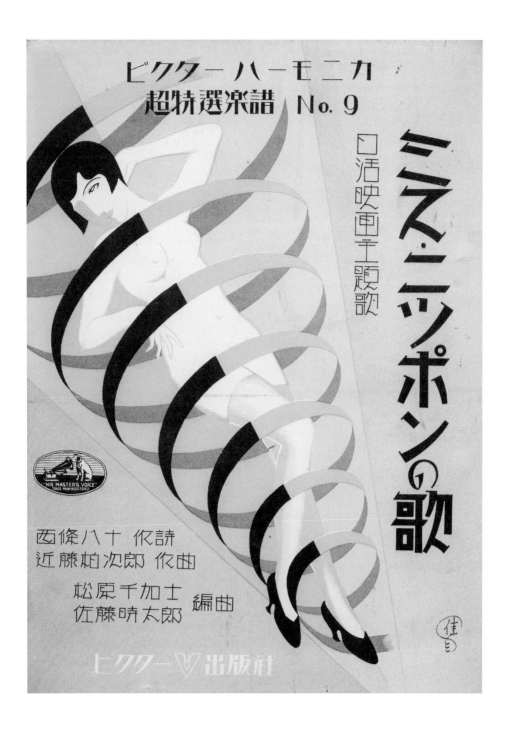

ビクターハーモニカ
超特選楽譜 No. 9

日活映画主題歌

ミス・ニッポンの歌

西條八十 作詩
近藤柏次郎 作曲

松原千加士
佐藤晴太郎 編曲

ビクター ♥ 出版社

magazines, and films, these media reached the masses. Consequently, there was a shift in how collective identity was constructed: from a top-down approach attempted by the ministerial bureaucracy during the modernization process in the Meiji period to more liberal options in the 1920s where the Japanese state seemingly had lost control over the effects of modernization. However, the pervasiveness of all these new ideas and the debates about them in mass media, despite conflating reality, seriously impacted the search for the supposedly true "Japanese" identity. For many, the authentic lay in the culture of "Edo Japan". Ironically enough, even that past was not free of intellectual, political, and commercial contestation and was molded in the context of the massification of the 1920s.[34]

Arriving in Leuven in the mid-1920s, the donation of over 3,000 prevalently early modern titles in 14,000 volumes should therefore be understood in the context of Japan's vibrant mass culture. Even if the books themselves were centuries old, their selection was, in a unique way, eminently modern.

▲ 8. Cover of sheet music titled for the film 'Miss Nippon' (*Misu Nippon no uta*) of 1930 by Nikkatsu. Private collection of Aurel Baele.

Jan Schmidt

Selected Objects from 1920s Japan: Modernity in Popular Culture, Media, Society and Politics as Background to the Donation

The 1920s book donation represented Japanese culture as the Japanese elite wanted it to be perceived in the West. Most eye-catching are the high-quality illustrated books of the Edo period (1600-1868), as well as a selection of more recent literary works and academic studies published after 1868. For the majority of the Japanese population, however, the premodern past became commodified and integrated into the upcoming modern mass culture and mass consumption of the 1920s. Fragments of the Edo period could be found, for instance, as a frame of reference for popular historical novels, theatre plays, silent movies and songs on the radio and on gramophone records.

In the rapidly growing urban areas of 1920s Japan, which were as modern as their Western counterparts, there was increasing access to luxurious department stores, cafés and dance halls, cinemas, and public transportation. The modern way of life resonated with the tunes of new popular music, often jazz, which emanated from the speakers of the gramophone and the radio. It was also a time of cosmopolitanism. Japanese artists and intellectuals began to intensify their activities in and exchanges with the West in ever higher numbers. One example for this was the modern art exhibition held in 1929 in Brussels, mentioned by Freya Terryn in her essay in this volume, which was sponsored by the Japanese philanthropist Satsuma Jirōhachi, who around the same time financed the Satsuma Chair at the University of Louvain.

The 1920s were also the era of the so-called *Taishō demokurashī* 大正デモクラシー (Taishō Democracy), a time when steps towards further democratization were taken and social movements

demanded reforms on many levels of politics and society. They were also an era of extremely volatile economic development, which culminated in Japan already in 1927 in a first major banking crisis, the Bank of Taiwan Crisis, and ultimately in the global "Great Depression", which started in 1929. The subsequent trajectory towards the Second World War, which in Japan is called the Asia-Pacific War, started in East Asia with the Japanese invasion of North-East China in the so-called "Manchurian Incident" in September 1931. Given the events that then unfolded, including the failure of the system of collective security that had been attempted with the foundation of the League of Nations after the First World War, cultural diplomacy lost much - though never all - of its traction until after the end of the Second World War. It is therefore not surprising that the 1920s Japanese Book Donation moved out of sight for decades once the destructiveness of the political tensions that had accumulated manifested itself. The following gallery of descriptions of objects displayed in the exhibition is intended to shed further light on this side of the multifaceted background of the book donation to the University of Louvain.

1920s Consumer Culture in Japan: Popular Music, Department Stores, Fashion, Media

"Dancing to jazz, whiling away the time with booze,
You take the subway, I take the bus, but the stops are not made for lovers."
(Song *Tōkyō kōshinkyoku* 東京行進曲 / Tokyo March, 1929)

Popular music like this song text echoed the fast changes in Japan of the 1920s. Many of these were global, i.e. the arrival of jazz from across the

▸ Cover of Kon Wajirō/Yoshida Kenkichi (1930). *Modernologio – kōgengaku* (Modernology). Tōkyō: Shun'yōdō.

Pacific Ocean. Jazz was connected to other, new forms of leisure, such as dancing to live jazz in the dance hall or to a record on a gramophone in a café. *Jazuru*, 'to jazz around', was even a term to denote this lifestyle. Meanwhile, artists and composers experimented with their own music traditions and jazzy sounds, spawning new popular music genres like *ryūkōka* 流行歌. The quick tempo of jazz also symbolized the speed and mass consumption of contemporary technological advancements like the subway and radio. Moreover, the music itself was transformed into a mass product with the development of the big Japanese record companies.

Perhaps nowhere else is the complex situation of 1920s modernity in Japan reflected better than in the clothes worn. It would be a mistake here to simply see a juxtaposition between 'traditional' *kimono* and 'modern' Western clothing. Clothes increasingly became - at least for the upper and rising middle classes - a 'projection screen' of modern patterns. The *kimono*, too, was imprinted with modern(ist) designs. Western-style clothing became increasingly popular in modern Japan, especially by the end of the 1920s. Even so, the majority of Japanese women still wore the 'traditional' *kimono*, which was not only more affordable but also deemed more practical for daily life, though it was often combined with modern accessories or hairstyles. Men, especially in the rising middle class, began wearing coats and suits.

They adopted the practice from the elites who, since the late 19th century, had been expected to wear Western clothing while working. While older children usually dressed in Western-style clothing, children under the age of six or seven as well as those of poorer upbringing often still wore traditional Japanese clothing. Once the children started school, they switched to school uniforms to become what Mark Jones has called "small national citizens". Fashion(s) and mass media mutually influenced each other. A constant stream of imagery in magazines or department store advertisements stimulated the demand and fed the hunger for novelty and consumption.

The following objects, many of which were lent to the exhibition by the National Museum of Japanese History in Sakura, and their descriptions aim to highlight key tendencies of 1920s politics and consumer culture in Japan, which was part of mass culture in Japan's modernity. Although not mutually exclusive these items can complement the concept of "Japanese culture" that lay at the heart of the elite project of the book donation to the University of Louvain, and they point to a heterogeneous, multi-layered, and never stable "cultural identity" in the 1920s, which was typical of a modern society of that time.

Literature: Atkins 2001; Dickinson 2013; Francks 2009; Fuess 2005; Gordon 1991; Gordon 2020; Iriye 1997; Iriye 2002; Jones 2010; Koresawa 2008; Mathias 2010; Minami/Shakai shinri kenkyūjo 1977; Minichiello 1998; Nagamine 2001; Nakamura and Odaka 2003; Narita 2007; Richter 2004; Silverberg 2007.

1. Hō-Ō daihikō kinen hikō sugoroku
訪欧大飛行記念飛行双六

**Board game; appendix to *Ōsaka asahi shinbun* 大阪朝日新,
10/12/1925**

"Board Game Commemorating a Flight to Europe".
Sugoroku 双六 were board games, either printed on
wood or paper. They were often attached to newspapers or magazines as giveaways, as also in this
case. This particular *sugoroku,* as an addendum to
the newspaper *Ōsaka asahi shinbun,* allows the players to re-enact a flight by four Japanese aviators to
and around Europe, starting in Tokyo and ending in
Rome. The flight was made by two airplanes and was
most likely the reverse version of a historic flight
from Rome to Tokyo in 1920, which was similarly
conducted in two airplanes with four Italian aviators. The Japanese flight was funded by the newspaper *Ōsaka asahi shinbun* in cooperation with the
Imperial Army and Navy. The reasoning was that
the flight - with ultimately only 111 hours in the air
- would put Japan on the map in terms of the global
aviation industry, and that it was meant as a sign of

international cooperation. The Japanese airplanes
Hatsukaze 初風 (First wind) and 東風 *Kochikaze*
(East Wind) also passed through Belgium, and the
newspaper *Het Nieuws Van Den Dag* reported on 20
October 1925: "Abe and Kawachi (pilots)" had left the
airfield in Croydon (England) and arrived in Evere,
Belgium. They were welcomed by the Japanese Ambassador Adachi Mine'ichirō and various Belgian officials with "the whole of the Japanese colony in Belgium gathered in the square to meet them". The two
bi-planes were met by and escorted by nine Belgian
military aircraft who guided them in. On 25 October 1925 the Belgian Minister of Foreign Affairs met
them and received from them a "wonderful piece of
'borduur' (embroidery) in the Japanese style, which
has been paid for by the *Asahi* newspaper. In 1916
the *Asahi* had already given an old sword to the Belgian Royal house as a gift of friendship."

229

2. Kaimono sugoroku ichimei depātomento sutōa
買い物双六　一名デパートメントストーア

"Board Game: Shopping at a Certain Department Store", appendix to
Shōjo no tomo 少女の友 **7/1 (1 January 1914)**

This board game takes the players on a race through a department store and to the marvels to be consumed there. Anything from Western clothes, cosmetics, Japanese *kimono*, stationery and shoes to sweets, toys and music instruments, among other things, could be purchased there. In addition, family photos or portraits could be taken, a restaurant and a rest area offered food and beverages, while on the rooftop a small garden and a "zoo" offered views of exotic plants and birds. In the 1910s and 1920s *sugoroku* were often sold as supplements to magazines or newspapers. This particular one, advertising modern consumer habits and consumption worlds, was a supplement to a magazine for girls.

3. Mitsukoshi *No. 5/9* 三越5巻9号

Advertisement magazine *Mitsukoshi* of the Mitsukoshi department store,
1.09.1915, pp. 26–27

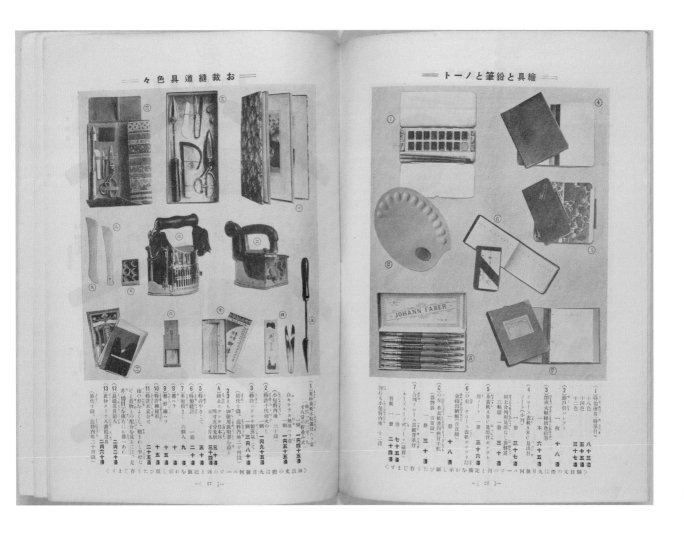

The Mitsukoshi Department Store chain was a trail-blazer in modern Japan, introducing a new form of consumerism. The company established several research teams, including one which analyzed trends and how to create new ones. The *Mitsukoshi* 三越 house magazine served to advertise new products, lifestyles and special exhibitions. Although the magazine targeted a more upper-class clientele, just visiting Mitsukoshi and the desire to go shopping there became part of the consumption culture of the rising middle class. The pages shown here feature on the right stationary and writing materials, among which products by the renowned German company Johann Faber, as well as materials for painting, and on the left sewing tools.

231

4. Mitsukoshi *No. 5/10* 三越5巻10号

**Advertisement magazine *Mitsukoshi* of the Mitsukoshi department store,
1.10.1915, pp. 38-39**

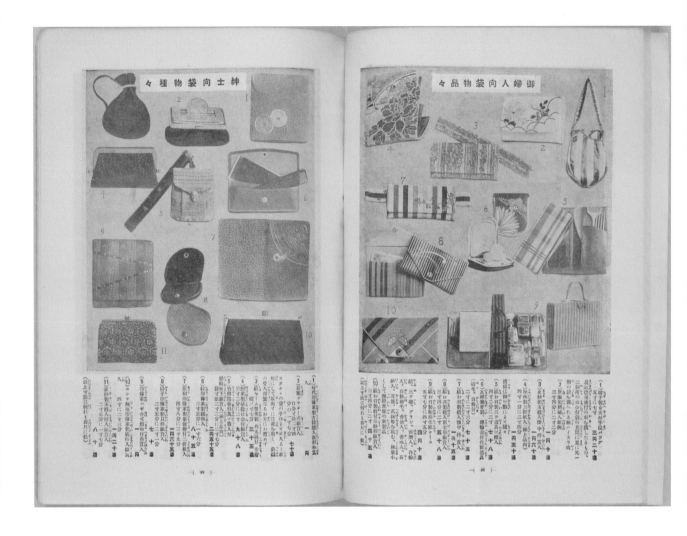

These pages of the *Mitsukoshi* magazine show, on the
right, "Bags and purses for ladies", and on the left,
"Bags and purses of different kinds for gentlemen".
It is typical that more "traditional" Japanese designs
and products of high quality are displayed alongside
expensive Western imported products.

5. Mitsukoshi *No. 16/1* 三越*16*巻*1*号

**Advertisement magazine *Mitsukoshi* of the Mitsukoshi department store,
1.1.1926, table of contents**

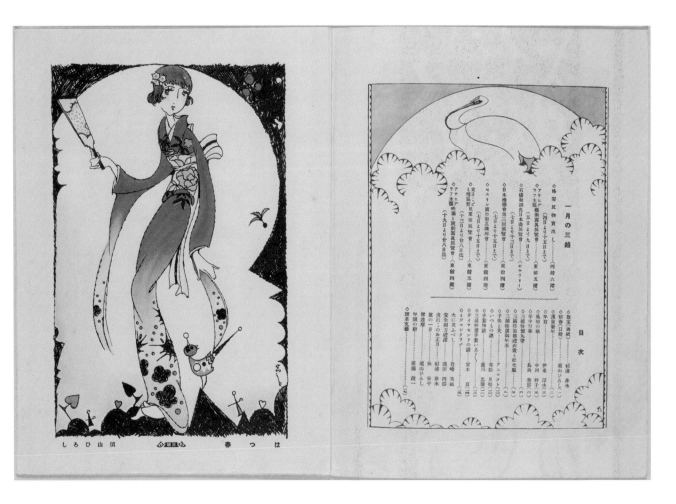

On the top right of this double-page spread is a list of events that would take place inside the Mitsukoshi Department Store in January 1926, such as a sale in the early days of January and exhibitions of art photography and of photos of theatre plays that were both organized by the new photo magazine *Asahi gurafu* (Asahi Graph) 朝日グラフ and, for instance, the "Third Japanese Manga Exhibition." The latter alludes to the fact that *manga* did only in the 1920s find their way into the mainstream of society and were also more and more consumed by the middle and upper classes. The table of contents at the bottom right guides the reader to articles by various authors not only on fashion but also on "children and dogs," on "diamonds," etc. The left page features a coloured drawing entitled *Hatsuharu* はつ春 ("New Year") by artist Suyama Hiroshi 須山ひろし, who often produced drawings and designs for magazines as well as for sheet music similar to that introduced in Aurel Baele's essay in this volume.

233

6. Kimono 着物

Part of a 1920s women's *kimono*, 1926

SELECTED OBJECTS FROM 1920S JAPAN

234

As the street surveys of Kon Wajirō 今和次郎 (see
No. 10) and other contemporary evidence showed,
throughout the 1920s the majority of women in Japan still wore a *kimono* like this one, which was selected by the National Museum of Japanese History
because it is fairly representative of its time.

Men's *kimono*, ca. 1920-1930

Leuven, Japanese Studies KU Leuven, donated
by Mrs. Gokita Mitsuko 五木田美津子, Sakura

235

This item belonged to an affluent member of the local elites in Chiba Prefecture in the 1920s, produced with lavish materials and using a classical pattern in a modern way. While many men in the urbanized areas but also in the regional centres, especially the growing multitudes of white-collar workers, wore Western-style suits, it remained common that lavish *kimono* were worn for celebrations but also in private, casual settings. The design on this kimono is inspired by *Ataka no matsu* 安宅の松, a *naga-uta* 長唄 (a song accompanying a theatrical dance), first performed in 1769, which took its subject matter from the famous story of the deadly feud between Minamoto no Yoshitsune 源義経 (1159-1189) and his older brother Minamoto no Yoritomo 源頼朝 (1147-1199), later to become the first *shōgun* 将軍 of the Kamakura period (1192-1333). Originally adapted from a 15th century *nōgaku* 能楽 theatre play, the theatrical dance subsequently garnered huge popular acclaim and was ranked as one of the *kabuki* evergreen plays, known as *kabuki jūhachiban* 歌舞伎十八番 ("best 18 kabuki plays"). This 1920s *kimono* is a vivid testimony to how classical *topoi* of initially elite and later popular culture are incorporated into very modern, everyday life designs, becoming part of an always evolving – and never unified – cultural identity.

8. Haori 羽織

Children's *haori* with iconic images of modernity, 1928-1931

236

The *haori* is a coat worn over a *kimono* as a form of jacket. Very concrete images of modern icons and depictions of actual contemporary events were very popular in the 1920s as part of *kimono* designs called *omoshirogara*, 'novelty' or 'cool designs.' This one was produced at the end of the 1920s or in the early 1930s. It seems to herald US-Japanese Friendship by displaying the flags of both countries, a Japanese airplane, and a battleship, as well as a skyscraper skyline, representing either New York or San Francisco. One possibility is that the airplane, as well as the pilot goggles and pilot's leather cap that can be seen on the head of one of the two boys depicted, allude to a daring trans-Pacific flight that was conducted by two US aviators in response to an offer of 25,000 US Dollars by the Japanese Newspapers *Tōkyō asahi shinbun* in October 1931. The flight – and the offer by the newspaper – came at an auspicious time, since US-Japanese diplomatic relations were heavily strained by the Japanese invasion in North-East China in the aftermath of the "Manchurian Incident", which had started on 17 September 1931. In reaction to criticism of Japan's actions in the US public, not only Japanese diplomats but also private citizens and companies, like the afore-mentioned newspaper, tried to amend the relation by friendship campaigns, which then became part of the everyday material culture, here in fashion for children.

9. Seifuku 制服

Children's uniform (male), 1926

In 1879, uniforms were introduced in the Gakushūin 学習院 school for the children of aristocrats, strongly inspired by the sailor outfits of the French and British Navies, which by that point had been adopted as the uniforms for the Imperial Japanese Navy as well. This compulsory wearing of uniforms at the Gakushūin school was the start of the spread of the uniforms throughout Japan for, by the late 1880s, ultimately all levels ranging from primary education up to the Imperial Universities. In the Taishō period (1912-1926) the various styles became consolidated into the now-typical *gaku-ran* 学ラン (学欄) school uniform for boys. For girls, uniforms only came into widespread use in the 1930s. The uniforms were in line with what the historian Mark Jones has called the discourses of the *shō-kokumin* 小国民, the 'little (national) citizen' and of the *yūtōsei* 優等生,

the 'superior student', although he also identified another discourse of 'childlike children' (*kodomo-rashī kodomo* 子供らしい子供). The first one was connected to the idea of being of service to the nation. During the 1910s and 1920s, education was increasingly seen as a tool to climb the social ladder in a complex modern society by parents in all social classes. Thus, pushing children to achieve 'superior' results in school gradually became a social norm, especially in the elites but also in the emerging middle class. School uniforms became a normal sight on any street, with some of them worn by students who were affiliated to universities that participated in the 1920s donation to the University of Louvain. In addition, uniform-like children's dresses were worn outside of school as well. This one is most likely from an elementary school boy.

10. Modernologio – kōgengaku モデルノロヂオ：考現学 / Kon Wajirō 今和次郎, Yoshida Kenkichi 吉田謙吉, 1930

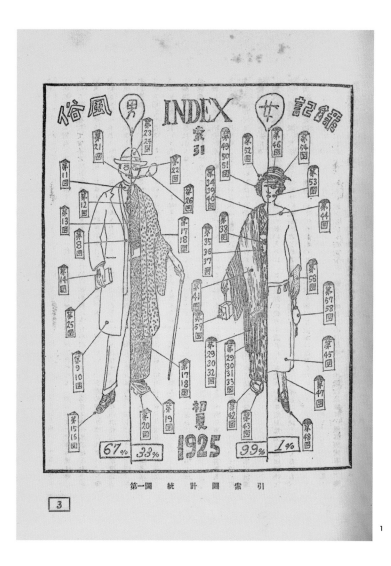

The title "Modernologio - Studies of Present Times" refers to the concept coined by the folklore studies and ethnography scholar Kon Wajirō (1888-1973). He is primarily known for his extensive ethnographic research on changing material culture in light of Tokyo's rapid urban transformation following the Great Kantō Earthquake of 1923. In this, he applied a method he framed with the neologism 考現学 *kōgengaku*, the 'study of the contemporary', as an antonym to the long-established 考古学 *kōkogaku*, 'study of the old', which to this day is the standard Japanese word for 'archaeology'. He also used the Esperanto word *modernologio*, to express the global meaning of his approach of a "modernology". The use of Esperanto alludes to the fact that many members of Japanese academia were intrigued by the appeal of one unified language to be used globally – which shows their transnational connectedness to the cosmopolitan avant-garde movements of their times. Together with his students and various other

volunteers, Kon held large-scale surveys around the Ginza street (May 1925), Tokyo's counterpart to New York's Fifth Avenue, but also in the working-class slum areas of Honjo and Fukagawa, Tokyo (October 1925), meticulously capturing their observations of everyday life with annotated sketches and statistics. The same method was applied to surveys in Japan's colonies and rural areas of Japan, including extensive studies on architecture and the material culture inside buildings of all kinds.

The first page [ill. 1] displayed here is taken from his 1925 Ginza survey that was originally published as the index to the July 1925 issue of the women's magazine *Fujin kōron*, summarizing the fashion of strolling men and women, including a distinction between Western-style clothing and more traditional Japanese garments. The rectangular boxes with numbers attached to different elements on both the female and male model sketches guide the reader of the survey to numerous tables with

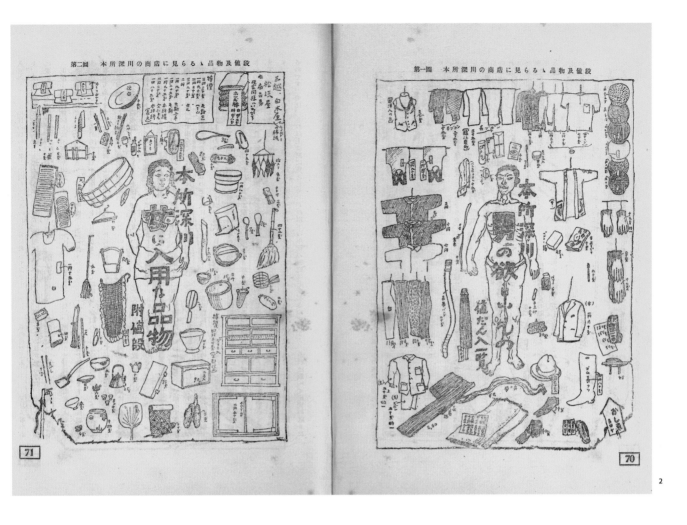

71

70

statistics on percentages of anything ranging from different types of hats, of hair or beard styles, of glasses, purses, parts of the respective dress, down to the different types of shoes worn by anybody who walked past Kon Wajirō and his fellow surveyors. The sketches on this index page already show by the percentages given below, that the clothing styles of the most likely more elite or middle-class passers-by differed radically between the genders at the time of the survey: while 99% of the women wore *kimono*, 67% of the men wore Western suits. At the same time *kimono* were not unaffected by modernity either: new color schemes and graphic patterns were rapidly being introduced by the modern department stores and found attention through distribution to local smaller stores throughout the Japanese Empire and through mail-order catalogues or popular magazines. A significant number had modernist graphic patterns or depicted icons of modernity as can be seen in the case of the children's *haori* among the objects included in this catalogue here.

The second page [ill. 2] is taken from the survey *Honjo Fukagawa hinminkutsu fukin fūzoku saishū* 本所深川貧民窟付近風俗採集 (Collections regarding customs from around the slum areas of Honjo-Fukagawa), depicting a radically different material culture than that seen on the Ginza shopping street. In the 1920s, Honjo and Fukagawa in Tokyo, two areas that stretched from north to south, occupying a vast stretch of land east of the Sumida River, were full of smaller factories and over-crowded living quarters for working class families, who often lived in precarious conditions. Only a few kilometers away from Ginza, everyday livelihood situations could hardly be more different. Seen through the lens of what was sold in shops in the Honjo-Fukagawa area and for what prices, the left side depicts the "Items that women of Honjo-Fukagawa need" in everyday life, while the right side shows what "Things men of Honjo-Fukugawa want" to buy in the shops surveyed, and what the average prices were.

Both pages were reprinted as part of a collection of Kon's surveys in 1930 under the title "Modernologio – Studies of Present Times", which he published together with Yoshida Kenkichi (1897-1982), his former fellow junior student at the Tōkyō bijutsu gakkō 東京美術学校 (Tokyo Academy of Fine Arts), who had become a theatre scenographer. Yoshida was similarly intrigued by contemporary material culture and habits and collaborated with Kon in developing the concept of "Modernology".

239

11. Kirin bīru *(Kirin Beer)* キリンビール

Advertisement poster, 1923

This 1923 poster features a girl in *kimono* enjoying a glass of Kirin Beer with other patrons at the neighboring tables in suits and a lady in traditional dress in the background. Japan's beer production and consumption had increased tremendously since the introduction of German brewery techniques in the 19th century. Although it was considered an exotic luxury beverage before 1900, by 1920 the average consumption of beer per capita had risen fivefold. The Kirin Beer Company, which was established in 1887, had a share of 18.9% of Japan's beer market in 1920. The first place (64.1% in 1920) was taken by Dai Nihon Beer, which was the result of a merger of Kirin's three competitors Sapporo, Ebisu, and Asahi in 1906. That producing beer was a profitable business was also reflected in Kirin Beer's and Dai Nihon Beer's positions (89th and 39th respectively in 1918) in the top 100 of Japan's largest industrial firms.

The consumption and cultural representation of beer in fact rose in parallel with the social and economic transformation that Japan experienced between 1900 and 1920. The image of beer remained exotic, but in a different way. With the expansion of cities, the foreign nature of beer became linked with trends in a modern urban lifestyle that were globally oriented. In beer halls Japanese salarymen could be found savoring beer that was served by the *jokyū* 女給 (waitresses). Another contemporary image in the weekly illustrated magazine *Asahi gurafu* 朝日ブ ラフ featured a combination of beer, waitresses, cigarettes, and commuter trains to symbolize the life of salaried men. What Kirin attempted to do with this poster and other similar ones in the 1920s was to create such imagery of the modern life, in which the consumption of beer and other modern beverages was to be deeply entangled. An image like this, in which the woman in the poster is alone and radiates self-confidence while indulging in her beer, would have been impossible even a short while before and was probably still provocative to a certain extent in 1923, but it also shows that Japanese companies saw women and their independent consumption choices as an increasingly important market segment.

12. Fujokai 婦女界

Advertisement poster for the magazine *Fujokai* (Women's World), 1927

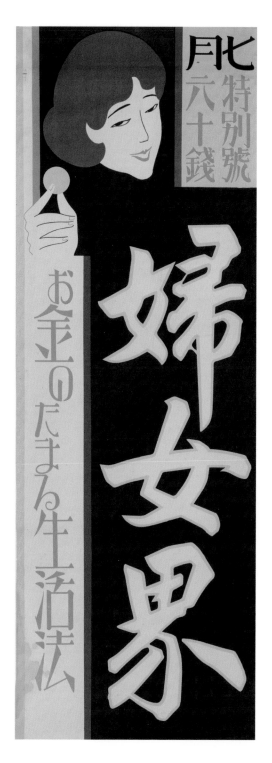

Fujokai, "Women's World", published between 1910 and 1950 (briefly revived in 1952), was one of the many thriving women's magazines in the 1920s. The magazine featured a variety of items, including serialized novels and practical advice for everyday life. This poster advertises the July 1927 issue of the magazine, which was a special issue focusing on *O-kane no tamaru seikatsu-hō* お金のたまる生活方, on a "lifestyle which allows saving money". It was part of

a general trend to encourage accumulating savings that was often fueled by government campaigns. Women were ascribed a crucial role in this endeavor as they were deemed more trustworthy in administrating the family savings than their husbands. The relative success of encouraging thrift and savings led to a path-dependency in spending habits that turned Japan, up to today, into one of the nations with the highest rates of private savings.

Advertisement poster for the "7th Children's Fair", 1915

Sakura, National Museum for Japanese History, F-457-45

242

Mitsukoshi, the most renowned Japanese department store, with its main branch located on the Ginza street, Tōkyō's 'Fifth Avenue', organized so-called *Jidō hakurankai* 児童博覧会 "Children's Fairs" or "Children's Exhibitions" from 1909 to 1921. This is an advertisement, in a playful graphic design playing with the graphic elements of the Japanese characters, for the 7th edition, taking place between March 20 and May 5 1915. The exhibition focused on children's toys and other products from both in and outside Japan. In the 1910s and 1920s a new type of modern childhood was invented – with children forming a new category of consumers. The last event in 1921 featured a lavish display of toys of all kinds, domestically produced and imported from all over the world, clothes for children, sweets and items related to education, books, photos, modern school desks and chairs etc., and also articles for improving hygiene.

14. Jikkai 十誡

Advertisement poster for the film "The Ten Commandments", 1923

Poster advertising a special screening of the American silent film "The Ten Commandments," directed by Cecil B. DeMille. The character for 'ten' 十 is stylised to resemble the Christian cross. "The Ten Commandments," grossed over $4,000,000 in the USA, which made it into one of the commercially most successful movies for Paramount in the early 1920s. In Japan it was screened even still in 1925, for instance in the Cinema Teikokukan 帝国館, the 'Imperial' Cinema in Tōkyō's Asakusa cinema district.

This advertisement poster is from the Shin-sekai Iroha-za 新世界いろは座 cinema in Ōsaka, which originally was a traditional theatre that had been remodelled into a modern cinema specializing in premieres. It is an example of the popularity of Western films, which were shown in mixed programmes with Japanese productions, usually consisting of traditional sword-fighting movies, set mostly in the Edo period (1600-1868), and contemporary dramas or comedies.

15. Hatsu-hōsō 初放送

Illustration "First Broadcast", in: *Meiji Taishō Shōwa Dai-emaki* 明治大正昭和大絵巻**, Tokyo: Kōdansha, 1931**

This is one of the many contemporary illustrations which shows the radio as a gathering point for the whole family in the 1920s. The picture was part of a collection of images which depicted what the editors in 1931 saw as historical milestones of the Meiji (1868-1912), Taishō (1912-1926) periods and the early years of the Shōwa (1926-1989) period. It was a supplement to the January issue of the very popular general-reader magazine *Kingu* キング and demonstrates that many even very recent events were seen as "historical" already, which Japanese historians have ascribed to a keen awareness of the contemporaries in the late 1920s of having entered *gendai* 現代, which means "modern/modernity" but also "contemporary". It shows the very first Japanese radio broadcast in 1925, with all household members of a Japanese multi-generation family gathered around. The text above states:

"'J.O.A.K., J.O.A.K., this is the Tokyo Broadcasting Station.' It was on March 1 that the announcer's cheerful voice could first be heard in the East [=in East Asia]. The people in the capital gathered in front of the amplifiers and could not help but marvel and rejoice at this wonder of scientific civilization."

16. Gramophone Nipponophone 'Harmony'

Taishō period (1912-1926)

The displayed model is a 'Harmony' manufactured by the Japanese company Nihon chikuonki shōkai (Nipponophone) with the manufacturer's logo inside under the lid. In the 1920s gramophones became an accessible commodity for many Japanese, with prices going as low as about 19 yen for a basic model. Already in 1920, the sales volume for domestically produced gramophones peaked at about 5.6 million yen. That year imports of foreign-made gramophones such as the 'Victrolas' (the models produced by the Victor Talking Machine Company)

and Grafanolas (Columbia) totaled 350,000 yen, but would increase fivefold by 1925.

Where earlier types before 1920 still possessed a horn on top of the machine, the Harmony uses a different technique. The vibrations that the needle picks up from the disc's grooves are amplified and sent from inside the opened box. This gramophone is an acoustic model where one has to wind a handle several times to tighten a metal coil to play the record. Electricity-powered devices were only introduced from 1925 onwards.

17. Taihei Record タイヘイレコード

Advertisement poster, Taishō period (1912–1926)

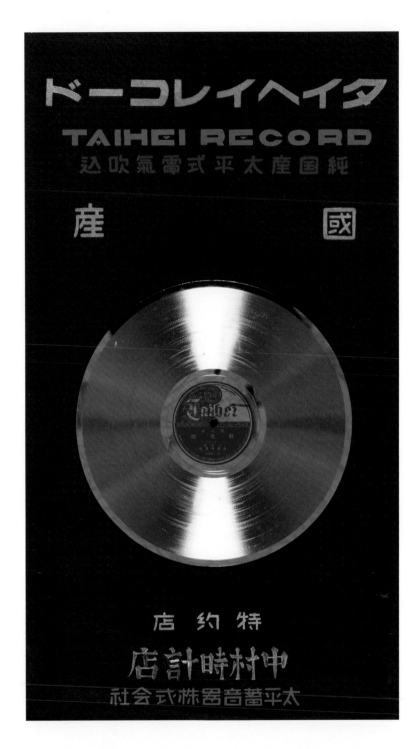

SELECTED OBJECTS FROM 1920S JAPAN

In the 1920s, smaller specialized stores and whole-salers promoted and sold gramophone records of manufacturers under an exclusive contract system. In some cases these were shops that combined the sales of music instruments and gramophones, such as Yamano Gakki and Nippon Victor. This poster show-cases the sale of Taihei records by the watch store Nakamura that mentions its exclusive relationship with Taihei as a "special contracted store". The poster is lavishly executed with a replica of a disc physically mounted on it, showing the innovativeness of the ad-vertising industry at that time. Their products are praised as being "genuine domestic electrical record-ings". This was due to two reasons: Before the 1920s many Japanese songs had been recorded and printed in overseas studios before being imported to Japan. From 1925 onwards, electrical recording was intro-duced in Japan, which improved the sound quality. Domestic record companies used the new technology in their advertisements to boost their sales.

18. Tōkyō kōshinkyoku 東京行進曲

Shellac gramophone record, Nippon Victor, 1929

This is a gramophone record with the song that accompanied the silent film *Tōkyō kōshinkyoku* (Tokyo March), directed by the renowned director Mizoguchi Kenji 溝口健二 (1898-1956). The record sold over 300,000 copies. The film was based on a novel by Kikuchi Kan 菊池寛 (1888-1948), which was serialized in one of the most popular Japanese magazines at the time, *Kingu* キング. Set in 1929 Tokyo, the story depicts a tragic love story between an upper-class boy and a lower-class girl. Sound was an integral part of the cinematic experience in silent films. Such films were accompanied by *benshi* 弁士, live narrators, who guided the story and added to the experience, as well as music from gramophone records that were played before, during and at the end of a screening. It was exactly the hit "Tokyo March" that elevated the film's success. The allure of "Tokyo March" was its jazzy tunes and the catchy lyrics both reflecting the fast transformation of Japan's society. The tie-up that the film company Nikkatsu formed with the American-owned record company Nippon Victor was crucial here. The latter's introduction of new American market strategies and an exclusive contract system influenced the practice of increasing the tempo at which films and the accompanying songs were produced. "Tokyo March" is thus exemplary for the media mix that formed in Japan's 1920s mass entertainment.

247

19. Kokunan ni men shite 国難に面して

Record sleeve with shellac gramophone record produced by Dai-Nihon Nittō chikuonki kabushiki gaisha 大日本日東蓄音機株式会社, **1924**

248

This 1924 record was produced by one of the big domestic Japanese record and gramophone companies, Dai-Nihon Nittō chikuonki kabushiki gaisha. Nittō was the biggest competitor of Nihon chikuonki shōkai (Nipponophone), the company that produced the gramophone on display here (see: 16) in the 1920s. Nittō was established in Ōsaka and occupied a strong position in the record market of Western Japan. This record featured a speech by Lieutenant General Gondō Denji on the *hai-Nichi mondai* 排日問題, the "Anti-Japanese Problem," entitled "Facing a National Crisis". The title referred to the recent outcry within the Japanese public when news reached the country of the Immigration Act of 1924, a US federal law often called the "Asian exclusion act" since it targeted Japanese and

Chinese immigrants, especially those residing on the US West Coast. General Gondō was a veteran of the Russo-Japanese War (1904-05) and also the head of the Dai-Nippon kokkō sen'yō kai 大日本国光宣揚会 (Association for the enhancement of the national glory of Great Japan), an ultranationalist organization that exploited the legitimate criticism of the racist and discriminatory US legislation that led to lasting mistrust and anger in the Japanese public. This example illustrates that records were not only used to distribute music but also educational or, as here, political content. The 1920s Japanese book donation can be seen as one attempt at cultural diplomacy to counter rising international tensions and to improve Japan's image in the world, as Lieven Sommen argues in his essay in this volume.

20. Chikuzen biwa "Ishidōmaru" 筑前琵琶 石堂丸

Record sleeve with shellac gramophone record produced by Dai-Nihon Tōa chikuonki kabushikigaisha 大日本東亜蓄音機株式会社, **1922 (?, judged from the matrix number of the record)**

Dai-Nihon Tōa chikuonki kabushikigaisha was a minor gramophone company and label from Ōsaka. This record features a recorded traditional tale performed as *Chikuzen biwa* 筑前琵琶 narrative storytelling. The *Chikuzen biwa* is a lute-like instrument with four strings and four frets or five strings and five frets. Originally this form of storytelling had been performed by the *biwa-hōshi* 琵琶法師, blind monks, since the late medieval period. The *Chikuzen biwa* came into use in the Meiji period (1868-1912) and was very popular in the 1920s, when many older tales were adapted to a more modern style of narration and distributed on gramophone shellac records. The tale is about Ishidōmaru 石童丸, a legendary figure who features in the temple founding myth of

the Karukaya-dō 苅萱堂, a temple hall which is part of the famous Shingon buddhist temple complex around the Kongōbu-ji 金剛峯寺 on Mt. Kōya 高野山. The story was performed for this recording by a certain Madono (or Shinden) Asahiyama 真殿旭山, which was the pseudonym of a performer about whom not much information can be found nowadays. The modernized versions of such tales in narrative performance accompanied by a *biwa* or other forms of oral narrative performances were a very popular genre for gramophone records and existed in parallell to equally popular modern music like the jazzy tunes of the "Tōkyō March" (see No. 18), or imported Western music.

249

21. Chikuzen biwa "Ishidōmaru" 筑前琵琶 石堂丸

**Record sleeve with shellac gramophone record produced by Dai-Nihon
Tōa chikuonki kabushikigaisha** 大日本東亜蓄音機株式会社**, 1922
(?, date based on the matrix number of the record), reverse side of No. 20**

The reverse side of the sleeve that holds the *Chikuzen biwa* performance of the tale about *Ishidōmaru* (see No. 20) provides a hint at the range of genres on sale by domestic Japanese record companies and how they – at least in the language of their advertisements – rationalized their own existence. The text on the sleeve proudly announces:

> "The five great missions of East Asia Gramophone Inc., which were born out of our times:
> - The production of gramophone records for education.
> - The study and proliferation of music for children.
> - The study and proliferation of popular music.
> - The preservation and improvement of Japanese music.
> - Enhancing the practical uses of gramophones."

An interesting detail is that the company pledged not only to preserve more traditional forms of Japanese music but to "improve" it, which points to a process of adapting – or in many cases quite substantially reinventing – "traditional" music to align it with the modern tastes of the 1920s.

22. Shosei-bushi Sonezaki shinjū 書生節 曾根崎心中

Nittō record sleeve with Nipponophone shellac gramophone record, 1920 (?, date based on the matrix number of the record)

This record by Nipponophone was mistakenly placed in the wrong sleeve by its previous owner. Nipponophone was a label of the Nihon chikuonki shōkai 日本蓄音機商会 (short: Nitchiku). With the name change it came into the hands of exclusively Japanese owners and would remain so until the company was acquired by Columbia and subsequently became its subsidiary in 1927. This record features a *shosei-bushi* which was a form of popular song for the masses that had been adapted around 1900 from an earlier, more political form. That earlier form had been used to disguise demands and critique directed at politicians in the 1870s at the time of the government-critical 'Movement for Freedom and Popular Rights' (*jiyū minken undō* 自由民権運動). In the 1910s, the musical style of these often witty

and ironic songs was used to also convey premodern stories, such as, here, the famous traditional puppet theatre play *Sonezaki shinjū* (Love suicide at Sonezaki). This play had first been performed in Ōsaka in 1703 and was written by none other than the Edo period playwright and dramatist Chikamatsu Monzaemon 近松門左衛門 (1653-1725), whose work deeply influenced Japanese theatre through the various forms of puppet theatre. The latter developed into the *kabuki* 歌舞伎 theatre, which then, by the 1920s, was already seen as "traditional Japanese" theatre in contrast to contemporary plays. Chikamatsu plays are also present in books that were sent to the University of Louvain in the 1920s to represent Japanese culture, while they were integrated into modern mass media consumption in Japan at the same time.

23. Satsuma biwa "Hitachi-maru" 薩摩琵琶 常陸丸

Record sleeve with shellac gramophone record produced by Nihon chikuonki shōkai, 1916-1918 (?, based on the matrix number of the record)

This record features another narrative song performance accompanied by a *Satsuma biwa*, a lute that has four strings and four frets and is played with a bigger plectrum than the *Chikuzen biwa* lute. It was also the older, longer established version of the two. The record demonstrates well the merger of a premodern form of lute and song performance with a modern subject: the piece recorded here is about one of two ships that were named *Hitachi-maru*. Both were sunk, the first in June 1904 during the Russo-Japanese War when transporting Japanese troops with 1,091 lives lost, the second in September 1917, with 16 lives lost and the rest of the crew and passengers interned by the German auxiliary cruiser SMS *Wolf*. It is not clear which of the two ships the song is about, but it is certainly a song about the ravages of war and loss of Japanese life at sea, performed with a modernized version of a very old lute tradition. The map on the sleeve shows the core of the Japanese Empire, Japan as we know it today, and the colonies Korea and Taiwan. The label Nipponophone boasted 15 branch offices marked on the map, from Otaru on the northern Japanese main island Hokkaidō to Hakata in Southwestern Japan and Dalian (Jap.: Dairen) in Manchuria, Seoul (Jap.: Keijō) in Korea, and Taipei (Jap.: Taihoku) in Taiwan. Although a simple record sleeve that was to advertise the record company, it gives an impression of how widespread the awareness of being part of an Empire was, which was also part of the basis of the self-confidence manifest in the joint efforts of Japanese politicians, academics and entrepreneurs to support the donation to the University of Louvain.

Domestic Politics Through the Lens of Posters

The political and socio-economic dynamics and tensions of late 1920s Japan finds ample expression in graphically powerful posters. Many of the posters introduced here stem from the 1928 national election and are testimony to the so-called "Taishō Democracy". The term refers to the promising democratic tendencies of the Taishō period (1912-1926) and, in a wider sense, to the period from 1905 to 1932, which became also an important source of inspiration for post-1945 democracy in Japan, similar to to the role the Weimar Republic played for postwar Western Germany. Other posters – often illegal ones – advertised labor and peasant movements or called for the liberation of the so-called *burakumin* 部落民, the former pre-modern "outcasts". They represent the rising radical social and political movements of the 1920s. The conservative government bureaucracy was afraid of a possible future revolution from the left, due to having the example of the Russian Revolution and the emerging Soviet Union literally next door geographically, with the Russian Far Eastern provinces located on the opposite site of the Sea of Japan. The infamous Chian iji hō 治安維持法 (Peace Preservation Law) that was promulgated together with the revision of the election laws to universal male suffrage in 1925 provided the state with far-reaching instruments to censor and punish anything that was violating a deliberately vaguely defined *kokutai* 国体, which means "national body" or "national polity" in a narrower sense but could also be translated as "national essence," which centered around the Imperial Institution. The mighty conservative bureaucracy, often in alliance with the employers and with academics, also tried to engage in what historian Sheldon Garon has called 'moral suasion campaigns' that were designed to induce certain behaviors in the population and to ease social tensions. The posters by the Industrial Welfare Association displayed here represent this tendency. These domestic – but also global – political tendencies have to be taken into account when asking why in the 1930s the priorities of Japanese politics – and politics elsewhere – ultimately shifted away from cultural diplomacy, which the Japanese 1920s book donation is an example of. The latter never fully ceased to exist, but with the rising domestic and ultimately global political tensions the world began to march into the direction of a second, even more devastating World War, due to which the Japanese donations and many similar Interwar period efforts were forgotten, sometimes for decades.

Literature: Berger 1977; Duus 1968; Garon 1987; Garon 2011; Griffin 1972; Lewis 1990; Neary 2010; Shimizu 2019; Silberman and Harootunian 1974; Vanoverbeke 2004; Vos 1967.

Poster by the Home Ministry encouraging people to vote in the national elections, 1928

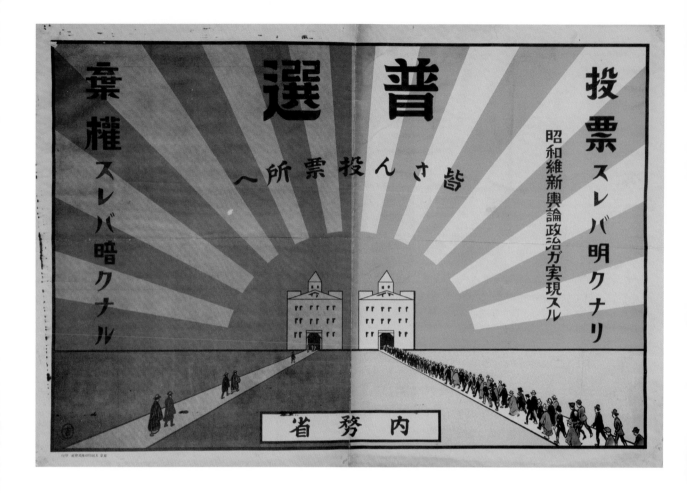

"Universal Suffrage – Everybody, go to the ballots!" This poster, issued by the Home Ministry, calls to vote in the 1928 election, the first with male universal suffrage, further stating on the brighter right-hand side of the poster: "Vote and the future will be bright! The politics of a Shōwa Period Restauration based on public opinion will be realized." This is juxtaposed with the darker tones on the left-hand side of the poster, which states "Abstain from your right, and darkness shall fall!" The usage of the phrase "Shōwa Period Restauration" was rather conspicuous since, although the poster was issued by the Home Ministry that was supposed to be politically neutral, this phrase was also used in right-wing discourse. There, it expressed the idea of renewing the Meiji Restauration of 1868, this time 'completing it' by aspiring to put the population in a more direct connection with the Emperor, which could mean to devaluate parliamentarism. But in the context of this poster it rather means that the Shōwa era, which had started in 1926, was to usher in a more democratic era of widened participation by the public via the elections and the political campaigning for votes surrounding them.

25. Tattoki kika no ippyō o Minseitō kōhosha
Masutani Torakichi e 尊き貴下の一票を　民政党候補者桝谷寅吉へ

Election campaign poster, 1928

On this poster, Masutani Torakichi (1878-1953) is depicted asking for "your precious vote". He was the candidate of the progressive Rikken Minseitō, the Constitutional Democratic Party, one of the main democratic political parties in interwar Japan. Ever since universal male suffrage was granted in 1925, it was clear that the coming election campaigns would have a very different character. Before, the limited number of elite voters had meant often exclusive back-chamber talks in all localities in Japan to convince local elites to give their votes *en bloc*, sometimes even through bribes. But with the first election under universal male suffrage, the candidates had to compete for a suddenly massively enlarged electorate, hence also the graphically ever more appealing posters in order to get attention.

26. Kiyoki ippyō o Hiraga Shū 清き一票を　平賀周

Election campaign poster, 1928

"Give your pure [uncorrupted] vote to Hiraga Shū!"
Hiraga (1882-1957) was a lawyer and House of Commons candidate of the conservative democratic party Rikken Seiyūkai for an election district of Ōsaka.
Before that election, votes were often exchanged for
political favors or money by all established parties.

27. Tenka o saiyū su kika no ippyō – kika no shimei o hatasu mono Tsutsui Tamijirō
天下ヲ左右ス貴下ノ一票, 貴下ノ使命ヲ果ス者　筒井民次郎

Election campaign poster, 1928

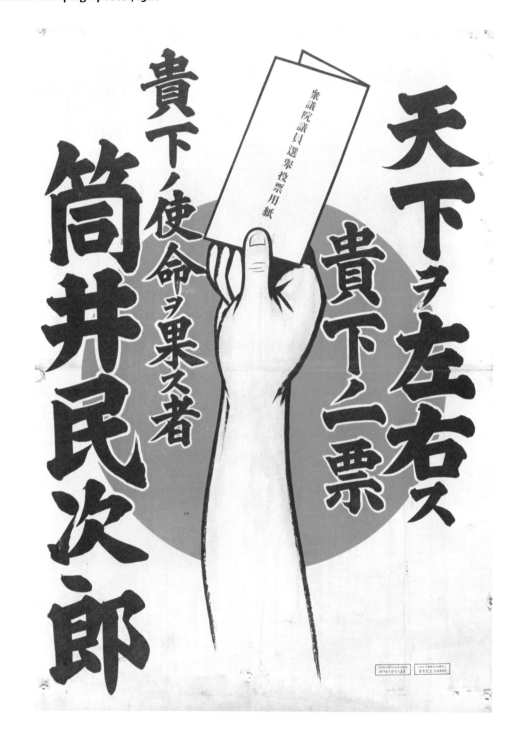

Campaign poster for Tsutsui Tamijirō (1875-1941) of the progressive Rikken Minseitō Party for the 1928 Lower House Elections under universal male suffrage. The text reads: "It is your one vote that will influence the world! It is the person who will accomplish your mission – Tsutsui Tamijirō." Tsutsui had been elected before for the Ōsaka City Assembly and in 1924 to the House of Commons, although for another party, the Seiyū hontō 政友本党. His campaign in 1928 for the Ōsaka No. 1 election district was not successful. The raised hand on the poster holds a ballot for the house of commons, which the vast majority of the (exclusively male) voters had in their hands for the first time. It was a considerable leap forward to further democratize Japanese politics and the campaigning for votes was fierce.

**28. Subete no hito ni shoku to shoku o ataeyo,
kitaru nijūnichi ni wa zehi go-tōhyō o!**
すべての人に食と職を与へよ, 来る二十日には是非御投票を！

Election campaign poster, 1928

The candidate Sumi Gensen (1871-1943), was a former colonial bureaucrat-turned politician, a member of the Lower House, and later the mayor of Shingū city from 1933 until 1935. The poster promises to give everyone food and work, hinting at the social hardships of the late 1920s. Above his name the phrase "strict and righteous neutrality" can be found to set him apart from colleagues of the established political parties and claim that he was impartial to the usual strife between the political parties.

29. Bungeika ni mo giseki o ataeyo – dokusho kaikyū no hito wa Kikuchi Kan-shi o erabe

文芸家にも議席を与へよ　読書会級の人は菊池寛氏を撰べ

Election campaign poster, 1928

This poster with its avant-garde style demands: "Give parliamentary seats also to men of letters! Members of the reading class – vote for Kikuchi Kan!" The novelist, playwright and journalist Kikuchi Kan (1888-1948) had won nationwide acclaim for his 1920 novel *Shinju fujin* 真珠夫人 (Madam Pearl), which was first serialized in the major newspapers *Ōsaka mainichi shinbun* and *Tōkyō nichinichi shinbun*. He was also the author of the novel on which the screenplay for the film *Tōkyō kōshinkyoku* 東京行進曲 (Tokyo March) with its immensely popular soundtrack was based (see item 18). The novel was serialized in the popular magazine *Kingu* from June 1928 onwards, the same year that Kikuchi was – ultimately unsuccessfully – running as candidate for the House of Commons in the general election, the

first election under universal male suffrage. He was supported by the Socialist People's Party, one of a number of left-leaning parties with a background in the proletarian movement that were allowed for the first time. However, this party ultimately managed to win only four out of 466 seats in the House of Commons, the lower chamber of the Imperial Diet. After the Second World War he was purged by the US Occupation forces for his strong involvement in wartime propaganda, but his influence is lasting, with many of his novels and theatre plays having been turned into movies and later into TV dramas, and his tutelage for the foundation of two of the most prestigious literature prices in Japan, the Akutagawa Price and the Naoki Price, while another one, founded in 1938, was named after him.

30. *Fukai no senkyo kosakunin wa, koakindo wa, rōdōsha wa,*
Yatsushiro Tomozō – warera wa warera no tame ni warera no daihyōsha e
府会の選挙　小作人は, 小商人は, 労働者は八代智蔵　我等は我等の為に我等の代表者へ

Election campaign poster, 1927

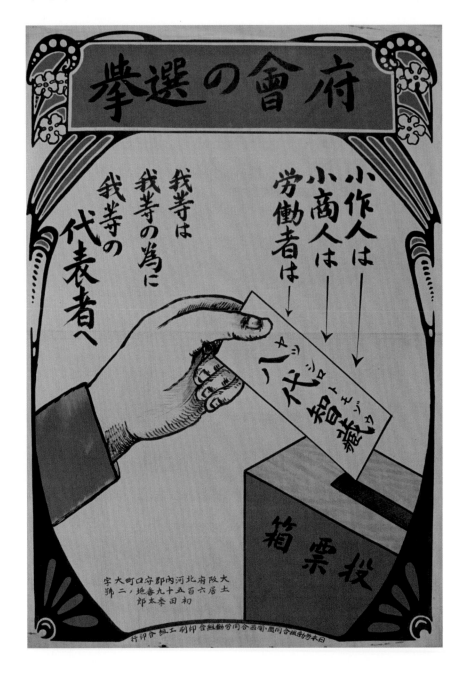

This poster was issued by the Nihon rōdō kumiai dōmei - Kansai gōdō rōdō kumiai 日本労働組合同盟・関西合同労働組合, the League of Labor Unions of Japan - Kansai Joint Labor Union, stating: "Tenant farmers, shopkeepers and workers [vote for] Yatsushiro Tomozō. We - for us - for our representative!" The poster points to the rising social tensions in the rapidly urbanizing areas of Japan, here the Kansai region with Ōsaka being the economic hub, only rivaled by Tōkyō. Many peasants had lost proprietorship of their own land over the previous centuries and were degraded to tenant farmers, often working on the same fields their ancestors had once owned for an upper stratum of wealthy lenders, burdened by high taxes. In the aftermath of the First World War and the drastic rise in domestic prices that the unprecedented wartime boom had ushered in, tenant farmer strikes and violent clashes with landlords and the police became common, and some also sought legal actions supported by lawyers solidarizing with them. Here they and the urban small business owners and factory workers are called upon to unite behind a candidate from their own social background.

31. Nihon Rōnōtō 日本労農党

Poster of the Japanese Labourers and Farmers' Party, 1926-1928

261

The Rōdō nōmin tō, the Japanese Labourers and
Farmers' Party, active between December 1926 and
December 1928, was a proletarian political party
with a centrist socialist stance.

**32. Shūgiin giin Nihon rōnōtō kōnin kōho Fukuda Kyōji –
Nōmin rōdōsha hōkyū seikatsusha koakindo no mikata
tadashiki ippyō o tōzeyo!** 衆議院議員日本労農党公認候補　福田狂二
農民, 労働者, 俸給生活者, 小商人の味方　正しき一票を投ぜよ!

Election campaign poster, 1928

This poster, which used the same basic layout as the advertisement for the "Japan Laborers and Farmers newspaper" (No. 33) and was most likely also used for other candidates of the Japanese Labourers and Farmers' Party with just the name and the photo exchanged, states: "Authorized candidate of the Japanese Labourers and Farmers' Party for the House of Commons Fukuda Kyōji". The writing on the flyer that the worker holds in his hands with a portrait photo of Fukuda says: "A friend of peasants, workers, salary earners, shopkeepers. Cast the right vote!"

**33. Shūkan jitsugen no tame kikin 3,000 en boshū –
Musan taishū no sentō-teki seiji shinbun – Nihon rōnō shinbun o yome!**
週刊実現の為め基金三千円募集、無産大衆の戦闘的政治新聞、日本労農新聞を読め*!!*

Poster advertising the "Japan Laborers and Farmer's newspaper", late 1920s

263

This poster advertises the "Japanese Labourers and
Farmers' Newspaper." The text reads "To realize
a weekly publication, we are collecting a fund of
3,000 yen. Read the militant political newspaper
of the proletarian masses: the 'Japan Labourers and
Farmers' Newspaper'!!"

34. Rōnō Roshia tenrankai – tōkei, posutā, manga, chōkoku, shinbun, zasshi, shoseki, sono ta. Miyo! Chikara to nozomi ni michita jūnen-kan no kensetsu no ato o! 労農ロシア展覧会、統計、ポスター、漫画、彫刻、新聞、雑誌、書籍、その他。見よ！力と望みに充ちた十年間の建設の跡を！

Poster for the Labourers and Farmers' Russia Exhibition, 1927

This poster announces a "Laborers and Farmers' Russia Exhibition" encouraging the visitors to see the "evidence of the construction of ten years that were filled with power and hope." The exhibition commemorated the 10th anniversary of the Russian Revolution, displaying statistics, posters, caricatures, sculptures, books and magazines from Soviet Russia. The exhibition was sponsored by several leftist organizations of the proletarian movement. It is obvious that the main design of the poster itself was influenced by Soviet aesthetics. In the lower left corner a suggestion for further reading can be found: a Japanese translation of Karl Marx' Capital, *Shihon-ron* 資本論, by the famous Kyōto University professor of economics Kawakami Hajime 河上肇 (1879-1946) and his former student Miyakawa Minoru 宮川実 (1895-1985), who had become a marxist economist himself. This translation had been published as an affordable paperback by the left-leaning major publishing house Iwanami 岩波.

35. Nihon Nōmin Kumiai Ōsaka-fu rengōkai dai-gokai taikai
日本農民組合大阪府聯合会第五回大会

Poster of the fifth assembly of the Japan Farmers' Union in Ōsaka, 25/01/1928

The Japan Farmers' Union campaigned for direct
ownership by farmers of their land and recognition
of their cultivation rights.

36. Dai-nanakai Zenkoku Suiheisha taikai
第七回全国水平社大会

Poster announcing the 7th Zenkoku Suiheisha general assembly, 1928

The Zenkoku Suiheisha, the 'National Levelers Association', founded in 1919, fought for the emancipation of the *burakumin* 部落民. They were outcasts discriminated against since the pre-modern era because their occupations were associated with death, such as grave-digging or tannery. The bottom of the poster features the exhortation "'Special village people' of the entire country – unite!", with the term 'special village people' being used to describe the discriminated.

Poster issued by the Industrial Welfare Organization, 1934

Poster stating "Take good care of the machines, pay attention to your work" issued by the *Sangyō fukuri kyōkai* 産業福利協会, the Industrial Welfare Organization. This association was founded in 1925 under the tutelage of the Naimu-shō shakai-kyoku 内務省社会局, the Social Bureau of the Home Ministry, which itself had been founded in 1921 as a reaction to rising inequality and social tensions in Japan but also around the world. The Home Ministry bureaucrats feared possible left-wing activism or even an attempt at revolution. One should not forget that the Russian Revolution of 1917, leading to the foundation of the Soviet Union, had happened "next door" to Japan, which shared a water border with the Russian Far-Eastern regions. Throughout the 1920s

these tensions experienced a further rise also in Japan, and the government in liaison with the business world tried desperately to find ways to amend them – without granting workers too wide-ranging rights to self-organize. The Association, which was later merged with the Kyōchōkai 協調会, the 'Conciliation Society,' that had a similar purpose of mitigating conflicts between employers and employees, had a paternalistic character which can be easily discerned from this and the other posters issued by it. The slogan on the poster alludes to the many accidents in factories, here essentially blaming the workers and encouraging them to be more attentive to avoid accidents, in an attempt that historian Sheldon Garon has described as 'moral suasion'.

38. Kichinto shita fuku tsune ni anzen
キチンとした服　常に安全

Poster issued by the Industrial Welfare Organization, 1927

The text in bold red print on this poster reads: "Proper clothes – always safe". This winning poster design was, according to the text at the bottom, submitted by a worker in the Kure Naval Arsenal close to Hiroshima by the name of Iwamoto (or Ishimoto) Nobukata (or Nobumasa) 石本信方 (since, as an 'ordinary' worker, he is not to be found in any bibliographical lexicon or database, the reading of this name cannot be confirmed). The design was one of the many submitted to the Industrial Welfare Organization as part of a competition it had advertised. The three examples show the disastrous consequences of wearing improper garments for work, resulting in accidents because of parts getting caught in machines, while the upper, superior example features a workman's apron and tight sleeves.

39. Migaita shiraha ni hikaru kenkō みがいた白歯に光る健康

Poster issued by the Industrial Welfare Organization, 1934

269

This poster shows a female factory worker who is ostentatiously showing her white teeth as the result of frequently using a toothbrush, stating "To brushed white teeth – [comes] shining health". The poster alludes to the many maladies induced by inferior oral hygiene among factory workers, against which ministerial bureaucrats, employers and the medical profession campaigned in order to raise the average health level of the workers.

40. *Shokudō wa seiketsu ni, yamai no moto no hai o tore*
食堂ハ清潔ニ　病ノ基ノ蠅ヲ取レ

Poster issued by the Industrial Welfare Organization, 1927

This graphically appealing poster, stating "The hygienic canteen - take out the flies which are at the basis of diseases", was a winning poster of the 6th poster competition of the Industrial Welfare Association, lobbying for stricter hygiene measures in factory cantinas. Insects are abundant especially in Japan's humid summers, and high rates of diseases associated with insects had been a constant problem in factory eateries for decades. Modern hygiene studies, often related to research undertaken in Japan's colonies on behalf of the prestigious Imperial Universities - many of which supported the 1920s book donations to Leuven - resulted in ever intensifying attempts to change behavior in order to avoid diseases.

41. Saigai wa tsune ni nanji no suki ni jōzu
災害ハ常ニ汝ノスキニ乗ズ

Poster issued by the Industrial Welfare Organization, 1927

This poster in an abstract style announces: "Natural disasters always strike when you least expect them". It was a winning poster of the 11th poster competition of the Industrial Welfare Association and part of a campaign by the Home Ministry aimed at changing the behavior of the population in the event of disasters, encouraging them to always be on the guard to not be engulfed in calamities. This is demonstrated here in a humorous way with a housewife in a kitchen, but literarily with a serious background, it being set ablaze, while a cat, through the ages accused of stealing but also loved, is taking advantage of the situation.

Notes

The First World War as Precondition to the Japanese Donation to the University of Louvain (pp. 18-31)

1 In documents of the 1910s and 1920s "Louvain" is used to refer to the name of what is nowadays known as the KU Leuven in Leuven and the UCLouvain in Louvain-la-Neuve, after the split of their common ancestor university. To reflect the historical usage here, University of Louvain will be used.
2 On the perception of Belgium in Japan since the late nineteenth century, see Kurosawa 2016.
3 On the impact of the First World War on Japan in general, see Dickinson 1999; Dickinson 2013; Frattolillo/Best 2015; Minohara/Hon/Dawley 2014; Schmidt/Schmidtpott 2020; Schmidt 2021.
4 Yamamuro 2020.
5 Dore 1965.
6 Hufmann 1997; Yamamoto 1981; Nagamine 1997.
7 Blaker 1964.
8 Hufmann 1997, pp. 224-270.
9 Sharf/Morse/Dobson 2005; Shimazu 2009.
10 Schmidt 2021, pp. 117-257.
11 Ariyama 2009, p. 125.
12 Togiya 2013, pp. 33-69.
13 High 2003, p. 8.
14 Yamamuro 2020, p. 40.
15 Kurosawa 2016, p. 203.
16 Izao 2007, pp. 103-128.
17 On the symbolism of the Japanese Red Cross nurses in representing Asia on the European war theatre, see Schmidt 2012, pp. 131-154.
18 Wilson 2005, pp. 35-51.
19 Nakamura/Odaka 2003, pp. 1-54.
20 Takagi 2014, pp. 241-265.
21 On the *narikin*: Umezu 1978.
22 Nakano 1977.
23 Schmidt 2014, pp. 239-265.
24 It is not to be confused with its sister institute - originally the Kurashiki rōdō kagaku kenkyūjo (Kurashiki Institute of Labor Science), later often shortened to Rōken - which was created in 1921 also by Ōhara from profits made during the First World War and known today as the Ōhara Memorial Institute for Science of Labor.
25 Murakami 2009.
26 Nitobe 1899.
27 Hobsbawm/Ranger 1983.
28 Gluck 1998.
29 Rūven kokusai jigyō iin kai 1926, p. 1.
30 Schencking 2013.
31 A good example is an article in the renowned public opinion magazine *Chūō kōron* by Maida Minoru; Maida 1923.

An Empire of the Mid-Tier: The Japanese Ministry of Foreign Affairs and the New Mass Public-Focused Diplomacy of the Early Twentieth Century (pp. 32-39)

1 Iriye 1997, p. 51.
2 Rubinger 2000, pp. 164-165; Kornicki/Rubinger 2001: pp. 383-385.
3 Van Waarden 2019, pp. 2-3; Voerman/Wijfjes 2009, pp. xv - xvi.
4 Ariyama 2014, pp. 73-74.
5 Throntveit 2001, p. 446.
6 Robson 2015, pp. 140-141; Chiba 2008, pp. ii-iii.
7 Akami 2008, p. 106; Komatsu 1937, p. 157.
8 Iriye 1997, pp. 61-62.
9 Esthus 1959, p. 436.
10 Iriye 1997, pp. 61-62.
11 O'Connor 2010, p. 159.
12 Shimazu 1998, pp. 66 - 67.
13 Matsumura 1971, pp. 76 - 77.
14 Matsumura 2002, p. 49.
15 Shimazu 1998, pp. 66 - 67.
16 Akami 2008, pp. 108, 110.
17 Burkman 2008, pp. xi, xii - xiii, 210.
18 For another good example of public diplomacy in the 1920s by Japan, see the 1927 Doll Exchange with the United States of America, in for instance: Kohiyama 2019, pp. 282-304.
19 Koyama 2013, p. 16.
20 Koyama 2013, pp. 17-18.
21 De Cooman/Vande Walle 2016, p. 132.
22 Koyama 2013, p. 20.
23 Kamiya 2018, pp. 32-52.
24 Koyama 2013, pp. 18-19.
25 Koyama 2013, p. 20.
26 Iriye 1997, pp. 79-80.

The Japanese Book Donation to the University of Louvain (pp. 40-65)

1 The use of the toponym Louvain/Leuven is confusing. I will use "Louvain" when talking about the unitary university, at least for the period when French was either the only, the dominant, or the default institutional language. This usage coincides more or less with the period up to 1945. Only from the end of the Second World War did Dutch become a significant language for instruction, not to mention for research. Even so, though Dutch was increasingly used in teaching, for internal communications French remained the default language. Faculty councils, for example, were exclusively conducted in French until 1961. For the city name I will use "Leuven". In connection with the Japanese donation I will use "Louvain collection" and "Louvain University" or "Louvain University collection". "Louvain" in this context can be read as either English or French. When dealing with the period after the Second World War, Louvain/Leuven University is probably better, although the official name is Université Catholique de Louvain/Katholieke Universiteit

Leuven. After the legal split in 1968, it becomes Université Catholique de Louvain (present official abbreviation: UCLouvain) or Katholieke Universiteit Leuven (official abbreviation: KU Leuven), depending on the context. The Université Catholique de Louvain relocated to the city of Louvain-la-Neuve in 1970.

2 E. Van Cauwenbergh. "La bibliothèque de l'université de Louvain 1425-1914", *Alumni* Deel XX, nummer 1-2 (1951): 92-93.

3 Universiteitsarchief KU Leuven, Archief rector Paulin Ladeuze, *Circulaire van het Leuvensch Boekenfonds*; Mark Derez, "Furore Teutonico: De Brand van een Bibliotheek", *Tijdschrift voor Filosofie* 76 (2014): 691-692.

4 *Bulletin de l' Oeuvre Internationale de Louvain*, published by the Commissariat général, no. 10 (May 1922): 288-289.

5 All important information on the organizational aspects can be found in *Bulletin de l' Oeuvre Internationale de Louvain*, published by the Commissariat général, no. 1 (1919): 32.

6 All documentary data relating to the donation held at the Diplomatic Record Office, Tokyo, can be found in the following two digitized sets of documents: *Japan Center for Asian Historical Records National Archives of Japan* (JACAR, digital archive Ajireki) Reference code B12082010100: 3-2498 (0186-0287); B12082010200: 3-2498 (0288-0371).

7 Japanese names are given in the Japanese order, i.e. family name followed by personal name.

8 See *Gaimushō Gaikō shiryō-kan* 外務省外交史料館 (Diplomatic Record Office, Tokyo), Toshokan kankei zakken III-10-2-30 図書館関係雑件, 三門１０類二項三〇号4-16-21-4: Ambassador Matsui Keishirō 松井慶四郎 to Minister of Foreign Affairs Uchida Kōsai 内田康哉 (Paris, April 27, 1919). Also *Japan Center for Asian Historical Records National Archives of Japan* (JACAR, digital archive Ajireki) Reference code B12082010100: B-3-10-2-30 (Diplomatic Record Office, Tokyo): 3-2498 (pp. 0186-0287), pp. 0187-0188. The full list as of March 19, 1922 included, besides Saionji and Hozumi: Dr Yamakawa Kenjirō, president of the Imperial University of Tokyo; Dr Araki Torasaburō, president of the Imperial University of Kyoto; Dr Tanakadate Aikitsu and Dr Miura Kinnosuke, professors at the Imperial University of Tokyo; Baron Furuichi Kimitake, Member of the House of Peers and the Imperial Academy; Dr Inoue Tetsujirō, member of the Imperial Academy; Dr Sakurai Jōji, senator, secretary of the Imperial Academy; Dr Mori Rintarō, president of the Imperial Museum; Mr Kamata Eikichi, member of the House of Peers, president of Keiō University; Dr Hiranuma Yoshirō, president of Waseda University; Dr Tomii Masaaki, Privy Councillor, professor at the Imperial University of Tokyo; Dr Kinoshita Tomosaburō, president of Meiji University, and Dr Okano Keijirō, president of Chūō University. This list is based on the article "Japan Will Aid in Restoring Louvain", *The Japan Advertiser* (Tokyo, Sunday, March 12, 1922); also in *Bulletin de l' Oeuvre Internationale de Louvain* 10 (May 1922): 289.

9 In the French correspondence, he is variously called "capitaine de vaisseau" or "commandant"; in the *Bulletin de l'Oeuvre International de Louvain*, he is referred to as "commandant". His rank at the time was that of taisa 大佐 which corresponded to a captain in the US and UK navies. By 1925 he had been promoted to shōshō 少将, equivalent to a rear admiral in the US and UK navies. See *Taishō jinmei jiten* II vol. 2 大正人名辞典II下巻, Tokyo: Nihon tosho sentā 日本図書センター, 1989, p. 105. He is the author of a book titled *Sesshō denka no go-nichijō o haishite* 摂政殿下の御日常を拝して (Having the honour of serving His Imperial Highness the Prince-Regent in his everyday life). Tokyo: Nihon keisatsu shinbunsha, 日本警察新聞社: 1925. It contains little if any real information and is, not surprisingly, an endless flood of sugary statements about the character and intellect of its subject.

10 *Bulletin de l' Oeuvre Internationale de Louvain*, published by the Commissariat général, no. 1 (1919): 31-32.

11 Documents concerning his promotion in *Japan Center for Asian Historical Records National Archives of Japan* (JACAR, digital archive Ajireki) Reference code A03023417000 and Reference code B16080366500: 6-0204, pp. 0007-0026.

12 Universiteitsarchief KU Leuven, Archief rector Paulin Ladeuze C163-2, Ambassade impériale du Japon, Adachi to Stainier, February 26, 1921.

13 Universiteitsarchief KU Leuven, Archief rector Paulin Ladeuze C163-2, Ambassade impériale du Japon, Adachi to Stainier, February 26, 1921, and internal note from Stainier to Ladeuze, dated March 3, 1921.

14 For more details about this visit, see David De Cooman, "Crown Prince Hirohito's Visit to Belgium", in *Japan & Belgium: An Itinerary of Mutual Inspiration*, eds. Willy Vande Walle and David De Cooman (Tielt: Lannoo, 2016), 129-145.

15 *Bulletin de l' Oeuvre Internationale de Louvain*, no. 10 (May 1922): 290.

16 Signed Joseph Ageorges, "Billet Parisien", *La Libre Belgique*, May 17, 1919; id., June 24, 1921.

17 *Bulletin de l' Oeuvre Internationale de Louvain*, no. 10 (May 1922): 290; also Universiteitsarchief KU Leuven, Archief rector Paulin Ladeuze C165-3.

18 Universiteitsarchief KU Leuven, Archief rector Paulin Ladeuze C163-2, Ambassade impériale du Japon, Vicomte Mushakoji to Ladeuze, Brussels, December 21, 1922.

19 Wada Mankichi 和田万吉, "Rūven daigaku toshokan fukkō ni kiyo-seru waga kokusai jigyō iinkai no jigyō ni tsuite" ルーヴェン大学図書館復興に寄与せる我が国際事業委員会の事業に就いて, *Toshokan zasshi* 図書館雑誌 XXI-5 (May 1926), 167.

20 *Ueno kōen Tōkyō bijutsugakkō bunko nai Rūven kokusai jigyō iinkai* 上野公園東京美術学校文庫内ルーヴェン国際事業委員会.

21 Wada, "Rūven daigaku toshokan", 167.

22 Ibid.

23 Ibid.

24 "Pour la Nouvelle Bibliothèque de l'Université de Louvain", *Indépendance Belge*, July 1, 1924.

25 *Bulletin de l' Oeuvre Internationale de Louvain*, no. 19-20 (May 1928): 532-533.

26 Wada, "Rūven daigaku toshokan", 168.

27 As an advocate of romanization he spelled his name in *hiragana* rather than in *kanji*.

28 Mori Kiyoshi 森清, *Nihon Jisshin Bunruihō: Wa-Kan-Yō Sho Kyōyō Bunruihyō oyobi Sakuin* 日本十進分類法：和

漢洋書共用分類表及索引 (Sendai: Mamiya Shōten 間宮商店, 1929), 212.

29 Wada Mankichi 和田萬吉, "'Bunruihōshiki no kakuitsu ni tsuite' no ikkōsatsu" 「分類法式の画一に就いて」の一考察, *Toshokan Zasshi* 図書館雑誌 25, no. 2 (1931): 41-43.

30 Suzuki Masachi 鈴木賢祐, "Dore ga Hyōjun Bunruihyō ka? (1) Otobe-an / Mōri-an / Mori-an" どれが標準分類表か？(一)乙部案-毛利案-森案, *Toshokan Zasshi* 図書館雑誌 119 (1929): 262-265. Suzuki Masachi 鈴木賢祐, "Dore ga Hyōjun Bunruihyō ka? (2) Otobe-an / Mōri-an / Mori-an" どれが標準分類表か？(二)乙部案-毛利案-森案, *Toshokan Zasshi* 図書館雑誌 120 (1929): 292-294. "Nihon Jisshin Bunruihō (NDC) no Rekishi Zenpen" 日本十進分類法（NDC）の歴史 前編, *NDL Shoshi Jōhō Nyūsuretā* 39 NDL書誌情報ニュースレター39号 (April 2016), https://www.ndl.go.jp/jp/data/bib_newsletter/2016_4/article_02.html.

31 Wada Mankichi 和田万吉, *Toshokan Kanri-hō Taikō* 図書館管理法大綱 (Tokyo: Heigo shuppansha 丙午出版社, 1922), 123.

32 Wada, "Rūven daigaku toshokan", 168.

33 Universiteitsarchief KU Leuven, Archief Ladeuze, rapport "L'acquisition des livres japonais offerts à la Bibliothèque de l'Université de Louvain", f. 1; *Japan Center for Asian Historical Records National Archives of Japan* (JACAR, digital archive Ajireki) Reference code B12082010200: B-3-10-2-30 (Diplomatic Record Office, Tokyo): 3-2498 (pp. 0288-0371), p. 0339.

34 The figures vary according to the sources. The Japanese final report/communiqué has 14,000, while the French version of it mentions "about 13,000". See "Orientalia: Oosterse Studies en Bibliotheken te Leuven en Louvain-la-Neuve", in *Symbolae Facultatis Litterarum Lovaniensis B*, vol. 20, eds. Willy Vande Walle and Paul Servais (Leuven: Leuven University Press, 2001), 74.

35 Receiving a grant from the Japan Society for the Promotion of Science, he spent one month in the library of UCL, from June 20, 1998 through July 20, 1998. Letter from José Traest, Secretaris-generaal of the Fonds voor Wetenschappelijk Onderzoek Vlaanderen, dated October 24, 1997 (reference v 4/212A - MW. D 12520, in the possession of the author. In this letter his name is spelled 'Yamazaki', hence my use of this spelling throughout).

36 Yamazaki Makoto 山崎誠, ed., *Ruvan Ranūbu Daigaku-zō Nihon Shoseki Mokuroku* ルヴァンラヌーブ大学蔵日本書籍目録 (Tokyo: Bensei shuppan 勉便誠出版, 2000).

37 Original in the National Diet Library, Sassa Hiro'o Kankei Bunsho 佐々弘雄関係文書52-12. "Sassa Hiro'o Kankei Bunsho" 佐々弘雄関係文書, *National Diet Library Monthly Bulletin* 国立国会図書館月報 703 (November 2019): 8-9.

38 Gaimushō Gaikō Shiryōkan 外務省外交史料館 (Diplomatic Record Office), Toshokan Kankei Zakken III-10-2-30 図書館関係雑件三門, *Rūven Kokusai Jigyō Iinkai Jigyō Seiseki Hōkoku* ルーヴェン国際事業委員会事業成績報告.

39 The 'Five Mountain' temples (five in Kyoto and five in Kamakura) were a network of state-sponsored Zen Buddhist temples, both protected and controlled by the Ashikaga shogunate. As centres of learning, they not only became a sort of governmental bureaucracy for the Ashikaga *shōgun* but were also at the vanguard of cultural innovation.

40 See *Vijf Jaar Aanwinsten 1974-1978, Tentoonstelling Georganiseerd in de Koninklijke Bibliotheek Albert I van 22 September tot 31 Oktober 1979* (Brussel: Koninklijke Bibliotheek Albert I, 1979), 1-4 (notice contributed by Ch(antal) K(ozyreff); D. Chibbet, *The History of Japanese Printing and Book Illustration* (Tokyo-New York-San Francisco: Kodansha, 1977), 29-33.

41 Literally "General Catalogue of National Books" is a Japanese reference work that indexes books published in Japan or written by Japanese before the Meiji Restoration (1868). First published by the Iwanami Shoten publishing company in 1963, an expanded edition was released in 1989. The catalogue was put together by compiling over one million library catalogue cards from over 600 libraries across Japan. It catalogues books published before the Meiji Restoration still in existence and written in Japan or by Japanese nationals. It does not include Chinese classics, Buddhist scriptures, or books from non-Japanese sources.

42 Afterwards superseded by *Nihon Kotenseki Sōgōmokuroku Dētabēsu* 日本古典籍総合目録データベース, Union Catalogue of Early Japanese Books, also accessible to the public. It has absorbed all data in the revised edition of *Kokusho Sōmokuroku* 国書総目録 (1989〜1991) as well as of *Kotenseki Sōgōmokuroku* 古典籍総合目録.

43 Wada, "Rūven daigaku toshokan", p. 168.

44 Due to his father's illness the crown prince had been proclaimed Regent of Japan on 25 November 1921.

45 See Willy Vande Walle, "De vaas van Hirohito", *Ex Officina*, jaargang 14/1 (April 2001): 4-5.

46 *La Libre Belgique*, January 16, 1924. The gift of money is known in Japanese as *onaidokin* 御内帑金.

47 The first file *Toshoroku* 図書録, dates from Taishō 13 (1924), has the registered number 290, and is supposed to be kept for 30 years. It includes several documents related to the donation of books to the University Library of Louvain. The second file equally contains a set of documents related to the library. The file is dated Shōwa 31 (1956), and bears the notice "to be kept eternally". The fourth document in that file is in French and bears the title: "Notes explicatives sur les titres des ouvrages offerts à la Bibliothèque de Louvain". It is a document of 15 pages format B5.

48 "Un Don du Japon à l'Université de Louvain", *La Libre Belgique*, September 10, 1924.

49 Ibid.

50 Wada, "Rūven daigaku toshokan", 168.

51 Ibid., 167.

52 Ibid.

53 Kitasato and Emil von Behring, working together in Berlin in 1890, announced the discovery of diphtheria antitoxin serum. Von Behring was awarded the 1901 Nobel Prize in Physiology or Medicine because of this breakthrough, but Kitasato was not.

54 Yamazaki erroneously notes that *Shōka Kojitsu Roku* is a reprint (*atozuri*) from Bunka 5 (1808), but it is a reprint from Meiji 15 (1883).

55 Yamazaki, ed., *Ruvan Ranūbu Daigaku-zō Nihon Shoseki Mokuroku*, 255.

56 77 volumes according to the interim report of the committee.

57 Wada, "Rūven daigaku toshokan", 168.

58 Ibid., 167.

59 Gaimushō Gaikō Shiryōkan 外務省外交史料館 (Diplomatic Record Office), Toshokan Kankei Zakken III-10-2-30 図書館関係雑件三門, Rūven kokusai jigyō iinkai ルーヴェン国際事業委員会, ed. (1926), pp. 5-7, 14-16.

60 Koyama Noboru 小山騰, "Rūvan Daigaku Toshokan e no Nihongo Shoseki Kizō Jigyō" ルーヴァン大学図書館への日本語書籍寄贈事業, *Shibusawa Kenkyū* 渋沢研究 10 (1997): 3-23.

61 *Bulletin de l' Oeuvre Internationale de Louvain*, published by the Commissariat général, no. 2 (January 1920): 45.

62 Satsuma Jirōhachi 薩摩次郎八 also donated the Maison du Japon (Nihonkan 日本館) in the Cité Universitaire in Paris. He was commonly referred to as "Baron Satsuma", but the title had no legal ground. Murakami, Kimio 村上紀史郎. *'Baron Satsuma' to yobareta otoko: Satsuma Jirohachi to sono jidai*「バロン・サツマ」と呼ばれた男—薩摩治郎八とその時代. Tōkyō: Fujiwara Shōten, 2009. Kobayashi, Shigeru 小林茂. *Satsuma Jirohachi: Pari Nihonkan koso waga inochi* 薩摩治郎八 —パリ日本館こそわがいのち. Kyōto: Minerva Shobō, 2010.

63 Letter from Adachi to Ladeuze, dated Brussels, November 21, 1927, Archives of the Algemeen Beheer, Katholieke Universiteit Leuven; undated note by Baron Descamps in the Archives of the Algemeen Beheer.

64 Japan-related publications by Pierre Charles include: Pierre Charles, S.J., "L'Avenir Catholique du Japon", *Xaveriana* 40 (Leuven: Xaveriana, 1927); Pierre Charles, S.J., "L'Avenir Catholique du Japon", *Xaveriana* 40, 2nd ed. (Leuven: Xaveriana, 1931); Pierre Charles, S.J., "Les Premiers Japonais en Europe", *Xaveriana* 122 (Leuven: Museum Lessianum, 1934); Pierre Charles, S.J., "Le Premier Jésuite Japonais", *Xaveriana* 138 (Leuven: Museum Lessianum, 1935); Pierre Charles, S.J., "Kwannon de Blanc Vêtue", *Xaveriana* 146 (Leuven: Museum Lessianum, 1936); Pierre Charles, S.J., "Yamaguchi au Temps de François Xavier", *Xaveriana* 167 (Leuven: Xaveriana, 1937); Pierre Charles, S.J., and Joseph Masson, S.J., *Japon: Études Détachées* (Leuven: AUCAM, 1937).

65 As Minister of Foreign Affairs of China, he had joined the honorary committee of the Œuvre International de Louvain.

66 Letter of April 25, 1935 from Dom Lou to Raoul Pontus, Institut belge des hautes études chinoises, archives Raoul Pontus box 1, map 8.

67 *Tianjin Yishibao* 天津益世報 disizhang 第四張 Minkoku 17th year, July 27, July 28, and July 29 editions carried reports on the contents of the library, the grand inauguration ceremony, and the speeches of the VIP's respectively (Mullie number 56 B01).

68 J. Schoonjans, *Universiteitsbibliotheek, een Bijdrage tot Haar Geschiedenis* (Leuven: eigen beheer, 1977), 44 and 50.

69 Universiteitsarchief KU Leuven, Archief rector Paulin Ladeuze C163-2, scrap note reading: "En nov. 1937, deux caisses envoyés par governement japonais, contenant 120 grands volumes (sur le Mandchoukuo), pareils à ceux de la collection japonaise. N'avons eu qu'à payer la post. Par remercie... du 28 nov, 37."

Incidentally, the East Asian Library of KU Leuven owns a few wrappers (numbered LSIN-22/0500 MANJ 1948) of *Daiqing Shilu (Daishin Jitsuroku)* 大清実録 that once belonged to the great Mongolian scholar Antoine Mostaert CICM, and bearing his signature and dated 5-9-48. They evidently date from the donation made by Mullie to KU Leuven. Including the index volumes the collection presently counts 122 volumes.

70 A Catholic students' periodical, published under the auspices of *L'Action Catholique de la Jeunesse Belge* (A.C.J.B.), a sub-group of the *Action Catholique*. The issue in question is now rare. I could locate it in "Archives du monde catholique (ARCA)", a documentation centre on Catholicism in Francophone Belgium during the nineteenth and twentieth centuries, attached to l'Université Catholique de Louvain.

71 Gonzague Ryckmans, "Bis Diruta, Bis Restituta: Contribution à l'Histoire de la Bibliothèque de Louvain", in *Scrinium Lovaniense: Mélanges Historiques Etienne Van Cauwenbergh; Scrinium Lovaniense: Historische Opstellen Etienne van Cauwenbergh* (18-50), 38; Em. Prof. dr. Jan F. Vanderheyden, "Het Herstel van de Leuvense Universiteitsbibliotheek 1940-1945", *Onze Alma Mater* 2 (1987): 119.

72 The inventory was drawn up on August 30, 1940. It is now in the Leuven municipal archives in the file "Oorlog 1940. Bibliotheek der Hoogeschool. Geredde kunstwerken" (file 15.655).

73 Letter from Van Cauwenbergh to Rector Van Waeyenbergh, dated Louvain, July 1, 1941, UCL Archives de la Bibliothèque centrale BE A4006 FI 067\rapport annuel 1941-1942, stating "Vers la mi-juillet, les livres échappés à l'incendie dans le bâtiment sinistré purent en être enlevés et furent alors transportés au Collège Américain, sauf les ouvrages de l'Institut de Toponymie, qui trouvèrent un abri à l'Institut de Pharmacie et les collections japonaises et chinoises, qui furent déposées aux Halles Universitaires."

74 After the First World War, the university made an attempt to acquire the block between Naamsestraat and Oude Markt on the one hand, and Krakenstraat and Collegeberg on the other. That was not successful, because many café owners fronted onto the Oude Markt refused. However, the university has managed to acquire a few plots, and the Institut de Spoelbergh was built on one of those plots.

75 Note pour monsieur le Ministre des Affaires étrangères de Belgique au sujet de la Bibliothèque de l'université de Louvain, in Archives de l'Université catholique de Louvain, Archives de la Bibliothèque centrale, Fonds BE A4006 FI 067, Archives Mgr Van Waeyenbergh.

76 KU Leuven, archief Algemeen Beheer, Fonds Satsuma, letter from Van Cauwenbergh to rector, dated Louvain, April 11, 1946.

77 Em. Prof. dr. Jan F. Vanderheyden, "Het Herstel van de Leuvense Universiteitsbibliotheek 1940-1945", *Onze Alma Mater* 2 (1987): 120.

78 UCL Archives de la Bibliothèque centrale BE A4006 FI 067 kort ook Fonds FI 067\map 13 Service des Assurances, relevé de la bibliothèque centrale.

79 Rodica Doina Pop, *Bibliothèque de l'Université Catholique de Louvain: Trentième Anniversaire de la Première*

Restauration (4 juillet 1958) et Lettre de Son Excellence Mgr Honoré Van Waeyenbergh, Évêque Titulaire de Gilba, Évêque Auxiliaire de Malines, Recteur Magnifique (Louvain: UCL. Centre international de dialectologie générale, 1958, planche V). According to Mark Derez, archivist of KU Leuven, the photo was taken by Jean Schoonjans, director of the 'Service photographique de la Bibliothèque'. He was Van Cauwenbergh's amanuensis and is the author of a creditable book about the history of the Leuven/Louvain library.

80 See "Catholic University of Louvain Service des Assurances, Library, Relevé du 21 September 1959", in UCL Fund FI 067 Archives de la Bibliothèque central BE A4006 FI 067, folder 13.

81 Universiteitsarchief KU Leuven Archief Universiteitsbibliotheek KU BIB 22/11 M: Letter from Mullie to W. Dehennin, dated Korbeek, 2-3-1971.

82 Archives de l'Université catholique de Louvain, Archives de la Bibliothèque centrale Letter from J. Ryckmans to the Head Librarian of the University (i.e. professor Joseph Ruwet), dated February 9, 1971. It is written and signed by J. Ryckmans, who is the president at that time of the Institut Orientaliste, located at 16 Redingenstraat in Leuven.

83 Ibid.

84 A total of 20,000 volumes (presumably fascicles) according to his own testimony. See Universiteitsarchief KU Leuven Archief Universiteitsbibliotheek KU BIB 22/11 M: Letter from Mullie to W. Dehennin, dated Korbeek, 2-3-1971.

85 Universiteitsarchief KU Leuven Archief Universiteitsbibliotheek KU BIB 22/11 M.

86 Gonzague Ryckmans, "Bis Diruta, Bis Restituta: Contribution à l'Histoire de la Bibliothèque de Louvain", in *Scrinium Lovaniense: Mélanges Historiques Etienne Van Cauwenbergh; Scrinium Lovaniense: Historische Opstellen Etienne van Cauwenbergh* (18-50), 50.

87 Willy Jonckheere & Herman Todts, *Leuven Vlaams: Splitsingsgeschiedenis van de Katholieke Universiteit Leuven* (Leuven: Davidsfonds, 1979).

88 Archives de l'Université catholique de Louvain, Archives de la Bibliothèque centrale: Letter from J. Ryckmans to the Head Librarian of the University (i.e. Professor Joseph Ruwet), dated February 9, 1971. It is written and signed by J. Ryckmans, who is the president at that time of the Institut Orientaliste, located at 16 Redingenstraat in Leuven.

89 Universiteitsarchief KU Leuven Archief Universiteitsbibliotheek KU BIB 22/11 M: letter from Mullie to (unnamed) dated Leuven, 21 januari 1970 and unsigned note attached to letter from Mullie to W. Dehennin, dated Korbeek, 2-3-1971.

90 Universiteitsarchief KU Leuven Archief Universiteitsbibliotheek KU BIB 22/11 M: letter from J. Ryckmans to the Head Librarian of the University (i.e. Professor Joseph Ruwet), dated February 9, 1971.

91 See the photograph of the First International Conference on Chinese Science in September 1981, the first conference held by the section of Chinese Studies of KU Leuven in this new room.

92 Peter F. Kornicki, "The Union Catalogue of Early Japanese Books in Europe: History and Progress", *Journal of East Asian Libraries* 1995, no. 105, art. 5 (January 2, 1995).

93 Koyama Noboru (Cambridge University Library, UK), "Japanese Books Donated to the University of Louvain, 1924-26".

94 Koyama, "Rūvan Daigaku Toshokan".

95 I contributed a more comprehensive article on the subject in *Higashi to Nishi no Bunka Kōryū* 東と西の文化交流 ('The Cultural Exchange between the East and the West'), ed. Fujiyoshi Masumi 藤善眞澄 (Suita: Kansai daigaku shuppanbu 関西大学出版部, 2004), 191-223.

96 http://base1.nijl.ac.jp/~oushu/readme.html

Selected Books from the Japanese Donation (pp. 66-207)

1 See Lutz 1994. The *Recueil des voyages au Nord* comprises in total five volumes, published between 1715-1727.

2 Unit of gold currency, also considered equivalent to 1 *koku* of rice, i.e., the amount of rice needed to feed one person for one year.

3 Zhang came from the region of the present-day province of Sichuan.

4 Pacheco 1971, p. 441.

5 Toyoshima 2013, Appendix, 1-10.

6 Existing editions were cut up and the pages were pasted face down onto a woodblock. The engraver then cut out the block following the lines of the printed characters. Because most Chinese and Japanese paper is quite transparent, the engraver could still make out the characters through the paper. fairly well.

7 Sugimoto 1998, p. 28.

8 *The Lotus Sutra* (Takakusu/Watanabe 1924-1934, vol. 9, no. 262), translated from the Chinese of Kumārajiva by Kubo and Yuyama 2007, p. 47.

9 Genbun 元文 era [1736-1741] is a copyist's error. The quoted source has Genkyū 元久 (1204-1205). The Keichō 慶長 era ran from 1596 to 1615.

Japanese Art in Belgium in the 1920s: Hidden Treasures and Public Celebrations (pp. 208-215)

1 Freya Terryn is an art historian who specializes in Japanese visual and print culture of the nineteenth century. She holds a PhD in Japanese Studies from the University of Leuven (KU Leuven) and her research is funded by the Research Foundation - Flanders (FWO). Acknowledgments: I would like to thank Adrien Carbonnet and Jan Schmidt for their comments on earlier versions of this essay.

2 For an in-depth discussion, see Vande Walle's essay in the present volume.

3 Takagi 2005, p. 194.

4 Together with the Chinese Pavilion, this is today one of the departments of the RMAH and is known as the Museums of the Far East. Vandeperre 2016, p. 319.

5 This collection of approximately 6,700 pieces consists of woodblock prints, illustrated books, *netsuke, tsuba*, combs, porcelain, bronzes, lacquered works, and arms. Takagi 2002, p. 68.

6 Takagi 2002, p. 67.

7 The groundwork listed here is only the tip of the

iceberg. The craze for Japanese art was also cel-ebrated, for example, by the painter Alfred Stevens (1823-1906) and in the Belgian Fin de Siècle literature such as Max Elskamp's *L'eventail japonais* (1886) and Emile Verhaeren's *Images japonaises* (1896).

8 He was the minister from 2 December 1919 until 24 October 1921. At the time, the museums were required to inform the ministry of any kind of acquisition.

9 Letter Dupieurreux to Van Overloop, 20 April 1921, Archives RMAH, Brussels, dossier no. 1680.

10 Report Bommer, no date, Archives RMAH, Brussels, dossier no. 1680.

11 Letter Bommer to Van Overloop, 24 November 1919, Archives RMAH, Brussels, dossier Bommer and letter Bommer to Van Overloop, 12 January 1920, Archives RMAH, Brussels, dossier Bommer.

12 Report Bommer, no date, Archives RMAH, Brussels, dossier no. 1680.

13 Report Bommer, no date, Archives RMAH, Brussels, dossier no. 1680.

14 Letter Bommer to Van Overloop, 5 July 1921, Archives RMAH, Brussels, dossier no. 669.

15 No files concerning this exchange remain in the archives of the RMAH. The number of prints was derived from a list composed by Ms. G. Craps on the provenance of the Japanese woodblock print collec-tion. I am indebted to Nathalie Vandeperre, curator of the East-Asian collections of the RMAH, for provid-ing this list.

16 Another lacuna in the archival material is that Bom-mer never disclosed where he found the prints or who provided them.

17 Letter Bommer to Van Overloop, 5 July 1921, Archives RMAH, Brussels, dossier no. 669.

18 Jules Destrée, "Foujita et l'art japonais d'aujourd'hui," *Le Soir*, 24 October 1924.

19 Tsujiokaya Kamekichi 辻岡屋亀吉 (Amaterasu and Emperor Yūryaku), Morimoto Junzaburō 森本順三郎 (Empress Jingū, Emperor Kameyama, Emperor Takakura, and Emperor Antoku), Maruya Tetsujirō 丸屋鉄次郎 (Emperor Sutoku and Emperor Go-Daigo), Yamaguchiya Tōbei 山口屋藤兵衛 (Emperor Jinmu), and Yamanaka Kitarō 山中喜太郎 (Emperor Keikō).

20 Newland 2011, p. 29; Uhlenbeck 2011, p. 17.

21 Although the RMAH holds eight prints, it is beyond the scope of this essay to provide a detailed analysis of each print. Instead, two prints are discussed.

22 Keyes 1982; Ing/Schaap 1992; Kozyreff 1998; Uhlen-beck/Newland 2011.

23 Vansina 2019, p. 33.

24 Vansina 2019, pp. iv, 30-32.

25 For an in-depth discussion, see Vansina 2019, pp. 34-35.

26 Vansina 2019, p. 15.

27 L.P., "La vie artistique : Un salon d'artistes japonais," *Le Peuple*, 19 June 1929.

28 For a thorough analysis of Fujita, see Buisson 2011 and Buisson/Buisson 2001.

29 Mestré, "Artiste japonais," *La Meuse*, 25 June 1929.

20 L.P., "La vie artistique."

31 Vansina 2019, p. 35 and especially footnote 125.

32 Buisson 2001, p. 600.

33 Buisson 2001, pp. 600-601.

34 C.B., "Les expositions: T. Foujita au Centaure. Le 1er salon des artistes anciens combattants," *La Nation Belge*, 16 January 1922; "Les expositions," *Le Peuple*, 16 January 1922; "Exposition d'un peintre japonais," *Le Soir*, 12 January 1922.

35 Buisson 2001, p. 600. Reports of the acquisition: 1922. "Au Musée royal des Beaux-Arts de Bruxelles," *Le Peuple*, 2 July 1922; "Uit Brussel : Koninklijk Muzeum van Schoone Kunsten," *De Schelde, 3 July 1922.*

36 C.B., "Les expositions."

37 In 1928 he produced a series of 8 aquarelles on his vices, which were steeling, games, tobacco, gluttony, and greed. Buisson/Buisson 2001, p. 404 (catalogue no. 28.66-28.73).

38 Buisson 2001, pp. 387-388 (catalogue no. 26.01-26.67), 391 (27.02-27.03), 404-405 (28.63, 29.01), 420 (31.12-31.13).

39 "Chronique artistique: Au Musée royal des Beaux-Arts," *Gazette de Charleroi*, 11 November 1923; "Nos echos: Divers," *La Dernière Heure*, 12 November 1923; "Beaux-Arts," *Le Vingtième Siècle*, 13 November 1923; "La vie artistique: Au Musée des Beaux-Arts," *Le Peuple*, 14 November 1923.

40 Aude Alexandre, archivist at the RMFAB, confirmed that the museums have no documentation whatsoever.

41 Destrée, "Foujita et l'art japonais d'aujourd'hui."

42 "Petit gazette," *Le Soir*, 25 October 1924; "Petit gazette," *Le Soir*, 8 November 1924.

43 I am indebted to Marieke Vansina for this information.

44 Buisson/Buisson 2001, pp. 392-402 lists 12 nudes for 1927 and 8 for 1928, whereas Buisson 2001, pp. 238-277 lists 36 for 1927 and 58 for 1928.

45 "Un don au Musées des Beaux-Arts," *Le Peuple*, 1 Feb-ruary 1928; "M. SATSUMO Heeft een der Schoonste Werken van FOUJITA, den Japanschen Schilder ten Geschenke Gegeven aan het Modern Museum te Brus-sel," *De Volksgazet*, 2 February 1928.

Japan's Sonic Modernity: Popular Music and Culture in the 1920s (pp 216-225)

1 PhD Fellow, Research Foundation - Flanders. Affilia-tion: University of Leuven (KU Leuven). Acknowledgments: The author wants to thank Jan Schmidt for his comments on earlier versions of this essay and Mōri Masato for his many critical comments and suggestions on Japanese recordings of the 1920s.

2 Horiuchi Keizō, preface to *Jazu Ongaku* by Shio'uri Kamesuke (Tōkyō: Keibunkan, 1929), 5; for a short introduction to a global outlook, see: Gumbrecht 1997, pp. 120-125.

3 For more on Japanese diplomacy, see the essay by Lieven Sommen in this volume.

4 For more on the Japanese book donation, see the essay by Willy Vande Walle in this volume.

5 Gluck 1998, pp. 270-271; Tanaka 2004, pp. 17-24.

6 Francks 2009, pp. 156–159.

7 For more on the intricacies of Japan's 1920s moder-nity, see: Minichiello 1998.

8 Harootunian 2000, p. 8; Young 2013, pp. 16-23.

9 Harootunian 2000, p. 7.

10 Sato 2003, pp. 114-151; Tipton 1997, p. 4.

11 Young 2013, pp. 23-32.

12 Taira 1997, p. 274.
13 In his "modernology", a study on modernity in society, Kon Wajirō only reported an extremely small minority of women (one percent) who could be identified as *moga*. See Image no. 5 in Silverberg 2006, p. 172; Sato 2003, p. 49; see also pp. 238-239 in this publication.
14 Silverberg 2006, p. 28-30; Atkins 2017, pp. 102-104.
15 Jazz was first recorded by the Original Dixieland Jazz Band and released by the Victor Talking Machine Company in 1917 on record with number. The same band toured in the United Kingdom in 1919. Moreover, African-American soldiers, such as James Reese Europe and his military band of the Harlem Hellfighters, brought it to Europe in the last year of the First World War and recorded in France for Pathé Records.
16 For a visual and written example, see: Okamoto Ippei, "Sekai isshū: jazu," *Tōkyō Asahi Shinbun*, Evening Edition, 15 September 1922, p. 1.
17 Atkins 2001, pp. 45-46 & 91.
18 This transformation also happened because the "police authorities pronounced dancing in cafés to gramophone music inappropriate for a place where food and drink were served." See: Tipton 2008, p. 718.

19 Young 2013, p. 198.
20 Atkins 2001, pp. 56, 68-74; Sato 2003, pp. 61-69.
21 "Dansu hōru saisho no torishimari kisoku – zenkoku kakutoshi ni sakigake, Hyōgo-ken de kenrei happu," *Tōkyō Asahi Shinbun*, Morning Edition, 6 November 1928, p. 3.
22 White 2012, pp. 7-58.
23 Atkins 2001, pp. 68, 74-75.
24 Ōkubo 2015, pp. 28-30.
25 Azami 2016, pp. 98-99.
26 Yano 1998, pp. 247-264.
27 Pope 2003, pp. 154-156.
28 Kami Kyōsuke, "Jazu-gaku nyūmon," *Kinema Junpō*, 1 January 1935, p. 180.
29 Young 2013, pp. 220-221.
30 Toshio 2016, pp. 117-118.
31 Kan's story was serialized in the magazine *King* before and during the release of the film.
32 Terakawa Shin, "Gendaisō to eiga shudaika: Rekōdo no ureyuki wo mite," *Eiga Kyōiku* 55, 9 (1932), p. 24.
33 Young 2013, p. 194.
34 Gluck 1998, p. 264.

About the Editors and Authors

Aurel Baele is a PhD candidate with the Japanese Studies Research Group at the East Asian and Arabic Studies Research Unit, KU Leuven Faculty of Arts. His research explores the history of record companies and the development of jazz in Japan considering the changing political conditions, 1920-1952. He is currently a beneficiary of a four-year PhD fellowship from the Research Foundation – Flanders (FWO) and co-founder of the popular science magazine *Wasshoi!* Between April 1, 2022, and March 31, 2023, he is a visiting researcher at Aoyama Gakuin University, Tokyo. His main research interests are the modern history of Japan, media history, and jazz history.

Angelika Koch is Assistant Professor in Premodern Japanese History at Leiden University. She completed her PhD at the University of Cambridge and is in the process of completing her first book project: *Sexual Healing. Sexuality, Health, and the Male Body in Early Modern Japan*. Specializing in the cultural history of early modern Japan, one of her research interests is the representation of health and disease in popular fiction from the late-Edo period.

Eline Mennens obtained an MA in Japanese Studies at the KU Leuven Faculty of Arts in 2018, with a thesis on "Kusunoki Masashige and Ninomiya Sontoku as 'Lieux de Mémoire' in Modern Japan". Her research focused on collective memory within the modern history of Japan. In 2019 and 2020, she worked as an assistant preparing the special exhibition "Japan's Book Donation to the University of Louvain. Japanese Cultural Identity and Modernity in the 1920s". She additionally served on the campaign for establishing what became the "Japan Mirai Fund, a Joint Initiative of KU Leuven & UCLouvain", before becoming an elementary school teacher.

Jan Schmidt is Associate Professor for Modern and Contemporary History of Japan and Head of the Japanese Studies Research Group within the East Asian and Arabic Studies Research Unit at the KU Leuven Faculty of Arts. He obtained his MA in Medieval and Modern History and Japanese Studies at Heidelberg University and his PhD from the Faculty of East Asian Studies of Ruhr University

Bochum, where he worked as lecturer from 2006 to 2015. He specializes in political and media history, having published a monograph, co-edited volumes, and several articles on the impact of the First World War in Japan and East Asia from a global perspective.

Lieven Sommen is a PhD candidate in Japanese Studies at the East Asian and Arabic Studies Research Unit, KU Leuven Faculty of Arts. His research delves into the history of mediatization of the Japanese Ministry of Foreign Affairs during the interwar period, with a focus on the evolving consciousness towards public diplomacy, propaganda policies, and new media within the ministry. His research has been supported by a four-year fellowship from the Research Foundation – Flanders (FWO) until September 2022. From October 2022, he will continue his research in Japan with a one-year scholarship from Kokugakuin University (Tokyo).

Freya Terryn is a postdoctoral fellow at the Japanese Studies Research Group at the KU Leuven Faculty of Arts and specializes in Japanese visual and print culture of the nineteenth century. She holds a PhD in Japanese Studies from KU Leuven (2021) which was funded by the Research Foundation – Flanders (FWO). Her primary research interests lie in the arts and material cultures of eighteenth- and nineteenth-century Japan, with a particular focus on prints, illustrated books, and paintings. She is currently reworking her PhD thesis into a book.

Willy Vande Walle is professor emeritus of Japanese Studies at KU Leuven. His publications - in Dutch, English, French, and Japanese as well as Chinese - cover a wide range of Japan-related topics, including Buddhism, Japanese diplomatic history, Sino-Japanese relations, societal issues, language, and art history. He was the chair for the Scientific Committee of *Europalia Japan 1989*. He is the recipient of the Japan Foundation Special Prize, the Yamagata Bantō Prize, holder of an honorary doctorate from Kansai University, and has been awarded the Order of the Rising Sun. He currently serves as the chairperson of the European Association of Japanese Resource Specialists.

Bibliography

Akami, Tomoko **(2008)**. "The Emergence of International Public Opinion and the Origins of Public Diplomacy in Japan in the Inter-War Period." In: *The Hague Journal of Diplomacy* 3, pp. 99-128.

Aoki, Kunio 青木国夫 **(1977)**. "Kaisetsu: Nōgu benri-ron to Ōkura Nagatsune" 解説農具便利論と大蔵永常, Nōgu benri-ron 農具便利論, Tawarakasane kōsaku emaki shō たはらかさね耕作絵巻(抄), Tōkyō: Kōwa shuppan 恒和出版, 1977 (Edo kagaku koten sōsho 江戸科学古典叢書, eds. Aoki Kunio 青木国夫 & Matsushima Eiichi 松島栄一, vol. 4).

Ariyama, Teruo 有山輝雄 **(2009)**. *Kindai Nihon no media to chiiki shakai* 近代日本のメディアと地域社会. Tōkyō: Yoshikawa kōbunkan 吉川弘文館.

Ariyama, Teruo 有山輝雄 **(2014)**. "Nihon no dai-ichiji sekai taisen sansen to mō hitotsu no sensō" 日本の第一次世界大戦参戦ともう一つの戦争. In: *Momoyama gakuin daigaku kurisutokyō ronshū* 桃山学院大学キリスト教論集 49, pp. 73-74.

Asahina, Sōgen 朝比奈宗源 **(1982)**. Transl. *Hekiganroku* 碧巌録, 3 vols. Tōkyō: Iwanami bunko 岩波文庫.

Atkins, Taylor E. **(2001)**. *Blue Nippon: Authenticating Jazz in Japan*. Durham: Duke University Press.

Atkins, Taylor E. **(2017)**. *A History of Popular Culture in Japan: From the Seventeenth Century to the Present*. London: Bloomsbury.

Azami, Toshio 生明俊雄 **(2016)**. *Nijū seiki Nihon/Rekōdo sangyō-shi: gurōbaru kigyō no shinkō to shijō no hatten* 二〇世紀日本レコード産業史：グローバル企業の進攻と市場の発展. Tōkyō: Keisō shobō 勁草書房.

Beans, George H. **(1951)**. *A List of Japanese Maps of the Tokugawa Era* (Tall Tree Library Publication No. 23). Tall Tree Library: Jenkintown.

Beans, George H. **(1955)**. *A List of Japanese Maps of the Tokugawa Era, Supplement A* (Tall Tree Library Publication No. 24). Tall Tree Library: Jenkintown.

Beans, George H. **(1958)**. *A List of Japanese Maps of the Tokugawa Era, Supplement B* (Tall Tree Library Publication No. 25). Tall Tree Library: Jenkintown.

Beans, George H. **(1963)**. *A List of Japanese Maps of the Tokugawa Era, Supplement C* (Tall Tree Library Publication No. 26). Tall Tree Library: Jenkintown.

Berger, Gordon Mark **(1977)**. *Parties out of Power in Japan 1931-1941*. Princeton, N.J.: Princeton University Press.

Buisson, Sylvie **(2001)**. *Léonard-Tsuguharu Foujita*. Vol. 2. 2 vols. Paris: ACR édition.

Buisson, Sylvie/**Buisson**, Dominique **(2001)**. *Léonard-Tsuguharu Foujita*. Vol. 1. 2 vols. Courbevoie: ACR édition.

Burkman, Thomas **(2008)**. *Japan and the League of Nations: Empire and World Order, 1914-1938*. Hawai'i: University of Hawai'i Press.

Blaker, Carmen **(1964)**. *The Japanese Enlightenment. A Study of the Writings of Fukuzawa Yukichi*. Cambridge: Cambridge University Press.

Chiba, Isao 千葉功 **(2008)**. *Kyūgaikō no keisei: Nihon gaikō 1900 - 1919* 旧外交の形成：日本外交1900-1919. Tōkyō: Keisō shobō 勁草書房.

Chibbett, David **(1977)**. *The History of Japanese Printing and Book Illustration*, Tōkyō: Kodansha International Ltd.

China hemel en aarde: *5000 jaar uitvindingen en ontdekkingen, 16 september 1988-16 januari 1989*. Brussels: Koninklijke Musea voor Kunst en Geschiedenis (exhibition catalogue).

Cleary, Thomas/**Cleary**, J.C. **(1977)**. *The Blue Cliff Record*, transl. from the Chinese *Pi Yen Lu* by Thomas and J.C. Cleary, 3 vols. Boulder/London: Shambala.

Collection Hayashi: Dessins, Estampes, Livres illustrés **(1902)**. Paris: Imprimerie de Charles Herissey.

De Cooman, David/**Vande Walle**, Willy, eds. **(2016)**. *Japan & Belgium: An Itinerary of Mutual Inspiration*. Tielt: Lannoo.

Dickinson, Frederick **(1999)**. *War and National Reinvention. Japan and the Great War, 1914-1919*. Cambridge, MA/London: Harvard University Press.

Dickinson, Frederick **(2013)**. *World War I and the Triumph of a New Japan, 1919-1930*. Cambridge: Cambridge University Press.

Donegan, Patricia/**Ishibashi**, Yoshie **(1996)**. *Chiyo-ni: Woman Haiku Master*. Tōkyō/Rutland Vt.: Tuttle Publishing.

Dore, Ronald **(1965)**. *Education in Tokugawa Japan*. Berkeley, CA: University of California Press.

Duus, Peter **(1968)**. *Party Rivalry and Political Change in Taisho Japan*. Cambridge, MA: Harvard University Press.

Esthus, Raymond **(1959)**. "The Changing Concept of the Open Door, 1899-1910." In: *The Mississippi Valley Historical Review* 46/3, pp. 435-454.

Forrer, Matthi/**Effert**, Fifi **(2000)**. *De hofreis naar de Shōgun van Japan*. Leiden: Hotei Publishing.

Francks, Penelope **(2009)**. "Inconspicuous Consumption: Sake, Beer, and the Birth of the Consumer in Japan." In: *The Journal of Asian Studies* 68/1, pp. 135-164.

Frattolillo, Oliviero/**Best**, Antony, eds. **(2015)**. *Japan and the Great War*. Basingstoke/New York: Palgrave Macmillan.

Fuess, Harald **(2005)**. "Investment, Importation and Innovation: Genesis and Growth of Beer Corporations in Pre-war Japan." In: Janet Hunter and Cornelia Stolz, ed. *Institutional and Technological Change in Japan's Economy: Past and Present*. London: Routledge, pp. 43-59.

Fujikawa, Hideo 富士川英郎, ed. **(1991)**. *Kikō Nihon kanshi* 紀行日本漢詩, vol. 2 (*kaidai*: Sano Masami). Tōkyō: Kyūko shoin 汲古書院.

Fujikawa, Hideo 富士川英郎/**Sano**, Masami 佐野正巳, eds. **(1992)**. *Kikō Nihon kanshi* 紀行日本漢詩, vol. 3 (*kaidai*: Fujikawa Hideo). Tōkyō: Kyūko shoin 汲古書院.

Fujisawa, Murasaki 藤澤紫 **(2003)**. *Suzuki Harunobu ehon zenshū* 鈴木春信絵本全集 3 vols. Tōkyō: Bensei shuppan 勉誠出版.

Fukuda, Mahito 福田眞人/**Suzuki**, Noriko 鈴木則子, eds. **(2005)**. *Nihon baidokushi no kenkyū. Iryō, shakai, kokka* 日本梅毒史の研究：医療・社会・国家, Kyōto: Shibunkaku shuppan.

Fumoto, Yasutaka 麓保孝 **(1984)**. *Teihan shinki* 帝範・臣軌, Chūgoku koten shinsho 中国古典新書. Tōkyō: Meitoku shuppansha 明徳出版社.

Funakoshi, Kinkai 船越錦海 **(1831)**. *Baisō sadan* 黴瘡茶談 (Keio University Collections).

Garon, Sheldon **(1987)**. *The State and Labor in Modern Japan*. Berkeley/Los Angeles/London: University of California Press.

Garon, Sheldon **(2011)**. *Beyond our Means: Why America Spends while the World Saves*. Princeton: Princeton University Press.

Gluck, Carol **(1998)**. "The Invention of Edo." In Stephen Vlastos, ed., *Mirror of Modernity: Invented Traditions of Modern Japan* (Berkeley, CA: University of California Press), pp. 262-284.

Gordon, Andrew **(1991)**. *Labor and Imperial Democracy in Prewar Japan*. Berkeley/ Los Angeles/ Oxford: University of California Press.

Gordon, Andrew **(2020)**. *Japan. A Modern History*. 4th edition. New York: Oxford University Press.

Griffin, Edward G. **(1972)**. "The Universal Suffrage Issue in Japanese Politics, 1918-1925." *The Journal of Asian Studies* 31/2, pp. 275-290.

Gumbrecht, Hans **(1997)**. *In 1926: Living at the Edge of Time*. Cambridge, MA: Harvard University Press, pp. 120-125.

Hakubunkan henshūkyoku 博文館編輯局, ed. **(1902)**. *Kōtei Asahina Juntōki* 校訂朝夷巡島記. Tōkyō: Hakubunkan 博文館.

Harootunian, Harry **(2000)**. *Overcome by Modernity: History, Culture, and Community in Interwar Japan*. Princeton: Princeton University Press.

Hattori, Unokichi 服部宇之吉, ed. **(1984)**. *Senkai kobun shinpō kōshū; zōchū santaishi; senchū tōshisen* 箋解古文真宝・増註三体詩・箋註唐詩選; vol. 2 of Hattori Unokichi et al., eds. 服部宇之吉 校訂. *Kanbun taikei* 漢文大系 第2巻. Tōkyō: Fuzanbō 冨山房 (増補版 普及版).

Hattori, Toshirō 服部敏良 **(1978)**. *Edo jidai igakushi no kenkyū* 江戸時代医学史の研究. Tōkyō: Yoshikawa kōbunkan 吉川弘文館.

Hayashi, Razan 林羅山/Ugai, Sekisai 鵜飼石斎 **(1910)**. *Kobun shinpō kōshū genkai taisei* 古文真宝後集諺解大成, vol. 12 of *Kanseki kokuji-kai zensho* 漢籍国字解全書. Tōkyō: Waseda daigaku shuppanbu 早稲田大学出版部.

Heine, Steven **(2016)**. *Chan Rhetoric of Uncertainty in the Blue Cliff Record: Sharpening a Sword at the Dragon Gate*. Oxford: Oxford University Press.

High, Peter B. **(2003)**. *The Imperial Screen. Japanese Film Culture in the Fifteenth Years' War, 1931-1945*. Madison, WI: University of Wisconsin Press.

Hillier, Jack Ronald **(1980)**. *The Art of Hokusai in Book Illustration*. New York: Sotheby Parke Bernet.

Hioki, Kazuko **(2009)**. "Japanese Printed Books of the Edo Period (1603-1867): History and Characteristics of Block-printed Books", *Journal of the Institute of Conservation* 32/1, pp. 79-101.

Hirata, Takashi 平田高士 **(1982)**. *Butten kōza 29 Hekiganshū* 仏典講座 29 碧巌集. Tōkyō: Daizō shuppan 大蔵出版.

Hobsbawm, Eric/Terence Ranger, eds. **(1983)**. *The Invention of Tradition*. Cambridge: Cambridge University Press.

Horiuchi, Annick **(1994)**. *Les mathématiques japonaises à l'époque d'Edo (1600-1868)*. Paris: Librairie philosophique Vrins.

Hoshikawa, Kiyotaka 星川清孝 **(1963)**. *Kobun shinpō (kōshū)*: 古文真宝(後集), Shinshaku Kanbun Taikei 新釈漢文大系 16. Tōkyō: Meiji shoin 明治書院.

Hoshikawa, Kiyotaka 星川清孝 **(1967a)**. *Kobun shinpō (zenshū): Jō*. 古文真宝(前集):上, Shinshaku Kanbun Taikei 新釈漢文大系 9. Tōkyō: Meiji shoin 明治書院.

Hoshikawa, Kiyotaka 星川清孝 **(1967b)**. *Kobun shinpō (zenshū): Ge*. 古文真宝(前集):下, Shinshaku Kanbun Taikei 新釈漢文大系 10. Tōkyō: Meiji shoin 明治書院.

Huffman, James L. **(1997)**. *Creating a Public. People and Press in Meiji Japan*. Honolulu: University of Hawai'i Press.

Ichiko, Teiji 市古貞次 **et al.**, eds. **(1995-1996)**. *Kokusho jinmei jiten* 国書人名辞典. Tōkyō: Iwanami shoten 岩波書店.

Iguchi, Tsunenori 井口常範/**Ōya**, Shin'ichi 大矢真一 **(1980)**. *Tenmon Zukai* 天文図解 (Edo kagaku koten sōsho 江戸科学古典叢書 33). Tōkyō: Kōwa shuppan 恒和出版.

Imai, Kingo 今井金吾 **(1997)**. *Edo no tabi fūzoku; dōchūki o chūshin ni* 江戸の旅風俗 道中記を中心に. Tōkyō: Ōzorasha 大空社.

Ing, Eric van den/**Schaap**, Robert **(1992)**. *Beauty and Violence: Japanese Prints by Yoshitoshi 1839-1892*. Bergeijk: Society for Japanese Arts.

Iriya, Yoshitaka 入矢義高/**Kajitani**, Sōnin 梶谷宗忍/**Yanagida**, Seizan 柳田聖山 eds. **(1981)**. *Zen no goroku 15 Setchō juko* 禅の語録15 雪竇頌古. Tōkyō: Chikuma shobō 筑摩書房.

Iriye, Akira **(1997)**. *Cultural Internationalism and World Order*. Baltimore: Johns Hopkins University Press.

Iriye, Akira **(2002)**. *Global Community: The Role of International Organizations in the Making of the Contemporary World*. Berkeley: University of California Press.

Iwasa, Ryōji 岩佐亮二 **(1982)**. "Atogaki" 後書き. In: Hirano Mitsuru 平野満, ed. *Tachibana Yasukuni Ehon Noyamagusa* 橘保国 絵本野山草 (Seikatsu koten sōsho 生活古典叢書 25). Tōkyō: Yasaka shobō 八坂書房.

Izao, Tomio 井竿富雄 **(2007)**. "Dai-ichiji sekai taisen to minshū ishiki. Futatsu no kan-min gassaku bokin undō o megutte"「第一次世界大戦と民衆意識 二つの官民合作募金運動をめぐって」. In *Nihonshi kenkyū* 日本史研究 535, pp. 103-128.

Jones, Mark **(2010)**. *Children as Treasures: Childhood and the Middle Class in Early Twentieth Century Japan*. Cambridge: Harvard University Asia Center.

Kamiya, Makiko 紙屋牧子 **(2018)**. "Saishoki no 'Kōshitsu eiga' ni kansuru kōsatsu: kakusareru/sarasareru 'shintai'" 最初期の「皇室映画」に関する考察:隠される／晒される「身体」. In: *Eizōgaku* 映像学 100, pp. 32-52.

Katō, Totsudō 加藤咄堂 **(1939)**. *Hekiganroku daikōza* 碧巌録大講座, 15 vols. Tōkyō: Heibonsha 平凡社.

Kawase, Kazuma 川瀬一馬 **(1943)**. *Nihon shoshigaku no kenkyū* 日本書誌学之研究. Tōkyō: Dai-Nihon yūbenkai kōdansha 大日本雄弁会講談社.

Keene, Donald **(1978)**. *World Within Walls, Japanese Literature of the Pre-modern Era 1600-1867*. New York: Grove Press Inc. (reprint of Holt edition, Rinehart and Winston, New York, 1976).

Keyes, Roger Start **(1982)**. "Courage and Silence: A Study of the Life and Color Woodblock Prints of Tsukioka Yoshitoshi, 1839-1892." PhD diss., Cincinnati: Union for Experimenting Colleges and Universities.

Kinsei joshi kyōiku shisō 近世女子教育思想 (Nihon kyōiku shisō taikei 日本教育思想大系16) **(1980)**. Tōkyō: Nihon tosho sentā 日本図書センター.

Kitamura, Shirō 北村四郎/**Tsukamoto**, Yōtarō 塚本洋

太郎/**Konoshima**, Masao 木島正夫 **(1986)**. *Honzō zufu sōgō kaisetsu* 本草図譜総合解説 1. Kyōto: Dōhōsha shuppan 同朋舎出版.

Koakimoto, Dan 小秋元段 **(2010)**. "Kokatsujiban no engen o meguru shomondai: iwayuru Kirishitan-ban kigensetsu o chūshin ni" 古活字版の淵源をめぐる諸問題 所謂キリシタン版起源説を中心に. *Kokusai Nihon gaku* 国際日本学 (Monbu kagakushō 21 seiki COE puroguramu saitaku Nihon hasshin no kokusai nihongaku no kōchiku kenkyū seika hōkokushū 文部科学省 21世紀COEプログラム採択日本発信の国際日本学の構築研究成果報告集).

Kohiyama, Rui **(2019)**. "The 1927 Exchange of Friendship Dolls: U.S.-Japan Cultural Diplomacy in the Inter-War Years." In: *Diplomatic History* 43/2, pp. 282-304.

Koike, Masatane 小池正胤 **(1994)**. "Jiraiya gōketsu mono-gatari" 児雷也豪傑譚. In: *Nippon daihyakka zensho (Nipponica)* 日本大百科全書 (ニッポニカ). Tōkyō: Shōgakukan 小学館.

Komatsu, Taka'aki 小松孝彰 **(1937)**. "Manshū Jihen o kataru Shinagawa puropaganda" 満州事変を語る支那側プロパガンダ. In: *Chūō kōron* 中央公論 52/9, p. 157.

Kokushi daijiten henshū iinkai 国史大辞典編集委員会, eds. **(1979-1993)**. *Kokushi daijiten* 国史大辞典. Tōkyō: Yoshikawa kōbunkan 吉川弘文館.

Kondō, Haruo 近藤春雄 **(1978)**. *Chūgoku gakugei daijiten* 中国学芸大事典. Tōkyō: Taishūkan shoten 大修館書店.

Konishi, Masayasu 小西正泰 "kaidai" 解題; **Ōkura** Nagatsune 大蔵永常, *Kōeki kokusan-kō* 広益国産考 (Nihon nōsho zenshū 日本農書全集 14), (Yamada Tatsuo 山田龍雄, Iinuma Jirō 飯沼二郎, Oka Mitsuo 岡光夫, Morita Shirō 守田志郎), (Kōchū 校注, shippitsu 執筆: Iinuma Jirō 飯沼二郎), Tōkyō: Nōsan gyoson bunka kyōkai 農山漁村文化協会, 1978: Iinuma Jirō 飯沼二郎, "kaidai" 解題.

Koresawa, Yūko 是澤優子 **(2008)**. "Taishō-ki ni okeru Mitsukoshi jidō hakurankai no tenkai" 大正期における三越児童博覧会の展開. Bulletin of Tokyo Kasei University Museum 東京家政大学博物館紀要 13, pp. 39-46.

Kornicki, Peter/**Rubinger**, Richard **(2001)**. "Literacy Revisited: Some Reflections on Richard Rubinger's Findings." In: *Monumenta Nipponica* 56/3, pp. 383-385.

Kornicki, Peter **(1998)**. *The Book in Japan: a Cultural History from the Beginnings to the Nineteenth Century.* Leiden/Boston/Cologne: Brill.

Kosoto, Hiroshi 小曽戸洋 **(1999)**. *Nihon kanpō tenseki jiten* 日本漢方典籍辞典. Tōkyō: Taishūkan shoten 大修館書店.

Kosugi, Keiko 小杉恵子/**Pigeot**, Jacqueline **(1995)**. *Nara-ehon-shū, Pari-bon* 奈良絵本集: パリ本 (Koten bunko 古典文庫 dai 582 satsu 第582冊). Tōkyō: Koten bunko 古典文庫.

Koyama, Akira 小山亮 **(2013)**. "Senkyūhyaku nijūichi nen Hirohito Kōtaishi gaiyū to shikaku media: satsuei kitei no kanwa to no kakawari kara" 一九二一年裕仁皇太子外遊と視覚メディア：撮影規定の緩和との関わりから. In: *Jinmin no Rekishigaku* 人民の歴史学189, pp. 16-31.

Kozyreff, Chantal **(1992)**. *Deux siècles de livres japonais: le Fonds Hans de Winiwarter*, Exposition organisé à la Bibliothèque royale Albert Ier du 27 mai au 11 juillet 1992, catalogue établi par Chantal Kozyreff, premier assistant aux Musées royaux d'Art et d'Histoire. Bruxelles: Bibliothèque royale Albert Ier.

Kozyreff, Chantal **(1998)**. *Tradition et transition: le Japon de 1842 à 1912 = Tussen traditie en vernieuwing: Japan van 1842 tot 1912.* Brussel: Koninklijke Musea voor Kunst en Geschiedenis

Kracht, Klaus **(1974)**. *Kyūō-dōwa - Predigten des Shibata Kyūō (1783-1839). Ein Beitrag zur Lehrpraxis der Späten Shingaku.* Eingeleitet von Klaus Kracht. Wiesbaden: Otto Harrassowitz.

Kubo, Tsugunari/**Yuyama**, Akira **(2007)**. *The Lotus Sutra*, rev. ed. Berkeley, CA: Numata Center for Buddhist Translation and Research.

Kurosawa, Fumitaka **(2016)**. "Japanese Perceptions of Belgium in the Meiji and Taishō Periods." In: Willy Vande Walle and David De Cooman, eds. *Japan & Belgium. An Itinerary of Mutual Inspiration.* Tielt: Lannoo, pp. 187-212.

Lequin, Frank, ed. **(1990)**. *The Private Correspondence of Isaac Titsingh.* Amsterdam: Gieben, (1990). - XLIX, 534 p., 8 p. pl; 24 cm. - Japonica neerlandica; vol. 4. Vol. I: (1785-1811) / introd. and ed. by Frank Lequin.

Lequin, Frank, ed. **(1992a)**. *The Private Correspondence of Isaac Titsingh.* Amsterdam: Gieben, (1992). - XXVII, p. 535-931, 33 p. pl; 24 cm. - Japonica neerlandica; vol. 5. Vol. II: (1779-1812) / introd. and ed. by Frank Lequin.

Lequin, Frank, ed. **(1992b)**. *Private Correspondence of Kutsuki Masatsuna and Isaac Titsingh, 1785-1807*: compiled in celebration of the friendship between Kutsuki Masatsuna and Isaac Titsingh, Fukuchiyama, November 1992 / by Frank Lequin. Amsterdam [etc.]: Gieben, (1992). - vi, 58 p.; 24 cm.

Lequin, Frank **(2002)**. *Isaac Titsingh (1745-1812): een passie voor Japan: leven en werk van de grondlegger van de Europese japanologie* / Frank Lequin. - Alphen aan den Rijn: Canaletto/Repro-Holland. - 290 p.: ill., krt; 25 cm. - Titsingh studies; [dl. 1].

Lequin, Frank **(2003)**. *A la recherche du Cabinet Titsingh: its history, contents and dispersal: catalogue raisonne of the collection of the founder of European Japanology.* Alphen aan den Rijn: Canaletto/Repro-Holland. - 409 p.: ill., krt; 25 cm. - Titsingh studies; [dl. 2].

Lewis, Michael **(1990)**. *Rioters and Citizens. Mass Protest in Imperial Japan.* Berkeley/Los Angeles/Oxford: University of California Press.

Lutz, Walter, ed. **(1994)**. *Japan: A Cartographic Vision*, Munich/New York: Prestel Verlag.

Maida, Minoru 米田實 **(1923)**. "Taisen-go no Sai-Haku-Futsu-Ei to shinsai-go no Nihon"「大戦後の塞、白、佛、英と震災後の日本」. In: *Chūō kōron* 中央公論 38/12, pp. 102-108.

Maison franco-japonaise eds. **(1990)**. *Dictionnaire historique du Japon.* vol. 16. Tokyo: Kinokuniya.

Marks, Andreas **(2011)**. *Publishers of Japanese Woodblock Prints: A Compendium.* Leiden/Boston: Hotei Publishing.

Marks, Andreas **(2012)**. *Japanese Woodblock Prints: Artists, Publishers and Masterworks: 1680-1900.* Clarendon, VT: Tuttle Publishing.

Markus, Andrew Lawrence **(1992)**. *The Willow in Autumn: Ryūtei Tanehiko, 1783-1842.* Volume 35 of Harvard-Yenching Institute monograph series. Cambridge, MA: Harvard University Asia Center.

Mathias, Regine **(2010)**. "Das Entstehen einer modernen städtischen Gesellschaft und Kultur, 1900/1905-1932." In: Kreiner, Josef, ed. *Kleine Geschichte Japans.* Stuttgart: Philipp Reclam, pp. 332-380.

Matsumura, Masayoshi 松村正義 (1971). "Gaimushō jōhōbu no sōsetsu to Ijūin Hikokichi shodai buchō" 外務省情報部の創設と伊集院彦吉初代部長. In: *Kokusai hō gaikō zasshi* 国際法外交雑誌 70/2, pp. 76-77.

Matsumura, Masayoshi 松村正義 (2002). "Washinton kaigi to Nihon no kōhō gaikō" ワシントン会議と日本の広報外交. In: *Gaimushō chōsa geppō* 外務省調査月報 1, p. 49.

Minami, Hiroshi 南博/ **Shakai shinri kenkyūjo** 社会心理研究所, eds. (1977). *Taishō bunka* 大正文化. 2nd. ed., Tōkyō: Keisō shobō 勁草書房.

Minichiello, Sharon A. ed. (1998). *Japan's Competing Modernities: Issues in Culture and Democracy, 1900-1930.* Honolulu: University of Hawai'i Press.

Minohara, Tosh/**Hon**, Tze-ki/**Dawley**, Evan, eds. (2014). *The Decade of the Great War: Japan and the Wider World in the 1910s.* Leiden/Boston: Brill.

Miyoshi, Tadayoshi 三好唯義/**Onoda**, Kazuyuki 小野田一幸, eds. (2004). *Zusetsu Nihon kochizu korekushon* 図説日本古地図コレクション. Tōkyō: Kawade shobō shinsha 河出書房新社.

Mizuno, Kōgen 水野弘元 et al., eds. (1977). *Butten kaidai jiten* 仏典解題事典. Tōkyō: Shunjūsha 春秋社 (second print).

Mizutani, Futō 水谷不倒 (1973). *Mizutani Futō chosakushū* 水谷不倒著作集, vol. 5. Tōkyō: Chūō kōronsha 中央公論社.

Montblanc, Comte Charles de (1878). "Extraits du Kiu-o dau-wa, traduit du japonais," *Mémoires de la Société des Études Japonaises* 2, pp. 135-153.

Munemasa, Iso'o 宗政五十緒 (1972). *Kinsei kijinden, Zoku kinsei kijinden* 近世畸人伝・続近世畸人伝. Tōkyō: Heibonsha 平凡社.

Munemasa, Iso'o 宗政五十緒 (1977). *'Kinsei kijinden' no seiritsu*『近世畸人伝』の成立. Tōkyō: Miraisha 未来社.

Murai, Masahiro 村井昌弘/**Ōya**, Shin'ichi 大谷眞一 (kaisetsu) (1978). *Ryōchi shinan* 量地指南 (*Edo kagaku koten sōsho* 江戸科学古典叢書 9). Tōkyō: Kōwa shuppan 恒和出版.

Murakami, Kimio 村上紀史郎 (2009). *'Baron Satsuma' to yobareta otoko: Satsuma Jirohachi to sono jidai*「バロン・サツマ」と呼ばれた男：薩摩治郎八とその時代. Tōkyō: Fujiwara shoten 藤原書店.

Murakami, Shigeyoshi 村上重良, ed. (1980). *Kōshitsu jiten* 皇室辞典. Tōkyō: Tōkyōdō shuppan 東京堂出版.

Mutō, Motoaki 武藤元昭 (1994). "Kanamajiri musume setsuyō" 仮名文章娘節用. In: *Nippon daihyakka zensho (Nipponica)* 日本大百科全書 (ニッポニカ). Tōkyō: Shōgakukan 小学館.

Nagamine, Shigetoshi 永嶺重敏 (1997). *Zasshi to dokusha no kindai* 雑誌と読者の近代. Tōkyō: Nihon editā sukūru shuppanbu 日本エディタースクール出版部.

Nagamine, Shigetoshi 永嶺重敏 (2001). *Modan toshi no dokusho kūkan* モダン都市の読書空間. Tōkyō: Nihon editā sukūru shuppanbu 日本エディタースクール出版部.

Nagoya-shi hakubutsukan 名古屋市博物館, ed. (1988). *Meisho zue no sekai* 名所図会の世界. Nagoya: Nagoya-shi hakubutsukan 名古屋市博物館.

Nagoya-shi Hōsa bunko 名古屋市蓬左文庫, ed. (1982). *Buppin shikimei, Buppin shikimei shūi, Itsubi honzō-e buppin mokuroku, Taisei honzō meiso* 物品識名・物品識名拾遺乙未本草会物品目録 泰西本草名疏 (Na-

goya sōsho series 3 vol.19). Nagoya: Nagoya-shi kyōiku iinkai 名古屋市教育委員会.

Nakagawa, Kiun 中川喜雲 (1976). *Kyō warabe* 京童 (kohan chishi hen 古板地誌編 1). Tōkyō: Benseisha 勉誠社, (*Kinsei bungaku shiryō ruijū*: 近世文學資料類從:)

Nakagawa, Kiun 中川喜雲/Yamamoto, Taijun 山本泰順/Asai, Ryōi 浅井了意 (1967). *Kyō warabe, Kyō warabe ato-oi, Rakuyō meisho shū, Kyō suzume* 京童・京童跡追・洛陽名所集・京雀 (Shinshū Kyōto sōsho vol.1 新修京都叢書1). Tōkyō: Kōsaisha 光彩社.

Nakamura, Takafusa/**Odaka**, Kōnosuke (2003). "The Inter-war Period: 1914-37, an Overview." In: Nakamura, Takafusa/Odaka, Kōnosuke, eds. *The Economic History of Japan: 1600-1990. Vol. 3: Economic History of Japan 1914-1955. A Dual Structure.* Transl. by Noah S. Brannen. Oxford: Oxford University Press, pp. 1-54.

Nakamura, Takafusa/**Odaka**, Kōnosuke, eds. (2003). *The Economic History of Japan: 1600-1990. Vol. 3: Economic History of Japan 1914-1955. A Dual Structure.* Transl. by Noah S. Brannen. Oxford: Oxford University Press.

Nakamura, Tsukō 中村士/**Itō**, Setsuko 伊藤節子, eds. (2006). *Meijizen Nihon tenmon rekigaku sokuryō no shomoku jiten* 明治前日本天文暦学・測量の書目辞典. Tōkyō: Daiichi shobō 第一書房.

Nakano, Akira 中野光 (1977). *Taishō demokurashī to kyōiku* 大正デモクラシーと教育. Tōkyō: Shin-hyōron 新評論.

Nakano, Kōichi 中野幸一 (1988). *Ōeyama; Gyōshun; Hachikazuki* 大江山・堯舜・鉢かづき (*Nara-ehon emaki-shū* 奈良絵本絵巻集 10). Tōkyō: Waseda daigaku shuppanbu 早稲田大学出版部.

Nakayama, Hisao 中山尚夫 (2002). *Jippensha Ikku kenkyū* 十返舎一九研究. Tōkyō: Ōfū おうふう.

Nara kokuritsu hakubutsukan (1997). *Nara kokuritsu hakubutsukan no meihō — isseiki no kiseki* 奈良国立博物館の名宝――一世紀の軌跡. *Nara kokuritsu hakubutsukan* 奈良国立博物館.

Narita, Ryūichi 成田龍一 (2007). *Taishō demokurashī* 大正デモクラシー. Tōkyō: Iwanami shoten 岩波書店.

Neary, Ian (2010). *The Buraku Issue and Modern Japan: The Career of Matsumoto Jiichirō.* The Nissan Institute/Routledge Japanese Studies Series. London: Routledge.

Needham, Joseph (1954). *Science and Civilisation in China.* Cambridge, UK: Cambridge University Press.

Newland, Amy Reigle (2011). "'The Great Authority of Ukiyo-e Masters': The Making of Tsukioka Yoshitoshi's Public Persona." In: Uhlenbeck, Chris/Newland, Amy Reigle, eds. *Yoshitoshi: Masterpieces from the Ed Freis Collection.* Leiden: Hotei Publishing, pp. 25-46.

Nichiran gakkai 日蘭学会/**Numata**, Jirō 沼田次郎 et al., eds. (1984). *Yōgaku-shi jiten* 洋学史事典. Tōkyō: Yūshōdō 雄松堂.

Nihon gakushiin Nihon kagaku-shi kankōkai 日本学士院日本科学史刊行会, eds. (1978). *Zōtei fukkoku-ban Meiji-zen Nihon igaku-shi* 増訂復刻版明治前日本医学史. Tōkyō: Nihon ko'igaku shiryō sentā 日本古医学資料センター.

Nihon jinmei daijiten 日本人名大事典, 7 vols. Tōkyō: Heibonsha 平凡社, 1977 (reprint of 1937 edition).

Nihon koten bungaku daijiten henshū iinkai 日本古典文学大辞典編集委員会, ed. (1984). *Nihon koten bungaku daijiten* 日本古典文学大辞典. Tōkyō: Iwanami shoten 岩波書店, vol. 5.

Nishi, Yayoi 西弥生 (2018). "Kōbō daishi den o kataru

baitai: Emaki, hanpon, mandara ni chūmoku shite"「弘法大師伝を語る媒体: 絵巻・版本・曼荼羅に注目して」. In: *Shigaku* 史学 87/3, pp. 225-256.

Nishitani, Keiji 西谷啓治/**Yanagida**, Seizan 柳田聖山, eds. **(1974)**. *Sekai koten bungaku zenshū* 世界古典文学全集36B, 禅家語録 Zenka goroku. Tōkyō: Chikuma shobō 筑摩書房.

Nitobe, Inazō **(1899)**. *Bushido: The Soul of Japan: An Exposition of Japanese Thought*. Rutland, Vt./Tōkyō: Charles E. Tuttle.

Nojima, Jusaburō 野島寿三郎, ed. **(1990)**. *Kabuki jōruri gedai yomikata jiten* 歌舞伎・浄瑠璃外題よみかた辞典. Tōkyō: Nichigai Associates 日外アソシエーツ.

O'Connor, Peter **(2010)**. *The English-language Press Networks of East Asia, 1918-1945*. Folkestone: Global Oriental.

Okamoto, Kidō 岡本綺堂 **(2002)**. "Jiraiya no hanashi 自来也の話". In: Okamoto Kidō. *Kidō zuihitsu Edo no omoide* 綺堂随筆　江戸の思い出. Tōkyō: Kawade shobō shinsha 河出書房新社.

Ōkubo, Izumi 大久保いづみ **(2015)**. "Dai-niji sekai taisen izen no Nihon rekōdo sangyō to gaishi teikei: 6 shataisei no seiritsu" 第二次世界大戦以前の日本レコード産業と外資提携—6 社体制の成立—. In: *Keiei shigaku* 経営史学 49/4, pp. 25-51.

Ōkura, Nagatsune 大蔵永常/**Yamada**, Tatsuo 山田龍雄/**Iinuma**, Jirō 飯沼二郎/**Oka**, Mitsuo 岡光夫, **Morita**, Shirō 守田志郎, eds. **(1977)**. *Jokōroku* 除蝗録 (zen-go hen 前後編), *nōgu benriron* 農具便利論 (*jō-chū-ge* 上中下), *menbo yōmu* 綿圃要務 (*Nihon nōsho zenshū* 日本農書全集 15). Tōkyō: Nōsan gyoson bunka kyōkai 農山漁村文化協会.

Ōkura, Nagatsune 大蔵永常/**Ōita kenritsu sentetsu shiryō-kan** 大分県立先哲史料館/**Rai**, Ki'ichi 頼祺一/**Toyota**, Kanzō 豊田寛三, eds. **(1999)**. *Ōita ken sentetsu sōsho ōkura nagatsune shiryōshū (dai 2-kan)* 大分県先哲叢書 大蔵永常 資料集 (第2巻). Ōita ken kyōiku iinkai 大分県教育委員.

Ono, Tadashige 小野忠重 **(1978)**. *Hon no bijutsushi: Nara-ehon kara kusazōshi made* 本の美術史: 奈良絵本から草双紙まで. Tōkyō: Kawade shobō shinsha 河出書房新社.

Ono, Genmyō 小野玄妙, ed. **(1978)**. *Bussho kaisetsu daijiten* 佛書解説大辭典. Tōkyō: Daitō shuppansha 大東出版社.

Ono, Noriaki 小野則秋 **(1988)**. *Nihon zōshoin kō* 日本蔵書印考. Tōkyō: Rinsen shoten 臨川書店.

Ōta, Shinsai 太田晋斎 **(2011)**. *Anpuku zukai: gendaigoyaku* 按腹図解—現代語訳, trans. into modern Japanese by Wakuda Tetsuji. Tōkyō: Ōun kaitenji shuppanbu 桜雲会点字出版部.

Ozaki, Masayoshi 尾崎雅嘉 **(1993)**. *Hyakunin isshu hitoyogatari* 百人一首一夕話, Ozaki Masayoshi jihitsu kōhon (zen 2 kan), (Kaidai: Suga Sōji) 尾崎雅嘉自筆稿本 解題: 管宗次. Kyōto: Rinsen shoten 臨川書店 (H. 5).

Ozaki, Yūjirō 尾崎雄二/**Chikusa**, Masa'aki 竺沙雅章/**Togawa**, Yoshio 戸川芳郎, eds. **(2013)**. *Chūgoku bunkashi daijiten* 中国文化史大事典. Tōkyō: Taishūkan shoten 大修館書店.

Pacheco, Diego **(1971)**. "Diogo de Mesquita, S.J. and the Jesuit Mission Press." In: *Monumenta Nipponica* 26/3-4, pp. 431-443.

Pope, Edgar W. **(2003)**. "Songs of the Empire: Continental Asia in Japanese Wartime Popular Music." PhD Dissertation, University of Washington.

Richter, Steffi **(2007)**. "Kaufhausjournale als Quelle japanologischer Forschung zum ‚Alltag' der 1920/30er Jahre." *Bochumer Jahrburch zur Ostasienforschung* 28, pp. 27-44.

Robson, Christopher **(2015)**. *The Rise of Democracy: Revolution, War and Transformations in International Politics since 1776*. Edinburgh: Edinburgh University Press.

Rubinger, Richard **(2000)**. "Who Can't Read and Write? Illiteracy in Meiji Japan." In: *Monumenta Nipponica* 55/2, pp. 164-165.

Rūven kokusai jigyō iinkai ルーヴェン国際事業委員会, ed. **(1926)**. *Rūven kokusai jigyō iinkai jigyo seiseki hōkoku* ルーヴェン国際事業委員会事業成績報告. Tōkyō: Rūven kokusai jigyō iinkai ルーヴェン国際事業委員会.

Saigusa, Hiroto 三枝博音 **(1956)**. *Nihon no Yuibutsuronsha* 日本の唯物論者. Tōkyō: Eiōsha 英宝社.

Saigusa, Hiroto 三枝博音, ed. **(1957)**. *Nihon Tetsugaku Shisō Zensho* 日本哲学思想全書 (Library of Japanese philosophical thought, vol. 1). Tōkyō: Heibonsha 平凡社.

Sakakibara, Kōshū 榊原篁州 **(1910)**. *Kobun shinpō zenshū genkai taisei* 古文真宝前集諺解大成, vol. 11 of *Kanseki kokuji-kai zensho*. Tōkyō: Waseda daigaku shuppanbu 早稲田大学出版部.

Sakamoto, Tarō 坂本太郎 **(1964)**. "Teihan to Nihon" 帝範と日本. In: *Nihon kodai-shi no kisoteki kenkyū* 日本古代史の基礎的研究, vol. 1: Literature 上 文献篇. Tōkyō: Tōkyō daigaku shuppankai 東京大学出版会.

Sato, Barbara **(2003)**. *The New Japanese Woman: Modernity, Media, and Women in Interwar Japan*. Durham: Duke University Press.

Sato, Hiroaki **(2007)**. *Japanese Women Poets: An Anthology*. New York: Routledge.

Schencking, Charles **(2012)**. *The Great Kantō Earthquake and the Chimera of National Reconstruction in Japan*. New York: Columbia University Press/Hong Kong: Hong Kong University Press.

Schmidt, Jan **(2012)**. "Infirmières japonaises et 'coolies' chinois ? - La quête japonaise pour la suprématie dans le contexte de la contribution de l'Asie orientale à la Grande Guerre." In: Ma Li, ed. *Les travailleurs chinois dans la première guerre mondiale*. Paris: CNRS éditions, pp. 131-154.

Schmidt, Jan **(2014)**. "Der Erste Weltkrieg als vermittelte Kriegserfahrung in Japan: Mediale Aneignungen und Studien durch Militär und Ministerialbürokratie." In: *Geschichte und Gesellschaft* 40, pp. 239-265.

Schmidt, Jan **(2021)**. *Nach dem Krieg ist vor dem Krieg. Medialisierte Erfahrungen des Ersten Weltkriegs und Nachkriegsdiskurse in Japan (1914-1919)*. Frankfurt am Main/New York: Campus.

Schmidt, Jan/**Schmidtpott**, Katja, eds. **(2020)**. *The East Asian Dimension of the First World War. Global Entanglements and Japan, China, and Korea, 1914-1919*. Frankfurt am Main/New York: Campus.

Schönbein, Martina **(1994)**. *Die Michiyuki-Passagen in den Sewa-Jōruri des Dramatikers Chikamatsu Monzaemon (1653-1724): Struktur, literarische Stilmittel und Rezeption*. Wiesbaden: Harrassowitz Verlag.

Sekai daihyakka jiten 世界大百科事典 **(1993)**, 2nd ed. Tōkyō: Heibonsha 平凡社.

Sekida, Katsuki **(1977)**. *Two Zen Classics: Mumonkan and Hekiganroku*, transl. with commentaries by Katsuki Sekida, ed. and intro. by A.V. Grimstone. New York/Tōkyō: Weatherhill.

Sharf, Frederic/**Morse**, Anne Nishimura/**Dobson**, Sebastian, **(2005)**. *A Much Recorded War: The Russo-Japanese War in History and Imagery*. Boston: MFA Publications.

Shibata, Minoru 柴田実, ed. **(1970)**. "Kaisetsu" 解説. In: *Kyūōdōwa* 鳩翁道話. Tōyō Bunko 東洋文庫, vol. 154. Tōkyō: Heibonsha 平凡社.

Shimazu, Naoko **(1988)**. *Japan, Race and Equality – The Racial Equality Proposal of 1919*. Oxfordshire: Routledge.

Shimazu, Naoko **(2009)**. *Japanese Society at War. Death, Memory and the Russo-Japanese War*. Cambridge: Cambridge University Press.

Shimazu, Norifumi. "Nakatominoharae." *Encyclopedia of Shinto*. Last accessed 28 Mar 2020. http://k-amc. kokugakuin.ac.jp/DM/

Shimizu, Yuichirō **(2019)**. *The Origins of the Modern Japanese Bureaucracy*. Transl. Amin Ghadimi. London: Bloomsbury.

Shinchō sekai bijutsu jiten 新潮世界美術辞典 **(1985)**. Tōkyō: Shinchōsha 新潮社.

Shinozaki, Kazuko 篠崎和子 **(1968a)**. "Honkoku Tōryū Kaisei Setsuyō Ryōri Taizen" 飜刻 當流改正節用料理大全. In: *Atomi gakuen tanki daigaku gaiyō* 5 跡見学園短期大学紀要 (5), pp. 26-54.

Shinozaki, Kazuko 篠崎和子 **(1968b)**. "Honkoku Tōryū Kaisei Setsuyō Ryōri Taizen (jōzen)" 飜刻 當流改正節用料理大全 (承前). In: *Atomi gakuen tanki daigaku gaiyō* 5 跡見学園短期大学紀要 (5), pp. 41-70.

Shinozaki, Kazuko 篠崎和子 **(1969)**. "Honkoku Tōryū Kaisei Setsuyō Ryōri Taizen (jōzen)" 飜刻 當流改正節用料理大全 (承前). In: *Atomi gakuen tanki daigaku gaiyō* 6 跡見学園短期大学紀要 (6), pp. 41-58.

Shinozaki, Kazuko 篠崎和子 **(1971)**. "Honkoku Tōryū Kaisei Setsuyō Ryōri Taizen (kanketsu)" 飜刻 當流改正節用料理大全 (完結). In: *Atomi gakuen tanki daigaku gaiyō* 7-8, 跡見学園短期大学紀要 (7・8), pp. 85-115.

Shirane, Haruo **(2013)**. *Japan and the Culture of the Four Seasons: Nature, Literature, and the Arts*. New York: Columbia University Press.

Silberman, Bernard S./ **Harootunian**, Harry D., eds. **(1974)**. *Japan in Crisis. Essays on Taishō Democracy*. Princeton, NJ: Princeton University Press.

Silverberg, Miriam **(2006)**. *Erotic Grotesque Nonsense: The Mass Culture of Japanese Modern Times*. Berkeley: University of California Press.

Sugano, Noriko 菅野則子, ed. **(1999)**. *Kankoku-kōgiroku* 官刻孝義録, vols. 1-3. Tōkyō: Tōkyōdō shuppan 東京堂出版.

Sugimoto, Tsutomu 杉本つとむ **(1998)**. *Zōtei Nihon hon'yakugoshi no kenkyū* 増訂日本翻訳語史の研究, Sugimoto Tsutomu chosaku senshū 4 杉本つとむ著作選集4. Tōkyō: Yasaka shobō 八坂書房.

Sugimoto, Masayoshi/**Swain**, David L. **(1978)**. *Science and Culture in Traditional Japan, A.D. 600-1854* (The M.I.T. East Asian Science Series, No. 6). Cambridge, MA: MIT Press.

Suwa, Haruo 諏訪春雄 **(1981)**. "Chikamatsu no sewajōruri: sono higekisei no kōsatsu" 近松の世話浄瑠璃: その悲劇性の考察. In: *Kenkyū nenpō / Gakushūin Daigaku Bungakubu* 研究年報/学習院大学文学部 27, pp. 173-207.

Suzuki, Jūzō 鈴木重三 **(1957)**, "*Kanamajiri musume setsuyō shohanbon no hakken*"『仮名文章娘節用』初版

本の発見. In: *Nihon kosho tsūshin* 日本古書通信, vol. 22:10 (339), pp. 2-5.

Suzuki, Jūzō 鈴木重三 **(1979)**, "*Kanamajiri musume setsuyō shohanbon no hakken*"『仮名文章娘節用』初版本の発見. In: *Ehon to ukiyoe: Edo shuppan bunka no kōsatsu* 絵本と浮世絵 江戸出版文化の考察, Tōkyō: Bijutsu shuppansha 美術出版社.

Suzuki, Harunobu 鈴木春信/Suzuki, Jūzō 鈴木重三, eds. **(1981)**. *Ehon seirō bijin awase* 絵本青楼美人合 (Kinsei Nihon fūzoku ehon shūsei 近世日本風俗絵本集成 120). Kyōto: Rinsen shoten 臨川書店.

Suzuki, Rie 鈴木理恵 **(2004)**. "The Analysis of kō (filial piety) in the Edo period: through *Kankoku-kōgiroku* | Edo jidai no minshū kyōka: *Kankoku-kōgiroku* ni yoru kōkō no jōkyō bunseki" 江戸時代の民衆教化:『官刻孝義録』による孝行の状況分析. *Nagasaki daigaku kyōikugakubu shakai-kagaku ronsō* 長崎大学教育学部社会科学論叢 65, pp. 19-34.

Suzuki gakujutsu zaidan 鈴木学術財団, ed. **(1916)**. *Mahāvyutpatti Honyaku myōgi taishū* 飜譯名義大集. Tōkyō: Suzuki gakujutsu zaidan 鈴木学術財団, (Fukkan sōsho 1).

Taira, Koji **(1997)**. "Factory Labour and the Industrial Revolution in Japan." In Kōzō Yamamura, ed. *The Economic Emergence of Modern Japan*. Cambridge: Cambridge University Press, pp. 239-293.

Takagi, Hiroshi 高木博志 **(2014)**. "Dai-ichiji sekai taisen zengo no Nihon no bunkazai hogo to dentō bunka" 第一次世界大戦前後の日本の文化財保護と伝統文化. In: Yamamuro Shin'ichi 山室信一 et al., eds. *Gendai no kiten Dai-ichiji sekai taisen. 3 Seishin no hen'yō* 現代の起点第一次世界大戦 3 (精神の変容). Tōkyō: Iwanami shoten 岩波書店, pp. 241-265.

Takagi, Yōko **(2002)**. *Japonisme in fin de siècle art in Belgium*. Antwerp: Pandora.

Takagi, Yōko **(2005)**. "Japonisme: A Formative Influence on Belgian Art Nouveau." In: Vande Walle, Willy/De Cooman, David, eds. *Japan and Belgium: Four Centuries of Exchange*. Brussels: Commissioner-General of the Belgian Government, pp. 190-205.

Takakusu, Junjirō 高楠順次郎/**Watanabe**, Kaigyoku 渡辺海旭 et al., eds. **(2003)**. *Taishō daizōkyō* 大正大藏經. Tōkyō: Taishō issaikyō kankō kai 大正一切經刊行會, 1924-1934, vol. 48.

Tanaka, Stefan **(2004)**. *New Times in Modern Japan*. Princeton: Princeton University Press.

Tenri daigaku fuzoku Tenri toshokan, ed. **(2018-2020)**. *Tenri daigaku fuzoku Tenri toshokan henshū* 天理大学附属天理図書館編集, *Nara ehon-shū* 奈良絵本集, 8 vols. Tenri 天理: Tenri daigaku shuppanbu 天理大学出版部 / Tōkyō: Yagi shoten 八木書店. (Shin Tenri Toshokan Zenpon Sōsho Fourth Series 新天理図書館善本叢書 第4期, vols 23-30).

Throntveit, Trygve **(2001)**. "The Fable of the Fourteen Points: Woodrow Wilson and National Self-Determination." In: *Diplomatic History* 35/3, pp. 445-481.

Tipton, Elise K. **(1997)**. "Introduction." In: Tipton, Elise K., ed. *Society and State in Interwar Japan*. London: Routledge, pp. 1-16.

Tipton, Elise K. **(2008)**. "Cleansing the Nation: Urban Entertainments and Moral Reform in Interwar Japan." In: *Modern Asian Studies* 42/4, pp. 705-731.

Togiya, Norio 研谷紀夫 **(2013)**. "Gekkanshi *Rekishi shashin* to rekishi no imēji hyōshō. Taishō-ki no *Rekishi*

shashin no shimen naiyō to 'Rekishi shashin kai' no un'ei o chūshin ni"「月刊誌『歴史写真』と歴史のイメージ表象：大正初期の『歴史写真』の誌面内容と「歴史写真会」の運営を中心に」. In: *Fūzoku shigaku* 風俗史学 54, pp. 33-69.

Tokoro, Isao 所功 ed. (2018). *Kyōto no go-tairei: sokui-rei daijōsai-rei to kyūtei bunka no miyabi*「京都の御大礼-即位礼・大嘗祭礼と宮廷文化のみやび-. Tenji jikkō iinkai henshū 展示実行委員会編. Kyōto: Shibunkaku shuppan 思文閣出版.

Toyoshima, Masayuki 豊島正之, ed. (2013). *Kirishitan to Shuppan* キリシタンと出版 = *Cristianismo y edición*. Tōkyō: Yagi shoten 八木書店.

Tsukamoto, Tetsuzō 塚本哲三, ed. (1915). *Kottōshū* 骨董集, Enseki zasshi 燕石雑誌, Yōshabako 用捨箱 (Yūhōdō bunko 有朋堂文庫). Tōkyō: Yūhōdō shoten 有朋堂書店.

Tsukamoto, Tetsuzō 塚本哲三, ed. (1918). *Mukashigatari inazuma-byōshi* 昔話稲妻表紙 (Yūhōdō bunko 有朋堂文庫). Tōkyō: Yūhōdō shoten 有朋堂書店.

Tucker, Mary Evelyn (1989). *Moral and Spiritual Cultivation in Japanese Neo-Confucianism: The Life and Thought of Kaibara Ekken, 1630-1714*. Albany: SUNY Press.

Uhlenbeck, Chris (2011). "The Phases in the Career of Tsukioka Yoshitoshi: A Print Designer in a Time of Change." In: Uhlenbeck, Chris/Newland, Amy Reigle, eds. *Yoshitoshi: Masterpieces from the Ed Freis Collection*. Leiden: Hotei Publishing, pp. 8-24.

Uhlenbeck, Chris/Newland, Amy Reigle (2011). *Yoshitoshi: Masterpieces from the Ed Freis Collection*. Leiden: Hotei Publishing.

Umezu, Kazuo 梅津和郎 (1978). *Narikin jidai: Dai-ichiji sekai taisen to Nihon – 1* 成金時代：第一次世界大戦と日本 1. Tōkyō: Kyōikusha 教育社.

Van Alphen, Jan (1999). *Enkū 1632-1695: Tijdloze beelden uit 17de-eeuws Japan*, compilation and redaction by: Jan Van Alphen, with contributions by Jeroen P. Lamers e.a. (exhibition catalogue), Etnografisch Museum Antwerpen, 5 May-29 August 1999.

Vandeperre, Nathalie (2016). "The King's Dream: The Museums of the Far East and Their Collections." In: Vande Walle, Willy/De Cooman, David, eds. *Japan & Belgium: An Itinerary of Mutual Inspiration*. Tielt: Uitg. Lannoo NV, pp. 319-336.

Vansina, Marieke (2019). "Satsuma Jirohachi: A Case Study in Interwar Cultural Internationalism and Self-Orientalism." Unpublished MA thesis, Leuven: KU Leuven.

Vanoverbeke, Dimitri (2004). *Community and State in the Japanese Farm Village: Farm Tenancy Conciliation (1924-1938)*. Leuven: Leuven University Press.

Van Steenpaal, Niels (2009). "Kankoku kōgiroku: Bakufu jinsei no pafōmansu"『官刻孝義録』―幕府仁政のパフォーマンス. In: *Kokusai Nihon bungaku kenkyū shūkai kaigiroku* 国際日本文学研究集会会議録, *Japanese Literature in World Literature: Past and Future of Monogatari / Sekai bungaku no naka no Nihon bungaku: Monogatari no kako to mirai* 世界文学の中の日本文学：物語の過去と未来, ed. Ningen bunka kenkyū kikō Kokubungaku kenkyū shiryōkan 人間文化研究機構国文学研究資料館, vol. 32, pp. 35-52. Tachikawa (Tōkyō): Ningen bunka kenkyū kikō Kokubungaku kenkyū shiryōkan 人間文化研究機構国文学研究資料館.

Van Waarden, Betto (2019). "Public Politics: The Coming of Age of the Media Politician in a Transnational Communicative Space, 1880s-1910s." Unpublished PhD Dissertation, KU Leuven.

Voerman, Gerrit/Wijfjes, Huub, eds. (2009). *Mediatization of Politics in History*. Leuven: Peeters Publishing.

Vos, George A., De (1967). *Japan's Invisible Race: Caste in Culture and Personality*. University of California Press.

Wang, Helen (2010). "How Did Kutsuki Masatsuna's Coins Come to the British Museum?" In: *Catalogue of the Japanese Coin Collection (pre-Meiji) at the British Museum, with special reference to Kutsuki Masatsuna* (British Museum Research Publication 174).

White, Merry (2012). *Coffee Life in Japan*. Berkeley: University of California Press.

Wilson, Sandra (2005). "The Discourse of National Greatness in Japan, 1890-1919." In: *Japanese Studies* 25/1, pp. 35-51.

Yamada, Keiji 山田慶児, ed. (1995). *Higashi Ajia no honzō to hakubutsugaku no sekai* 東アジアの本草と博物学の世界. 2 vols. Tōkyō: Shibunkaku 思文閣.

Yamamoto, Taketoshi 山本武利 (1981). *Kindai Nihon no shinbun dokusha-sō* 近代日本の新聞読者層. Tōkyō: Hōsei daigaku shuppankyoku 法政大学出版局.

Yamamuro, Shin'ichi (2020). "The First World War in East Asian Thought: As Seen from Japan." In: Schmidt, Jan/Schmidtpott, Katja, eds. *The East Asian Dimension of the First World War. Global Entanglements and Japan, China, and Korea, 1914-1919*. Frankfurt am Main/New York: Campus, pp. 39-79.

Yamazaki, Makoto 山崎誠 (2000). *Rūvan ra nūbu daigakukura Nihon shojaku mokuroku* ルヴァンラヌーブ大学蔵日本書籍目録. Tōkyō: Bensei 勉誠.

Yano, Christine R. (1998). "Defining the Modern Nation in Japanese Popular Song, 1914-1932." In: Minichiello, Sharon A., ed. *Japan's Competing Modernities: Issues in Culture and Democracy, 1900-1930*. Mānoa: University of Hawai'i Press, pp. 247-264.

Yasuda, Kenneth (2011). *Japanese Haiku: Its Essential Nature and History*, North Clarendon, VT: Tuttle Publishing.

Yokoyama, Shigeru 横山重/Matsumoto, Takanobu 松本隆信, eds. (1983-1988). *Muromachi jidai monogatari taisei* 室町時代物語大成. 15 vols. Tōkyō: Kadokawa shoten 角川書店.

Yoshii, Motoko 吉井始子 (1978-1981). *Honkoku Edo-jidai ryōribon shūsei* 翻刻江戸時代料理本集成. Kyōto: Rinsen shoten 臨川書店.

Young, Louise (2013). *Beyond the Metropolis: Second Cities and Modern Life in Interwar Japan*. Berkeley: University of California Press.

Zengaku jiten 禅学辞典 (1974). Jinbō, Nyoten 神保如天/Andō, Bun'ei 安藤文英, eds. Kyōto: Heirakuji shoten 平楽寺書店 (second edition).

Acknowledgements

The exhibition and this publication would not have been possible without the support of numerous institutions and individuals. The following list cannot ever be considered complete because there were simply too many persons who kindly supported the exhibition and this publication. We would therefore like to assure those whose names could not be included below that we nonetheless extend our utmost gratitude to them.

Above all we thank the rectors of KU Leuven and UCLouvain, Professor Dr. Luc Sels and Professor Dr. Vincent Blondeel, for their continuous support for the exhibition. We also would like to thank Ambassador Shimokawa Makita (Embassy of Japan in Belgium) for his generous patronage and Hilde Van Kiel (Director of KU Leuven Libraries) for kindly hosting the exhibition. The incredible and tireless work of her team (Katrien Smeyers, Diewer van der Meijden, Wouter Daenen, Liesbet Peeters, Erna Lombaerts, Tjamke Snijders et al.), coordinated by Prof. Dr. Demmy Verbeke (KU Leuven Libraries Artes) and of Britt Kennis and Ward Denys of Exponanza, was crucial for the success of the exhibition. For many years now Emilie Vilcot (UCLouvain Libraries Central Service) and Charles-Henri Nyns (UCLouvain Chief Librarian) have ensured that the Japanese book donation is preserved in pristine condition at UCLouvain. Their generous help with the loans and with the planning of the exhibition, and their efforts for the digitization of the Japanese Book Collection was central to the success of the exhibition.

For the manuscript of this catalogue our heartfelt gratefulness goes first and foremost to the authors Aurel Baele, Angelika Koch, Jan Schmidt, Lieven Sommen, Freya Terryn, and Willy Vande Walle. Maren Barton and John Eyck were of the greatest help with a native speaker check and further copy-editing. We further thank the following PhD students and postdoctoral researchers for their help in editing the manuscript: Aurel Baele, Charlotte Théa Bekkers, Maj Hartmann, Stevie Poppe, Lieven Sommen, and Jorinde Wels, as well as MA student Siebe Goris as intern. Without the tireless work and immense patience, which we more than once stretched to its limits, of Veerle De Laet and her team of Leuven University Press, this publication would never have seen the light of the day.

Our gratitude goes to all the following institutions and private persons who trusted us with items on loan for the exhibition or gave us the rights for digital reproductions for this catalogue as well as to colleagues and students who gave us crucial support in other capacities:

Prof. Dr. Akashi Tomonori (Kyushu University Archives); Archives of the Federal Public Service Foreign Affairs, Brussels; Archives of the Royal Palace, Brussels; Arvid Eykens; the Belgium-Japan Association (BJA); Cinematek – Royal Film Archive of Belgium (Bruno Mestdagh, Regina De Martelaere); Dr. An Descheemaeker (KU Leuven, Manager of the International Office); Federal Public Service Foreign Affairs: Diplomatic Archive, Brussels; FelixArchief, Antwerp; Gokita Mitsuko (Shinra, Sakura); In Flanders Fields Museum, Ieper (Dr. Dominiek Dendooven); Dr. Klaus Friese (Ludwig-Maximilians-Universität Munich); KU Leuven Digitisation and Document Delivery (Jesse Huiskamp, Bruno Vandermeulen, Frédéric Van Cutsem); KU Leuven Faculty of Arts; KU Leuven University Archives, Leuven; members of the "Seminar on Modern and Contemporary History of Japan", KU Leuven (Aurel Baele, Ilja Blondeel, Laure Brys, Arend Bucher, Gladys Coenen, Brent De hornois, Jordy De Leender, Arvid Eykens, Nasser Fathi, Amber Frederickx, Joyce Gilissen, Hana Iwamoto, Maj Hartmann, Anthe Herweyers, Akiha Ichihashi, Dilhan Ismail, Wouter Lausberg, Eline Mennens, Alexandra Nozdrina, Hannah Patteet, Benjamin Poelmans, Jen Romero Alvarado, Imane Saidi, Brecht Scherens, Nicolas Stassar, Freya Terryn, Fouad Toumi, Merel Tuytte, Tomoya Uejima, Jan Ulrichts, Floor Vaartjes, Thibault van Acker, Ella Van Aken, Arno van Boxem, Lotte van den Bogaert, Sara Vandenhoeck, Stan Vanderbruggen, Arne van der Veken, Marieke Vansina, Fabio Wauters, Jorinde Wels, Jolien Winters, Adam Zuidam); Museum Fünf Kontinente, Munich (Anka Krämer); National Film Archive of Japan, Tokyo (Alo Joekalda, Kamiya Makiko); National Museum of Japanese History, Sakura (Prof. Dr. Gotō Makoto); Nofuji Tae (Seinan Gakuin University); Ohara Institute for Social Research, Hosei University (Nakamura Mika); Japanese Studies Research Group (Prof. Dr. Adrien Carbonnet, Hans Coppens, MA, Prof. Dr. Dimitri Vanoverbeke); Royal Library of Belgium (Prof. Dr. Johan Van Heesch, Fran Stroobants); Royal Museum of the Armed Forces and Military History, Brussels (Céline Quairiaux); Royal Museums of Art and History, Brussels (Anja Van Lerberghe); Royal Museums of Fine Arts, Brussels; Prof. Dr. Stefan Schorn (KU Leuven, Faculty of Arts); Shibusawa Eiichi Memorial Foundation, Tokyo; The Japan-Belgium Society (JBS); The State Archives in Belgium, Brussels; UCLouvain (University Archives), Louvain-la-Neuve; Völkerkundemuseum der J. & E. von Portheim-Stiftung, Heidelberg (Dr. Margareta Pavaloi); ZBW – Leibniz Information Centre for Economics, Kiel.

Classification List of Selected Books

The following list provides an overview of the (limited) selection of books as distributed across the various thematic divisions of the original catalogue.

List of Selected Objects

List of Background Explanations

Alphabetical List of Selected Books

Alphabetical List of Selected Objects

Colophon

The publication of this work was supported by
the KU Leuven Fund for Fair Open Access and
KU Leuven-UCLouvain Japan Mirai Fund.

Published in 2022 by Leuven University Press/Presses
Universitaires de Louvain/Universitaire Pers Leuven.
Minderbroedersstraat 4, B-3000 Leuven (Belgium).

ISBN 978 94 6270 228 8 (Flexcover)
ISBN 978 94 6166 328 3 (ePDF)
https://doi.org/10.11116/9789461663283
D/2022/1869/8
NUR: 644

Layout: TopicA Graphic Design
Illustration cover: see pages 71, 244, 112, and 216
Illustration page 2-3: see page 58